VOICES FROM THE FIRING LINE

A Personal Account of the Pittsburgh Civil Rights Movement

THIRD EDITION

Ralph Proctor, Jr.

With contributions by John Brewer, Jr.

Photographs by Charles "Teenie" Harris

Social Context Series

Learning Moments Press
Oakmont, PA

VOICES FROM THE FIRING LINE
A Personal Account of the Pittsburgh Civil Rights Movement

Third Edition

Published by Learning Moments Press
Publishing Arm of the Scholar-Practitioner Nexus
Social Contexts Series
Oakmont, PA 15139
scholarpractitionernexus.com

ISBN: 13 978-1-7349594-6-8

Photographs courtesy of the Carnegie Museum of Art, Charles "Teenie" Harris Archive © 2014

Charles "Teenie" Harris

Book Layout: Mike Murray, pearhouse.com

BISAC Subject:

Education/History (EDU 016000)
History/Social History (HIS 054000)
Social Science/Ethic Studies/American/African American & Black Studies (SOC 001000)
Social Science/Discrimination (SOC 031000)
Social Science/Race & Ethic Relations (SOC 070000)
Education/Multicultural Education (EDU020000)
Political Science/Civil Rights (POL004000)

Onix Audience Code:
01 General Trade
06 Professional & Scholarly

1st Edition (January 2014) & 2nd Edition (December 2014) published by Introspec Press, Pittsburgh, PA.

Table of Contents

MY JOURNEY

I think of life as a journey

Along a sandy beach

And as I travel I worry

Is my goal beyond my reach?

You see the nagging worry

That burns ever in my mind

Is that at the end of the journey

I will have left no footprints behind.

Ralph Proctor, 1993

DEDICATION

This book is dedicated to my parents, Ralph Proctor, Sr., and Ruby Morrison Proctor, for all the years of guidance, care and love, and for allowing me to follow my own path and to march to the beat of a different drummer. It is also dedicated to my sons, Shawn and Vance Proctor. I wish I could leave you more than a legacy of hard work. The work I did in the movement described in this book was so that you would have a life that was less defined by virulent racism. Know that I have always loved you and will continue even beyond my last breath. I am proud of you. I ask that you do whatever you can to make this world a better place. You need not do incredible things; you only need to do ordinary things incredibly well. I will always be near you; just call my name and I will be there.

This book is also dedicated to the many friends I met in the Pittsburgh civil rights movement who allowed me to capture their words and stand on their shoulders. I am keeping my promise that their names would be written down so future generations could read about their selfless, brave contributions to justice and freedom. I have been honored to stand with you.

ACKNOWLEDGEMENTS

I want to give great thanks to Patricia Buddemeyer who encouraged and pushed me to publish this book when I had grown tired of begging others to realize that this story of heroes had to be told. In addition, she provided valuable help with editing, proofreading, and layout. Had it not been for Patricia, this book would never have been published.

I also want to acknowledge the role of Dr. Joseph Trotter, Professor of History at Carnegie-Mellon University. He was there from the first draft, encouraging my alma mater, the University of Pittsburgh, to publish the book. Dr. Trotter was always a voice of encouragement. He believed that what I was doing was of significant importance, and continued to offer support when others turned their backs.

There is another person I must mention and to whom I extend my eternal gratitude. That person is Morton "Moe" Coleman who is featured as one of the "voices" in this book. Moe has been my friend for more years than I can remember. He has provided encouragement in times of trouble and comfort when I had little hope. From the beginning of this project, more than twenty years ago, Moe encouraged me to complete the project when I had given up. Moe, thank you, my friend; thank you! It is done.

FOREWORD

Ralph Proctor is one of the foremost historians of African American life and history in Pittsburgh. Scholars, policy makers, and students of black urban history are indebted to his pioneering study of black educators, *Racial Discrimination Against Black Teachers and Black Professionals in the Pittsburgh Public School System 1834-1973*. Completed as a doctoral dissertation at the University of Pittsburgh in 1979, this study documented the long-run fight for racial equality in both the education of black children and the employment of black teachers and other education professionals in the Pittsburgh public schools. Building upon Proctor's extensive knowledge of the city's African American community and civil rights struggles, *Voices From the Firing Line: A Personal Account of the Pittsburgh Civil Rights Movement* illuminates the social and political history of blacks in the 20th century urban North "from the inside out."

Based upon the oral recollections of prominent and not so prominent black freedom fighters and their white allies, this book is currently the single richest source on the Steel City's Modern Black Freedom Movement. This study is not limited to Proctor's own extensive interviews with movement activists. It also includes voluminous newspaper accounts from the black weekly *Pittsburgh Courier* as well as interviews from the Trolley Station Oral History Center, directed by local historian John Brewer. Moreover, drawing partly upon the author's own recollections of African American culture, economics, and politics in Pittsburgh, this book is also a memoir of the personal, intellectual, family, community, educational, and activist struggles of Ralph Proctor himself. Most important, however, this study adds the voices of Black Pittsburgh to the expanding historiography of the nation's Modern Black Freedom Movement.

In 2003, civil rights historians Jeanne Theoharis and Komozi Woodard published their seminal collection of essays, *Freedom North: Black Freedom Struggles Outside the South, 1940-1980*. As the 20th century came to a close, they noted a firm southern bias in research and writing on the Black Freedom Movement. Existing scholarship placed the southern movement at the dynamic center of the nonviolent direct action phase of the black freedom struggle and rarely ventured above the Mason-Dixon Line. Moreover, rather than documenting the persistence of the nonviolent direct action movement beyond Martin Luther King's assassination in 1968, established scholarship emphasized the decline of the Civil Rights Movement under "the twin forces of Black Power and white backlash," when the movement presumably finally turned North after 1965. Over the past decade, however, scholars have expanded our knowledge of the Modern Black Freedom Movement into the urban North and West, including such diverse cities as New York, Philadelphia, Detroit, St. Louis, the San Francisco Bay Area, and Los Angeles.[1]

Despite the recent outpouring of scholarship on the freedom movement in the North and West, Pittsburgh remains underrepresented in the recent transformation of research on the Modern Black Freedom Struggle. *Voices from the Firing Line* not only brings Pittsburgh's civil rights movement into sharper focus, but also establishes an important baseline for future research on the subject. Proctor discusses a broad range of civil rights organizations, leaders, and grassroots campaigns against Jim Crow North. In varying degrees of detail, *Voices from the Firing Line* offers first-hand accounts of nearly 70 black and white participants in Pittsburgh's Civil Rights Movement. These include video-taped recollections of such well known individuals as Byrd Brown, attorney and president of the Pittsburgh chapter of the NAACP; Alma Speed Fox, executive director of the NAACP; Fr. Charles Owen Rice, the white labor and civil rights activist priest; Rev. LeRoy Patrick, the militant black minister of the Bethesda Presbyterian Church in Homewood, who helped to integrate the Highland Park public swimming pool; and Nate Smith, leader of "Operation Dig" and the fight against the discriminatory building and construction industry. Alongside such widely known figures, the book discusses the activities of Ewari Ellis, Mary Gloster, Harriet McCrea, and James "Swampman" Williams, all relatively "unsung" grassroots activists.

Closely aligned with microscopic details on numerous individual activists, Proctor illuminates the organizational landscape of the modern black freedom struggle. Pittsburgh's civil rights network included local chapters of the NAACP and Urban League, the Greater Pittsburgh Improvement League, the United Negro Protest Committee, the Black Construction Coalition, Forever Action Together (FAT), a short-lived Black Panther Party, and the Democratic Association of Black Brothers, to name only a few.

In an exceedingly revealing chapter on his own life in Pittsburgh, Ralph Proctor offers compelling insight into his struggle to demolish the city's Jim Crow order. Born and raised in the Hill District by southern-born parents of the Great 20th Century Black Migration to Pittsburgh, Ralph graduated from Schenley High School and attended college for a while before dropping out and joining the U.S. Army. In addition to service in Korea, his tour of duty included stints on southern army bases, particularly Fort Campbell, where he not only helped to organize black soldiers to fight injustice within the military, but also joined the larger black freedom movement in the nearby city of Nashville, Tennessee.

Although Dr. Proctor initially adopted the nonviolent direct action tenets of the Modern Black Freedom Movement, his journey from Martin Luther King's nonviolent direct action philosophy to Malcolm X's ideology of armed self-defense had commenced before he departed the South and returned to Pittsburgh. "It was fortuitous," he said, "that my time in the army was drawing to an end at about the time I had concluded that I still believed in non-violence as a tactical method to be used in demonstrations, but I could no longer accept it as a way of life....I had decided that I would be non-violent as long as no one was violent towards me!...I left the South a profoundly changed and angry young man, with a chip on my shoulder."

As suggested by Ralph Proctor's personal engagement in the black freedom struggle, Pittsburgh's fight for equal rights and social justice offers a unique opportunity to revisit the debate over the origins, character, and demise of the Modern Black Freedom struggle. In her 2004 Organization of American

---

1 Sundiata Keita Cha Jua and Clarence Lang, "The 'Long Movement' As Vampire: Temporal and Spatial Fallacies in Recent Black Freedom Studies," *Journal of African American History* 92, no. 2 (2007): 265-88.

Historians' Presidential Address on the subject, Jacquelyn Dowd Hall pointedly argued for a more expansive view of the civil rights movement, one that not only pushed the time frame back before the landmark Civil Rights events of the 1950s and 1960s, but also extended the timeline beyond the assassination of Martin Luther King, the escalation of violence in the streets, and rise of the explicitly Black Power phase of the modern black freedom movement.[2] Hall's plea for a "long movement" perspective inspired the vigorous outpouring of new scholarship on this important moment in African American and U.S. urban history. In recent years, however, following a critical assessment of "long movement" studies by historians Sundiata Cha Jua and Clarence Lang, contemporary scholars are beginning to worry that the "long movement" thesis may have inadvertently obliterated vital distinctions between violent and nonviolent approaches to social change; between northern, western, and southern components of the movement; and between the post-World War II years and earlier interwar struggles against the segregationist system.

Voices From the Firing Line reinforces the "long movement" thesis, while also offering substantial evidence that no single interpretive model can fully account for black social struggles on the ground. Upon returning to Pittsburgh, for example, Ralph soon joined the city's expanding black freedom movement. His civil rights activities included establishment of the University of Pittsburgh branch of the NAACP, which he spearheaded and served as first president. The organization soon launched vigorous campaigns to desegregate the University of Pittsburgh. As Ralph recalled, the organization became "so militant in its early days," the national office threatened to rescind its charter. In addition to co-hosting a popular radio show titled, "NAACP On The Line" between 1963 and 1968, Ralph later developed WQED-TV's ground-breaking, nationally recognized African American talk show, *Black Horizons*, from 1968-71. *Black Horizons* aimed to redress the imbalance between blacks and whites in the electronic media. While WQED's popular *Mr. Rogers Neighborhood* generated revenue for the station and gained resources for "a very expensive set, complete with trolley tracks, trees and such," Ralph recalled, for the innovative and pioneering *Black Horizons*, there were few resources. The station "simply turned *Mister Rogers* set around, revealing black panels, splashed colorful lights on it, put a platform in front of them, put a few chairs on the platform and 'behold'! *Black Horizons* was created." As Ralph intensified his efforts to desegregate radio and television programming and hiring in Pittsburgh, he later lamented that his day-to-day involvement in escalating street level demonstrations dissipated.

Based upon the individual and collective memories of civil rights movement activists, *Voices From the Firing Line* advances a series of compelling statements about Pittsburgh's black freedom struggle. First and perhaps most important, Proctor illuminates the emergence of the black freedom struggle against the broader backdrop of what he describes as Pittsburgh's rise to prominence as the "Birmingham (Alabama) of the North." The city's civil rights leaders often referred to Pittsburgh as "a small Southern town that broke away from the Mississippi Delta, floated up the river and got stuck!" In Proctor's view, only by recognizing the socioeconomic, political, and cultural toll that Jim Crow took on the lives of northern blacks will we be able to understand the principle underlying catalyst and motivation for the Modern Black Freedom Movement.[3]

Voices From the Firing Line also aims to deepen the social consciousness of the next generation

2 Jacquelyn Dowd Hall, "The Long Civil Rights Movement and the Political Uses of the Past," *Journal of American History* 91, no. 4 (March 2005): 1233-63.
3 Sundiata Keita Cha Jua and Clarence Lang, "The 'Long Movement' As Vampire: Temporal and Spatial Fallacies in Recent Black Freedom Studies," *Journal of African American History* 92, no. 2 (2007): 265-88.

of young people, policy makers, and activists in Pittsburgh and elsewhere. Young people, as Proctor puts it, too often believe that their accomplishments are the products of their own intellect, energy, and resources—"I did it all on my own. Nobody helped me!" Students reading this book will learn about the legions of Pittsburgh's men and women who made extraordinary sacrifices to open up jobs, neighborhoods, and schools heretofore off limits to black people. It will change the way you think about Pittsburgh, African Americans, race, and life in the new millennium.

Joe William Trotter, Jr.
Giant Eagle Professor of History and Social Justice,
Carnegie Mellon University, December 4, 2013

Prologue

A Desire to Write

This is a very personal account about the civil rights movement that took place in Pittsburgh, Pennsylvania, primarily between 1945 and 1980. It is told against the background of the national civil rights movement that swept the nation beginning in the mid-1950s and has waxed and waned since then.

The desire to write *Voices from the Firing Line* stems from my concern that many of today's young people have no knowledge of the battles fought to gain the freedoms they enjoy. That many rights are now taken for granted speaks to the progress made by the early activists. Yet, as an historian, I believe that understanding the past provides a crucial foundation for current and future actions. And much action is still needed.

As a teacher, I draw upon the oral traditions of African Americans who preserved our history through the stories they passed from one generation to the next. Such stories created collective memories and honored those whose deeds deserved to be commemorated. As I and my comrades-in-arms grow older, I fear time to capture memories is running out. Indeed, some of the great warriors of the movement have already passed away. For this reason, I embarked on an oral history project which I have transformed into *Voices from the Firing Line*.

Each revolution produces its own warriors—the heroes who place themselves at risk in order to change an unjust society. Those who gained prominence as leaders as well as those who work quietly behind the scene deserve our gratitude and remembrance.

Whose Voices Are Heard

For oppressed people whose voices have been marginalized and silenced, the issue of who can speak is highly charged. Deciding whose voices should be heard in this book was a matter of great concern, and I did not want to make that decision alone or arbitrarily. As I began the interviewing process for my oral history project, I asked each interviewee for the names of the five most important leaders in the movement. Among the most frequently named were Byrd Brown, James McCoy, Alma Fox, Harvey Adams, and Reverend Leroy Patrick. Beyond these key leaders, many others were mentioned. In all, I interviewed approximately 70 individuals whose voices appear throughout the book.[4] I've also drawn from my own memory and news accounts for additional information.

I am deeply indebted to the following individuals who graciously shared their time and memories with me. Each played an important role in Pittsburgh's civil rights movement. In many cases, complete biographies could be written about these extraordinary individuals and their dedication to the cause of equality and justice. What I present in *Voices* are short "cameo" portraits that convey a sense of their experiences of discrimination, what led to their involvement in the movement, and their key contribution.

Harvey Adams, Jr.	Mal Goode	Herman Mitchell
Lloyd Bell	Phylis Moreman Goode	William "Mugsy" Moore
Byrd Brown	Robert Goode	Reverend Leroy Patrick
Homer S. Brown	John Hannigan	Robert Pitts
Wilhelmina Byrd Brown	Pauline Hall	Father Charles Owens Rice
Frank Bolden	Phillip Hallen	Reverend James Robinson
Canon Junius Carter	K. Leroy Irvis	William Russell Robinson
Morton Coleman	Hubert 'Coop" Ivey	Roland Saunders
Ronald Davenport	Clyde Jackson	Henry Smith, Jr.
Arthur Edmunds	Bernard Jones	Nate Smith
Ed "Ewari" Ellis	Charles Kendle	Delores Stanton
Bishop Charles Hubert Foggie	Thomas Kerr	Tim Stevens
Alma Speed-Fox	Louis "Hop" Kendrick	William Strickland
Richard Gilcrist	Robert LaVelle	James Tyler, Jr
Dr. Charles Greenlee	Harriet McCrae	Herbert Wilkerson
Mary Gloster	Father Donald McIlvane	

In presenting their thoughts, I have remained faithful to the spirit in which they shared their recollections and in most cases have used the actual words they spoke, even when their comments were laced with profanity. Readers may be puzzled that so many intelligent men and women spoke in what seems to be broken or substandard English. This manner of speaking was not indicative of lesser education or intelligence. Rather, it reflects the speech patterns among Blacks who share a sense of comfort, camaraderie, and respect.

Honoring the Unsung Heroes

I fervently wish I could name every individual who fought for equal justice in Pittsburgh. That, of course, is impossible.[5] Therefore, I urge readers to keep in mind the millions of individuals who participated in marches, demonstrations, and protests that made change possible. Those listed below

---

4 All interviews for this project were conducted from 1991 to 2002. Unless stated otherwise, all comments attributed to these individuals were drawn from these interviews.

5 Freedom Corner is a monument at the corners of Centre Avenue and Crawford Street. It commemorates the contributions of those who participated in the Pittsburgh Civil Rights Movement. Jake Milliones, a city council member, conceived the idea for the monument, but died before the idea could be brought to fruition. That task was left to Sala Udin who was Milliones assistant and later was elected to city council. The artist for the project was Carlos Peterson and the architect was Howard Graves.

deserve recognition in their own right, but they also serve as representatives for those whose names have been lost to history.

Mattie Addis	Ruth Goode-White	Pharoah
Gail Austin	Dr. Leon Haley	Herman Reid
Roy Bates	Jody Harris	Luther Sewell
Millugetta Birru	Dr. Nelson Harrison	Sam Silberman
John Brewer, Sr.	John Heinz, III	Cecile Springer
Shelia Britton	James Henry	Eric Springer
Elmo Calloway	Dr. James Johnson	Stu Strothers
Harry Carroll	Dr. Norman Johnson	August Taylor
Dr. Alice Carter	Anne Jones	Dr. Arthur Tuden
Dr. Nathan Davis	Linda Kittle	Theodore Vasser, Sr.
Dr. David Epperson	Elmer McClung	Mildred Wade
Jesse Fife	Dr. Matt Nelson	Attorney David Washington
John Ford	Alice Nixon	

My Voice

As I said above, this is a highly personal account of the Pittsburgh civil rights movement. I am not a dispassionate researcher gathering "data" for a verifiable account of events. Rather, this has been a process of evoking memories—my own and those of others. After reviewing some of the early interviews, a good friend commented, "Wow! These people have given you a piece of their souls. These people were speaking to a trusted colleague, a friend. Why else would they reveal such personal information?" I believe she is right and feel honored that they entrusted their memories to me.

Readers who are looking for independent verification of the events I recount will be disappointed. My aim has been to convey each person's unique experience. Yet, many commonalities exist—from the indignities of racism to participation in the same demonstrations. In a sense, our collective memories corroborate my reconstruction of the Pittsburgh civil rights movement.

SECTION 1

PIERCING THE ILLUSION
OF INCLUSION

Pittsburgh, "The Promised Land"

CHAPTER 1

Introduction

From Slavery to Jim Crow Culture

When I began my oral history project upon which this book is based, almost all existing accounts of the civil rights movement focused on the southern states. Much less attention had been given to the struggles for civil rights north of the Mason-Dixon Line. Undoubtedly many factors contributed to this lack of attention. From my personal experience, however, and based on many formal interviews and informal conversations with my contemporaries, I attribute the lack of attention to a condition I call "the illusion of inclusion."

Largely because there were no Jim Crow signs screaming "White Only" and "Colored Only," those of us who were raised in northern cities believed that racial segregation did not exist here. We did not realize that we experienced much the same treatment as our Black sisters and brothers in the south. We, too, lived in segregated communities, attended segregated schools and churches, and were restricted in all aspects of life. However, if we stayed in our own segregated communities, we did not face the constant, in-your-face racism that southern Blacks endured. We could be born, reared, attend school, buy goods, be married, have children, vote in elections, die and be buried without facing overt racism. We then could delude ourselves into believing that we were included in all aspects of life, when in fact, we were excluded from White folks' lives just as much as those who lived in the South. Such self-induced blindness is the *Illusion of Inclusion*.

The Roots of Racism

From the founding of this country, Blacks have endured centuries of demeaning, dehumanizing, and deadly racism. The English system of "chattel" slavery persisted well into the 1800s, finally erupting in 1861 in the Civil War. Contrary to the common perception that the Civil War was fought to free the slaves, history documents that it was a fight about the expansion of slavery into the new western territories. History also shows, for all who care to know, that Abraham Lincoln did not believe in the equality of Blacks.[1] Nevertheless, the emancipation proclamation and the passage of the 13th Amendment

---

1   Lerone Bennet, Jr. *Forced Into Glory* (Chicago: Johnson Publishing, 2000).

to the United States Constitution brought an official end to slavery. The reality of the situation was far more complicated.

When the war ended in 1865, the North and South reconciled. President Andrew Johnson re-admitted the seceded states into the Union under the most lenient terms. As soon as the last northern troops departed, southern leaders moved to re-establish slavery by instituting a series of punitive measures, including a loophole that made slavery legal as a punishment for criminal behavior. Vagrancy laws, for example, allowed for the arrest and incarceration of anyone who could not show gainful employment.[2] When former slaves were incarcerated as vagrants, they could be leased under the convict leasing system to anyone who needed cheap labor. In order to "lease" a convict, a person needed only to pay the fine levied against the incarcerated person.

Once the "Compromise of 1876" ended Reconstruction and the electoral college "selected" Rutherford B. Hayes as President of the United States, southerners lost no time in re-establishing a system akin to apartheid in South Africa. Until the beginning of the modern civil rights protests (marked by the 1955 Montgomery, Alabama bus boycott), this system controlled virtually all aspects of Black life: whom they could marry, where they could be buried, where they went to school, where they could sleep, and where they could eat. Next came the voter suppression laws:

> The *Grandfather Clause* prohibited voting unless you could prove that your grandfather voted prior to 1865.

> The *Understanding Clause* required Black folks to interpret a section of a southern state constitution in order to vote. Of course, the Black person had to perform to the "satisfaction" of the White voter registrar.

> The *Good Character Clause*, a loophole that allowed illiterate Whites to vote, because the White voter registrar could determine who was of good character.

Black voting power was further negated by the free-rein given to terrorist organizations that soon spread throughout the South. In addition to the well-known Ku Klux Klan (KKK), other sinister groups operated under such seemingly benign names as the Knights of the White Camellia, Mother's Little Helpers, the John Birch Society, the Red Shirts, and the Baseball Club of the First Baptist Church.

When vagrancy laws and the convict leasing system were declared unconstitutional during Radical Reconstruction, southerners initiated a "sharecropping system," in which landowners could "lease" a portion of farmland to people who had no money. The tenant farmers would pay from one-third to one-half of their crop as "rent" to the landowners.[3] While on the surface that seems fair, farmers also owed money for the provisions they had to buy in order to plant and cultivate their first crop. Sharecroppers were forced to borrow from the land owner, because no White-owned establishment would extend credit to Blacks. By the time the sharecropper paid off all the debt, it was time to borrow for the next season's crop. Thus "renters" were never able to work their way out of debt. At the same time, they faced living conditions not much better than those that existed during slavery. In fact, the housing rented to the

2   Lerone Bennett, Jr. *Before the Mayflower* (Chicago: Johnson Publishing, 1962).
3   Joe William Trotter, Jr. *The African American Experience.* (Boston: Houghton Mifflin, 2001).

sharecroppers was often the old slave quarters. In most instances, sharecropping was the equivalent of lifelong slavery enforced by armed White men with orders to shoot any Blacks who tried to leave before their debt was satisfied.

When Black Codes became unconstitutional, every southern state began to pass a complex system of Jim Crow laws that continued to control virtually every aspect of Black lives.[4] Laws prohibited Blacks and Whites from playing checkers together, looking out of the same windows in textile factories, and drinking from the same water fountains. When a river or creek flowed through a southern town, Whites were permitted to swim, wash clothes, and drink upstream from the Blacks. White nurses could not treat Black male patients and, of course, there were Black hospitals and White hospitals. Blood was separated by race. If a hospital treated both Black and White patients, the wards were strictly segregated as were "insane asylums." Phone booths, schools for the blind, prostitutes, and cemeteries were separated by race. In court, Blacks and Whites swore to tell the truth on "Colored" and "White" bibles. Black and White school textbooks were kept in separate warehouses. Blacks were forced to sit in the back of the bus and in the "peanut heaven" balcony in movie theatres. Blacks could not rent rooms in White-owned hotels, nor could they get their hair cared for in White barber shops or beauty shops. Blacks could not eat in certain restaurants, could not worship God in White churches, and could not marry White folks.

The Jim Crow laws carried with them the additional insult of humiliation. No matter where Blacks travelled in the south, the symbols of White supremacy—**COLORED ONLY** and **WHITE ONLY** signs—served as constant reminders of their second-class citizenship.

Up North in the Land of Promise

As far back as I can remember, I heard older family members and neighbors sharing stories about the horrible conditions "down South": beatings, lynching, the "disappearance" of Blacks who "sassed" Whites, riding in the back of buses, the "Colored Only" and "White Only" signs, and the humiliation of a self-protective demeanor that allowed Whites to believe the "Negras" were happy. I witnessed discriminatory treatment during my family's summer visits to relatives in North Carolina. And I remember the amazement in the voices of Black folks down home when they asked me about life in "The Promised Land":

You mean Black folks got good jobs, and they can dress up in Sunday-go-to-meeting clothes and the White man don't bother them?

You mean y'all work right next to the White folks?

Y'all don't know nothin bout them goddamned signs that tells ya where you can eat or take a piss!

Boy, you sure is lucky to be living there! Soon as I kin save some money, I'm gonna come on up to Pittsburgh and git me a good job, buy me an automobile, and dress up in good clothes. I know iffin I kin make it to Pittsburgh, everything would be alright!

---

4   Trotter.

But I knew Pittsburgh was no promised land. Despite my telling them "Colored folks are discriminated against in Pittsburgh, the same as you are here," most folks clung to the belief (hope) that a promised land did exist somewhere up north.

In a sense, however, I was wrong. Discrimination in Pittsburgh *was not exactly the same* as the discrimination under which southern Blacks lived. There, racism was overt and sanctioned through a constellation of *Jim Crow laws*. Here in Pittsburgh, it appeared that we had more freedom and equality. For example, we had a bit of political power; my dad and mom voted, and Dad was active in local politics. Absent were barriers of the *Grandfather Clause*, the *Understanding Clause*, and *the Good Character Clause*. Northern Blacks did not endure poll taxes and literacy tests.[5]

Absent such blatant racist practices, we *were* free, were we not? Considering the network of blatant control that governed even the most trivial aspects of southern Black lives, northern Blacks seemed to enjoy a life free of discrimination. Beneath the surface, however, a covert, strongly entrenched *Jim Crow culture* constricted the rights and freedoms of northern Blacks. Major companies did not hire Blacks. City, county and state governments were controlled by Whites; few Blacks served on the police force. Public schools were segregated and practiced discrimination in the hiring, assignment, and promotion of Blacks as well as the omission of any information about Black history and culture in the curriculum. Colleges and universities limited the number of Black students admitted—if Blacks were admitted at all. Blacks could not swim in public pools, dine in restaurants, stay in hotels, enjoy any number of entertainment venues. Black women could not try on dresses in local department stores and none of these stores hired Blacks as clerks. Shoe stores in downtown Pittsburgh did not employ a single Black clerk. There were no Black bank tellers or loan offices; acquiring a mortgage was impossible. Discrimination limited the options of where Blacks could buy homes or rent apartments. The southern plantation system, that so effectively controlled Blacks, was replicated in northern steel mills, factories, and mines which were among the few industries where Blacks could find work.

One year, I engaged students in a classroom activity in which we wrote on a chalkboard every Jim Crow law we could find and how each law impacted behavior. Next we looked at the restrictions on Black behaviors in Pittsburgh. The students were stunned to learn that for every Jim Crow law that plagued southern Blacks, there was an equally devastating Jim Crow custom firmly in place in Pittsburgh. I call this constellation of unspoken customs a Jim Crow *culture*.

The virulence of this cultural racism rivalled that of the south. When Martin Luther King, Jr., held demonstrations in the northern city of Cairo, Illinois, he and his protestors were confronted by screaming White women, men, and children. In press conferences following the near-riots, King said he was stunned that northern Whites were as hateful as southern Whites. Until Cairo, even Martin Luther King had succumbed to the Illusion of Inclusion!

In northern cities located closer to the Mason-Dixon Line, the Jim Crow culture was more pervasive, more tightly woven, and exerted greater control. Blacks who visited or moved to Pittsburgh frequently expressed shock at the extent to which racial discrimination was so blatantly practiced here. Actually, this should not have been a surprise. Many of the Whites who lived in Pittsburgh had migrated from Southern states and carried their prejudices with them. For the most part, Whites who had always lived

---

5   Bennett, *Before the Mayflower.*

here did not object to the racist practices. It was easier to go along with the attitudes and behaviors of their White neighbors.

Submitting to Jim Crow Culture

Unlike the south where many Jim Crow practices were legal, in Pittsburgh the Jim Crow customs were often contrary to legislation specifically enacted to prohibit discrimination. Nevertheless, culturally embedded norms exerted tremendous control to let Blacks "know their place" and to keep Blacks in their place. From housing, to education, to law enforcement, to religion, to business, to recreation and entertainment—the older generation let the younger generation know where they could go, what they could do, and how they had to behave in order to be safe. Older Blacks knew how the system operated and passed on the knowledge of where Blacks could swim, dance, sit, use the restroom, get their hair taken care of, watch a movie, look for a job, try on clothing, sit on a bus, or even drive their car.

Despite such degrading treatment, it appears that Blacks did little, at least on an organized basis, to openly challenge the system. The roots of this apparent acquiescence go back centuries to the subjugation, dehumanization, and violence of slavery. Nowhere was this debasing violence more manifest than in the rape of Black women and the lynching of Black men. Typically, rapes took place in the slave quarters, away from the view of the White women. When the master came "to visit," he let it be known that any Black man present would be severely punished or killed. While Black men had a natural instinct to protect their women, women begged their husbands and sons to leave rather than face almost certain death.[6] This dynamic caused major problems between Black men and Black women across multiple generations.

In *100 Years of Lynchings*, Ralph Ginzburg details the White-sanctioned atrocities committed against Black males. Even after the Emancipation of slaves in 1865, Black men lived under the constant threat of beatings, a lifetime of legal slavery, and death. Any allegation of rape was sufficient justification for hanging. According to Ralph Ginzburg, many lynchings were treated as a social event. At times the lynching would be delayed until people could go home, pack a picnic lunch, gather the family, and return to watch the blood sport. Often, the murdered Black man was subjected to further indignities; his penis was severed, as a warning to Black men to "don't even ***look*** at White women." Ginsberg reports that it was not uncommon for some local participant in the lynch mob to carry the severed penis in his pocket as a trophy. In one instance, a mob was unable to locate the Black man who was accused of raping a White woman. Angered by this turn of events, the mob hanged the man's pregnant wife. As she was dying, a White man stepped from the crowd, brandishing a knife and cut the unborn child from the near-dead woman's womb. The infant was stomped to death by the frenzied crowd. When Blacks were no longer valuable chattel, lynchings and other forms of murder escalated.[7] Living generation after generation in a perpetual state of vulnerability gave rise to self-protective, non-threatening behaviors and demeanors. Submission was necessary to survive, but it left deep psychological scars.

The level of blatant and violent racism in the south contributed to a feeling among northern Blacks that they were living under less discriminatory conditions. Many Blacks who migrated to northern cities

---

6   Bennett, *Before the Mayflower.*
7   Ralph Ginzburg, editor, *One Hundred Years of Lynchings* (Baltimore: Black Classic Press, 1996).

felt they actually were better off. With no trust in city government, the judicial system, or police, many Blacks felt it was wiser to do nothing than to risk further trouble. Painful experience had taught that protesting discrimination provided all the excuse needed to arrest "troublesome" Blacks for "disturbing the peace," trespassing, disorderly conduct, or other trumped-up charges. Violating the cultural norms carried the risk of beatings, incarceration, and death. Survival depended upon submission. Perhaps this is so, but it also made us complicit in perpetuating Pittsburgh's Jim Crow culture. Yet, beneath the surface was a seething cauldron of resentment and anger that was eventually bound to boil over. First in small, isolated acts, resistance began to crack the tacit illusion of equality. Gradually, mass protests created a movement for integration of Blacks on an equal status with Whites. After the civil rights movement failed to produce the wholesale changes for which many Blacks had hoped, many Blacks withdrew from efforts towards integration and turned instead to the Black Power movement that excluded Whites.

CHAPTER 2

Life Cycle of the Pittsburgh Civil Rights Movement

In the early decades of the 20th century, Blacks suffered the indignities of Jim Crow culture in apparent silence. Behind the faint smiles and poker faces, however, was a seething anger that eventually erupted and gave rise to the Pittsburgh civil rights movement. Just what constitutes a movement can be understood by considering several fundamental dimensions—when it happened, what actions were taken, and who was involved.

Cracks in the Wall of Discrimination

The first visible cracks in the wall of racial discrimination on the national scene took place in 1954 when the US Supreme Court overturned the 1898 Court ruling in the case of *Plessey v. Ferguson*. *Plessey v. Ferguson* had upheld the constitutionality of the "separate but equal" mandate for schools. In 1953-1954, the NAACP mounted the challenge through their Legal Defense Fund. Thurgood Marshall,[8] a brilliant Black lawyer, was among those who argued that the concept of separate but equal schools was a sham and unconstitutional.

The fact of the matter was that there was no such thing as separate but equal schools in either the South or the North. Although Jim Crow laws in the South mandated such separation, in the North Jim Crow culture segregation was accomplished by virtue of "neighborhood schools." Because Blacks and Whites lived in separate enclaves, requiring children to attend schools in their own neighborhoods resulted in *de facto* separation. In neither the South nor North were the separate schools equal in term of education provided. In the landmark case of *Brown vs. the Board of Education of Topeka Kansas*, the Supreme Court ruled that all school systems in the nation should be desegregated *at all deliberate speed.*[9] Unfortunately, "all deliberate speed" was never defined and, consequently, many schools remained segregated. Nevertheless, the 1954 ruling represented a significant crack in the centuries-long legal wall between Blacks and Whites.

The second crack in the wall took place in 1955, when a simple act of defiance publicly challenged the notion of White Supremacy. In that year, a Black woman, Rosa Parks, refused to observe the segregated seating in a public bus in Montgomery, Alabama. Throughout the South, Blacks were permitted to ride

---

8   Eventually, Marshall became the first Black appointed as a justice to the US Supreme Court.
9   Trotter, *The African American Experience.*

only in the "colored" section at the rear of the bus. When Whites entered the bus and found no seats in the "White" section, they simply had the driver move the "Colored" sign. At that point, the law dictated that any Blacks now seated in front of the sign had to move further to the rear of the bus. On that fateful day, Rosa Parks, who was already seated in the colored section, was ordered to move further toward the back to afford a seat to a White man who had just boarded the bus. When Parks refused to do so, she was arrested and jailed. Blacks demanded her release, and she became a symbol of a new-found sense of righteous indignation. The Black citizens of Montgomery demanded to meet with bus company officials. Initially, all they asked for was that the segregated bus seating system be honored, meaning that if a White person boarded the bus and found no seats in the "White" section, that person would have to take a seat anywhere in the bus, even if it meant sitting behind Black folks. Believing that Blacks had neither the power nor the will to do anything about the situation, the bus company officials refused to grant this modest request.

Blacks called for a boycott of the bus company. Blacks policed themselves and put pressure on one another to stay away from the buses. On television stations across the nation and perhaps around the world, grainy black and white newsreels showed virtually empty buses and scenes of White bus drivers opening their doors at stops where Blacks refused to enter. Private vehicles picked up the former bus riders, and Blacks also walked, rode bikes, and even roller-skated around town. Finally, the bus company contacted the leaders of the movement and agreed to honor the status quo of bus discrimination. But it was too late. Now the Black citizens of Montgomery demanded the end of all forms of racial discrimination on buses. They had also expanded the boycott to include demands for better treatment by White merchants and jobs in downtown stores.

By the end of the boycott it was apparent that Blacks had faced off against the racists and **won**. Blacks in the South and the North stood a little taller. This marked the beginning of the modern civil rights movement. While the hard-fought victory over the racist system in Montgomery was important to the local community, the victory had several unforeseen and powerful impacts on the entire nation. First was the rise of the Reverend Doctor Martin Luther King, Jr. On the basis of this one victory, King and his organization, the Southern Christian Leadership Conference, rose to national prominence and importance.[10]

Second, the Montgomery boycott provided a very important psychological boost for Blacks. This was the first time Blacks could remember facing the racist system and winning. Although the Supreme Court decision was important on the legal front, it did not have the same visceral impact as the Montgomery boycott. At first, many of us were only vaguely aware of the Montgomery boycott. However, watching the old black and white newsreels made us feel proud. Across the nation, Montgomery became the rallying event. For instance, I was on the track team for Schenley High School. One day we badly defeated an all-White school. When we changed to our street clothes and were walking to our bus, some of the Whites from the other school decided they were going to "whip our Nigger asses." Suddenly, years of pent-up anger exploded. Each time my teammates and I hit a White player or fan, one heard a new battle cry, "this ain't Montgomery, motherfucker!" Soon the civil rights movement became national in scope, and news reporters from all over the world came to cover the movement.[11]

---

10 Bennett, *Before the Mayflower.*
11 Bennett, *Before the Mayflower.*

Beginnings of the Pittsburgh Movement

Pinpointing a specific time when a movement begins is difficult. Many people and some scholars mark the beginning of Pittsburgh's modern civil rights movement with the demonstration against Duquesne Light in 1963. Yet, as early as 1931, Black citizens had begun a 20-year battle for the right to swim in the Highland Park pool. Without undue concern for precise dates, several pivotal moments serve to delineate the life cycle of the Pittsburgh movement.

Prior to the mid-1950s, resistance to Jim Crow culture consisted primarily of small, sporadic protests directed toward a particular discriminatory event. This can be viewed as an antecedent to a full-blown movement with the involvement of large numbers of participants targeting a wide spectrum of institutionalized racism, over an extended period of time. From this standpoint, 1954 signaled a new, tumultuous era of race relations in the United States. Out of this turmoil, a movement was forged. Although it is impossible to trace all of the factors that contributed to the emergence of the movement, several deserve mention.

Across the country Blacks became less accepting of their status as second-class citizens. The horrific murder of Emmet Till helped to ignite simmering outrage. Black soldiers returning from the Korean War refused to submit to discrimination as they had before serving their country. If they had fought and died for the freedom of a country halfway around the world, surely they should be accorded respect and freedoms at home.

FIGURE 2.1
LEADERS OF PITTSBURGH'S 1ST MASS DEMONSTRATION

- Reverend Isaac Green, Pastor of Central Baptist Church and meeting host
- Reverend C. Leroy Hacker, Pastor, Shiloh Baptist Church
- Earl Belle Smith, President of the Pittsburgh Catholic Interracial Council
- Attorney Byrd Brown, President of The Pittsburgh NAACP
- Assistant City Solicitor Livingston Johnson
- James McCoy, Chairman of The United Negro Protest Committee
- Reverend Herbert Wilkerson, Executive Secretary of the NAACP
- C.E. McFadden, President of the Greater Pittsburgh Improvement League
- Gladys McNairy, Civic Leader
- Jackson Wright, Jr., Head of the NAACP Youth Council
- Charles Harris
- Bill Powell, local radio personality

The 1954 US Supreme Court ruling for school desegregation fostered a belief in the dawn of a new world in which racial equality would be rapidly achieved. The success of the Montgomery bus boycott also contributed to a mounting resistance to Pittsburgh's Jim Crow culture. The first mass demonstration in Pittsburgh was held in 1963, marking the start of five years of intense and widespread activism. This was such a pivotal moment, it deserves a more detailed description.

A Pivotal Moment—1963 Demonstration against Duquesne Light

The July 27, 1963, edition of *The Pittsburgh Courier* carried the headline, "Mass Protest Rally Set." The article announced plans for a mass rally to be held on Sunday, August 1, at Central Baptist Church on Wylie Avenue. The rally was a response to Reverend Andrew Young's (SCLC) criticism that there was no leadership in the North. Representatives of the planning group said, "We feel that there is no better time than now to show the world that Pittsburgh has leaders who are just as capable and articulate in presenting the grievances of the Negro Community as there are anywhere in the United States."

One of the tasks of the "unity" group, as it was called, was to use this meeting as a springboard for future mass demonstrations. Among the targets discussed against which demonstrations were likely to be launched were: Duquesne Light Company, the new Federal Building, Equitable Gas Company, People's Gas Company, the City-County Building, and the Washington Plaza Project.

Duquesne Light Company was chosen as the first target for a mass demonstration in Pittsburgh and took place under the aegis of the United Negro Protest Committee. According to NAACP President Byrd Brown, "Duquesne Light employed about 4,000 people. Only 35 of them are Black. Of those, 34 are in custodial positions. The other one is a secretary they hired so that when we came, they would have a Black person to meet with us." The demonstration took place at Mellon Park between Cherry Way and Smithfield Street, the location of Duquesne Light's headquarters. The following is my firsthand experience of the demonstration.

As I approached the site, I was surprised and pleased to see thousands of Black and White protestors ringing the Park. I had not seen so many Blacks in one place since I left the southern movement in 1961. Yet, as I joined the protestors, I flashed back to the horrors I had experienced during my time in the south. I thought about the pain from the beatings I had taken for the "crime" of seeking equality for Black folks. Images of fire departments hosing us down played before my eyes. The cries of women and children being beaten echoed from the past. I saw the image again of the southern sheriff with his knee pressing forcefully into the neck of a downed Black woman. In the throes of these memories, I stood no more than ten feet from a red-faced cop in riot gear and holding the leash of a police dog. I thought, "I may die today, because if that son-of-a-bitch turns that dog on me, I am going to try to kill it." The other thought that came flooding back was the training that I had received as a hand-to-hand killer, courtesy of Uncle Sam. I tried to find my center by silently singing the old Negro spiritual "Before I'll be a slave, I'll be buried in my grave and go home to my Lord and be Free!"

As I stood there, I noticed a movement to my left. A large, black van like those used to drop off riot-control cops stopped just across from me. "Damn, don't they already have enough cops to handle us?" Then the doors opened, and I stood in stunned silence as a Black man, dressed in a black military uniform complete with a beret, jumped from the back of the van. At his side, held firmly on the end of a short leash, was one of the largest dogs I had ever seen. Another brother followed the first; then another and another. Each one walked proudly, made a sharp military turn, and faced off against one of the police officers. I later learned this was a Black paramilitary group called The Democratic Association of Black Brothers.[12]

A cry filled the air as the marchers raised clinched fists skyward in the traditional "black power" salute. The hair on the back of my neck stood up; a chill played up and down my spine; a tear ran down my cheek. I straightened up and assumed the military "parade rest" stance. I felt ten feet tall. I was not going to be in the battle alone. I was ready. Let the battle begin! Fortunately cooler heads prevailed, and the cops did not attack us. The march proceeded without incident.

Democratic Association of Black Brothers

That demonstration of 5,000 people forced Duquesne Light Company to deal with us. As a result of the demonstration, the Urban League of Pittsburgh got a call to refer job applicants to Duquesne Light Company. The league referred 900 people within six or seven months. They had not referred 900 people in the previous six to seven years!

Many White Pittsburghers were stunned that "The Negroes are making trouble. They thought Pittsburgh Negroes knew their place." Indeed we did know our place on that hot summer day. Although subsequent demonstrations were larger, *this one* sent a clear message—hire Blacks *now*, or we will soon be at your doorstep. In a 1991 interview with Byrd Brown, he reminisced, "Ralph, you remember the day when I could put out a call, and we could put 8,000 people on the street?" Indeed, I did remember, with great pride.

---

12 I never saw these men again, but I hope they know how important they were in those most difficult days. They had to have known that they risked harm, or death, at the hands of rogue White cops that often showed up for riot duty ready to harm Blacks. Still they came! I hope they know that they saved lives that day. Diane Perry mentioned this group in a 1969 story about a violent confrontation between demonstrators and police that became known as "Black Monday." Writing for *The Pittsburgh Courier,* Perry reported, "At one time, during the stopover at the Steel Building, the crowd applauded and cheered as members of the controversial Democratic Association of Black Brothers marched, in single file, in front of the line of policemen with vicious looking dogs on leashes, and took positions directly in front of them."

The Movement Gains Momentum

From 1963 to 1965, scores of other demonstrations took place in Pittsburgh and surrounding communities such as Wilkinsburg, Homestead, Braddock, Homewood, and Rankin. In the beginning, the press covered most of the demonstrations. Later, as the number of protests increased, some were missed. Efforts to coordinate actions were not always successful as more than one event might occur on any given day. Local groups, wanting to control demonstrations in their own communities, did not necessarily inform the NAACP and/or the United Negro Protest Committee, so competing events could not always be avoided.

Nationally, the mid-1960s saw a new, more violent form of protest—riots in the Black ghettos[13] of major American cities, including:

1965—Watts in Los Angeles, California
1966—Detroit, Michigan
1967—Newark, New Jersey

When the urban riots of the 1960s first started, much of White society responded with disbelief. Some scholars put forth the "riff-raff" theory, explaining that the riots were caused by 5% of the Black community consisting of malcontents, communists, and criminals. With this theory, the solution was simply to incarcerate the "riff-raff" and life could return to normal. President Lyndon Johnson, however, was sufficiently alarmed by the riots that in 1967 he created the 11-member Kerner Commission, the National Advisory Commission on Civil Disorders charged with studying all the urban riots in order to determine the root causes and to suggest remedies to prevent their recurrence. Many officials, including the president, privately expressed the belief that the cause for the riots rested in the pathology of Blacks and the Black communities. They were shocked and disappointed when the Commission released its findings in 1968.

The Commission's report was a ringing indictment that concluded, "White society is deeply implicated in the ghetto. White society created the ghetto; white society condones the ghetto, and white society maintains the ghetto." The Commission warned that without changes, "We are moving towards two societies, one Black, one White—separate and unequal." The Commission recommended the passage of federal legislation that would promote true integration and enrich the lives of Black citizens. It further suggested job training, the creation of jobs to which Blacks would have equal access, and the creation of decent housing for Blacks. The Commission also cautioned that, if conditions remained unchanged, the United States would perpetuate a "system of apartheid" in its major cities. Despite the dire warnings, the findings of the Commission were ignored. National policies that exacerbated the problems delineated in the Commission's report continued unabated.

Waning of the Movement

---

13 Previously, urban riots were protests by Whites against Blacks. In New York, during the early days of the Civil War, Whites rioted against being drafted into a war they saw as a war to free Blacks. Mobs roamed the streets beating, lynching, and murdering Blacks. They screamed that they were not going to war to free *niggers*. In Pennsylvania, when steel mill owners brought in Black workers to replace striking Whites, angry White workers attacked Blacks. There had also been riots in the southern part of the United States after the Civil War when Whites, angry that Blacks were free, indiscriminately killed Black people. In all the riots mentioned, Blacks were the *targets* of mob violence. In the riots of the 1960s, Blacks were the rioters.

The accuracy of the Commission's assessment was proven when riots broke out across the country in the aftermath of the assassination of Reverend Martin Luther King, Jr., in 1968. Dr. King's assassination marked a pivotal moment, which some think brought an end to the civil rights movement in Pittsburgh. Dr. King's death certainly precipitated changes in the movement, both nationally and locally. In the years following the riots, the days of massive demonstrations with thousands of people taking to the streets waned. (Chapter 23 gives a more detailed account of the riots in Pittsburgh; Chapter 24 summarizes demonstrations that took place in the years following Dr. King's assassination.)

Many Whites, who had previously supported the movement, turned their attention elsewhere, becoming involved in anti-war efforts, the women's movement, and the fight for gay rights.[14] Many college students left the civil rights movement to take positions in corporate America. Other Whites lost interest because they believed that Blacks now enjoyed equality. Many White men no longer embraced the civil rights movement, because they found themselves, for the first time, competing with Blacks for jobs.

Blacks had changed as well. Some Black activists found meaningful employment in federal government programs such as Model Cities and the so-called Anti-Poverty Program. Many others became disenchanted with the movement because they felt that too little progress had been made. Many Blacks watched as Martin Luther King, Jr. met failure as he attempted to move his successful operation to Northern cities. Others felt that America was never going to live up to its promise of "life, liberty and the pursuit of happiness" for Black citizens. Many joined the rising chorus of Black voices demanding Black Power. For them the movement now was less about integration and more about building Black economic and political power.

Just as it is difficult to pinpoint the start of the civil rights movement, it is difficult to say when it ended. To help me answer the question, I examined *The Pittsburgh Courier* editions 1952 to 1982, looking for any stories that focused on civil rights activities. I noted events, whether big or small, and discovered that activities continued, at a very high level until 1971; then declined sharply. Beginning in 1972, instead of dozens of civil rights actions, *The Courier* reported only 13 events; then 11 in 1973; 14 in 1974. Throughout the remainder of the 1970s, the downward slope continued. From 1980 to 2002, the number of published stories about civil rights activities ranged from about 3 - 10 per year. Although the movement never died completely, it slowed to a crawl. Perhaps the movement no longer commanded the attention it once garnered. Perhaps *The Pittsburgh Courier* no longer had the resources to cover as many stories as it had in the past. Perhaps the movement lost its leadership. Perhaps the movement turned from a mass movement as individuals experiencing discrimination sought redress by filing complaints with the Pittsburgh Human Relations Commission, the Pennsylvania Human Relations Commission, and/or the Federal Office of Equal Employment Opportunity. This certainly was the case when I served on the Pittsburgh Commission for eight years in the 1980s.

 Thus, while Pittsburgh's civil rights movement continued for a number of years beyond 1968, by 1980 the movement was a mere shadow of itself. The NAACP continues today, but is a much changed organization; both in terms of the number of members and the respect afforded the organization even by Blacks. The Youth Division is a thing of the past, as is the very powerful Young Adult Chapter. Another

---

14 It is worth noting that many of those who became leaders in other movements had received their leadership training during their involvement in the civil rights movement. Many techniques they used had been part of the civil rights arsenal.

organization, The Black Political Empowerment Project also continues to operate. Civil rights activities still take place; however, the tactics and the participation have returned to a style very similar to that of the pre-1963 days. No calls go out for a mass meeting or a major direct-action exercise. Most of the work is done by writing letters or having small negotiation sessions.[15]

---

15 Since completion of the 2nd edition of *Voices*, the killing of Black men by police has provoked the *Black Lives Matter* movement, a new outpouring of mass protests across the country and, in some cases, around the world.

CHAPTER 3

Anatomy of the Pittsburgh Civil Rights Movement

Many forces shaped the structure and processes of the civil rights movement as it evolved. Pittsburgh did not have one unified civil rights group and tensions both within and among various groups exerted pressures that sculpted the nature of the city's movement.

Geography

Geography played a role in delaying the emergence of a full-blown civil rights movement in Pittsburgh. From its earliest founding, the rivers, hills, and valleys of the city's terrain fostered the development of racial and ethnic enclaves (Figure 3.1). Each community had its own distinctive culture, customs, folkways, and socio-economic characteristics. Contributing to the insular nature of the various communities was the custom of newcomers moving to neighborhoods where family and friends from "down home" already lived.

The largest Black community was centrally located in what is called The Hill District. Even that community had three subareas—the lower, middle, and upper Hill. The upper hill, in an area referred to as "Sugar Top," was home to most of Pittsburgh's wealthier, more highly educated, professional Blacks. Working class Blacks and merchants tended to live in the lower and middle hill. Residents in the widely dispersed public housing projects were lower-income Blacks.

Because Blacks were so widely scattered, folks in one community might not interact much with those from other communities. Even though many Blacks (and Whites) came to The Hill District to frequent bars, nightclubs, and speakeasies, normally they would return to their home community after an outing. Thus, they knew little of one and another. Regardless of where Blacks lived, negative attitudes and images emerged about "those folks" who lived in other communities. Sometimes physical confrontations occurred; often between youth gangs that flourished between 1945 and 1960.[16] This fragmentation of Black residents of Pittsburgh led to the emergence of many community-based leaders, rather than any one clearly identified and unifying leader.

Pittsburgh has always been a very provincial town, causing Black communities to distrust outsiders. It was much harder for folks with no Pittsburgh roots to be taken seriously as leaders. Beneath the

---

16 These gangs were substantively different than gangs that developed later. They were loosely organized and did not engage in selling and using hard drugs; nor were they involved in organized crime like prostitution.

FIGURE 3.1

DISPERSION OF BLACK ENCLAVES THROUGHOUT PITTSBURGH AREA

Center City
- Lower, Middle Hill & Upper Hill
- The Strip District
- Polish Hill
- Herron Hill
- Soho
- Hazelwood
- Bedford Dwellings
- Terrace Village 1 & 2*

East Side of the City
- Homewood
- Brushton
- East Liberty
- Wilkinsburg
- Lincoln/Larimer
- Stanton
- Garfield Manor*

South Side of the City
- Beechview
- Beltzhoover
- Chicken Hill
- Arlington Heights*
- St. Clair Village

North Side of City
- Manchester
- Chateau
- Woods Run
- Lower Northside & sections of Upper Northside
- Perry South
- North View Heights*

West Side of City
- Broadhead Manor*
- West End

*Public Housing Project

surface, one could hear the whispers, "What the hell do they know? How can they lead us? They ain't even from Pittsburgh." Newcomers did lead, but not without being put through some pretty strong tests of approval. Even today in the 21st century, Blacks who come from "out of town" have a difficult time being accepted by Black Pittsburghers.

The fact that there were so many leaders, from so many areas, made achieving consensus difficult. Fortunately, most disagreements took place behind closed doors where we could call each other names, debate strategy, and then emerge to face the world with a united front.

On rare occasions, things did escalate beyond closed-door arguments. In one instance, two prominent young activists each decided that the other was a spy for the CIA. During these times, the FBI and the CIA were infiltrating nearly every civil rights organization. At one meeting at the United Black Front on Wylie Avenue, one of the men burst into the room, sweating profusely, and screamed, "There's a fucking contract on my head!" He kept pacing back and forth, occasionally glancing towards the door. "They're claiming that I am a fucking CIA agent. They said a dude in Ohio and I are informants. They just fucking gunned him down, and are on their way to get me. You people have to help me."

This might seem like histrionics, except for the fact that earlier I had received a phone call from a former girlfriend who had married and moved to Ohio. She had warned me to stay away from the very activist who had burst into the meeting. Holding back sobs, she said, "Ralph, I know what I am talking about. That man and my husband were very tight. My husband was just gunned down in a public park.

As he lay dying, one of the shooters said, 'Now, motherfucker, we're going to Pittsburgh to get your friend.'"

I wasn't privy to the details, but someone at the meeting said they'd take care of the situation. Sure enough, the contract was lifted. But this incident is an example of just how dangerous those internal rivalries could be. You could be killed or harmed as a result of forces within the Black community as well as racists from outside our community. It was difficult to know who you could trust. I slept with a handgun close by.[17]

Despite the divisions I am going to describe, the fact is that the public and our enemies never knew about the divisions. Although we had differences, we settled them behind closed doors. We would go into a room, lock the door, bar the media and engage in conversation. That conversation sometimes was very strong, often loud, sometimes vulgar; despite this, when we came out of the room, we spoke with one voice. We adopted a policy that we would cease verbal assassination of Black folks for the entertainment of Whites.

Strategies of Resistance

Just as different communities followed different leaders, various groups used different tactics to challenge racist practices. The NAACP, especially before the 1960s, favored court litigation. As the movement became more militant, other groups, like the Congress of Racial Equality and the United Negro Protest Committee, preferred direct action such as picketing, sit-ins, and boycotts. At the height of the movement, many groups came together to mount massive demonstrations involving thousands of protestors.

In addition to confrontations, a number of more passive strategies proved effective. For example, when racist companies failed to negotiate in good faith, a telephone call-in tactic might be used. This entailed many individuals repeatedly calling the company and then hanging up when the phone was answered. Periodically, one of the callers would ask the switchboard operator if the company was ready to negotiate. Eventually, the company got the message, called the organization behind the protest, and requested a meeting.

This technique was still effective years later. In 1998, I was hosting a radio show on WCZJ in Homewood. Some callers complained that a funding organization was awarding grants to not-for-profit organizations, but gave little money to Black organizations. When I suggested that those with concerns should call the funder's executive director, I had no idea that hundreds of folks would do just that and tie up the phones for hours. Some callers succeeded in speaking with the executive director and one of them later reported, "Ralph, you will enjoy this. The director was so angry that his phone lines had been tied up for two days. He said, 'We can't get any work done because *you people* keep calling. Ralph Proctor put you up to this didn't he?'"

Another passive technique was used against the utility companies, which in those days sent their bills on computer-type cards clearly marked, "Do not fold, bend or mutilate." After hundreds of people proceeded to punch holes, fold, spindle, and mutilate their bills, the companies agreed to meet with civil

---

17 Despite conclusive evidence, many find it hard to believe that our own government would spy on its citizens. History has proven that J. Edgar Hoover spied on Martin Luther King. The federal government railroaded Marcus Garvey so that they could jail and deport him. The FBI targeted and destroyed the Black Panthers. Many ordinary citizens have a dossier compiled on them by our government.

rights groups. In another, brilliantly conceived move, many people would go to utility companies, banks, and other establishments to pay their bills with dimes, nickels and pennies. Boy, it took a long time to count out the required amount. I should know, because for some reason, I seemed to miscount the coins and had to start all over again.

Once, when I was working for the poverty program in The Hill, we had a great deal of difficulty getting the City to pick up the garbage on the stipulated date. Complaints to the City's Sanitation Department were ignored. On the next scheduled pickup date, the same lack of service occurred. Some "malcontents," as the city called them, suddenly appeared dragging garbage bags and cans and dumped them in the middle of the street. Oddly enough, the garbage was strewn over several blocks along Centre Avenue, including right in front of City Police Station #2, which was located about five doors away from my office. By mid-day, the city crews came and cleaned up the mess. Someone called the Sanitation Department and suggested that the same thing might happen every week should the garbage be ignored again. I wonder who would do such a terrible thing.

The good citizens of Homewood used a similar approach when City officials ignored requests to remove a number of abandoned cars. Not only were they an eyesore, but they were also a danger to the children of the community. Out of frustration, someone hired a private tow firm and had all the junk cars hauled into the middle of the main street, Frankstown Avenue. Strangely enough, all the vehicles were towed to the city-owned car pound on the very same day.

"Good cop, bad cop" was another effective strategy, because many Whites became unglued during confrontations with angry Black men. The toughest team members would be sent to a meeting with instructions to be as unyielding and obnoxious as possible—screaming, yelling, threatening; anything short of actual physical assault was okay. After the "bad cops" left, the firm would be contacted by the "good cop," who would listen sympathetically to the sorrowful tale of intimidation and say something like, "I am so sorry that Nate upset you. We know how difficult he can be. But, you know, he does have a point; your hiring record is not very good. I'll tell you what. I'll talk to Nate about his manners and ask that he not come back to see you again. Of course, you'll have to give me something that I can use to show your good faith efforts. Can we agree that in the next 30 days you will set up a training program for minorities and hire five Black folks? NO? Well, thank you for your time. I am sure Nate will be back tomorrow." You would be surprised how quickly the company was willing to make some concessions rather than see Nate again.

One of my favorite techniques was the sit-in, where members of a team would take over an office or a facility and shut it down until specific demands were met. Curtis Porter and Jack Daniel used this at the University of Pittsburgh where they and other students walked into the computer center, barricaded the doors, and vowed not to come out until the demands of Black students were met. The bold action led to the establishment of the Black Studies Program.

The tactic proved successful again in having Pitt set up a program to help older poor and minority students who were returning to college after a long absence. Officials had refused to negotiate, so I suggested that one person should make an appointment to see the provost. Once the meeting was secured, they should conduct a sit-in in the provost's office. Then I left for the Christmas break. Soon I got a call from my boss who asked me to return to work to help settle a dangerous situation. The women had followed my suggestion, but never divulged my part in the plot. The result was the New Careers Program.

The Organization of Black Administrators, Faculty and Staff met frequently to plan efforts to change the treatment of all Blacks on campus. The Black Action Society monitored treatment of Black students.

It is impossible to know the full extent of demonstrations, negotiations, and other protests that took place during the movement. Everyone was too busy making history to even think about documenting it. So much was going on, it actually looked as if we might achieve total equality. We came *soooo* close. Then our hopes were dashed by the assassination of Dr. Martin Luther King, Jr.

Internal Tensions

Within the movement, tensions arose based on a number of issues, some minor, some major. Although we were fighting common enemies in the larger society, we had to overcome a natural tendency to be competitive. We also had to overcome the lessons of slavery that taught us to mistrust and hate one another. As mentioned above, one source of tension arose from the mistrust among the various Black enclaves dispersed throughout the Pittsburgh area. In addition, tensions arose over differences in philosophy, color, gender, and age.

While all leaders cooperated with one another on major issues, it would be a mistake to assume that there was no tension. Many of the leaders were strong-willed individuals. Some of them rose to leadership positions by defeating equally strong-willed individuals. Sometimes residual tensions could be seen between winners and the vanquished. Some of those who lost their positions as leaders, simply left the group. Others formed their own organizations.

Tensions within the Movement—Philosophical Divides

Despite the effectiveness of a full range of active and passive strategies, they pointed to an underlying philosophical divide among various members within groups and among various groups. Illustrative of this divide are the attitudes of Homer Brown and his son Byrd, both of whom served as president of the Pittsburgh NAACP. As Byrd told me:

> Dad never understood why we would be willing to take to the streets, risk getting beaten
> or jailed, when all we had to do was take our case to the courts. I couldn't understand or
> accept the slow, deliberate, resource-gobbling approach used by the NAACP.

Although the NAACP was the oldest civil rights group, some viewed it as an elitist, middle class organization that was out of touch with the masses. This was particularly true of younger, emerging leaders like Byrd Brown who were impatient with the slow progress gained through legal channels. More militant members of the movement favored direct, and if necessary, violent confrontation. This sentiment in Pittsburgh led to the formation of other groups that challenged the NAACP for leadership. These included the Greater Pittsburgh Improvement League, United Black Front, Black Construction Coalition, Forever Action Together, United Movement for Progress, Operation Dig, Halfway Art Gallery, Congress of Racial Equality, and the Direct Action Coalition.

Following the murder of Martin Luther King, Jr. a philosophical divide deeper than that of strategy emerged. This concerned the very purpose of the civil rights movement and what equality truly meant.

In the early years, most civil rights groups and many liberal Whites saw integration as the desired goal of the movement. Even so, different groups had differing definitions of "integration." Blacks were seeking the integration of the entire Black population into White society; all Blacks were supposed to benefit from the movement. Many Whites, however, were seeking to admit only the most "desirable" Blacks—those who were educated, adhered to White cultural norms, were well-groomed, spoke "good" English, and were "light, bright and almost White."

Other Blacks openly criticized efforts aimed toward integration, saying in effect, "Come on, get real. If they would kill someone who stood for *peace,* what would they do to the rest of us? We need to quit this bullshit, and concentrate on Black Power, Black Liberation, and self-determination." Previously, this philosophy of separation had been embraced only by so-called "militants." Later, however, new voices such as those of Black intellectuals were being added to the separatist chorus. The Black Muslims said we should have expected that Whites would do something to keep us out of their communities, jobs, churches, and away from their women. Essentially, they were saying, "I told you so!" After the riots, I was interviewing Dick Gregory, comedian and civil rights activist, on my show, *Black Horizons.* When I asked about his feelings about integration, he said, "It is entirely possible I could leave this show, go downtown to my hotel, enter my room, lie down in bed, have the place catch on fire, die. But it is not likely, at all, that I would go downtown, see that the place is on fire and enter my room, and lie down in my burning bed!" I understood all too well what he was saying.

Many who had been fighting racism believed discrimination persisted because so many were oblivious to it—especially in the North with its illusion of inclusion. In the early years, many naively thought the solution was simply to raise awareness. When this failed, many became disenchanted. Out of that disenchantment came the shift from integration to self-determination and the emergence of the Black Power movement.

It was difficult, in my research, to determine who belonged to the integrationist and the separatist groups. In fact, some individuals were identified as having belonged to **both** groups. Attorney Richard Jones said, "All the Negroes involved in the separatist group were initially from the South. That group reached the conclusion that Negroes had to accept separate schools." His next remarks were revealing with respect to the animosity between the two groups. He took an intellectual swipe at the opposing group by saying, "No intellectual effort had been made by Pittsburgh Negroes to obtain employment in mixed schools, and we should accept no less. They [the separatists] were ready to consummate a deal for Pittsburgh, and I was fearful that the separate school system would come about. I had become a lawyer to become independent, and not have to live in mental or physical slavery." For the most part, Homer S. Brown agreed with Jones' observations. What is telling about the conversation is that the interviews took place in 1973 about a situation that occurred in the 1930s; it was obvious that both men still harbored anger towards the individuals who had been a part of another Black leadership group. This animosity and distrust obviously continued until the time of the civil rights movement, which took place thirty years later.

Tensions—A Matter of Name

One ramification of self-determination was a painful process of claiming and naming our own identity. From the time Blacks first arrived in America on slave ships, we were called by various names—Neger,

Niger, Negra, Negro, Black Ivory, Nigger, Darkie, Sambo and so forth. Over time, Negro and Colored came to be the commonly accepted terms. With the rise of the Black Power movement, however, many of us wanted to define ourselves differently with names like Afro-American, African-American, and Black.

"Black" was a bit of a surprise, because for eons it carried negative connotations. When I was a young man, calling someone Black was grounds for a fist fight. I, like others, was initially confused by the idea of upending the status quo by claiming Black as a positive identity. Yet, the word did seem to fit, and I adopted it on my radio and television shows. On one show, I engaged in a conversation with a conservative man who was upset with me for, as he called it, "Africanizing" Negroes. He said that all Negroes did not come from Africa. Further, he did not appreciate being called "Black." "We are not black, we are brown." When I pointed out that he had called himself "Black" for many years but just didn't know it, he became agitated and insisted that "Negro" was the correct term. I thought he would have a coronary when I showed him a page from a dictionary that indicated that Negro was a Spanish word for the color black. He left the show in angry denial. Years later the same man chaired the African Heritage Room Committee at the University of Pittsburgh. He was still struggling with "Black," but now admitted that Blacks came from Africa—direct descendants of Cleopatra and other queens and kings of Egypt. He simply could not deal with the thought that we may have been descendants of dark-skinned, ordinary folks from West Africa.

According to an October 19, 1969, article in *The Pittsburgh Courier*, a growing dissatisfaction with progress and an increasing sense of Black pride led the United Negro Protest Committee to change its name to The United Black Protest Committee. Along with the name change, UBPC adopted a ten-point program; among the points was an agreement to push for a Black president for the national NAACP. All previous presidents had been White.

Tensions within the Movement—Matters of Color

Some Whites also had difficulty calling us "Black." Friends would say something like, "Ralph, you're not Black; you're brown. I just can't bring myself to call you Black." Phrases like "Say it Loud; I'm Black and I'm Proud," created emotional dissonance. They would say things like, "You don't want to use that word. Yes, I understand that you feel you must re-define yourself, but why don't you let us help you?" My response was usually, "Well now, it is true that I am not black as a color, but neither are you white, as a color. In fact, you are pink. But you have no problem calling yourself White; perhaps because whiteness connotes privilege. No thanks, we do not need you to help us re-define ourselves. It is your definitions that got us into this mess in the first place!" Black power—two simple words—caused broken friendships and the exodus of some Whites from the movement.

There is a saying in a movie with an all-Black cast—"If you White, you alright; if you Brown, you can stick around; but if you ***Black***, get back." This alluded to a system of color discrimination and preference expressed not only by Whites, but also by Blacks. The system originated during slavery, when light-skinned Blacks had slightly more status than their darker skinned brothers and sisters. The system held that the lighter you were, the "prettier" you were. The preference seemed to be for Colored people who were "light, bright and almost White." This caused many battles between Blacks of various shades. "High Yellow" was preferable to "Deep Blue/Black." Very dark folks were not beautiful, or so they were taught. As a young man, I was rejected as a suitor by one young lady because as she said, "You're too light. A man as light as you are would never marry a girl as dark as I am." Another woman rejected me, because I was "too light, and could produce a White baby!" This color-consciousness found its way into the civil rights movement. Nate Smith, a powerful, important leader who was also very dark, recalled being told that he could never be a leader because he was too Black.

While many people treat the civil rights movement as an exclusively Black effort, this is an erroneous idea. Clearly, the movement was a collaborative effort between Blacks and Whites. In fact, much of the information we used to negotiate with companies, government agencies, and other organizations came from White people who had access to information denied to Blacks. We owe these folks, who risked much for no personal gain, an eternal debt of gratitude. That said, tensions did arise when Whites felt they were better positioned to lead organizations and projects than Blacks. Those who understood the importance of Blacks claiming power for themselves continued as valued allies; those unwilling to grant Blacks their right of self-determination often left the movement.

Probably the most charged areas of the color issue concerned inter-racial marriage. Two friends, Elmer McClung, who ran for city council, and Byrd Brown, who ran for mayor of Pittsburgh, both lost their bids, in part, because they had White wives. It seems that more Black women than Black men simply refused to vote for them because of the color of their wives' skins. Black men who dated/married White women were accused of "talking Black and sleeping White." Any attempt to reason with these folks was fruitless.

Tensions within the Movement—A Matter of Gender

Another source of tension was the role of women versus men as leaders. There is some disagreement as to the genesis of this problem, but it did cause contentious moments during the movement. Traditionally, Black women held many leadership positions in churches, schools, and social organizations. According to some who were willing to speak about the subject, the lack of men in key positions was due to the preference Whites had for hiring Black women rather than Black men. Some women with whom I spoke said they stepped forward because Black men would not. Many people were unwilling to broach the subject for fear of being accused of harboring negative feelings towards one gender or the other. In fact, most would not speak to me on the issue until I agreed that I would not use their exact words or attribute the words to them. At any rate, in the beginning of the civil rights movement locally and nationally, there was tension as men assumed leadership roles, often pushing women aside. Many of the women with whom I spoke said that they were happy to step aside and let Black men lead, because they believed that it was about time Black men stepped up to the task.

Tensions within the Movement—A Matter of Age

Other problems arose as a result of age differences. Many of the young folks, including me, grew weary of older leaders holding on to the reins for too long. Each generation felt the "old heads" had no fire and engaged in more moderate (some would say insignificant) forms of protest. Each new generation questioned the value of what the previous generation considered as dangerous and militant. I had my time on both sides of the age issue. Many young folks thought the approach of using the courts as a way of addressing Black problems was too slow, too cumbersome. Around the country, young folks were expressing displeasure with the NAACP, its old, middle class leadership and its slow tactics. The NAACP found itself running to catch up with the young people. As Byrd Brown, a key leader of the Pittsburgh movement put it, "When you used the litigation approach, it only affected a few people. By the time you took it through the Court, you had exhausted huge resources in terms of money, which we didn't have, and it took years."

The Pittsburgh Courier reported on January 31, 1970, that there was friction between the United Black Protest Committee and the national NAACP because the national NAACP suggested that the United Black Protest Committee might not be legal. In 1963, the charter of the University of Pittsburgh chapter of the NAACP was questioned by the national NAAP, based on the fact that the Pitt chapter was engaging in "questionable activities," such as picketing and mass demonstrations.

Despite these tensions, those who dedicated themselves to the movement tried as best as they could to make life better for both the present and next generations. What led each individual to become involved in the fight for equality may have differed; however, their sacrifices cannot be denied or ignored. While I cannot speak to the experiences that led each individual to shed the illusion of inclusion, I share some of my own story. In the following chapter, I trace my evolution from a naïve youth to a militant activist.

CHAPTER 4

Shedding Illusions – Finding My Voice

AUTOBIOGRAPHICAL SKETCH OF AN ACTIVIST

An Unlikely Activist

I did not decide, early in life, that my ambition was to be involved in efforts to secure equal rights for Black folks. I most certainly never gave a moment's thought to leading any kind of civil rights organization. Neither, as a matter of fact, did any of my friends harbor any such ambition. Oh sure, in our early teens we became aware of the discriminatory treatment to which people of color were subjected in Pittsburgh. My closest friends and I often spoke about being aware that our fathers were somehow held back because of their race. We vowed to "do better" and go to college so that we would not have to work as hard and make as little money as our fathers. We even promised that we would not accept the same kind of racist treatments we saw our fathers endure. Never did we talk about being a leader.

It is somewhat of a surprise that I became involved in any sort of activity that required me to speak in public or lead any kind of process. Until the eighth grade I was an extremely shy child, who spoke only what is now called "Black English." I could barely stammer a coherent sentence in public and felt like I was dying each time I had to speak in the front of the class. A White teacher, Gladys Donahue, decided that she "saw something" in me and made me one of her "projects." She taught me Standard English, without ever communicating that the language I already spoke was inferior. She convinced me to drop the art classes I loved, so that she could enroll me in a group of "leadership" classes. She pushed me to take leadership roles in which I was forced to speak in public. She succeeded in turning me from a natural introvert into a manufactured extrovert. Even today I am still shy to a fault.

It is equally amazing that I became a talk show host. I hated my voice. In the 8th grade our English teacher, who also taught public speaking and mass communication, took us to the auditorium where we had to go on the stage and read a news article from one of Pittsburgh's newspapers. When I heard my voice bouncing off the walls I was embarrassed and appalled by the sound. My God, I sounded like a *girl!* I was so relieved when the ordeal was over. I went back to my seat, fighting back tears and afraid to look up. Then I heard the applause and heard the teacher say, while he was applauding as well: "See, Ralph has the kind of voice that would be very successful on the radio." "Sure," I thought, "and pigs fly!" And yet, years later, his pronouncement proved to be true.

In this chapter I explain the forces that shaped my involvement in the civil rights movement and why I felt compelled to act when I saw racism, discrimination or other unfair treatment, even if I was not the victim. I always knew there would be a penalty for fighting my bosses, the army, school administrators, government agencies and other establishment entities. The cost of militancy was lost jobs, denied pay raises, physical harm, and social censure. So, given all that, what led to my involvement in the civil rights movement?

Two of the forces were my mother and father. Mom raised me to be the kind of person who helped others without thought of personal risk. She told me I had an obligation to help others. Dad raised me to be a rough, tough person capable of holding my own in any type of confrontation. Actually, holding my own was not enough. He and my uncles taught me that once hostilities began, my job was to wipe out my opponent in such a way that they would think long and hard about ever bothering me again. They said, "When you have to fight, make certain that you hurt the other person enough so they know that each time they fight you they will leave with a memory of pain!" The lessons from my mom, my dad and my uncles formed the base for my fight for social justice. In the remainder of this chapter, I recount key events that led me from naiveté, to anger, to activism.

The End of Innocence

For the most part, many of my family, neighbors, friends and I were simply living our lives while being somewhat insulated from racism, because we spent most of our time in Pittsburgh's Hill district. There one could avoid some aspects of visible racism. After all, prior to a disastrous urban "renewal" program, The Hill District provided most of what we needed. We were educated there, sought entertainment there, and got our first jobs there. We had grocery stores, pharmacies, cleaners, bowling lanes, night clubs, bars, hotels, clothing stores, shoe stores, jewelers, and many other establishments. In fact, if one wanted to, one could purchase most necessary goods and services without stepping outside The Hill. I was born into this sheltered community with no awareness of the harsh realities to come.

Herron Avenue, circa 1940s

I was talking with Mrs. Russell, an older lady with whom I was friends, when my mother called me to come back home. As I climbed the front steps, Mom asked, "Why were you going to kick Mrs. Russell?" Despite my denials, Mom had clearly recognized that my right leg was locked and ready to deliver a swift kick to the shins. Busted! "I was mad 'cause she was accusing me of something I didn't do and wouldn't do."

"What on earth—," Mom started to ask as I continued in an aggrieved tone. "She asked me who that White boy is who's always playing at my house. I told her I didn't know no White boys, and if I did, I wouldn't play with them. I hear what you and daddy say about White people doing bad things to Colored people. You say that sometimes they hurt and kill Colored people, and they won't give Colored people jobs and they are mean. So I just decided that I wouldn't have nothing to do with those White people. But Mrs. Russell kept saying she saw the same White boy around my house a lot. Then I got real mad when she asked me who that boy was at my house yesterday? I remembered that Jimmy was here for dinner. I told her that wasn't no White boy. That was Jimmy! But she kept saying that Jimmy was White, and I got mad and was going to kick her."

Mom said, "Honey, Jimmy *is White!*" I could not believe Mom could say such a thing, and we argued back and forth for a couple of minutes. Finally, Mom asked what color I thought Jimmy was. "Jimmy is *PINK!*" I replied with a certainty that is reserved for youth.

"No, Honey, Jimmy is White!" Now I found myself getting angry and continued to argue back and forth: "WHITE!" "PINK!" "WHITE!" "PINK!" Then I asked, "What color is Carol?"

"Your sister is *Colored.*"

"I know she's colored; but what color is she colored? Jimmy is colored and Carol is colored, and they are both colored *pink!* What you're saying just don't make sense. How can Jimmy be White and Carol be Colored when they are both the same color?" We argued until my dad came home and asked what all the ruckus was about. Mom told him, and he had a good laugh at my expense. He joined the opposition, by also insisting that Jimmy was a White boy. We were getting nowhere. Dad suggested that I get out of Mom's way and go read my comic books. This I did, and as I was reading *Superman*, I came across the ultimate defense of my position. Mom was at the dining room table fixing something to cook. I walked up to her, placed my comic book on the table, and pointed to the border around the pages. "What color is this?" I asked.

"White."

Now I had her. In the most condescending voice a 10-year-old could muster, I said, "Right! Now what color is this, as I pointed to Superman."

"White," she said.

"Mommy," I gasped, "Superman can't be white if he's not the same color as the edge of the page. This is white; Superman is pink, and Carol is the same color, so *she* is pink. Jimmy is the same color as Carol and Superman, so he is *PINK, TOO!* So I wasn't playing with no White boy."

By now Mom and Dad had endured just about enough of their precocious son and said in unison "Why don't you go outside and play?" Feeling victorious, I was ready to confront Mrs. Russell with my well thought out proof. I was stopped short, however, when I overheard Mom ask Dad, "How do you get your child ready for what is going to happen to him as he gets older? How do you tell your son that he will be hurt every day of his life because he is Colored and most of the world is White?" I waited for Dad's response. There was nothing but silence!!

A day or so later, I went to the public housing project to see if Jimmy wanted to play. When he opened the door, I said, "Hey, Jimmy, come on out and play. Ask your mom if you can come home with me and spend the night. Mom is fixing your favorite dinner, fried chicken."

"I can't," Jimmy informed me. "My mother told me that I was too old now to play with Niggers."

I replied, "That's okay 'cause I ain't no Nigger, whatever that is!"

"I already told you that my mom said I was too old to keep playing with Niggers." With that he shut the door in my face.

At this point, I was more confused than angry. Jimmy and I were in the sixth grade and had been friends since kindergarten. He had eaten at my house many times, and had even spent the night on several occasions. I thought about that for a moment and then realized that I had never eaten at or spent the night at Jimmy's home.

After standing there for a few minutes, I walked home, bounced up the steps, and finding Mom in the kitchen, said almost in one breath, "Hi, Mommy. The chicken sure smells good. Can I have a drumstick? Jimmy can't come to dinner tonight because his mommy told him he's too old to be playing with Niggers. Do we have some Kool-aide? Mommy, what's a Nigger?"

Mom stopped cooking and became very sad. "I'm sorry, Honey" she said, folding me in her arms. "I am so sorry that you were hurt by Jimmy, but like we told you, Jimmy is White, and most White folks think they are better than Colored folks." What was she talking about? I wasn't hurt; I had plenty of friends. I would just play with them. Then she explained what a Nigger was. I did not understand all the words, but I did know that most of them were hurtful. I knew that Jimmy had insulted me. I told Mom

I would be right back as I ran down the steps and out the front door. I ran all the way back to Jimmy's home and knocked as loudly as I could. "Come on out, Jimmy," I screamed. He finally came to the door and said, "I already told you I'm too old to play with Niggers." I grabbed his collar and screamed, "In the first place, I ain't no Nigger, and I didn't ask you to come out to play. I asked you to come out so that I can kick your White ass!" Unfortunately, I did not get a good grip on his shirt. He broke away, slammed the door and ran to his mother shouting: "Mommy, Mommy, Ralph is going to kick my White ass! Help me, help me." The little punk never could fight! I always had to rescue his butt from other kids. A short time later his family moved. Good!

The Shock of Recognition

The year I learned Jimmy was White, I was in art class working on a mural-sized image of a child on a swing. I was a good artist and teachers delighted in showing me how to improve. Often I was assigned to help out by painting backdrops for stage plays or other such special projects. I enjoyed the work and the special attention. At the direction of the teacher, I began adding more red coloring to the boy's cheeks. Suddenly I stopped and stared at the image. Something was wrong, but what? Slowly it dawned on me that I was painting a pale-skinned, red-cheeked, blue-eyed White boy. I realized I had never painted a picture of a Black person. I didn't even know how to paint a Black person. My teachers had taught me to paint what they knew; humans in their own image. Confused, hurt, and angry, I vowed never to draw another human figure until I learned how to draw Black figures. By holding up a mirror and drawing what I saw, I learned to draw big noses, thick lips, and kinky hair. I do not believe my teachers had intentionally meant me harm, but still the shock of realizing Blacks were never included in our school's artwork took me one step closer to anger and activism.

The "Kindness" of Strangers

Each summer my family traveled to North Carolina to visit relatives. We were somewhere below the Mason Dixon line when the car ran low on fuel, and Dad stopped at a rural gasoline station. While the attendant was putting fuel in the car, I noticed a restaurant inside the station. Starving, I asked if we could go inside to get some food. Dad did not respond, and I watched in confusion as his posture changed—his shoulders slumped, and he stared at the ground. After paying for gas, Dad drove around to the back of the station where the man who had fueled our car, came out of the back door, walked over, and handed him a cardboard box containing sandwiches and soft drinks. We ate in silence as I fumed at the indignity of having to eat outside. My anger grew when I told Dad I had to go to the bathroom. "You'll have to go in those woods," he said. "The restrooms are only for White folks."

As we continued our journey, my sisters and I began to complain we were thirsty. Tired of our complaining, Dad finally pulled off the road near a small farmhouse. After talking to the elderly White woman who answered the door, Dad told us to follow him to the back of the house. We stopped at a well; Dad dropped the bucket into the depths, and pulled up cool, fresh water. As we drove away from the house, Mom and Dad kept remarking about how nice the woman had been, how kind she was to allow us to drink from her well. "What was the big deal," I thought. "After all, if that lady had come to our house and was thirsty, I would have given her a drink of cold water from the jug we kept in the refrigerator."

Later I realized that Jim Crow laws had forbidden us from eating at the gas station's restaurant and the elderly woman had violated southern norms by letting us drink from the same dipper she used. My proud father's slumping posture was necessary to assure his family's survival in hostile territory. We had been given food and drink by the "kindness" of strangers.

Minding My Place

I really liked spending time at Grandma Amy's farm. Everyday breakfast was huge—eggs, bacon, ham, chicken, pancakes, biscuits, jam, honey, and all manner of good things. So, the summer I was about 10, on the day before we were to start home, I stayed with Grandma while the rest of the family went to see other relatives. My plan was to enlist Grandma in my plan to extend my visit, so I was trying to be on my best behavior when I answered a knock on the door. As I opened the screen door, an elderly White woman entered and was greeted warmly by Grandma. I was left to visit with the stranger while Grandma went to the kitchen for iced tea. I wasn't paying much attention as I contemplated the possibility of running down a chicken and wringing its neck so we could have it for dinner. My cousin Charles and I had done this the week before and claimed that the chicken had fallen over dead. Grandma had been skeptical, but the fried chicken was so good I wanted to risk the ruse again.

At any rate, the White lady asked me a question, and I replied, "no." Surprised at my response, she and asked, "What did you say?" Again I replied, "no," but with a little more emphasis. She said, "Didn't you forget something?" Now the lady was getting on my nerves. I said, "I didn't forget nuthin'. The answer is 'NO'."

Just then Grandma called, "Come here, son, I need you to do something for me." When I entered the kitchen, she said in a low voice, "Baby, down here, when a White person says something to you, you're supposed to answer by saying, 'yes ma'am, no ma'am, or yes sir and no sir."

"Why would I say 'yes ma'am' to that old dried up White lady when I don't even say that to my mother?" My young voice bounced off the wall. Grandma was appalled and went into the living room and apologized to the woman, "Please excuse the boy. He's from up North, and he ain't accustomed to our ways." The woman said she understood and sat with Grandma sipping on some cool tea. I was HOT! Why was Grandma apologizing for me when I had done nothing wrong? When Mom and Dad returned, I heard Grandma telling them that they had better take me back up North because I was going to get hurt, or worse, because I did not "know my place."

I was so angry, I refused to travel down home again. It was fine by me that the visits to North Carolina came to an end. My step towards militancy drew ever nearer.

Lessons in Racism

My education in racism continued courtesy of the Pittsburgh Public School system. Admittedly, elementary school was not so bad. We had both Black and White teachers at Robert L. Vann Elementary School, and as noted above, I was too young and naive to recognize racism. At Herron Hill Junior High School, however, I began to notice the differences in the way Black and White students were treated. A memory from English class still remains vivid. I had been absent from class one day and missed a homework assignment. Hating to fall behind in my work, I received permission to complete the assignment while the student teacher and the class went over some new material. Sitting in the front row, right under her nose, with only two sheets of lined paper and a #2 pencil I wrote a one-page essay about visiting a cemetery at night. I was stunned when the paper was returned the next day with a big, red "F" emblazoned across the top and a cryptic sentence: "See me." I demanded an explanation, and the student teacher said, "I failed you, because you plagiarized this paper!"

"How could I have copied this paper when I sat right under your nose and wrote it? You never moved from in front of me, and you would have seen me copying from something!"

"There can be no other explanation," she asserted. "No eighth grade child can write this well. You had to copy it." The ensuing shouting match was interrupted by my regular English teacher. "What the hell is going on here? I can hear the two of you screaming way out in the hall." The student teacher and I both yelled our explanations. Again we were interrupted. "You just came to this damn school and you don't know my students. Why the hell didn't you check with me before accusing the student of doing something wrong? Give me the damn paper."

I handed it to him; he perused it for a moment and looked at the student teacher in utter disgust. "Hell, this is the way he writes all the time. Give him his damn 'A' and an apology. And, Ralph, shut up." I got my "A," and a lesson in the racist belief that no *Black* student could write well.

In 1953, when we graduated from Herron Hill Junior High, we had two proms; one for the White Kids; one for the Blacks. Frankly, I don't recall and don't care where the White prom took place. We Black students held ours in the basement party room for residents of Knott Manor, a small apartment building on Centre Avenue in The Hill. That was another indelible lesson in discrimination.

In high school, teachers who acted as guidance counselors were supposed to advise students on what courses to take, how to complete college applications, where to seek scholarships, and other preparations for life beyond graduation. This tended to happen for students of color—"high yellow" color that is. These were light-skinned Black students who came from a so-called "good family." For the rest of us chocolate kids, things were quite different. Guidance counselors frequently steered Black students away from college courses, suggesting that Black girls take secretarial courses, while directing Black males to trade school courses so that they could get a job "working with their hands." Those of us who aspired to a college education attended the obligatory "guidance" sessions, listened politely, and then gave these "counselors" notes from our parents dictating what courses they wanted us to take.

I was targeted by Miss Fannie Pittler, one of these notorious practitioners of biased counseling. When asked about my plans after high school graduation, I informed Ms. Pittler that I was going to college. She seemed surprised and suggested that I would be better off taking some "trade" courses at Connelly Trade School. "Why on Earth would I do that?" I asked.

Her reply was, "Now, Kenneth, you know that you won't find jobs like the White kids will, unless you are prepared to work with your hands. It would be senseless to take academic subjects in the hope of getting a better job. Besides, you'll never get into college with *your* grades."

I was dumbfounded. "What are you talking about? I'm a straight-A student. My folks expect me to go to college and that is precisely what I am going to do!"

She interrupted me, claiming that I had some very low grades. I said, "I don't know what you're talking about. I am a straight-A student, and why do you keep calling me Kenneth? My name is 'Ralph'." At that, I grabbed the folder lying in front of her and said, "Lady, don't say another word to me. You don't even know who I am. Kenneth Proctor is my *cousin!"* I left her office and went to complain to the principal who dismissed it all as a "little misunderstanding."

Discrimination was not confined to classrooms and guidance counselor offices. I helped a friend design "Schenley Spartan," a mascot for the high school's football team. The mascot came complete with costume. When it came time for try-outs, Black males were not permitted to put on the costume, let alone audition for the part. Naturally, we protested our exclusion. The principal, Mr. McCormick, claimed it was for our own protection, since we played in some rough coal-mining communities that did not like Blacks. He went on to say that those White folks might become angry seeing a Black male on the field in a Spartan uniform. Unconvinced, we argued that we were perfectly capable of defending ourselves, especially given the fact that most of us Black males were gang members. Our protests went unheeded, and a White boy with no athletic ability took the field as the Schenley Spartan mascot. We seethed in anger as we watched this pudgy character prance around the field pretending to be a mighty warrior.

Not only did I learn lessons about racism in junior and senior high school, I also learned valuable lessons in resistance. Outrage over discrimination was not enough. Action was necessary, and valiant teachers prepared us for action.[18]

Herron Hill Junior High School had some of the best teachers in the entire high school system. They were determined that we Black kids were going to learn, and learn well. They accepted no excuses, even from those of us who were gang members. On the first day I entered algebra class, clad in my maroon and gray Cobra gang jacket, Mr. Calloway said to me, "Listen boy, folks have been telling me that you are supposed to be a tough son-of-a-bitch. Well, let me tell you, I don't give a damn how tough you are, you ain't hardly leaving my class being dumb. That would be a reflection on me, and I don't play that crap. You hear me, boy?"

Elmo Calloway, Middle Row, 3rd from Left

18 My book, *Racial Discrimination against Black Teachers and Black Professionals in the Pittsburgh Public School System: 1834-1973* (Oakmont, PA: Learning Moments Press, 2021), provides a detailed account of the long struggle of the Black community to integrate the Pittsburgh Public School System and the discrimination endured by the early educators who paved the way of students of my generation.

I had never heard a teacher swear, and I had never allowed anyone to call me "boy" without them getting hurt, but there was something about this man. I earned straight "A's" in higher math. He was a taskmaster. So were all the other Black teachers at Herron Hill.

I should add that we had some excellent White teachers, as well, such as my mentor, Gladys Donahue. She told me that she was proud to work with the group of youngsters with whom I went to school. "When I first met your group, I said to myself 'there is something different about these youngsters. They stare you right in the eye. I don't think they are going to accept the same treatment their parents accepted. I decided to help prepare you for what you were going to face by virtue of your demands." Many years later, I called Mrs. Donahue to thank her for all her hard work and to inform her that I had just earned my Ph.D. She said, "I already know that. I have followed your career since you left Herron Hill. I know about your radio and TV work and your efforts to free your people. I was right about your group of youngsters and I am so proud."

Beyond Pittsburgh—Military Lessons

After graduating from high school, I entered college, but dropped out after a year when I realized the financial burden I was creating for my parents. I bounced around Pittsburgh for a while, looking for some kind of employment that would lead to a career. However, it soon became obvious that there was not much of a future for me in a racist town where Blacks had to be far better educated than Whites to even be considered for a good job. After exhausting all the options I could imagine, I made the painful decision to join the Army. The draft was active, and nearly every male in the previous generation either was drafted or volunteered for active duty. I reasoned that, if I joined the service, I could better control what my life would be.

Most Blacks with whom I had spoken were either in the infantry or were cooks. Not imagining myself in those roles, I searched for alternatives and discovered a year-long training program that would qualify me to work in the newly-emerging field of rocket science. Volunteering for an additional year of service seemed like a reasonable tradeoff for training I could use in civilian life and for the G.I. education benefits that would allow me to return to college.

Blacks who enlisted or were drafted from Northern cities were assigned to training and duty stations in the southern part of the United States. Having experienced southern "hospitality" during my family's yearly visit to North Carolina, I thought I might have some problems. After all, as my grandmother often said, I did not "know my place." To southern racists, I was a "northern, uppity, arrogant Negro." Indeed, my grandmother's assessment proved all too true.

My first duty station was Fort Jackson, South Carolina, the base to which all new soldiers were processed and then sent on to their basic training stations. The Army's use of abusive control tactics to instill unquestioning obedience to authority was meted out to both White and Black enlistees. Blacks, however, were typically treated worse than Whites. I hated the way we were stripped of our dignity and began to organize a small group of Black soldiers so we could protect ourselves.

After a short stay in South Carolina, I was assigned for basic training to Fort Benning, Georgia, where the mistreatment was even worse. On and off the base, Black soldiers were treated like dirt. Everywhere I looked in the United States Army, I saw that Blacks were treated as third-class citizens. I could not accept that treatment and continued my unorganized protests that I had started at Fort Jackson.

"Nigger" rolled off the tongues of the White folks, whether from the South or North. Several of us decided that whenever a White person used that word, the closest of my little band of thugs would punch them in the face. As word got around, we heard "nigger" less and less often.

I was rapidly developing a "bad attitude," because I refused to conform to expected behaviors of "good nigras." Being defiant, challenging, and dangerous did not endear me to my superiors or the local townsfolk. Nevertheless, I continued to transform my anger into action. This included "messing" with racist, southern-born, redneck "leaders." I set up one such sergeant and got him busted in rank and re-assigned to a combat unit. The next leader was a young Black sergeant named Barnes. He saw what I was doing and called me his "educated, fuck-up." We clashed until he decided he was in danger of losing his rank, and I was in danger of spending years in a military prison. He said I was like a man with a high-powered gun with no idea of how to avoid shooting himself in the foot.

Deciding I needed to have some protection, he suggested I become an expert in the Army regulations 380-5 which controlled every aspect of the army life. By learning them, I could take action while knowing what the army could or could not do to retaliate. I was a bit suspicious and asked, "Why do you give a flying fuck about what happens to me?"

"I don't," he replied, "but I've been checking your records to see what makes you so determined to do in anyone who messes over you. I didn't find that out, but I did find that you have something I need. Watching you go after anybody who outranks you, I figure that you would never do what I am going to ask you unless I can give you something that will make it easier for you to keep messing up folks that try to mess with you. Knowing the Army regulations can protect your smart ass. Sooner or later, you're going to piss off somebody bad enough that they're going to grab you. Then you'll punch them out, and you're off to jail—unless you're able to quote the specific rule that says no one above your rank can even touch you without risking being brought up on charges. Most folks, including officers, don't know the regulations. Once you start quoting them, they will check the regulation out and see that you're right. Then they'll leave you alone, even when you're blowing smoke. I know this works, because it's what has kept my Black ass out of jail."

"Okay," I said, "I'm game. But we both know you ain't doing this out of your love for me, so what do you want?"

He laughed and said, "When I was checking your records, I found out that you used to be a damned *dance instructor.*"

"That ain't hardly funny. Besides what has that to do with what we are discussing?" Again he laughed and said, "Look, I been trying to score with this cute chick in town. She is *hot*, but she won't give me no action because she is a dancer and I can't dance a step. I figure if you teach me how to dance, I can score with this chick. Deal?"

A deal it was, and for the next few weeks, I taught him to dance, and he taught me Army regulations. It was a good trade; he scored with and married the object of his affection, and I stayed out of military jail.

It was during Basic Training that I was cheated out of the one-year school for which I had enlisted. They claimed that I was not qualified for the training because I wore glasses, even though I had worn glasses when the training was guaranteed. I was cheated, because the training was in Texas where Black soldiers were not welcome in the field of guided missiles. At that time, I did not know I had the right to demand an honorable discharge. This was the final straw, and I vowed to get even with any racists who crossed my path. As far as I was concerned, the war was on!

My next duty base was Aberdeen Proving Ground, Maryland, where I continued my one-man crusade against authority until I was shipped out to Korea. I was appalled to find that racism was alive and well in Korea. Koreans readily admitted that they learned negative stereotypes of Blacks from White soldiers and defense contractors. Here's an example. One evening I went to the base non-commissioned officers club with a White friend. When the call for the last round of drinks was made, Tater went to the bar leaving me with Peggy, his Korean girlfriend. Soon Peggy seemed to be suffering from an uncontrollable "tic" as she kept swiveling her head to look at a clock on the wall. After a few minutes of this, I asked, "Peggy, what the hell are you doing?" After an initial denial, she confessed, "Oh, I just wait to see if what White G.I. tell all Korean girls is true!"

Damn, do I really want to hear this? "Okay, Peggy, what do White soldiers tell you?"

"They say don't get caught with Black G.I. after 12 midnight, because Black G.I. grow horns and tail. I wait to see." She was most disappointed when no such appendages appeared on my head or ass as the clock struck midnight. Needless to say, the chip of resentment on my shoulder was getting larger. Here I was, in a foreign land, protecting South Koreans from North Koreans, while racist venom was being spread by my supposed comrades at arms.

That changed after I began to teach conversational English to Korean nationals at their equivalent of a junior college. Teachers were highly respected in Korean culture, which allowed me to escape much of the racism directed at other Black soldiers. Still, once I left my home base, I was subjected to racism by Koreans who did not know me. The racism took the form of name calling, poor service, exclusion from many Korean-owned establishments, and fights. Because I had learned to speak Korean before teaching English, I was able to eavesdrop on conversations about Black soldiers. The looks on folk's faces when they discovered that I understood every word they said were priceless. This gave me a way to counteract some racism.

Returning to the Jim Crow South

After a year in Korea, I returned to the states and was assigned to my last duty station, Fort Campbell, Kentucky. I had tried to convince my commander to allow me to finish out the remainder of my enlistment in Korea, where I enjoyed some modicum of respect as a teacher. Unfortunately, here I was, being sent in yet another racist Southern town.

After a month-long leave back in Pittsburgh, I was traveling by bus to Fort Campbell and had to change buses in Nashville, Tennessee. As required by military regulations, I was wearing what was called a "full-dress" uniform. Having time to kill, I went to a restaurant in the station and sat at a table. I immediately noticed two things. I was the only Black in the establishment, and the Whites were staring at me. I returned their stares with the most malevolent look I could muster. My anger grew as some White folks entered the restaurant and were immediately given service. Fed up, I marched up to the counter, slammed my open hand on the counter, and I spat out, "I want a ham sandwich and a coke." My actions shook up the staff; I was given my meal, and then returned to the waiting area.

Within a few minutes, I noticed a movement to my left and turned to see a red-faced, overweight, sweating local cop staring at me. I had violated the cultural norms of this Southern town by demanding to be served. Someone in the restaurant obviously called for reinforcement. My anger grew to a seething rage, as I recalled the way my family was treated on that Southern trip many years ago. Without saying a word, I rose from my seat and faced the cop, and returned his hateful glare, even though I knew that I was violating another Southern rule. Echoing in the back of my mind were the words of a hymn, "before I'll be a slave, I'll be buried in my grave and go home to my lord and be free." I was prepared to face death rather than accept one more humiliation. My glare sent the message, "Listen fool, you are in a very dangerous situation. I am one of Uncle Sam's hired killers, trained to kill with my bare hands. I have just returned from duty in Korea. I was there to protect the freedom of Koreans who often treated me and other Black G.I's like shit! I am your worst nightmare. I am an angry Black man; I have a bad attitude and the means to back it up. Best you back off, or one of us will die, and I do not intend to be the one." I knew my actions were dangerous, but damn it, I was more than a little ticked off. He must have gotten my message; he left without saying a word.

As I sat there fuming, I realized I was the only Black person in the waiting room. Puzzled, I carefully watched the next bus arrive, saw the Whites disembark first and proceed to the waiting room where I sat, followed by Blacks who headed to my left and disappeared. Deciding further investigation was warranted, I walked outside, looked up, and saw a faded sign, *"Colored Waiting Room."* With a shaking hand, I opened the door. As my eyes adjusted to the dim light, I saw a handful of Blacks quietly eating at the cramped lunch counter and three tables in a small, dingy room.

Ironically (infuriatingly), the large, clean, well-lit "Whites Only" dining room was separated from the dingy Black dining room by a shared kitchen. The menus carried the same items, but those handed to the Whites were clean; those for the Blacks were old and spotted. The same person passed food from two separate serving windows. This made me realize I had seen the same thing at the ticket/information booth.

One ticket seller sat on a swivel stool, in the middle of a long and narrow room with two windows. Whites were handed their ticket through the window opening into the White waiting room. When Blacks purchased a ticket, the seller spun around and sold the ticket through the Colored window.

All of this was taking place in 1960, *after* discrimination in the nation's bus system had already been declared unconstitutional. Even though Blacks no longer had to stay out of the White side of the facility, they continued to do so. I wanted to scream at the Black folks and urge them to resist. I kept my mouth shut, because I realized that they were doing what they had always done, behaving in a non-confrontational fashion to remain safe. I left the room, my heart hurting, and returned to the White side of the place. Later that year, I returned to Nashville and participated in the civil rights demonstrations. I was more than pleased to strike a small blow against this racist hell hole.

I was happy to see my bus arrive; I was happy to leave this ghost of Jim Crow behind. I took a front seat, ignoring the stares of the bus driver and soon I fell asleep. I was awakened when the bus stopped and the driver announced that the riders had only a few minutes to use the restroom. As I headed toward the exit, the driver fired at me, "Where you going, **boy?**" I turned, looked him straight in his eyes, and said. "I don't know how big they grow men where *you* come from, but where I come from, I am a *MAN.* I would strongly suggest that you refrain from calling me *boy* again. I am going to use the toilet facilities."

"They is for White folks," he informed me. Black folks were supposed to hold on until they got to a place that had a Colored bathroom, or they were supposed to relieve themselves in the bushes.

I said, "Tell you what, my man. I have to piss pretty badly. I can't hold it, and I ain't about to go in the bushes. In about 30 seconds, I am going to be taking a leak. Where I take that leak is entirely up to you. Now, I can go into that restroom in that little building, or I can leak on your shoe. I would suggest that you make up your mind very rapidly, 'cause I really have to go bad." I then reached for my trouser zipper in order to impress on him the seriousness of the situation. He turned away muttered under his breath, "Damn uppity Yankee nigra." As I stepped off the bus, I asked him to repeat himself, but he chose not to.

The rest of the journey was uneventful; a brief respite from what awaited me at Fort Campbell. Straddling the Kentucky and Tennessee border, the fort was within a short bus ride from other Southern states in which Blacks were mounting mass protests. Nearby Nashville was a hot bed of civil rights activities. Whites in Nashville were very surprised that "their happy and contented nigras" were suddenly picketing and demonstrating. Some very prestigious Black colleges[19] were located in Nashville and attracted students from both southern and northern states where Blacks were denied admission to White institutions. Many northern students (accustomed to more subtle manifestations of racism) had never seen the blatant display of Jim Crow "COLORED ONLY" and "WHITE ONLY" signs. Offended and angered by such overt, virulent racism, some became leaders in the Southern movement. It was here I became drawn to the broader civil rights movement.

One day, we were in military formation when a racist 1st sergeant announced some "radical Yankees" were stirring up trouble in Nashville and causing "nigras" to act up. The red-neck sergeant was the cause of most of the crap my unit went through as part of blatant racism practiced against Black soldiers. I loved to dog him and threaten to take him to the Adjutant General and charge his ugly behind with failing to promote Blacks.

Although soldiers were forbidden to participate in the demonstrations under penalty of imprisonment in a military jail, I hated this sergeant so much, he might just as well have handed me an engraved invitation to join the demonstrations. And join I did. I thought I could do something to change what I had seen in that Colored-only waiting room at the bus station. I marched, picketed and made myself available whenever I was needed. During demonstrations in small towns and large Southern cities, I was spat upon, beaten, shocked with cattle prods, and washed away with high pressure water hoses. I spent time in some of the best jails in the South.

These were extremely dangerous times. The five guys I hung out with at Fort Campbell were all tough, young Black dudes, like me, with chips on their shoulders. We traveled to several demonstrations within a day's journey of the base, but we needed a "cover story" for our frequent requests for weekend passes. Here my experience as a professional dance instructor once again served me well. My friends and I created a line-dance routine based on a dance called "the continental walk." Whoever said "all Blacks can dance" never worked with a couple of the dudes in our group. We finally became very good and showed off our techniques at some dances at the Black non-commissioned officers club on base. Soon we were the talk of the base as well as the town of Hopkinsville, KY and many small Black, nearby communities in Tennessee. We became very popular with the girls as we taught them to do the dance. Sure this was fun, but the dance routine was our way to get weekend passes and participate in demonstrations.

---

19 Mehary Medical School, Fisk University, Tennessee A&I University, and other Black colleges had reputations for providing a quality education in a welcoming, nurturing environment steeped in their own traditions and culture.

During the demonstrations we got extremely angry when women and children were beaten. Now and then we were able to take a measure of revenge. We made note of the White offenders and under cover of darkness we would leave some of these punks in an alley in less than perfect condition. One night, after completing a "pay back" mission, we hopped into Lou's car and headed back to camp. The car engine began to sputter and died in the middle of nowhere on a moonless night and no lights to be seen. If local cops found us, we would be in dire trouble. We considered sending someone in both directions to look for help, but decided it was safer to stay together. After what seemed like an eternity, the sun began to rise. Eventually, a Black farmer came by in an old truck, gave us a jump, and asked only one question, "What you city boys doing out on this road at night?" I suspect our silence was answer enough. The angels were looking out for us that night. We and the car could have easily vanished without a trace.

A War Within

As a foot soldier in the war on racism, I marched and demonstrated in the fashion dictated by the leaders. The more I participated, the more conflicted I became about which leaders to follow. I had met and heard Dr. Martin Luther King, Jr., speak about freedom, dreams, and non-violence. I had also met Malcolm X, the fiery leader of the Black Muslims, who spoke about self-determination, self-defense, and the right to protect yourself and your family. King spoke to my heart; Malcolm X spoke to my intellect.

As a former gang member, I was very philosophically aligned with Malcolm. My father and his brothers were terrors in the neighborhood; Uncle Sam had trained me to kill in ten ways with my bare hands. Allowing someone to beat me without defending myself was completely foreign to me. Yet, I elected to follow King—one of the most difficult things I have ever done. King's charisma captured me and convinced me to join the non-violent movement that was the very antithesis of my personal beliefs.

Still, each time I was struck by someone I could have easily annihilated, each time I saw a woman or child beaten, I remembered Malcom X's message that you were a fool and a chump if you didn't protect yourself and your family. With each new march, I struggled to remain non-violent. Others began to notice how close I skirted to the edge of violence during the demonstrations. They asked me to stop attending demonstrations, because I was too dangerous to the workers around me. My attitude and behavior could cause others to be hurt or killed. They were right. Each time my friends and I went out "dancing," we were appalled by the level of squalor that far exceeded even the deplorable conditions in the urban ghettos in which we grew up. As time wore on, with each beating I took, with each child or woman I saw beaten, I started to change. My heart knew hatred. I wanted to kill. Although I believed in non-violence as a tactical method, I could no longer accept it as a way of life. At that point, I decided that I would be non-violent as long as no one was violent toward me.

Fortuitously, my time with the army was drawing to an end. It was time to go home. I left the South a profoundly changed and angry young man, with a chip on my shoulder. I had seen the underbelly of America, and it was gut-wrenchingly ugly.

The Scars of War

Like others who have suffered traumatic experiences, I carry deep scars. Even today, I have an immediate, negative reaction to any White person with a Southern accent. As I write this I am aware of a rage that lies just beneath the surface. I am enraged by the inhuman treatment we were forced to endure simply because we wanted equal access to the so-called American dream. My years in the Southern movement became an American nightmare. I also promised that I would never march in a demonstration again. That's why I did not go on the March on Washington in 1963. I do not regret that decision. Still I was immersed in a battle that would continue for the rest of my life. Sometimes I would be joined by other warriors; other times I would be quite alone. Most painful were situations in which Blacks who bore the brunt of discrimination could not or would not join the battle.

The rage within me was never far from the surface. Late one evening, I was sitting on the couch in my living room, working on a speech I had to make during Black History Month. My dog lay at my feet. In the background, a movie was playing on the television. I was not paying much attention to the movie, or so I thought. The little part of me that is always alert—watching for danger—went on alert.

A White supremacy group was operating on a college campus somewhere in the United States. As part of the plot, one of the redneck White boys climbed to the top of a tall campus building, carrying a high-powered rifle. He aimed and fired a shot at a beautiful, young Black woman. Even though I knew this was fiction, I heard a scream of rage reverberate through the room, startling me and scaring the hell out of my dog. That trapped-animal scream had come from *me!* The fictional scene of violence touched a wound in the depths of my soul. I was a walking time bomb. Damn those Southern racist, Black-hating, sons of bitches. They stole my soul and changed me forever.

Returning to Pittsburgh's Jim Crow Culture
Connecting with the Pittsburgh Movement

When my Fort Campbell buddies first persuaded me to join the Nashville demonstrations, they said I'd have my pick of thousands of "fine, brown ladies." My old high school buddy, Jim Tyler, used the same ploy to recruit me into the Young Adult Chapter of the Pittsburgh NAACP. He was right; it was a young bachelor's paradise, and I was having a good time dating a variety of women. Unfortunately, Dorothy Williams, the group's advisor, would not let us get away with just socializing; she insisted that we join the NAACP. This reignited my activism. In the remainder of the book, I weave my own experiences with those of others who became active leaders in the Pittsburgh movement.

VOICES FROM THE FIRING LINE

Movement Leaders: Left to right: James "Swampman" Williams, Mike Desmond, Rev. Jimmy Joe Robinson, Lloyd Bell, Nate Smith, Dr. Norman Johnson, Attorney Byrd Brown, Vince Wilson, Chief William "Mugsy" Mooney

The battle for equality of Black Pittsburghers was led by a number of organizations. Some, like the NAACP, were old and well-established with national chapters. As mention above, philosophical differences led to the formation of other civil rights organizations; some more militant than others. At times, those with similar philosophies formed new groups to address specific areas of discrimination such as the construction industry or the police force.

The civil rights movement received support from a range of religious, community, and governmental organizations. Although the primary mission of these groups was not civil rights, they contributed in significant ways to the movement. Many provided services that supported efforts to secure housing, employment, and education for Blacks in Pittsburgh. Without their involvement, far less progress would have been made.

Within all these various organizations were key individuals who served as leaders, dedicating themselves to the fight for equality and justice. In many instances, individuals were involved in multiple organizations; in other cases, individuals worked more independently as community activists. While it is impossible to name every person who played a vital role in the movement, those included in this section are individuals who were actively involved in the Pittsburgh movement from 1950 until 1970. These individuals risked ridicule from family, friends and co-workers, because they did not hide their involvement in the civil rights movement. They also risked loss of livelihood, physical harm, and death. These are the people who were on the firing line of the movement.

CHAPTER 5

Greater Pittsburgh
Improvement League
(Founded 1949)

Members of GPIL, including K. Leroy Irvis (2nd from left) and William Powell (right)

FIGURE 5.1

GPIL FOUNDING MEMBERS

- Mary Carter
- Dr. Lafayette Davis
- Fulton Johnson
- James Jordan, 1st president
- Marion Jordan
- James McCoy
- Irene Roberts
- Manfred Sales, president
- Roger Taliaferro
- Bradford Williams
- John O'Holly, President, Cleveland Improvement League, served as an advisor

In the course of conducting research for this book, I spoke with John Brewer, Jr. who had established The Trolley Station Oral History Center. While Brewer was conducting an interview for his oral history project, he uncovered a forgotten chapter of the Pittsburgh civil rights movement—The Greater Pittsburgh Improvement League. As John excitedly shared what he had learned, I realized that he had uncovered an important story of the civil rights movement of which I knew little. I am indebted to John Brewer for so generously contributing the information about this key group for this chapter of *Voices*.

* * *

Blacks have been a part of Pittsburgh since its founding. However the population was rather small (823 in 1840) and did not show significant growth until 1880, when the population reached 4,077. In the next decade, the population more than doubled, and by 1890, Black residents of Pittsburgh numbered 10,359.[20]

No matter how much the population grew, Blacks faced a complicated system of racial discrimination. As discussed in Chapter 2, in the years following the Emancipation Proclamation and the Civil War, much of the discrimination in Pittsburgh was covert. Confronting the Jim Crow culture that permeated and controlled all aspects of Black life was confounded by Pittsburgh's topography. Known for its three rivers, Pittsburgh has a long-standing history of separation among those living to the north, south or between those rivers.

FIGURE 5.2

ADDITIONAL MEMBERS OF GPIL

- Anna and Marshal Brice
- Mal Goode
- Dr. Elmer Harrison
- Alma Illery
- Daisy Lampkin
- Rev. Leroy Patrick
- William "Bill" Powell
- Henry Smith

---

20 Population statistics from the United States Census Data

Further dividing the population is the hilly terrain and many valleys. The result was tightly knit ethnic enclaves where immigrants joined relatives as they moved to Pittsburgh. During the great migration from the South, Blacks followed this same settlement pattern, resulting in fragmented communities whose citizens often mistrusted each other. As a result, forming a cohesive alliance with united leadership was a long time coming.

This does not mean, however, that there was no resistance to the discriminatory Jim Crow culture. In the early decades of the 20th century, sporadic resistance occurred on a small and somewhat isolated scale. This began to change and one of the influential groups to emerge was the Greater Pittsburgh Improvement League (GPIL). Many accounts of the Pittsburgh civil rights movement make no mention of the GPIL, perhaps because it was overshadowed by the Pittsburgh Chapter of the NAACP. Fortunately, John Brewer, Jr., rediscovered this important group during an oral history interview with one of its early organizers.

Late in the summer of 1949, a group of blacks from Pittsburgh's East End attended a meeting at the Office of Dr. Lafayette Davis, who had recently returned from a trip to Cleveland, Ohio. During that trip, Dr. Davis had been given a tour by John O'Holly, President of the Cleveland Greater Improvement League. Not only did Dr. Davis witness Blacks confronting conditions similar to those in Pittsburgh, he learned about the non-violent boycotting strategy being used to protest discriminatory practices of large corporations. O'Holly explained that organizations like the NAACP and Urban League did not pose a significant threat to the status quo in either city.

Manfred Sales, one of the men who met in Davis' office, recalled, "Most of the time letters sent to companies like Sealtest, A&P, Kroger's, Kaufmann's, Gimbel's were never answered. Requests for meetings to discuss employment opportunities for blacks were disregarded. Many of our members had just served in World War II. We were full of passion about that double V sign the papers talked so much about. We had put our lives on the line for this country to bring victory home so that we would have victory here as well. We were all disappointed and frustrated over the lack of opportunity."[21]

Out of such frustration, the East Liberty Improvement League was formed. Among its early members were some of Pittsburgh's most prominent civil rights activists and many rank and file men and women who joined in the struggle against Pittsburgh's Jim Crow culture.[22] Anna and Marshal Brice are typical of the many "common" citizens who joined the movement. They were very well known in the Black church circles as a couple who would go to great lengths to support any uplifting effort. Marshall, an imposing, extremely strong man, was very soft spoken and full of love and understanding. At first glance, he appeared to be White with his straight, long, black hair and very light skin. He worked for Pepsi Cola Bottling Company in Pittsburgh. He would tell the story of how the man who hired him at Pepsi mistakenly believed him to be White. His wife, Anna, worked both as a domestic and part-time baker. Anna's entire family had set the example of involvement in causes from the women's suffrage movements in the early nineteen hundreds, to the 1954 Supreme Court decision of *Brown v. Board of Education of Topeka, Kansas*. They exemplified the dedicated soldiers in a war against discrimination and injustice. Figures 4.1 and 4.2 list some of the individuals whose names were not lost to history.

---

21 December 2003 John Brewer interview with Mr. Sales.
22 Although I had interviewed some of the individuals involved with the GPIL, I was not aware of the organization at that time. By the time John Brewer, Jr., brought this group to my attention, all those whom I had previously interviewed had already died, and I was unable to conduct follow-up interviews about the League.

After several meetings, the group decided to take action utilizing the skills and the sheer will of their members. Leadership roles were entrusted to James Jordan, Manfred Sales, and Doctor Lafayette Davis. To be successful, the League had to appear to be well organized and consistently focused on confronting problems caused by economic and social discrimination systems in Pittsburgh. They rallied behind the idea of confronting companies who discriminated against Blacks by organizing massive boycotts designed to shut the stores down. Prior to a boycott, each company's revenue sources were analyzed to document how much income Black customers were generating for the company. A company chosen for an upcoming boycott was sent a letter asking for a meeting to talk about employment opportunities for Blacks. The tag line "spend only where you are hired" was officially adopted as the League's motto. This slogan became a symbol on every picket sign and correspondence the League used from that point on.

In March of 1950, the League confronted the Thorofare Market located at Lowell and Frankstown Avenues. The organizers had already blanketed Black communities with flyers proclaiming the League's motto. The slogan spread like wildfire as it was repeated at monthly meetings conducted at several churches that were committed to becoming a part of the movement. Black whispers became louder from every barbershop to every bar. After attempts to discuss employment with Thorofare failed, a massive boycott by hundreds of people was held. It was successful.

Picketing A&P and Donahoe's Supermarkets

League planners decided to continue its focus on grocery store food chains, where they could measure the impact of Black dollars on the stores' revenue to justify employment requests. The largest chain of grocery stores in Pittsburgh was A&P, which stood for Atlantic and Pacific Tea Company. The chain's executive offices were located in New York City. Letters to A&P President R. W. Burger were met with indifference, evasions, or arrogance. The A&P Board's resistance to change discriminatory hiring policies resulted in a bitter four-year battle.

By March 13, 1952, a strong wave of boycotters from Black churches, fraternal organizations, and unemployed youth supported picket lines around thirty A&P stores throughout Pittsburgh. A&P attempted to stop this picketing by secretly offering to talk to the local branch of the NAACP. Their efforts to "divide and conquer" were quickly reversed by Improvement League President Manfred Sales with a request for the NAACP to "back off."

As the boycott continued, A&P branches felt the financial impact as Black and even some White shoppers took their money elsewhere. Still, A&P would not concede. Finally, after almost one year, A&P executives requested federal intervention. During the month of January 1953, federal officials, acting under the authorization of The Fair Employment Practice Commission, interceded in the conflict. This Commission had been created by Presidential orders of both Presidents Roosevelt and Truman. Representatives of both A&P and the Improvement League were asked to meet with federal representatives, call off the boycott, and allow negotiations to start. By February 18, 1953, GPIL attorney Henry Smith requested a halt to the boycott until a meeting with all parties was completed. The meeting results show a considerable change in attitude and respect for the Improvement League.

Over 22 employment interviews were quickly scheduled with Blacks for entry-level positions such as clerks. By then, the reputation for getting results led Blacks from other communities in the Pittsburgh region to request support and leadership. The East Liberty Improvement League changed its name to The Greater Pittsburgh Improvement League. GPIL continued to work on the low Black employment record at A&P until early 1956.

By late 1953, a long list of companies discriminating against Blacks had been compiled, including Sealtest, Sears and Roebuck, Rosenbaum's, G.C. Murphy 5&1O Cent stores, Donahue's, Isaly's, Kaufman's, Horne's, Gimbel's, and a host of manufacturing firms. To support the growing number of boycotts, the GPIL expanded operations and added staff. In 1954, the organization moved to a new office at 127 Larimer Avenue in the Lincoln-Larimer district of Pittsburgh. Manfred Sales continued to serve as GPIL's President. A new branch—the Mon Valley Greater Pittsburgh Improvement League—was established to serve Blacks living in Braddock, Rankin, Homestead, Clairton, and McKeesport. Local Black churches continued to act as hosts for the many raffles and informational meetings held for the public. Monthly executive committee meetings were held at the Green Hearth Restaurant in Homewood-Brushton to discuss issues, make future plans, and hear progress reports about ongoing campaigns.

By October 1955, despite the working relationship previously established with A&P Stores, employment committee chairman Dr. Elmer B. Harrison recommended action be taken against the Homewood A&P, where management had ignored all attempts to discuss employment of Blacks. The Black population in Homewood had risen to well over fifteen thousand people, and yet Blacks held no jobs in the store. By March 1, 1956, picket lines were placed around the A&P. Criticism of the boycott by White employees created an atmosphere thick with the threat of violence. After six intense days of boycotting, the management of A&P agreed to meet with GPIL and State Fair Employment Director George Culberson.

Culberson filed a complaint against A&P which he sent to GPIL via telegram. He asked the GPIL to remove picket lines temporarily by March 7, 1956. A subsequent meeting was held with representatives from A&P, GPIL and FERC. Final results were shared in a public meeting held March 11, 1956, at Mt.

Ararat Church in East Liberty. A&P had agreed to hire four Black clerks at two of the chain's stores. They also agreed to place Blacks in entry level positions never before available. Those who attended the meeting rejoiced and openly cheered the victory.

Before long, the entire Black community had heard the good news. In late May 1956, the GPIL took the opportunity to schedule recruitment and fund raising events at Holy Cross Episcopal Church in Homewood. Featured guest speakers included Emery F. Bacon, Commissioner from the Human Relations Board, and Mal Goode of *The Pittsburgh Courier*. Word of the GPIL victory even reached the powerful New York Congressman Adam Clayton Powell, who sent words of wisdom to Mal Goode for the occasion.

GPIL made history as the first self-supported, organized civil rights group in Pittsburgh to confront and defeat long-standing racial barriers to employment. During 1956 many Blacks became a part of the new work experience outside of their community. Black clerks began to appear at front counters around the city of Pittsburgh. Still, boycotts continued against resistant employers like Kaufman's, Murphy's, and Sealtest.

In 1957, the GPIL sent over 60 names of potential employees to the operators of Forbes Field food vending services. As Manfred Sales recalled, "Management at the stadium maintained that Blacks 'can't handle food with their bare hands. White folks ain't gonna buy from them and they would lose money.'" Sales just smiled and the next day more than sixty big guys from the sanitation department and construction crews volunteered to act as vendors. Forbes Field management and the union were caught off guard. The volunteers were respected, and GPIL supplied replacement workers that had been screened. Fans going to the ballgame from that point on became accustomed to Black vendors selling everything from popcorn to banners. Once again, the League could claim victory.

Operations like the Forbes Field campaign were very costly in terms of staff and temporary manpower. Many of the League members were also supporters of the local chapter of the NAACP and often suggested a merger of the two organizations to bring "better finances" to the fight against racial discrimination. At first, the GPIL rejected such proposals. However, executive board meetings to plan collaborations between the Urban League of Pittsburgh and the GPIL took shape in 1957.

Urban League Executive Director Gaines T. Bradford agreed to co-sponsor a Motherhood Celebration on Mother's Day, May 12, 1957. The idea was to generate new membership and raise funds for GPIL expenses. In the end, the program budget absorbed most of the funds generated. For months the expensive operations threatened to bring all activity to a halt. A suggestion was made to elect Bill Powell, WAMO disc jockey, to recruit members and raise funds for the GPIL. In October 1957, Powell announced the goal of raising $5,000 and signing up 1,000 new members for the GPIL. League staff kept the public informed about its activities by distributing over 3,000 copies of a monthly paper called *The Citizens Voice* which included announcements about League youth activities, scheduled meetings, and boycott objectives.

Efforts to increase operating revenues by Bill Powell were not successful as he also provided support to Pittsburgh's Chapter of the NAACP, which had launched a massive fund raising campaign from 1956 to 1960 to increase membership and rise to the forefront of the civil rights struggle. Powell was instrumental in connecting corporate giant Gulf Oil to assist the NAACP's efforts in exchange for "a positive corporate image." The GPIL executive Board rejected the concept of accepting funds from Pittsburgh corporations. "There are always strings attached," Manfred Sales said. "When you accept money from the same force that is keeping you down, then you lose the battle." The League's ongoing campaigns against companies like Meadow Gold, Kroger's, and Loblaw's became weak due to lack of funds. The League still conducted monthly meetings at Homewood's Green Hearth, but scaled down its staff and public campaigns and began to take an advisory role to the stronger organizations like NAACP and Urban League. By late 1959, ten years after its inception, the GPIL merged with the NAACP.

CHAPTER 6

Pittsburgh Chapter of the NAACP

T he national NAACP is the oldest civil rights group in the United States. During the timeframe covered by this book, the national leader was Roy Wilkens. The Pittsburgh Chapter of the NAACP was one of the earliest and largest civil rights groups in the region to protest the city's Jim Crow culture. Initially, the Chapter depended upon court litigation as the strategy for achieving equality. Later, more active and militant strategies such as demonstrations, marches, boycotts, and picketing were used.

Organizations and movements are shaped by the individuals who lead them and the causes these leaders feel compelled to champion. The willingness to accept what is often an onerous burden lies in the experiences that have ignited an individual's passion and given focus to their action. In the remainder of this chapter, I offer brief portraits of many key contributors to the NAACP's campaign against Pittsburgh's Jim Crow culture. These portraits include information I gathered in the course of interviews as well as my personal relationships with many of those involved in the movement. As will become apparent, many leaders of the movement had multiple organizational affiliations. These interconnections create a web of support that sustained on-going efforts on multiple fronts.

Judge Homer S. Brown
Founding Member of the Pittsburgh Chapter of the NAACP; served as 1st President for 24 years
First Black in the House of Representatives in Pennsylvania (1934)
First Black appointed to the Pittsburgh Public School Board (1941)
First Black to serve on the Allegheny Court and Court of Common Pleas (1956)
Pittsburgh Housing Authority, Member

As evidenced by the preceding list, Homer S. Brown was active in a number of civic organizations and broke a number of barriers to the involvement of Blacks in the legal/judicial system. Through the Barr/Brown Scholarship awards, he made it possible for many Black students to attend college.

I met Judge Brown in the 1960s when I was doing research on early Black pioneers in Pittsburgh. He was a very dignified man who exuded an aura of power, yet he graciously welcomed me into his home.

Judge Brown was a brilliant attorney who built a strong private practice. However, he is better known for his pioneering efforts in the public arena. He used this latter position to hold legislative hearings in Pittsburgh to investigate the Pittsburgh Board of Public Education's discriminatory hiring practices. When I interviewed him for my doctoral dissertation,[23] he gave me access to his personal papers and explained the strategy that he used to win the court battle:

> When they first heard about my efforts, they were very smug. They were not aware that I was going to use the power of the Commonwealth of Pennsylvania to attack them, by using state laws. I avoided the usual moral approach. I wanted to prove that they had violated state law." Now Blacks who wanted to teach could stop the treks to other cities and find employment right at home.

When Elmer McClung and I created a program to honor deceased civil rights pioneers, I made certain that Judge Homer S. Brown was one of the first people honored on the Wall of Fame, located in a quiet parklet at the East Liberty entrance to the Martin Luther King Busway. I later did the same for his wife, Wilhelmina Byrd Brown, and for his son, Attorney Byrd Brown.

Wilhelmina Byrd Brown
Pittsburgh Chapter of the NAACP, Member

Wilhelmina Brown was an elegant woman known primarily as the force behind the throne. Together with her husband, Judge Homer Brown, and son, Attorney Byrd Brown, they formed the most important civil rights family in Pittsburgh. Both Homer and Byrd spoke in glowing terms of the very powerful influence Mrs. Brown had on them.

I met Mrs. Brown when I first interviewed her husband for a project on important Black pioneers in Pittsburgh. I saw her again when I applied for a Barr/Brown Scholarship so I could attend the University of Pittsburgh. Mrs. Brown told me that, even though Byrd was a successful attorney and had inherited a law practice and the good name of his father, Byrd was still expected to be deeply involved in the movement. As Byrd put it, "There was simply no excuse for not being involved…no saying that I am tired, or angry, or discouraged."

In her own right, Wilhelmina was very active in the Pittsburgh NAACP and other civic and civil rights organizations. She was credited with an uncanny ability to choose leaders for the NAACP. She was instrumental, for example, in convincing Dorothy Williams to become an active leader in the Pittsburgh youth movement. Mrs. Brown was instrumental in awarding many scholarships that allowed Black students to attend college.

Attorney Byrd R. Brown
Byrd R. Brown, President of Pittsburgh Chapter of NAACP (1958-1971)
United Negro Protest Committee, Co-founder

In the course of my oral history research, I asked interviewees who they considered to be the top five leaders of the Pittsburgh civil rights movement. Among the many who were named, Attorney Byrd

---

23 A more detailed account of Judge Homer's role in the fight to integrate the Pittsburgh Public School system is provided in my book, *Racial Discrimination against Black Teachers and Professionals in the Pittsburgh Public Schools System, 1834-1973*. Oakmont, PA: Learning Moments Press, 2021.

Brown was the individual identified by everyone. He was, indeed, the heart of the movement and served as the Chapter's president during the height of the Pittsburgh movement.

Byrd Brown with his parents, Wilhelmina Byrd Brown and Homer S. Brown

I'm not sure when I first met Byrd Brown, but it seemed he had always been a part of my life. Our first encounter may have been when I interviewed his father, Homer Brown, for an undergraduate research project. I already knew him in 1961 when I established the University of Pittsburgh chapter of the NAACP. Byrd and I became friends and remained so until his death.

Byrd Brown was a handsome man whose presence demanded respect. As the son of Homer Brown, he inherited a lucrative law practice, which he built into an even more successful firm. He could have stayed out of the fray and enjoyed the status and privilege that wealth brings. Yet, at the urging of union leader James McCoy and attorney Henry Smith, Byrd ran for and was elected president of the Pittsburgh NAACP. He risked everything, including his life, to lead the quest for equality. He was always at the head of the line during demonstrations. He put no one in harm's way without being there himself. Government officials, business leaders, and the police had to deal him, because thousands of people would respond to his call for organized marches and demonstrations. At the height of the movement, Byrd had the ability to summon 8,000 for demonstrations. He organized the first massive public disobedience demonstrations in Pittsburgh, as well as many that were to follow.

Brown's parents taught him that he was "somebody," but that he had a responsibility to serve his fellow human beings and especially other Black folks. His father had not intended that Byrd "risk his career" by becoming the very vocal president of the Pittsburgh NAACP. However, Byrd's mom supported him in all that he did. "She was a communication system in her own right. She could contact more people in any given moment than radio, television and newspapers combined." Brown remembered the legislative hearings his father held against the Board of Education's racist hiring practices. "I was so proud of him during those hearings," Brown stated.

When asked why he had risked a lucrative career in order to lead the Pittsburgh civil rights movement, Brown replied:

> I was born Black. I must live as a Black. I will die Black. I didn't have to be a lawyer; I did not want to be a judge, so the risk was not that great. I really had no choice but to become involved. I would not accept living in a community where I was not respected. If I had not taken a leadership role, I would not have been able to live with myself; I would have had no self-respect. Many folks thought my father made a great deal of money, but he really did not. He was more concerned about helping Black folks. He took many cases for free, because people could not afford to pay.

Brown continued that tradition when he became a lawyer. Robert Lavelle, the realtor who broke the stranglehold of the White Pittsburgh realtors, spoke fondly of Brown's involvement in the federal anti-trust suit Lavelle won against the Greater Pittsburgh Multi-list Corporation. "People don't realize how hard Byrd worked on this case, for free. He didn't make a dime. I could never have done it without him."

Brown felt that Black Pittsburghers were treated with benign neglect. The power structure simply ignored them. "There were two societies in Pittsburgh: one Black, one White, and divided from one another by racist practices. A Black person could not go through the day without experiencing covert or overt racism. In all the years I went to Pittsburgh public schools, I never saw a Black teacher," he recalled. This was despite the fact that his father had successfully proven the case of racism and discrimination in the Pittsburgh Board of Education's hiring and promotion of Black teachers. During his tenure as president of the Pittsburgh NAACP, Brown led several demonstrations and negotiation sessions against the continued racism of this body of appointed gate-keepers.

Brown observed that Pittsburgh held itself out as a moral leader in the treatment of Black folks. The city was one of the early pioneers in creating a Human Relations Commission to investigate discrimination. It was also one of the first cities to pass fair employment and equal housing laws. "The passage of these laws did not erase discrimination and racism. It just pushed the perpetrators underground," Brown noted.

Charles Harris told Brown that he had the ability to get all of the disparate civil rights groups to come together for a common cause. After becoming president of the NAACP, Brown realized the NAACP limited the types of activities permissible for protesting discrimination. The winds of change were blowing and "we could not afford to be limited. So, remembering what Harris had said about my ability to call groups together, I sent out letters to all the Negro groups I could think of including block clubs, gardens…; 90% of them responded. That allowed us to form the United Negro Protest Committee. Many folks thought it was a separate organization, but it was the action arm of the NAACP, operating under a separate charter.

Brown, like thousands of other people, traveled to the 1963 March on Washington:

> So many folks from Pittsburgh wanted to go, we had to charter an entire train. When we arrived, it was a hot, miserable day. People are always playing back King's 'I Have a Dream' speech, and it was a fantastic, memorable speech. But those were not the words that resonated with me. King also said to America that "we have a check to cash today." I cried like a baby when he said that. Unfortunately, the check still has not been

cashed, and America still owes us the promised freedom, life, liberty, and the pursuit of happiness.

Brown said that he never really feared for his life or his livelihood when he was the leader of the Pittsburgh NAACP. "You simply accepted the fact that what you were doing was dangerous." He continued by saying that he had to frequently shut off the phone in his law firm, because the phones constantly rang with threats of death or bodily harm. "My boat was blown up and my vehicle was damaged more than once. If you let the danger get to you, you simply could not function as a leader."[24]

When asked, Brown stated, "Yes, I would do it over again. I would do some things differently. For example, I became weary after the murder of King and resigned from the movement twice. I became inactive; I should have remained involved." Brown did become involved again when, in 1987, at the urging of many Black leaders, he ran an unsuccessful mayoral campaign.[25]

He lost the election for two reasons. Whites, even though many admitted that Brown was the most qualified, could not bring themselves to vote for a Black man. He also lost many Black votes, especially those of Black women, because they felt he had "sold out" by marrying a White woman. Blacks who refused to vote for Byrd did a grave disservice to the Black community, because it has been shown that when Black mayors are elected conditions for Blacks improve dramatically.

When asked how he would like to be remembered, Brown said, "I tried to do what I could to open the society so that we could rush in. All I did was to say "open the gate for my people." I never asked for a job, and I *never sold out!"*

James "Jim" McCoy
Pittsburgh NAACP, Chairman, Labor and Industry Committee
Greater Pittsburgh Improvement League, Founding Member,
United Black Protest Committee, Co-founder and 1st President

No matter what the temperature, no matter what the demonstration, James McCoy was always dressed in a white shirt, a tie and a "snap brim" hat. When people spoke about him it was with great reverence, as if they were speaking about a saint. He exuded charisma, pride, confidence, and control even when standing silently.

---

24 According to the FBI, Brown was the number one target on the assassination list of The Minute Men, a para-military group dedicated to White Supremacy. An FBI agent told me I was number two on the list, because of my outspoken comments on the radio and television shows I hosted.

25 By any objective standards, Byrd Brown was the most qualified person ever to run for mayor of the city of Pittsburgh. Of this I am certain, because I served on a committee that examined the credentials of all the candidates that ever occupied the mayor's seat as well as the credentials of the candidates running against Brown. Having compared the credentials of all who occupied the position, no one matched Brown's education and experience as of the publication of the 2014 edition of this book.

**NAACP Youth Council picketing Pittsburgh shoe stores;
Vince Wilson & Dorothy K. Williams Youth Council Leaders**

To the best of my recollection, I first met Jim when he appeared on my television show, *Black Horizons* and renewed our acquaintance at one of the early meetings of the United Negro Protest Committee. I was a frequent visitor at his office and had many conversations with him, but was too much in awe of Jim to ever call him my friend (although he often referred to me in that way). I admired his courage and the "presence" he exuded when he entered a room.

One of my regrets is failing to gather his memories about the Pittsburgh civil rights era before he died. However, according to the people with whom I spoke, McCoy was the second most important leader in Pittsburgh. He was good friends with and a confidant to Byrd Brown. Because McCoy was active and well respected in the labor union movement in the steel mills, Byrd convinced Jim to chair the NAACP Labor and Industry Committee. In that capacity, McCoy became a feared negotiator with companies that discriminated against Blacks. He was highly effective, quite articulate and had a deep, booming voice that you could hear above the marchers as we demonstrated in the streets of Pittsburgh.

The National NAACP was quite clear that court litigation was the only approved strategy in the quest for Black equality. In the early years of the movement, no NAACP chapter was permitted to involve itself in tactics such as sit-ins, marches and boycotts.[26]

However, more and more organizations were adopting direct confrontation, causing many young folks to turn away from the NAACP. Byrd Brown and James McCoy saw the value of the youth movement and also wanted to be on the firing line of direct confrontation. Not wanting to risk the charter of the

---

26 I learned this when the national office threatened to revoke the charter of the University of Pittsburgh Chapter that I had organized. Byrd Brown interceded on my behalf and we were able to keep our charter.

organization in which both his father and mother were involved, Brown consulted with James McCoy and together they created the United Negro Protest Committee (UNPC).

Martin Luther King Jr., shaking hands with James McCoy; Mike Desmond (looking at paper) Charles Harris (between King and McCoy)

McCoy was not satisfied with the UNPC simply being one of the most effective civil rights groups; he wanted more. The "more" came in the form of a spin-off organization called Freedom House that operated out of the UNPC headquarters. Among the accomplishments of Freedom House was a set of trucks that sold fruits and vegetables throughout The Hill and an ambulance system that was the first of its kind in the country. Freedom House ambulance service was so good that the City of Pittsburgh bought it out, and it became the first paramedic service in the area.

As the term "Negro" began to fall out of favor with many in the Black community, the United Negro Protest Committee changed its name to The United Black Protest Committee in 1969. In 1978, the Pittsburgh civil rights movement suffered a great loss when James McCoy died, at the age of 58. Death did what many opponents of justice had been unable to do; it silenced the powerful, deep bass voice that cried out for justice. Jim, please accept my apology for my taking so long to realize how important capturing your memories was. Your eloquent words would have greatly enhanced this book.

Alma "Speed" Fox
Pittsburgh Chapter of the NAACP, Executive Director (1966-1971 during presidency of Byrd Brown)
Pittsburgh Human Relations Commission (longest serving member)
US Department of the Interior, Bureau of Mines, EEOC Manager (served for 12 years)
Recipient of the Greater Pittsburgh YWCA Lifetime Achievement Award

I'm not sure exactly when or how I met Alma Fox, but I certainly fell in love with this strong, beautiful Black woman. We worked together on many NAACP projects including the struggle for equality at the University of Pittsburgh and the Mayor's Commission on Human Relations. When Alma asked me to do something, I did so without a moment's hesitation. Alma was also a staunch feminist before such activities had a name. To know Alma was to love her, unless you were on the other side of the issue.

Alma Fox moved to Pittsburgh from Cleveland, Ohio. "I was very surprised by the treatment of Blacks in Pittsburgh when I first arrived," Fox said. "I had just spent some time in the South, and was shocked to find the same atmosphere, the same treatment of Blacks that I had seen in the Deep South. Blacks could not swim in Highland Park Pool; The Brass Rail did not serve Blacks. Even after the Brass Rail was forced to open its doors to Blacks, I refused to eat there. If my money wasn't good enough for them before, they sure as hell weren't going to get any of my money now." A look of disgust played over the otherwise very pleasant face of this charming lady. Fox said that, in Cleveland, she was accustomed to sitting "right up front" in the movies. She was stunned when she was told that Blacks were expected to sit in the balcony in theatres in White communities. When she arrived in Pittsburgh, some Blacks were working downtown, "but Whites apparently believed that these light-hued Blacks were actually White. Mine Safety Appliance Company employed Blacks only as housekeeping staff. Even Mal Goode, who later became an

Alma Speed Fox

internationally famous broadcaster, was working in the post office, along with scores of other highly-educated Black folks. Blacks were better off in Cleveland."

At first, Fox did not participate in the growing number of civil rights demonstrations being held in Pittsburgh. "I thought that such behavior was un-ladylike. Then I was watching a demonstration, and I thought 'hmm, they don't represent *me.*' Then I heard myself say I did know who did represent me. I picked my daughter up and, with her in my arms, I joined my first demonstration." After that, Fox participated in many demonstrations against all the public utility companies, Sears and a host of other organizations. "We surprised the Board of Education," she said. "They thought they could wait us out, because we had a reputation of picketing only in the summer. That demonstration lasted for a whole year. You have to be willing to give your all, because freedom is not free. Everybody put their necks on the line for the movement. We get no more than we demand!"

Picketing the Pittsburgh Board of Public Education

She demonstrated, picketed, planned demonstrations, and participated in negotiation sessions, all without fear. Yet she had plenty to fear, because those were dangerous times, even for a woman. Twice she went to jail. At that time, the role of many women was very different. Certainly, some took to the streets with other marchers, but according to Fox, women helped to plan the demonstrations. They also "handled the membership drive, without which the NAACP would not have survived. It was our only source of revenue; we accepted no government funds. Many major corporations supported our efforts by taking out lifetime memberships. We planned the annual Human Rights Dinner, a major source of income that was attended by thousands. We cooked food for marchers and supplied strength for the movement. We knew that our men needed to be out there, in front, leading the movement."

During the riots that took place in The Hill, Homewood and the Northside, the national guard was dispatched to help control the situation. Alma's son was a member of the unit sent to The Hill. He asked that he not be sent against his own people. Despite his request, he was ordered to join the line of foot soldiers that faced off against residents of The Hill. He was verbally abused by one Black man in the crowd. Fox was incensed by the man's actions. "Later on, I had a chance to tell the man off," she chuckled.

Fox is very proud of her association with the NAACP. "Some of the other groups that participated in the movement are gone. We're still here. We had the power to get people out of jail and to get them jobs. We helped to make major changes in Pittsburgh. There is no more discrimination in public accommodations. We can live in places that we could not live before the movement. We can take advantage of advanced degrees from all the colleges and universities. We can openly express ourselves without fear of retaliation. We negotiated agreements that led to many people getting good jobs, with good pay and benefits. Racism has not disappeared; it is more subtle today. I see it every day as the longest-standing member of the Pittsburgh Human Relations Commission."

Alma was a very attractive and cultured woman who surprised many with her fire and determination. She was fearless at times, even when it would have been prudent to be afraid. And we followed her into those highly charged situations. In later years, many of the NAACP leaders consider Alma to be our civil rights mother. She encouraged, mentored, and inspired Byrd Brown, Tim Stevens, Harvey Adams, me, and others. She was a warrior, a lady, a scholar, a counselor, a strategist, a leader, a listener, and a friend. I love her in a way that is difficult to explain.

When I asked if it was worth the effort, she replied, "Oh yes. As a result of my involvement I saw the attitudes of my children and other young people change. We broke up the discriminatory hiring practices of the Pittsburgh police. My sons are not sexist. My daughters promote equality. We invested our lives in the movement. We thought we had invested enough, but with the re-emergence of racism, we must re-invest."

Harvey Adams
Pittsburgh Chapter of the NAACP, Served as President from 1976 - 1992
Pittsburgh City Police Department, Sergeant
The Pittsburgh Black Guardians, Member

Harvey Adams was smart, shrewd, and fiery tempered. He was a forceful orator and a friend of all who labored for equal rights. I met Harvey when he was a sergeant in the Pittsburgh police department and admired his opposition to the racism of the police department and the Fraternal Order of Police (the all-White police union). He often risked his livelihood as an out-spoken critic of discrimination. He was feared, admired, and loved. I soon became Harvey's friend and a member of his family. His daughter called me "Uncle Ralph."

Many people, especially enemies of the movement, thought we were both cut from the same cloth of militancy. Not too many years ago, I was talking with one of Pittsburgh's rich, White leaders who said, "Ralph, one thing I can say about you is that at least you have matured in your old age; Harvey never did." I suppose he intended that as a compliment. I did not take it as one.

Adams was a member of The Pittsburgh Black Guardians, a group composed of Black police officers who were dedicated to trying to protect Black citizens and advocate for Black officers. He participated in many demonstrations during the first part of the civil rights movement. After Byrd Brown stepped down as president of the Pittsburgh NAACP, Alma S. Fox prevailed upon Adams to run for president. Adams served as a very powerful, confrontational president of the NAACP for 16 years. His bravery during the Pittsburgh riots of 1968 saved many people from serious injury or death.

Harvey Adams (3ʳᵈ from right), Karl Jackson (2ⁿᵈ from right), and other police officers by New Granada Theater in the Hill District

Adams was born in Pittsburgh. When I interviewed him he was living in Stanton Heights, once an all-White neighborhood near East Liberty and Highland Park. Adams remarked, "I remember when it took a federal law suit to allow Dr. Oswald Nickens to live in this community. Actually that should be no surprise; the racial climate in Pittsburgh has always been one of quiet accommodation to racism. And that's a tragedy."

Adams recalled the time he and his friends wanted to see a movie in Beltzhoover, but the Capitol Theater wouldn't sell tickets to Blacks. He stopped for a moment and chuckled, "The movie was *Snow White!* We didn't know any better. We shouldn't have been going to the movies that glorified White folks and had no Black folks in them. Anyway, my father went there and demanded a ticket. So there we sat, watching a movie that had nothing to do with us. We Black kids were so warped that when we watched westerns, we cheered for the White troops and the cowboys. But we didn't know any better; no one had ever taught us that the Indians were just trying to defend themselves against the slaughter of their people, the raping of their women, and the stealing of their land."

Adams continued, "There were no Black teachers, no Black truckers. I wanted to be a lawyer; my high school counselor told me that she guaranteed me a job as a custodian. In school, we were supposed to be happy singing 'Old Black Joe.' We were expected to accept the idea that there had been good masters and bad slaves. We were taught not to rebel. Blacks were better off in the South."

Despite saying that Blacks were better off in the South, Adams' father had to leave the South at night or face serious harm or death. "My father and grandfather recognized that we were treated badly and decided that we might be killed. But we weren't going to calmly walk to the gallows. My grandfather and my dad inspired me. My father told me about our history!"

Adams served in the United States military. He was assigned to attend Officer's Candidate School at Fort Benning, Georgia. "On the way there," he said, with a pained and angry look on his face, "we had a stop in Louisville, Kentucky. The Blacks on the train got up and moved to the back cars. This was in 1950. I was riding with a White kid, with whom I had become friends. When I did not move, the conductor told me 'Boy, get to the back of the train.' My White friend told the conductor, 'You'll have to kill us to get us to the back of the train.' Not wanting to cause trouble for my friend, I said, 'It's okay.' I *accommodated* the racism. I lost the friendship of the guy, who was willing to fight for my rights, because he no longer respected me. That was the turning point of my life. I resigned from Officers Candidate School and fought racism any time I found it in the Army. I refused to accept separate barber shops, clubs on the base, and any other discrimination. I was determined that never again would *I* accommodate racism."

Once, before 1968, Adams appeared on a talk show. After he had given his opinion about Pittsburgh racism, another guest said, "I am a talk show host, and I disagree with Adams." Adams replied, "We already know that you disagree with me; you are a **talk show host.** Those positions go to White folks. There are no Black talk show hosts in Pittsburgh. We know that you and others like you don't fight racism; you accommodate it."

Adams said that he became aware of the movement in the late 1950s, as a result of the friendship between his family and the Browns. "Funny," he said, "at that time, Whites respected the NAACP more than Black people did. I became involved with the civil rights movement when I was a cop. For one thing, I realized that I could not do enough dirt to my people to make me acceptable to White cops. Unfortunately, some of my brother Black officers tried so hard to be accepted, they were more oppressive to Blacks than their White counterparts. People were always blaming Blacks for being hurt and killed by racist White cops. They say 'Well, if he didn't do anything wrong, then why did he run from the cops?' Look! If you were Black and you had any brains, you were afraid of cops, and for very good reasons!"

Adams expressed deep concern about Black-on-Black crime. "It robs you of your dignity. It robs you of your reputation. We pay a high price when we attack one another. We fall on one another out of our frustration. It is easier to attack another Black, because we are right there, crowded in unsanitary conditions. It is easier to find a Black person than it is to hunt for a White one. I would say to other Blacks, be proud of who you are. A common thread runs between us, and we must collectively stand against those who would oppress us. Learn to respect yourself; get over your fears; make a better world for everyone. You cannot compromise yourself; if you see an injustice, say something! But don't become so bitter that you self-destruct."

"I am proud of my time in the movement. My people know that I never looked down on them, except to pick them up. I would do it all over again, but I would do it **better**. I want people to remember that when I take care of those for whom I am responsible, I will have also taken care of myself." What accomplishment gave him the most pride? "Being a parent. Also the fact that after swallowing stuff for years, my people realized that now they don't have to take it. While I am proud of that, I am disappointed that we have not come further than we have."

When asked how he would like to be remembered, Adams responded, "As a guy who was not exceptionally smart, but I worked hard. I'm a very private person, despite all the publicity. An average guy who cared as much for his people as he did for himself, and who demanded respect. That I was concerned about making wrongs *right!*"

Adams was a controversial leader in the eyes of many citizens, both Black and White. Some folks loved him; just as many hated him. Some Whites who hated him also feared him. Many Blacks who disliked him were jealous of his power. Whether loved or hated, revered or reviled, Adams was unquestionably one of the most powerful Black leaders in the Pittsburgh NAACP.

Matthew Moore, Sr.
United Negro Protest Committee, Founding Member
Pittsburgh Chapter of the NAACP, Member
First Recipient of the Homer S. Brown Humanitarian Award of the Pittsburgh NAACP
Southern Christian Leadership Conference, Board Member

Matthew Moore was repeatedly named as a leading figure in the Pittsburgh civil rights movement. He was a tall, powerful man, a natty dresser, and I never saw him without a snap-brim hat perched on his head. To many, however, he was a bit of a mystery. I met Matt at the offices of the United Negro Protest Committee. Although he died before I began this oral history project, I had interviewed him as a guest on both my radio and television shows. Matt and I had a cordial and professional relationship but never became friends.

**Dr. Martin Luther King Jr., seated at the table; behind are (left to right)
Charles Harris and Matthew Moore, Sr.**

Moore was one of several Pittsburghers who went to the march on Selma during the 1960s. I vividly recall those horrible black and white news films of the peaceful marchers being severely beaten by racist cops. As I watched, I saw the unmistakable image of Matthew Moore picking up a child and moving him to safety as the police tried to beat them both. He rescued several other people during the demonstration. He was a man of great courage.

Many found Mathew to be a mysterious figure, especially when it came to the source of his money and power. Some thought he worked for Gulf Oil, specifically for Roy Koehler. One person told me, "Matt was well-respected among the upper management of Gulf Oil. When money was needed for some project, if we needed a few dollars for some special event, Matt always came back with a few thousand dollars from Gulf Oil."

His access to power was not limited to Gulf Oil. Insiders of the Pittsburgh movement knew that Moore had a little black book filled with the names of important people in government, industry, and virtually every other walk of life. When folks in the local or national movement needed money, they called Moore and he pulled a name from his black book. Soon the money was there whether it was for $50 or $50,000. Despite his access to money, there was never any talk about his having used the money for his own gain. Unfortunately his apparently easy access to money caused some to speculate that he was connected, in some illicit way, to powerful government or industrial powers. I know of nothing that would lend credence to these dark rumors.

In the process of researching this book, I spoke with many individuals in the movement. When Moore's name came up, some spoke of him with great admiration, even awe; others expressed open suspicion. Matthew Moore, Sr., died in 1985, while attending a meeting of the Southern Christian Leadership Conference in Montgomery, AL. He was a good man whom I trusted without reservation.

Charles C. Harris
United Negro Protest Committee, Founding Member
Direct Action Coalition, Founder

Charles Harris was one of the small cadre of people who formed the inner-circle of Byrd Brown and James McCoy. He is considered to be one of the most influential leaders of the time. I met Charles at an NAACP meeting and had frequent contact with him in several civil rights-related activities. He, like many other leaders, was a guest on *Black Horizons*. We were more "comrades-at-arms" than friends.

Harris led a demonstration against Community College of Allegheny County in an attempt to get the organization to hire more Black staff and faculty. He also led a series of marches against local businesses that practiced racial discrimination. After the riots of 1968, Harris became disenchanted with the United Black Protest Committee and broke away, forming his own group called the Direct Action Coalition. Harris moved from Pittsburgh making it impossible for me to include his story in his own words. I deeply regret that.

Reverend Herbert Wilkerson
Pittsburgh Chapter of the NAACP, Executive Secretary
(now called Executive Director) beginning in 1962

Herbert Wilkerson was a close friend, a mentor, and the person responsible for my career in the media. We first met at a civil rights activity and connected again when he invited me to appear on the show he hosted on WAMO radio. He often told me that the evil he found in those who opposed the movement really tested his faith in God. He is considered one of the most influential leaders of the Pittsburgh civil rights movement.

As I neared completion of the oral history collection process for *Voices,* I was troubled by my inability to record the experiences of my mentor. Herb had left Pittsburgh for Atlanta, and we lost touch with each other. None of my strategies for locating him proved successful—and then the Creator intervened. In early 1997, I was teaching a class on Pittsburgh's civil rights movement in my course on African-American history at Community College of Allegheny County. After viewing an excerpt from one of the taped interviews, a Black woman raised her hand and said that her father, Reverend Herbert Wilkerson, had been involved in the movement. I nearly choked on the beverage I was sipping. I excitedly explained to the class how important this man was. After class, I asked Herb's daughter where he was. He was in Florida, but as luck would have it, he was coming to visit family in Pittsburgh. Herb and I reconnected and during our taping session, we laughed; we cried; we talked about incidents that I judiciously decided to omit from this book.

Wilkerson was born in Swissvale, a small suburb of Pittsburgh. His first recollection of racist treatment came in 1948, when he returned home after military service. He entered a drug store in downtown Pittsburgh, wanting to eat a hamburger and was told that he would have to eat the sandwich somewhere else. Herb was a strong, dedicated leader and was arrested several times during demonstrations. Although the NAACP Legal Defense Fund would bail protestors out of jail, Wilkerson refused bail, feeling that no point would be made if he simply accepted bail after each arrest. He forced the system to book him, charge him with a crime, and hold a hearing. Of course, each time he was released after a small fine was paid for him.

During one demonstration, Wilkerson stood in front of construction trucks to prevent them from entering a building site. He was promptly arrested, and when he refused bail, many civil rights organizations came to check on him. There was no need to fear, however, because Wilkerson was aggravating his jailers by trying to organize the men in the holding cell into a choir. The police were happy to see him gone.

Wilkerson recalled being involved in negotiations with and demonstrations against many Pittsburgh businesses. Among the targets he recalled were many hotels, the Coca Cola Bottling Company, and the Teamsters Union. At one point, two of the leaders of the teamsters burst into Wilkerson's office and screamed, "What do you want, Wilkerson, a WAR?" When their attempt at intimidation failed, they calmed down, and in Wilkerson's words, "we had a nice talk."

Because of his notoriety, Wilkerson was constantly followed home; death threats were common. Despite all of this, he stated that he never really feared for his life. The threats escalated when he began to appear on the radio. Wilkerson produced and hosted a very popular radio show, *NAACP on the Line,* on WAMO radio. The studio was located in a poorly constructed building in Homestead, PA. Broadcasts had a seven-second delay system so that threats or vulgarity could be "bleeped out." The studio was so poorly insulated that those in the broadcast studio could hear what they were saying, like an echo coming seven seconds later. Herb, a consummate professional, did not find this distracting. But when I appeared as a guest on the program, the constantly echoing feedback was so disorienting that my brain shut down.[27] Herb kept saying, "don't listen to that. Just keep talking." Well, I couldn't and made a complete ass of myself. I was flabbergasted when Herb invited me to co-host the show. For more than five years, Herb and I became a much listened-to duo on Sunday evenings. After each show, we had to be very cautious as we walked to our cars in the station's parking lot. No show was complete without a death threat. Callers would say something like, "We are tired of you *niggers* stirring up the other *niggers*. We know where you park your cars, and we are going to put a bullet in your heads *tonight!*" I don't know what Herb did, but I started carrying a gun!

When I asked my old friend and mentor if progress had been made, Wilkerson said, "The progress was more a moral victory than one of quantitative advancements. We proved that racism was immoral, but not enough Blacks benefited from that. The undertow of racism still exists. We did what we felt in our hearts was the best for our people. We believed that integration would solve most of our problems. Now I'm not so sure; the jury is still out. I hope I am remembered as someone who left footprints for others to follow, but I hope others will be inspired to leave their own. We must be careful. The time bomb of racism is still ticking." Sadly, his prophetic words have turned out to be all too true.

I had the pleasure of teaching my old buddy's daughter and grand-daughter. After class on February 13, 2007, his granddaughter informed me that Herb Wilkerson had died. Even after death, he remains forever in my heart as a cherished friend and an unsung hero in Pittsburgh's war on racism.

Louis "Hop" Kendrick
Pittsburgh Chapter of the NAACP, Member

Louis "Hop" Kendrick was a friend and confidant of Byrd Brown, Matthew Moore, Charles Harris, and Jim McCoy. As such, he was one of the "power brokers" of the movement, nearly always at the table when plans were being made. Many of the movement's leaders sought his advice and counsel.

I first met Hop at Carter's Chapel African Methodist Episcopal Church in The Hill District, where both of our families were active members. When the civil rights movement started, I had already known him for many years. He was dedicated to the movement, justice, and his family. Kendrick was born and reared in Pittsburgh. He recalled that he always knew that Blacks were not permitted to swim in Kennywood Park. "I never thought of that as being racism; I just thought that it was just the way things were," he said.

He thinks he first became aware of racism when he entered the United States armed services. "At one base, somewhere in the South, we could not eat at a restaurant on a base controlled by the United States government." By the time he returned to Pittsburgh in 1954, he was acutely aware of racism. "I decided that Pittsburgh was no different than Texas, Mississippi, or any other Southern state I had been in." Mal Goode, who later became the first Black employed by a major television network, was the first person he could recall who rallied Black folks.

Kendrick became involved in the Pittsburgh civil rights movement "because I just wanted to be part of the change." He chose politics as his initial means of involvement because "the ballot box is the way to achieve parity." He recalled with great pride the demonstration against Duquesne Light Company. "People from every walk of life came together for a common cause; even those who had no chance of

27 Herb frequently had members of the civil rights movement as guests on the show. At the time I appeared, I was the president of the University of Pittsburgh Chapter of the NAACP.

getting a job. It was the first time I saw that many people at a demonstration. It made me very proud." Kendrick participated in "damn near every demonstration, including the violent demonstrations at Three Rivers Stadium and the US Steel Building construction site." His fondest memory of the demonstrations was the 1963 March on Washington. He was "so proud to see oceans of people who came together to seek redress against America's own apartheid system."

His fervent, outspoken support of Black causes often had him at odds with his employers and government leaders. Once, while visiting my office, Kendrick related a story about a meeting with Mayor Sophie Masloff, at which Kendrick referred to the mayor as "a scrub woman." I nearly choked on my coffee. After I recovered from my shock and laughter, I reached across my desk and handed Hop an African sculpture that I kept on my credenza. "What's this?" Kendrick asked. "It's called a power figure; it's from the Congo in Africa. It is supposed to have magic power and the ability to protect its owner from all harm. Take it; when you go around talking about the mayor like that, it's obvious that you need it more than I do." Hop always had more courage than good sense, and he had a hell of a lot of sense.

About the 1968 riots in Pittsburgh Kendrick said, "Pittsburgh did not explode as early as other cities, because conditions were not as bad as in some other cities. The Democrats made some Black leaders into overseers. Blacks believed what the Democrats told us, but they never really delivered and never took us seriously."

Did Blacks make progress as a result of the civil rights movement? Kendrick remarked: "On a large scale, no! On a lesser scale, maybe! Blacks are better educated, but less informed. Many of those with good jobs really believe that they got where they are all by themselves. They don't remember the struggle."

Was it worth it? "You know, Ralph, my Daddy had the strength of Samson and the wisdom of Solomon. He told us that we were no better than anyone else, but we were as good as anyone. I'm as proud as any man who ever lived. Whatever I did, I would do again and again. When I see folk's kids in good positions, I can truly say that it's out there for you, as long as you believe. There is nothing in the world that you can't do, but you can't just say it, you have to believe it. I am rich in family, in children. All of my life I wanted my children to feel about me the way I felt about my parents. I want my kids to love me, respect me, tell their friends about me. If, at the end of life *you* remember me, Ralph, that would be nice, but as long as my kids remember me and love me, that's all that really matters"

Robert Lavelle
Pittsburgh Chapter of the NAACP, Member
Dwelling House Savings and Loan Association, Founder/Owner

I met Robert Lavelle and his family through Margaret Milliones, who lived with the Lavelles when she first moved to Pittsburgh. Margaret and I had become friends because of our experiences in the Southern civil rights movement. I would often pick Margaret up on the way to demonstrations and that's how I first became acquainted with Robert. There was a special quality about this gentle, yet courageous, man, and I soon grew to love him. He has been a great supporter of my efforts, as I have been of his. I have no doubt that he is one of God's special people.

Robert lived in Chicago, St. Louis, Indiana, and Ohio before coming to Pittsburgh with his parents. His father was a poor minister, and Robert recalled being delighted when one Christmas he and his six siblings received stockings containing an orange and a candy cane. Lavelle dropped out of public school in Pittsburgh in 1932, in order to take a job as a dishwasher at $10 a week. Later, he got a job at *The Pittsburgh Courier*, sweeping floors, wrapping the paper, and doing other small jobs. "*The Courier* job was a blessing. I saw Black people in control of their own lives. I noticed that they had a White accountant and thought someone Black ought to be in that position. I asked the editor, Robert L. Vann, to send me to school so that I could become *The Courier's* accountant. Vann refused my offer, saying I would then be a specialist and he wanted me to remain a generalist. I refused to let him stop me. My mother had two insurance policies worth $500 each. She gave me one, which I cashed in for $75. That let me start taking freshman English and accounting classes at Pitt. The courses cost me $50; I used the other $25 to buy books." While taking insurance courses at Pitt, he applied for life insurance, but was turned down because he was Black.

Right after Lavelle graduated from Pitt, he received an invitation to a social function from the National Honor Society of Accountants. "The letter said that I was the kind of person they wanted in their organization and invited me to a celebration at the William Penn Hotel. I was so proud. I took my letter and reported to the room indicated on the letter. The door was partially closed, but I could hear music and laughter. When I knocked on the door; a White man answered and asked, 'Yeah, what do you want?' I explained I had received an invitation to the event. '*You* received a letter?' the man said. When I showed him the letter, he took it and told me to wait there. Soon he returned with another White man who said, 'There's been a mistake. We had no idea that you were Colored.' With that, the man closed the door in my face. I just took it. What else could I do?" Lavelle said, with the pain of that 1939 incident reflected in his eyes.

Later, in 1953, Lavelle received his master's degree in Real Estate and Insurance and applied for a job with Union Fire Insurance Company. "Although I had seen the ad in the Sunday newspaper, I was told that they did not need any agents. When I referenced the ad, I was told, "We don't hire Negro people." Again Lavelle's face changed. He looked both sad and angry. He said "Here I was. I had played by all the rules and was not allowed to enter the game on a level playing field."

Looking back on the involvement, was it worth the effort? Lavelle, who was ill at the time of this interview, sat straight up in his chair. The years seemed to melt away from his face and body. Suddenly he seemed twenty or thirty years younger. His eyes glistened, "Yes, yes," came the reply. "That made life worth living. I have planted seeds and have had the privilege to live long enough to see them grow! Young people pass by my office, knock on the window, and wave. There is hope! All I can do now is pay tithes and be thankful." We who know what this unassuming man accomplished should be thankful for his courage.

Bishop Charles Hubert Foggie
American Methodist Zion Church, Bishop
Pittsburgh Chapter of the NAACP, President
Pittsburgh Board of Education, Member

Reverend Charles Hubert Foggie came to Pittsburgh in 1944 as the leader of Wesley Center AME Zion Church, located on Centre Avenue in The Hill. The church is one of the oldest and most prestigious churches in the Pittsburgh area. As soon as he arrived, members of his congregation introduced him

**Reverend Charles Foggie with
his wife and daughter**

to the racism problems they faced. Foggie himself experienced this racism upon his arrival. He was shocked that he could not get any cab driver to take him from the train station to The Hill. Someone arranged for him to get a jitney. Boston was not like that, so he knew that there was a lot of work to do.

From church members he learned about Pittsburgh's rampant culture of discrimination in jobs, education, and public accommodations. They told him about being important only during election campaigns, and that the politicians turned their backs to the Black community as soon as they were elected. It was apparent that the masses of Black people lived lives that were dramatically different from their White counterparts. Foggie listened to these stories against the backdrop of a painful memory from his early life. A white man told Foggie's father to shoe his horse and struck him when he did not move quickly enough. His father beat the man and was forced to flee with his family. They missed the lynch mob by ten minutes.

Wesley Center Church had many middle class Black members, and they had money and willpower. In the 1950s, Foggie asked them to retire the mortgage on the church. The amount was $92,000, a small fortune in those days. The church members paid off the entire amount in *eleven months!* This feat did not go unnoticed. At the time, the Pittsburgh NAACP was a small, financially strapped organization. A committee from the NAACP asked Foggie to head the organization. Foggie accepted and served as president. Marion Jordon joined the NAACP staff as Executive Secretary.

Foggie participated in a variety of civil rights activities. He and Jordon targeted the discriminatory policies at the South Park swimming pool. The county operated two pools in the park, but Blacks were allowed to swim in only one. The NAACP won a legal challenge to the segregated swimming pools and forced the County government to desegregate the parks. Foggie also served on the Pittsburgh school board and the Pittsburgh Housing Authority, where, "I had to battle racism even though they were governing bodies," he stated with a shrug of his shoulders. He said that Blacks even needed help to get into public housing.

When asked his opinion about why Blacks in Pittsburgh accepted such poor treatment, he stated that people needed someone to step out in dangerous areas before they would step out as well. "I was willing to step out. Martin Luther King stirred us up and made us want to want to do something about our treatment."

Early in his tenure as Chapter president, Foggie approached the Webster Hall Hotel in Oakland about holding a human rights dinner for 200 folks, most of whom would be Black. The hotel would not agree, because they thought that we would not be able to pay the bill. Florence Reizenstein, a Jewish leader, who was a member of the Mayor's Human Relations Committee, had to put up the money for the dinner. "We paid off that bill in one evening," he said proudly. "When we went to rent the place next year there were no problems. The manager of the hotel stated that the Black patrons from the previous year had been 'well dressed and well behaved.' What had he expected?"

Reflecting on all he had experienced and done, Bishop Foggie said, "It was worth it. If I had to do it over, I would come running! I did not like the city, but I did like the people. The good far outweighed the bad."

People were impressed with his oratory and his quiet, dignified leadership. He believed that, as Bishop, he had a responsibility to fight against any conditions that harmed the members of his church. During our interview, I commented, "You say that your feats were not impressive and neither were you. If this is so, how did you manage to impress so many people?" He smiled and said, "I was just trying to help"

When asked how he would like to be remembered, he said, "As a high school dropout who got converted; went back to high school; then lived a constructive life, and hopefully made a contribution to others' lives."

Marion B. Jordan
Pittsburgh Chapter of the NAACP, First Executive Secretary (later called Executive Director)
Negro Emergency Education Drive (NEED), Co-founder

Marion Jordan was another quiet leader whose contributions are likely to be remembered primarily by those who worked with her. She did not participate in demonstrations, preferring to work quietly behind the scenes. She helped Pittsburgh's fairly dormant NAACP chapter increase its membership by more than 20,000 members. She was an outspoken advocate of equal rights and worked with other mainstream organizations like the Urban League. By the time the Pittsburgh civil rights movement reached the stage of mass, law-defying demonstrations, Marion and her husband had left Pittsburgh.

Marion and I did not become friends, probably because she felt I had verbally beaten up on her husband during a WQED television show. Actually, I don't blame her. I was wrong, but too full of myself to realize it. You see, someone at the station decided to produce a one-shot program called *The New Negro*, focusing on the generational divide that was emerging among members of the civil rights movement. James Jordan was a middle-age Black man, who was a member of Pittsburgh City Council and worked for a large oil company. He represented the "old" leadership; William Robinson and I represented the new, young, impatient, emerging leadership. I can't recall exactly want was said, but I do remember that Bill and I did a pretty good job of ganging up on Mr. Jordan. My parting shot was, "Move over, old man, new leadership is coming." Marion called me the next day and angrily demanded an explanation about why we had been so disrespectful of her husband. I was arrogantly unsympathetic and replied, "If your husband can't take the heat, he needs to get out of the kitchen." I was very proud of my retort, *then!* A few years later, wisdom set in, and I became very ashamed by my behavior. I tried to find both of them to apologize, but had lost contact with them. I now realize that each generation becomes disenchanted with the older leaders and wishes them to move aside. The experience led me to adopt a policy to never again attack another Black person when Whites were present. I now counsel young folks to ask for the changes without the arrogance of youth that Bill and I exhibited so many years ago.

Judge Henry Smith, Jr.
In 1969, Henry Smith became the 3rd Black attorney appointed to the Pennsylvania Court of Common Pleas
Smith chaired the Legal Redress Committee that sued the City of Pittsburgh over discriminatory practices at the Highland Park swimming pool
Pennsylvania Bureau of Unemployment Compensation, Investigator
Pittsburgh Housing Authority

Henry Smith, Jr., came to Pittsburgh in 1941 and began working at the Kay Boy's Club in The Hill District. After holding a number of jobs, he enrolled in and graduated from law school, becoming one of a handful of prominent Black attorneys practicing in Pittsburgh. He was a personal friend and trusted advisor of Byrd Brown. Generally, his involvement in the Pittsburgh NAACP was behind the scenes as an ever-present figure at strategy meetings.

When Smith came to Pittsburgh, Blacks were treated as second class people. The Young Men's Christian Association, despite its name, was an unchristian, segregated organization. The organization not only barred Blacks from its buildings, it also prohibited Blacks from attending YMCA camps. Blacks, when they were permitted to enter theaters in White communities, were forced to sit in the balcony. In fact, Smith said, they had to sit in the far left or far right of the balcony; never in the center. In the Beltzhoover area and on the Southside, Blacks could not use the swimming pools. "We were prohibited from using most swimming pools in Pittsburgh. It was too dangerous to even think of using one of the restricted pools. You could walk for blocks in downtown and never see a Black face because there were relatively few jobs for Black folks. The first time I saw a large number of Blacks in downtown was when a group was picketing some stores. Black lawyers were about the only professional Blacks you saw downtown."

Smith explained that Blacks accepted their unfair treatment. "That's because it was the way folks were raised. Folks talked about it, but did nothing. I became aware of the movement pretty early. When I became a lawyer, I, like other Blacks before me, was expected to work for the NAACP. My personal involvement came because I had some very negative experiences; I wanted to make a contribution to the movement. The city fathers were very negative about the protests, and Mayor David L. Lawrence ignored them for as long as he could. He and the other city leaders did not even want to talk about the movement. Most of my activity was confined to doing the legal work: challenging laws, getting people out of jail. I did walk around Duquesne Light." Actually, Judge Smith may have forgotten how often he participated in demonstrations. I have seen photographs, taken by Teenie Harris, of Smith at demonstrations against Isaly's Dairy chain, The Pittsburgh Board of Public Education, and other demonstration sites.

Smith recalled that the riots of 1968 in Pittsburgh were fast and violent. "The first day was completely out of control. With all that was going on, I was never afraid. It was worth it; I had a lot of fun. I have some pride when I look back and see what has happened. It took us two years to break up swimming pool discrimination, beginning with Highland Park. The mayor hated all of us who forced him to desegregate the pools. He told us that we could never look to him for anything. Highland Park Pool was a rough place. Some young, White punks beat up the first Blacks who attempted to swim after the official desegregation. The police were not much interested in protecting us, so we took matters into our own hands. We sent some young Black toughs to swim at the pool. A few fights with the White thugs followed. The White boys lost each one and that ended the fights. We then filed 50 suits against various government and private groups. Whites hid behind the 'private club' ruse in order to discriminate against Blacks. We used the Pennsylvania public accommodations laws to bust them. We won them all. The publicity of the suits caused others to open their doors. We have made some progress. We were able to hold up funds for the court system, because the funds were being distributed on a basis that discriminated against Blacks."

How did he want to be remembered? "As a man who made a small contribution by using the legal system to open up society for Blacks."

Tim Stevens
Pittsburgh Chapter of the NAACP, Executive Director, Board Member, President
The Black Political Empowerment Project, Founder and Leader

Tim Stevens was born on Wylie Avenue, one of the main streets in the famous Hill District. His father, a postal worker, often talked about how badly Blacks were treated in Pittsburgh. I met Tim in the 1970s and learned that he was caught between two burning desires—his passion for justice and his love of singing. For most of his adult life he has pursued both dreams, splitting his time among singing, working at a facility for the mentally ill, and serving his people. He is good at all three activities. I have seen him dedicate his life to the cause of justice and have heard him sing on the *Mike Douglas Show*. He frequently appears at Pittsburgh entertainment venues. Tim became one of my best friends.

In 1967, Stevens was sent to Washington, D.C. as a trainee of Exxon Oil Company. While watching urban riots on television, the scenes made him very uncomfortable. Despite the considerable perks provided

Tim Stevens

by the oil company, Stevens returned to Pittsburgh and enrolled in the Graduate School for Public and International Affairs at the University of Pittsburgh. "Even though my decision would cost me thousands of dollars, I felt that I needed to be involved," he stated.

When he came back to Pittsburgh, Alma Fox encouraged him to apply for the executive director's position with the Pittsburgh NAACP and, at the age of 20 or so, became youngest director in the chapter's history. In addition to participating in demonstrations and leading negotiation teams, Stevens created the Black Political Empowerment Project, designed to convince Blacks to vote in every election.

Stevens placed a great deal of emphasis on recruiting more young people into the NAACP. In the early 1960s, the youth division of the Pittsburgh NAACP, under the leadership of Dorothy Williams, was large and active. Over time, however, youth had drifted away from the organization. Stevens wanted to recapture the energy of youth and felt strongly that his role was to bridge the gap between younger and older members of the Black community. He argued that the NAACP should not be segregated into older and younger divisions, but everyone should be included as fully functional members of the organization. To the discomfort of some older members, Stevens dubbed the Pittsburgh Chapter "The New Image NAACP." That action alone caused eyes to roll. He further exasperated older folks when he joined with many other young people in asking that the NAACP change its name to the "National Association for the Advancement of Black People." The idea was met with so much opposition, the word "Colored" remains.

One of Tim's early activities was to sponsor a three day Black arts festival. In an attempt to attract Whites, the third day of the festival was to be held in the predominantly White Oakland neighborhood. Opposition to the idea of catering to Whites was so strong, Stevens was forced to cancel the Oakland venue. During this time, Stevens' car windows were smashed as it sat in front of the NAACP's Hill District office. He wasn't certain if the damage was caused by his suggestion to rename the NAACP or the idea of holding part of a Black arts festival in a predominantly White community. This led Stevens to conduct a small survey to see what Blacks themselves wanted to be called. "Of my sample, 20 (young folks) wanted to be called "Black"; 40 to 50 (older folks) preferred "Negro," and about 60 (still older citizens) wanted to be called "Colored." These differences still persist to a lesser degree even today.

When asked whether he ever feared for his own safety, Stevens replied, "I used to look under the hood of my car to check for dynamite. I constantly received threats and, given the fact that Pittsburgh was and is one of the most racist cities in America, it made sense to be cautious. During this time, Blacks were trying to find our identity. Some Whites wanted to help us in that process. Some became a bit upset when we turned down their offers of assistance. They became confused and angry. At the same time, Blacks were becoming more and more frustrated, because the civil rights movement had not delivered on its promise of equality."

During the riots of 1968, many Blacks were frightened by the violent potential of the upheaval. "My brother and I sat on the front porch of our home, armed with rifles. Our house was attached to a White-owned store. After the riot, we bought the store in order to protect our investment in our home. We knew that part of the frustration of Blacks had to do with the fact that there were so many White-owned stores in The Hill. I understand why they burned the White stores, but 20 years later nothing has been replaced."

Was it worth the effort? "Without question, I would do it all over again. Of course, I might do some things a little smarter, but I would still do it again, without hesitation." As a matter of fact, Stevens did do it again. This interview was conducted in 1991; in 1995, Stevens ran a successful campaign for the presidency of the Pittsburgh NAACP. He remained the president until 2005, when he was defeated by a woman, in a very controversial election.

Stevens was devastated. He had devoted ten years of his life as president of the chapter, and now he was out on his ear. The day after the election, Tim called me to try to make sense of what had happened. He felt betrayed by more than one person he had regarded as a friend. After a very long discussion, Tim and I still found the situation incomprehensible. Seeing how hurt and upset Tim was, I suggested that he could still serve the people. "How?" he asked. "I just lost the election!"

"Look, Tim, just walk away from the NAACP. You started the Black Political Empowerment Project. Why don't you resurrect that project and put all your energy there?"

"But that project was about getting Black folks out to vote. It is not a civil rights organization," Tim protested.

"True. But look, man; you have some very faithful followers who will leave the NAACP, because you're no longer there. Have a meeting; get some input from your folks; decide what BPEP can do."

Tim took my words to heart and found a provision in the BPEP charter that allowed him to work with elected officials to make certain that they lived up to promises made to Blacks during political campaigns. He proceeded to shape the organization into a powerful force. When you see a protest meeting or a story about injustice in Pittsburgh, you also see Tim Stevens, a mature, articulate, well-spoken man who has never lost his zeal for righting wrongs. The Black Political Empowerment Program is now looked upon by many folks in government and in the public as the premier Pittsburgh civil rights organization.

Delores Stanton

Recipient of the NAACP Homer S. Brown Award for selling the most NAACP memberships in 1967 and 1968.

Although I frequently saw Delores Stanton during many actions taken by the NAACP and UNPC, I did not interact on a personal level until I interviewed her. This thoroughly delightful woman fought fiercely against the racist establishment that had belittled her when she when was growing up in Pittsburgh:

> You had to stand up and eat, or take your hot dogs outside, at those measly five-and-ten-cent stores! Black men were mostly laborers. One good job we had was as rubbish men—until Whites found out the job paid well and pushed us out.

Stanton, who became an engineer, had received no encouragement from school counselors, who tried to push her to become a teacher or a social worker, because those were acceptable positions for Black women. "I liked math. I did well in chemistry, but they would not encourage me."

Stanton's mother had been a member of Marcus Garvey's Universal Negro Improvement Association, a group that believed in self-determination and race-pride. Garvey preached, "Lift up your head, ye mighty race; you can be anything you will." Stanton believes that her mother's membership in the Garvey movement "made a difference in how I viewed myself."

Stanton became involved in the Pittsburgh movement "because I wanted to see better things for Blacks." She participated in a number of demonstrations, including those against Duquesne Light as well as Gimbel's, and Horne's department stores. She also participated in the march across the bridge to the construction site of Three Rivers Stadium. "At the demonstration against United States Steel, some of us sat down to block the construction trucks," she recalled. "The police came and said, 'if you don't want to go to jail, stand up.' I stood up, but Byrd Brown and Alma Fox just sat there. I tried to get Byrd to get up, but he wouldn't budge. I ran and called Byrd's mother; she called Attorney Utterback; he got Byrd out of jail." Then, with a twinkle in her eye, she added, "I thought someone had to be outside in order to get those other nuts out."

Asked about fear, Stanton stated, "I was not ever afraid for my job, even though I worked for the University of Pittsburgh. I always took vacation time when I was going to participate in a demonstration. It was time well spent. I wasn't afraid for my life either, but I didn't want to get hit or go to jail," she laughed. Her fondest memory was the March on Washington. "We sent nine buses and a train to the march. We had a nurse on every bus. All Star Chicken donated fried chicken to eat on the way down. It was a proud moment."

Was it worth the effort? "Yes, I would not change it. We did not always make progress. We took two steps forward and at least one step back. I hope that Black folks remember that we have to keep on fighting. The fight has just begun. We are nowhere near where we have to go."

Charles Kindle
Greater Pittsburgh Improvement League, Member
United Negro Protest Committee, Member
Pittsburgh Chapter of the NAACP, Member

I first met Charles Kindle when he appeared on *Black Horizons*. He could be funny and deadly serious at the same time. Whether he was calling in to my radio show, demonstrating with me, or accompanying me to see the King Tut exhibition in Cleveland, Charles never missed a chance to "harangue" me about civil rights issues. He held leaders accountable for their actions and never hesitated to confront them in public. Some folks ran in the opposite direction when Charles approached, because even though they were on his side, they knew they'd likely be trapped in a conversation on racism. Charles Kindle had a deep, powerful voice and whether he was singing, shouting, or praying, he could be heard above the din of demonstrations. He was a heroic voice of the movement; he was my friend.

Born in Pittsburgh's Hill District, Kindle recalled, "When coming up in The Hill, I did not notice much racism as a child, because The Hill was integrated. I did not realize that racism was such a devastating disease. That damn Urban Renewal took away our economic and cultural base in The Hill. It should have been called 'Negro Removal' rather than Urban Renewal. Actually, I didn't remain unaware of racism for very long; by 6 or 7 years of age, I began to notice that, outside The Hill, Blacks were treated very badly. I sat in my all Black school and could look out the window on Bedford Avenue and see the whole city. I saw that we didn't carry briefcases, and Whites did. I saw that they had on coats and ties, while we had on work clothes. Eventually, I took up with Mal Goode and worked with The Greater Pittsburgh Improvement League. I began to read books by European philosophers. They helped to open my eyes. I also read about the racism in Australia. Europeans have slaughtered indigenous people all over the world. We should all do whatever we can to be free. I *hate* evil people.

"Why did I become involved? Well, I looked at Asia and the old kingdoms of Africa and saw how we were exploited by Europeans. I was determined that they were not going to take back Africa; not as long as I was alive. Carl Redwood and I were raising money for guns. Folks thought we were crazy, but you can't defend yourself if you don't have guns." Charles was the first local leader to link the plight of South African Blacks to the civil rights of Blacks in the rest of the world.

"By the time I joined the NAACP in 1963, I was a full supporter of Nelson Mandela's attempts to free South Africans. This immoral country controlled all the coal mining in Africa by forcing Blacks into virtual slave labor, even though Blacks greatly outnumbered Whites. I was picketing, walking, and talking about freeing South Africa, long before others joined in the action. Folks told me I was crazy and made fun of me for identifying with Africans. They just didn't see that we couldn't be free as long as we permitted the oppression of our brothers and sisters in South Africa. Finally, some other folks began to join me, and the NAACP actually started an African Affairs committee. They even joined me in picketing stores that supported the corrupt South African government by selling gold krugerrands. How does it feel to be right after all the years of folks making fun of me? God has blessed me; I am on a *high* that I never got from booze." Kindle leaned back in his chair, and enjoyed a long, hearty laugh. Then he stopped laughing and became very quiet. After a moment of introspection, he looked at me and said, "Those who bring about change, including you Ralph, are living a dangerous life."

When asked about how racism had affected him on a personal basis, Kindle gave a surprising response: "At one time I believed that I could be president of the United States. I soon had my dreams dashed when I realized ain't no way this country's about to elect a Black president. Hell, we can't even elect a Black *mayor* in Pittsburgh. The FBI compiled a dossier on me because of my civil rights activities." His mood changed again as he laughed and said, "Hell, Ralph, they probably have one on you, with your radical self." Then his mood darkened again as he continued: "I worked in the Post Office for years. Based on my skills and knowledge, I should have been Post Master. Racism affects all of us. We are losing 25% of our youth to drugs. They want us to self-destruct."

Kindle was one of the people who worked with the United Negro Protest Committee. "We were out every day and every night demonstrating, picketing and negotiating. I was too dumb to be afraid when I was young. I was immortal; I even thought that I could be the salvation of the Black race. At 50, I started to get afraid, but I never let fear stop me from doing what was right. Jim McCoy of the United Negro Protest Committee was a hell of a leader. I would have followed him on a march into hell! Many folks, especially the young ones, don't even know who this great man was. We need to teach our history! I've been mad all my life; I'm mad just sitting here talking about it. A man asked me once why I was demonstrating. 'After all, you already have a good job.' He just didn't understand. We had some powerful leaders; Matt Moore could call the *president!* You know, we all have a responsibility to try to eliminate racism and discrimination. Evil only prevails when good men do nothing. When we were working to eliminate racism, we were often joined by our White brothers and sisters. They helped a lot. We could not have done it without them. Being on the inside, they could get information for us that we couldn't get ourselves."

"God did not intend for us to live in poverty. I have worked *hard.* I refused to let racism keep me poor. I have three cars, a home, and a motorcycle. God has been good to me. All you kids don't accept slavery. It's in your mind. I ain't gonna accept slavery from anybody! I don't give a damn what their color is." Kindle said that graduating from the University of Pittsburgh was his greatest accomplishment. "No one believed that I could do it. We must all pay our dues. When we make it, we need to come back and get somebody."

Charles vowed to demonstrate until freedom was won or he was dead. Sadly, he did not live to see the end of racism, but he certainly did his share in the war on racism. How would he like to be remembered? "Here is a man who made a contribution to the movement. A fighting soldier. A man who tried to do the right thing for *all* people."

Was it worth the effort? "YES! I am at peace with myself. I can die in peace. I know I am going to heaven. I am rich! I have seen the future. The price of freedom is eternal vigilance." Charles must have indeed been ready to meet his maker. Not long after this interview, death silenced this strong voice of protest. I still hear his voice ringing out above the crowd. If a powerful voice could kill racism, Kindle would have put it in its grave many moons ago. But then there is heaven, isn't there?

Elks Parade on Wylie Avenue

CHAPTER 7

Young Voices in
the Movement

The Young Adult Chapter of the Pittsburgh NAACP

Duuring the 1960s, the Pittsburgh NAACP had a very active Young Adult Chapter. The membership consisted primary of young Black professionals from ages 21–35. This group had two powerful leaders, Dorothy K. Williams and Herbert "Coop" Ivey. The Chapter was very active in investigating complaints about discrimination.

Dorothy K. Williams
Young Adult Chapter of the Pittsburgh NAACP, Founder
Wilkinsburg Youth Chapter, Advisor
Pittsburgh Youth Chapter, Advisor
Ike Small Award, 1965 Recipient

Dorothy Williams, the aunt of my best friend James Tyler, has always been a part of my life. My formal, working relationship with Dorothy began when she was organizing the Young Adult Chapter of the Pittsburgh NAACP. She recalled that, when she was a child, Blacks lived in alleys and above stores. They could not go to many restaurants or eat at lunch counters in five-and-dime stores. When she asked her mother about this, her mother said, "That's just the way we are treated in Pittsburgh." Dorothy's mother had graduated from Spellman College and taught in Atlanta. "Mom wanted one of her five girls to be a teacher," Williams recalled. "Since I was the last girl to be educated, she made certain that I became a teacher."

Dorothy's involvement in the Pittsburgh movement came when Wilhelmina Byrd Brown asked her to accept the position as youth advisor for the Pittsburgh NAACP. At Dorothy's request, her nephew James recruited "five fine young men, and the girls soon followed." She smiled and said, "One of the people Jimmy recruited was you, Ralph. You had just come home from the army and were always fussing with the officers of the chapter. One day I thought, 'Lord, if he had his own chapter, maybe he will stop all that fussing.' I knew you for a long time, because you and Jimmy had been friends since childhood. I knew that you were very intelligent, but, Lord, did you need somebody to help you channel all that energy! That's when I suggested that you start a chapter at Pitt.

Indeed, I remember that at one meeting a verbal battle broke out between the president, Coop Ivey, and me. I had just returned from military service, had participated in the southern civil rights movement, was carrying a big chip on my shoulder, and was full of myself. I tended to get into power struggles with other strong-willed Black men. As the argument grew louder and louder Dorothy jumped to her feet and challenged me to start an NAACP Chapter at Pitt. I took her suggestion to heart, started the Chapter, and was elected the first president.

One of the unsung heroes of the movement, Williams recruited members for and was the advisor to a total of four young chapters of the NAACP. She started the Young Adult Chapter for Black professionals between the ages of 21-35 that was highly effective in testing for racial discrimination in public accommodations and housing. Williams also was the advisor for the Wilkinsburg Youth Chapter and the Pittsburgh Youth chapter. Of this latter group, Dorothy recalled, "At one meeting, the youngsters were discussing jobs. One young man wanted to be a shoe salesman in downtown Pittsburgh. The others laughed and said, 'You know they don't hire colored people in those shoe stores.' Whenever my kids posed a problem, I always asked them what we should do about it. The solution to this problem was to picket the shoe stores. We had a lot of support from the adults in the NAACP, but we did all the picketing ourselves. Many White folks were moved by the sight of these cute, well-dressed, small, young Black children picketing. Many called the shoe stores and said that they would never buy another pair of shoes until the shoe stores hired Blacks. Many people refused to cross the picket lines. The campaign resulted in Blacks being hired, for the first time, as shoe sales clerks in Downtown Pittsburgh." My young people saw what was going on around the country, and they decided that they would become part of the solution. I was so proud of them!"

Williams was a very inspirational leader who moved her charges to do things about which they had only dreamed. Yet, her name does not appear in most accounts of the Pittsburgh movement. Perhaps it is because she did not seek the spotlight, but rather went quietly about her work of building the most powerful network of youth workers in the country. Her work was rewarded when her Youth Group received the Ike Small Award for having the largest and the best such group in the country. At the time, Williams had 6,500 youth in her groups.

When asked if it was worth the effort, she said, "Yes, I helped the kids do some of the things they wanted to do." How did she want to be remembered? "I tried to help my young folks make good choices." By mentoring so many young Black warriors, Dorothy Williams built a powerful coalition of Black young folks who were at the center of the revolution.

Herbert "Coop" Ivey
Young Adult Chapter of the Pittsburgh NAACP, President

Hebert "Coop" Ivey was a quiet young man who owned a business. Although his contributions were not well known, he led one of the most active chapters in Pittsburgh and the surrounding communities. When asked how he became involved, he said: "I was at the Loendi Club with some buddies, having a drink. James Tyler came up and told us that his aunt, Dorothy Williams, was putting together this civil rights group. It was going to be a branch of the Pittsburgh NAACP, but would have only young folks. I was hesitant, at first. Then on my way home from Korea, I was thinking how I could almost forget I was Black, because I was treated so much better than in the States. I got angry as I thought about the racist crap I was going to face when I got back. It made sense to join. So, I did, and folks elected me president. You remember; we thought the "old folks" in the adult chapter of the NAACP were moving too slowly. Court litigation was just too slow. We wanted change to take place faster. We wanted all of our rights now! So, we said 'let's take this direct.' Lots of young folks joined the group; we'd have 200-300 young people at the meetings. We did most of the testing and picketing of the housing market. We were a lot more active than the adult chapter. Our people were just not going to wait."

James Tyler, Jr.
Young Adult Chapter of the Pittsburgh NAACP, Member and Recruiter

Jim Tyler was my best friend from elementary school through our high school days. We spent many hours at one another's homes, went to movies together, and worked at the same laundry in the time between high school graduation and going off to college. We started at Lincoln University together. Jim graduated, but I quit and joined the army. We renewed our friendship when I returned from the army, and Jim was recruiting young people for membership in the Young Adult Chapter of the Pittsburgh NAACP.

When Jim's aunt, Dorothy Williams, enlisted his help he began with his friends who, in turn, recruited their friends. Soon there were hundreds of well-educated, young Black folks attending the meetings held at the Loendi Club, located in The Hill. "I suppose it helped," Tyler said, "that you could get drinks and dinner after the meetings. It also helped that many good looking, educated, single folks attended the meetings. Some came, looking at first for love, and later becoming involved in the movement."

Among the many people he recruited were his old high school buddies, Harriet McCrea and me. The three of us had encountered a racist teacher at Schenley High School who accused Harriet and me of helping Jim cheat on physics exams. Harriet recalled the incident this way, "I told the man that his accusations were ridiculous. Jimmy didn't need our help to pass any exams. All three of us were very intelligent people who made good grades. Jimmy was smart enough to complete medical school, why would he need our help? At graduation that teacher came up to me and said he had given us D's as a warning; he had intended to change them before submitting the final grades. But he didn't."

This man's callous act shook the confidence of all three of us. McCrea thought she did not have the talent to enter the field of science, which was her first love. Instead, she became a school teacher. Tyler said that the experience robbed him of a bit of his confidence. As a result of this lone 'D', I was robbed of my rank as the second highest student in the graduating class. That incident shook my faith in myself and led to my dropping out of college and joining the service. It would take five years before I regained enough faith in my intelligence so that I could return to college. This is just a small incident, but it clearly illustrates the damage racism has done to millions of Black youngsters across this land.

Tyler remembers that "Before the civil rights movement, most of us simply didn't venture into downtown Pittsburgh. All we needed was right there in The Hill. Even though our folks insisted that we were going to college, they sort of accepted their treatment at the hands of racists. I guess when you're trying to feed your family and take care of your kids, it's hard to do other things, like fight racism. I guess as long as they were able to get what they needed in The Hill, they accepted the unfair treatment."

"I was accustomed to seeing mostly Black folks in The Hill. I remember once taking the 87 Ardmore Bus and being surprised that all I saw were White folks. There were places we could not go in Oakland, where the University of Pittsburgh was located. The five-and-ten-cent stores employed Blacks only as bus boys. Once I was applying for a job and the person at the company asked for my zip code. When he recognized that the code was for The Hill, the job vanished." At the time about which Tyler was speaking, all newspaper ads were permitted to state that they wanted only White employees. Most Blacks did not bother applying for jobs that were so identified.

It soon became evident that the young Blacks in the chapter were vociferous fighters. Asked whether he had specifically recruited "radicals" Tyler replied, "No, I just recruited young Black males and females. We were not radical. We were simply what the times demanded. We were well-educated, but still could not find good jobs. We were not going to just sit by and accept the unfair treatment. We attacked racism with a vengeance born of righteous indignation. Our time had come, and we were not to be denied. You remember how all of us guys talked about the shit our fathers had to take, and we said that we were not going to take it. We were going to make some money, and no one was going to stand in our way! Now we were standing by our words and we were not afraid."

I reminded Tyler that we both had been in a gang, as had been most of the Black youth in our communities. "We were in gangs. That could have trapped us for life. But it didn't. We were in gangs, but they were not our whole life." The truth is that we did not pass the gang lore on to the younger guys in the neighborhood. We were taught that there was *hope!* As long as we had hope, we could work miracles and we did that!"[28]

Did we make sufficient progress? Tyler said "I don't think so. Before integration we were self-sufficient; now we're not. We who could afford it left the Black community. We lost a great deal under integration. We really were seeking economic integration; we did not achieve it. We did the best we could with what we had, and that is how I would like to be remembered."

Harriet McCrea
Young Adult Chapter of the Pittsburgh NAACP, Member

Harriet McCrea is one of the unsung heroes of the movement. I chose Harriet as the representative of the thousands of unnamed people who gallantly participated, without ever thinking that their contributions would be noticed. Although Harriet would argue that she was "nobody special" in the movement, she was very active in the Young Adult Chapter of the NAACP. Without people like Harriet, the movement could not have taken place.

She recalled an early incident of racism. "My father took me downtown to see a parade. I was too small to see over the crowd, so my father held me, straddling his shoulders. I was enjoying myself when a White man came along, picked up his child, placed her on his shoulders, and stood in front of Dad. He blocked my view on purpose! He could have chosen to stand anywhere else, but he chose to stand right in front of us. He knew what he was doing, because he looked right at us before he chose his spot. In

---

28 The gangs we belonged to were not violent, criminal groups. These early gangs stopped being a factor in 1956, when most of the members of the gang leadership either got jobs or went off to college. The gangs did not return until the 1990s when hope disappeared again.

very strong words, Dad told the man that he had better move. The man did not say a word and moved someplace else. I was very proud of my father. That White man thought he could get away with what he had done because, for the most part, Black folks in Pittsburgh did not speak up against White people. Well my dad did!"

McCrea remembered the Young Adult demonstrations against coffee houses in Shadyside, a very segregated neighborhood that catered to the hippy population. "We were surprised at the level of racism in this community. To be fair, most of the racism came at the hands of the home and apartment building owners and the shop owners, rather than the counter-culture folks themselves."

Asked why she had become involved in the movement, she replied, "I'm not sure that I had a choice. James Tyler recruited me," she said, smiling broadly. "Our generation was different. We more or less decided that we weren't going to accept the same treatment our parents had accepted. That's why we were so effective at attacking racism. We found it to be a personal affront, and we were just not going to take it. In the Young Adult Chapter, we were all young and ambitious; most of us were college graduates. We all had bad tastes in our mouths from the racism we had swallowed in high school. You remember how we were treated at Schenley?" Indeed I did remember, quite painfully.

Was it worth it? "Certainly! It expanded my support systems. All of my friends were fierce fighters. We demanded and required respect. We demanded and received a quality education. We made a difference!" McCrae would like to be remembered as a kind, honest person, who was willing to put herself on the line to help others.

The NAACP Youth Council

This group was the youngest of the Pittsburgh NAACP groups with members ranging in age from 6 to 18. It, too, was under the leadership of Dorothy Williams, who felt that even very young people should participate in securing their futures. I did not have much contact with the Youth Council, except through conversations with Dorothy. Consequently, I did not know the names of the young folks who were involved, and so, cannot acknowledge their important contributions.

The University of Pittsburgh NAACP

Dorothy Williams strongly suggested that I that I start a chapter of the NAACP at Pitt, where I was a student. She did this to keep me from constantly bickering with Hubert Ivey who was the president of the Young Adult Chapter. The group's advisor was Dr. Matt Nelson, the first Black faculty member hired by the University's dental school. The organization was officially recognized by the University and had offices in the William Pitt Student Union, in the heart of the Oakland Campus. The University wouldn't give us any furniture so a friend who worked for Alcoa made arrangements for us to pick out some furniture they were discarding. I chose a couple of chairs, a wooden file cabinet, and a beautiful, wooden, kidney-shaped desk. My eyes were bigger than my stomach, and when the desk was delivered it barely fit the space. In fact, in order to sit behind the desk I had to crawl over the top!

Initially, most members of the Pitt NAACP were White; Black students seemed more concerned with parties than with equal rights. We tried to recruit every Black student we ran into. For example, there was a small group of young Black men who played cards just outside the door of our office. We would invite them to participate in meetings and demonstrations, but to no avail; they either ignored us or laughed in our faces. Shortly after showing us nothing but disdain, one of the card players and his wife were discriminated against when seeking an apartment in Oakland. He beat a hasty path to our office door and asked us for assistance. I felt like telling him to kiss our collective behinds; good sense prevailed, and we helped him. Later this man became a high-ranking Pitt administrator and became very militant in seeking redress concerning racial discrimination at Pitt.

The Pitt Chapter investigated many cases of alleged discrimination at the university and in the surrounding Oakland community. At the time, the University practiced various forms of discrimination, including separate facilities for maintenance and housekeeping staffs, admission of students, and hiring and promoting staff and faculty. Ads specifying that apartments would be rented to only certain types of students were listed by Pitt's housing office. A woman dean of students was so disturbed by interracial dating that she called the parents of white students to tell them that their children were dating "Coloreds." She did not stop until the Pitt NAACP threatened to go public with the whole sordid mess. The Pitt Chapter tested public accommodations in restaurants, bars, night clubs, hair care businesses and other businesses in the Oakland community. In the early days the Chapter's rallies, meetings, and picketing were seen as so militant that the national Chapter threatened to revoke its charter.

At one point, I helped students and faculty prepare for a bus trip to Selma, Alabama, in response to the call by the leadership of the southern movement. As a result of my previous experiences in the south, I had vowed never again to participate in a non-violent demonstration. But I agreed to prepare those who were going on how to travel safely. Despite my instructions, a rabbi, who was a faculty member, took photographs of the group at one of their rest stops. The flashes of the camera attracted the attention of some local rednecks who vowed to follow the bus and "take care of the niggers and nigger-lovers." Fortunately, one of the students thought to call me, and I stayed by the phone until the group arrived at the rendezvous spot in Alabama. After consulting with some other faculty members on the trip and making a few phone calls, I was able to get the convoy escorted safely to their destination. When the group returned to Pittsburgh, the NAACP and other campus groups sponsored a campus meeting to allow the demonstrators to share their experiences with others. The rabbi and I had a heated public discussion about his "concern" over a remark that Stokely Carmichael made about "knocking the goddamn legs off the table if Whites would not permit Blacks to eat at the table in peace." Later, the rabbi would sell his "historic" account of the trip and demonstration to *Playboy* magazine. Suddenly, the purpose of the photos became abundantly clear.

Many of the White kids who worked with us were dedicated, at least initially. Soon, however, they drifted away. Truthfully, I was not upset about that. Those well-meaning young people did not experience racism in the same way those of us born with dark skin did. Around 1998, I was a panelist at a forum on racism. At the conclusion of the program, a White man approached me, shook my hand, embraced me, and began to weep. He stepped back and said, "I know you don't remember me, but I was a member of the University of Pittsburgh NAACP. I participated in demonstrations, meetings, and investigations. I was really dedicated. Then I graduated, got a new job in corporate America, and left all my dedication behind. Here you are, more than 30 years later, and you still are involved. Please forgive me, I am so ashamed."

I told him it was not my place to judge or forgive him. "You are not alone. Many folks, including some Blacks, left the movement in order to establish a good life. As for me, I had no choice. This is my life's work, and I do it because I really can't help myself. You can still be involved without picketing, demonstrating or risking your livelihood. Just look for the daily racism, gender bias, and anti-Semitism that are prevalent in all American corporations, and fight to eliminate such practices. Lead by example!" He thanked me, walked away, and I have not heard from him since. Such is life.

Unfortunately, I did not keep accurate notes on the number of people who were involved with the Pitt NAACP. When I graduated in 1963, I left the records behind, along with all other documentation. For several years, I tried unsuccessfully to retrieve the records for this project. It was as if the chapter had never existed. I sincerely hope some future historian will take up the challenge of finding and preserving the names of those who joined the fight for equality on campus.

Robert Goode
Pittsburgh Chapter of the NAACP, Member
University of Pittsburgh Chapter of the NAACP, Charter Member
1st Black hired as a top-level administer by Mellon Bank
The Pennsylvania State Human Relations Commission, Member

Robert Goode was the son of Mal Goode and the nephew of Ruth Goode-White, long-time director of the Western Pennsylvania Sickle Cell Anemia Society. I believe he felt an obligation to serve because of the fact that so many of his family were very prominent members of the Pittsburgh Black community.

Freedom House Headquarters of the United Negro Protest Committee;
James McCoy, Director (far right of group)

Bob came to one of the first meetings of the University of Pittsburgh NAACP. I was impressed with his "presence" and his serious nature. He was a quiet, unassuming man who never sought the spotlight. In this way, he was like many others who worked tirelessly in the movement, yet never gained a great deal of recognition. At Pitt, he was a moral compass, always bringing the group back to the fact that we were an NAACP chapter and had to live up to the ideals of the group. Among Goode's accomplishments was helping to organize a project called "Jazz for Freedom." Monies derived from jazz concerts performed by local musicians were used to sponsor students who were traveling to southern states to participate in "Mississippi Freedom Summer."

Citizen's Billboard warning about further incursion of the Hill Redevelopment Project, circa 1960

**Freedom House Traveling
Produce Vendor, circa 1965**

CHAPTER 8

The United Negro/Black Protest Committee

As mentioned in Chapter 5, many people did not realize that the United Negro Protest Committee (UNPC) was an arm of the NAACP. Because the national NAACP initially restricted the types of protest strategies the local chapters could use, Byrd Brown felt handcuffed as the movement took renewed energy. He wanted to have at his disposal any method available for addressing the evils of racial discrimination. After much discussion, Brown, James McCoy, and others created a new organization that would be the action arm of the NAACP. The new organization was called The United Negro Protest Committee. Its first leader was James McCoy, who was employed at United States Steel and was the chairman of the NAACP Labor and Industry Committee. Group tactics included boycotts, demonstrations, picketing, and economic activities. The group attracted more militant people, many of whom considered the NAACP to be too timid and middle-class. Because this group included the leaders of nearly every other Black group, it was well suited to handle the many mass demonstrations that became commonplace during the height of the movement. They called together 4,000 demonstrators to confront Duquesne Light Company. The largest demonstration took place in April, 1968 when 10,000 people gathered in a march to honor the slain leader Dr. Martin Luther King, Jr. In that same year, the United Negro Protest Committee became the United Black Protest Committee.

Vince Wilson
United Negro Protest Committee, Member

As was the case with so many other members of the movement, I met Vince through our participation in demonstrations. He also appeared as a guest on *Black Horizons*.

Vince Wilson was a bus driver for the Allegheny County Port Authority. By his own account, he was "just an ordinary guy." His involvement, however, was anything but ordinary. If there was a demonstration, Vince was there, participating vigorously while urging others to "come on out." He was a colorful person, and we all were comforted to see him standing tall at the demonstrations. He would like to be remembered as "someone who did the best with what he had."

Wilson became involved in the movement after "years of discrimination. It was around us everywhere. They were tearing down The Hill [for Urban "Renewal"] and the jobs went to White folks." He remembered with pride that the vast majority of Blacks who were involved in the movement were not famous. "Some were retired; some were winos, whores and homeless people. They were grass roots folks; they were the troops, the foot soldiers that came out by the thousands to protest Pittsburgh racism. One man, who carried a flag whenever he marched, said it was 'a symbol of our Americanism.' Then there was Red, a wino, who came to meetings and complained so bitterly about the lack of good medical care for Blacks that others began to pay attention. Almost everyone could recall an incident when someone died while waiting to be taken to the hospital. His concern eventually led to the establishing of the Freedom House Ambulance Service under the auspices of the UNPC."

Remembering the number of winos who joined the marches, Vince smiled, "They always got sober before taking part in any demonstrations. They marched even though they knew that they would never get any of the jobs that resulted from the civil rights movement. We marched because we wanted White folks to know that we were tired of the discrimination; we wanted them to know they didn't do right by us. We marched because it was the right thing to do!"

Wilson said that during a demonstration at Elmore Square, in the public housing projects, where no Black construction workers had been hired, "Father McIlvane [a White priest] lay down in the street in front of the construction trucks. He said that they would have to run over him. Me and some other folks lay down, too. I remember thinking, 'Lord, I sure hope these trucks stop!'"

Wilson admitted that he was frightened when he drove a truck full of food and clothing to Mississippi where people were evicted for trying to register to vote. "I knew how dangerous the situation was when the man who met me was carrying a 45 automatic. While in Mississippi, we went to Vicksburg to integrate a restaurant called Tambellini's. The White folks made us wait an hour. When they finally served us, we were put in a small room off the main dining room."

Asked about the results of the movement, Wilson expressed some discouragement. "Black students get a better education, but they don't come back to use that education to better their communities. The federal government bought off many in the civil rights movement by giving them jobs in the Poverty Program. I saw a whole bunch of folks get jobs in that program, and they only had to work for about two hours a day. We got to find a way to help our children learn to love one another. The work ain't over yet. We got to dig in and save what we got! We need to take care of our own young people."

Was it worth it? "Certainly." Would he do it again? "Hell yes!" Have we made progress? "Yes, but it is still open season on Blacks. We're all still taking a whipping! The cops is still killing us. I picketed all by myself against White cops' brutality against Blacks."

Was there a proudest moment? "Yes! When I drove that truck to Jackson, Mississippi and saw all these Black folks who owned their own businesses, owned their homes, and elected their own sheriff, I was proud. We've got to talk about the progress some of us have made."

Was there a greatest disappointment? "Yes! When Byrd Brown lost that election for mayor. We had a chance and we blew it! We failed to do our job in getting him elected. We also need to stop letting other folks pimp off our communities. It hurts me to see the lack of respect we have for one another."

Mary Gloster
NAACP, Member
United Negro Protest Committee, Member

I knew of Mary, but had not spent any time with her until our paths crossed briefly when I interviewed her for the oral history project. She was a quiet woman who did not draw attention to herself. Without women like Mary, there would have been far fewer successes in the Pittsburgh movement. When asked how she wants to be remembered, she said simply, "As a loving, compassionate, caring person."

Mary Gloster lived on the Southside, in Homewood, and in The Hill. She used to call the Southside, where racism was an everyday event, "Klansville." She recalled, "I used to shop at an Isaly's dairy on the Southside. Blacks and Whites could buy ice cream cones. Whites could eat in the store, but they always wrapped up Black folks cones so that they knew that they were supposed to eat them outside. Southside landlords made Blacks pay more for rent than Whites. We couldn't do *anything!*. That made me very angry."

"I thought segregation was a way of life everywhere. I kept hoping that, someday, I would be able to fight back, that's why I became an active member of the Pittsburgh NAACP. The NAACP was doing some of the things to fight discrimination that I had always wanted to do."

FIGURE 8.1

LEADERS FROM OTHER
ORGANIZATIONS WHO
SUPPORTED THE UNPC

- Byrd R. Brown
- Alma Fox
- James McCoy
- Matthew Moore
- Charles Harris

Gloster said that the riots of 1968 "were long overdue." White store owners in The Hill and in Homewood had a history of mistreating Black people. She did feel bad that the businesses were destroyed and never replaced.

Gloster also worked with Jim McCoy, the leader of the United Negro Protest Committee. "We started the first ambulance service because Black folks died waiting for police to take them to the hospital." She expressed sorrow that the city was allowed to take over the service. She was also angry that when White-owned companies were forced to hire Blacks, they would hire light-skinned Blacks and "sit them out in front so that everyone could see that they had hired ONE!" Interestingly, Gloster herself is very light-skinned and could have been among those that White businesses preferred to hire. When I pointed this out, she dismissed the idea. "No matter what shade I am, I'm still BLACK! I wasn't about to let those racists separate me from other Black folks. We worked hard, and I am so sorry that our youth did not pick up the ball and continue fighting discrimination."

Gloster was very proud of her civil rights work. "I realized that I could take all the years of anger and bitterness and *do something* about it! I was able to let it all out and *fight back!* That felt good! We made a little progress, but not enough. Us old folks are tired, and the youth did not take up the battle. Ralph, I sure hope this project reaches folks. We should be out on the street picketing *right now!*" Still, she felt that it was all worth the effort. "All the people I met in the movement were very important. They helped me so much! I was able to release all the frustration in my heart."

Was she ever afraid? "Yes, things got so bad that we had to meet in secret places at night."

The Direction Action Coalition

This organization broke off from the United Negro/Black Protest Committee in 1969. The split came when some members of the UNPC claimed that the group had acted irresponsibly in allegedly entering into an agreement with Mellon Bank without informing the entire membership. The leader of the group was Charles Harris who left the UNPC along with Father Donald McIllvane. The DAC operated for a number of years, at times mounting more protests than the NAACP or the UNPC. Like several other organizations, it disappeared.

CHAPTER 9

Allies in the Religious Community

Many of the first civil rights leaders came from the church. The pastors, deacons, priests, and imams were already in leadership positions. It was natural that they would heed the call for leadership when the civil rights movement began. Many churches contributed money to the movement. They provided space for meetings and training sessions as well as housing during demonstrations. Black churches led us in our first concrete steps to confront the two-headed dragon of racism and discrimination. For their involvement, some were bombed or burned to the ground.

Many churches in Pittsburgh and surrounding communities were identified with the Pittsburgh movement. Among some of the most prominent were Central Baptist, Grace Memorial, Ebenezer Baptist, Monumental Baptist and Bidwell Presbyterian Church. Not surprisingly, the more active churches were located in The Hill District, where many of the Black leaders lived and worshipped. Central Baptist and Ebenezer, as well as others, became known as "civil rights churches," because so many of the demonstrations began in their pews.

It is impossible to name all of the local religious leaders, but Dr. Laurence Glasco, an Assistant Professor of History at the University of Pittsburgh, did an excellent job of listing many of these courageous individuals.[29] Drawing from Glasco's work and my own recollections, I have compiled the following list of individuals who offered both their moral support and physical presence to the movement for civil rights in Pittsburgh.

Allies in the Presbyterian Churches

Dr. Reverend Leroy Patrick
Pastor of Bethesda Presbyterian Church in Homewood for 35 years
Member of the Pittsburgh Board of Education for 7 years
Moderator of the Pittsburgh Presbytery
Co-chair of the Allegheny County Committee on Fair Housing Practices
An Officer in The Allegheny County Council on Civil Rights
Member of The Mayor's Commission on Human Relations

---

29 Laurence Glasco, "The civil rights movement in Pittsburgh: TO MAKE THIS CITY 'SOME PLACE SPECIAL' Retrievable from the Internet.

Served on the Allegheny County Black Political Group and the Pennsylvania Black Political Caucus
Chair of various NAACP committees

Reverend Leroy Patrick was one of the top leaders of the Pittsburgh movement. I met him during one of the many Pittsburgh demonstrations and interviewed him on *Black Horizons*. I was somewhat in awe of his regal appearance and his quiet, dignified manner. During interviews for this project, I got to know him much better and enjoyed our interactions. When I showed his interview tape to some who had known him for years, they asked, "Ralph, what did you do to the Reverend? In all the years I have known him, I never heard him laugh out loud. You have him cracking up!" I had just assumed this was his manner in private conversations but was told they had never seen him in such a jovial mood.

Rev. Patrick not only preached about equality and racism from the pulpit, but also participated in many demonstrations, sit-ins, and other direct-action confrontations of the racist system in Pittsburgh. He and some of his young church members forced the integration of Highland Park Swimming Pool by holding a series of "swim-ins" in 1958.

Patrick was born in South Carolina, raised in Philadelphia, and came to Pittsburgh in January of 1951 to become the pastor of Bethesda Presbyterian Church. Patrick said, "I was very surprised by conditions in Pittsburgh. I did not realize that things were so segregated here. I took part in about 65 demonstrations—against slum landlords, construction sites, grocery chains, and just about anybody and everybody else in Pittsburgh. I was arrested several times. Once I was arrested for blocking a construction truck. There I stood, trying to look brave while being very frightened. We shut the place down, for which we were arrested. We picketed theaters, bowling alleys and pizza shops. We tested a bowling alley

FIGURE 9.1

RELIGIOUS LEADERS IN PITTSBURGH

- Reverend William Anderson
- Reverend Amos Bracken, Shiloh Baptist Church
- Reverend Amos Brecheen
- Reverend Casey, Ebenezer Baptist Church
- Reverend Ruben Eberhardt, Bethel AME Zion Church
- Reverend Charles Foggie, Wesley Center AME Zion Church
- Reverend Isaac Green, Central Baptist Church
- Reverend C. Leroy Hacker, Shilo Baptist Church

- Reverend J,G. Harris, Bethel AME Church
- Father Jack O' Malley, Citizen's Clergy Coordinating Committee
- Reverend Johnstone Patrick
- Reverend Albert Pugh, Pastor, Macedonia Baptist Church
- Reverend Obadiah Sims
- Father Augustus Taylor, Holy Rosary Catholic Church
- Reverend Twiggs, Macedonia Baptist Church
- Reverend Herbert Wilkerson.
- Reverend Elmer Williams

where the owners refused to allow the pin boys to set up the pins. We had White teams that would go into targeted places. They would take notes on their treatment so that we could compare it to how the Blacks who came after them were treated. We also demonstrated against the Pittsburgh Board of Public Education. This resulted in my being appointed to the school board, but I was really happy to leave at the end of seven long years."

"I enjoyed my civil rights work, because I believe the world is our parish, and we must be involved. You must see if you can help your people beyond the church walls. The only way to be a practicing Christian is to get out where the rubber meets the road. If the church is behind a preacher, he or she is independent of all other pressures. My church was always behind me."

Was it worth it? "YES! I would do it all again, but this time I wouldn't make the same mistakes. My wife was raising my boys while I was out saving the world. I would be more involved in raising my sons. One of my sons told me that he wanted to make an appointment with me so that he could talk to me about something. I should have spent more time with them." How does he wish to be remembered? "As a man who tried to be faithful to the gospel."

Forever Action Together

This organization was established by Canon Junius Carter and Nick Flournoy in reaction to what they perceived as the "too slow" movement by the mainstream civil rights organizations. Based in Homewood, there is little doubt that the organization was more militant than the NAACP and other historical organizations.

Canon Junius Carter
Pastor of Holy Cross Lutheran Church in Homewood-Brushton

I first met Canon Carter either at a meeting in Homewood or when he was a guest on *Black Horizons*. We grew to like one another very much.

When he moved to Pittsburgh, his first obligation was to get to know the people. "I found myself in the middle of a struggle for Black dignity. I met Nick Flournoy and David Owens. We established a local activist group called Forever Action Together (FAT). The group established Operation Better Block, a community improvement association that was erecting new middle- and low-income homes in Homewood. Nick and David threw me into the community. I wanted to guide, to lead, but found myself in the midst of a mighty struggle. I remember that WTAE television had just hired Cathy Milton as a reporter. She was being given a hard time by the station about her Afro hairstyle. They told her to cut her hair or else. A few of us paid a visit to the station; we changed their minds."

Canon Carter related that when he arrived at his new church, "The members of the parish exhibited class consciousness. They looked down on 'those people' [low income Blacks]. They were displeased when I brought Bouie Hayden to address them. He talked about jobs, unemployment, needing to open doors for Blacks. He had them listening. He told them that his job was to open doors for them." The church leadership considered him to be a maverick, but the people of Homewood considered him to be *their* leader. He was able to bring together groups that did not easily work together. Wherever he went, he was protected by a very visible, angry-looking group of young Black men.

Canon Carter's face was etched with pain, as he related how bad it was to be the only Black priest in his religious order. "The Lutheran Church was not responding to the people. I tried to make the Church respond, to open the doors to all who wanted to help." Perhaps it was this profound sense of loneliness that led Canon Carter to feel such kinships with the Blacks in his community, who were also lost in a monumental struggle against apathy and oppression. At one point during the struggle, Canon Carter was very pleased that his church embraced the struggle. "The Poor People's March came through Pittsburgh on its way to Washington D.C. We fed 2,000 people, and they all stayed in this church."

As to the aftermath of the movement, he said, "Some of those who walked through the doors we opened have forgotten how they got there. Racism today is still prevalent and is more detrimental than it was in the 1960s. For example, when Black organizations were boycotting Arizona over their refusal to allow a Martin Luther King, Jr., holiday, the Episcopal Church said that they were still going to hold their convention there. The excuse they used was that they were going to use their convention to fight racism. How were they going to fight racism when they had no Black priests in all of Arizona? Outsiders introduced dope and that was devastating to the community. Westinghouse is still an all-Black high school.

"The demonstration against the construction of The U.S. Steel building was nearly a catastrophe. White construction workers dropped hot rivets on the demonstrators and tried to urinate on them. The construction of the new Pittsburgh International Airport did not involve Blacks; all the construction that was going on in Homewood was being done by all-White crews. We did this to ourselves. We were prepared to fight, but stopped too soon. The universities destroyed Black people, yet we still ask them for help. The Beast does not sleep at night; he is constantly planning. When we get tired and try to rest, they plan while we sleep."

Was it worth it? After hesitating, he said, "I think so." He wanted to be remembered as a man who tried to bring about change. As I was packing up my video equipment, Canon Carter said, "Ralph, I am going to tell you something, but you can't tell anyone, because I haven't even told the members of my church yet. I'm leaving Holy Cross very soon." I asked if he was retiring. "No. but I've been thinking about what I want to do with the rest of my life. I've decided that this is definitely not it." I kept the secret, and that evening Canon Carter resigned as the pastor of Holy Cross Lutheran Church. Shortly afterwards, he left Pittsburgh.

Nick Flournoy
Forever Action Together, Founding Member
Young Adult Chapter of the NAACP, Member
Pittsburgh Chapter of the Congress of Racial Equality (CORE), Founding Member

Nick Flournoy and I called one another "friend," but we were more "comrades-at-arms." I met him at the height of the movement when we worked on some of the same projects. He was an intense, intelligent, extremely militant young man who took no prisoners. He was openly critical of the NAACP, which he considered to be too timid or conservative. He saw himself as a spokesperson of the "small people" who were left voiceless by the actions of less militant leaders. He and other likeminded members of the Young Adult Chapter of the Pittsburgh NAACP broke away and formed a local chapter of CORE with its more direct-action tactics. He and Canon Junius Carter were among the founders of Forever

Action Together. Flournoy's militancy was unacceptable to conservative Blacks as well as to Whites. Despite the misgivings of many, Flournoy was a very important leader in the Pittsburgh movement.

When I contacted Nick to request his participation in my oral history project, he refused and accused me of wanting to use him to make a "bunch" of money. Sadly, my request came when Nick was dying of cancer, and was suffering from the devastating physical and mental side effects of the treatment. That I had already invested more than 17 years and "bunches of money" in the project was really beside the point. The true pity was the loss of whatever he might have contributed to this account of a remarkable historical era. I hope he has finally found peace.[30]

Bidwell Presbyterian Church
The Bidwell Cultural and Training Center

The Bidwell Presbyterian Church was responsible for the birth of several important Northside institutions, including the Manchester Youth Development Center and Bidwell Cultural and Training Center. In addition to Jimmy Joe Robinson, the church responsibilities were shared by five other religious leaders.

Reverend James "Jimmy Joe" Robinson
Bidwell Presbyterian Church, Pastor
The Bidwell Training Center, Founder
The Citizen Clergy Coordinating Committee against Slum Housing
Langley Ministries
The Black Construction Coalition

Although I knew Reverend Robinson as a leader of the Northside civil rights movement, we did not really get to know one another until I interviewed him for this oral history project. During the interviews, I began to feel that I had known him all of my life. He, like others, appeared on *Black Horizons*.

Reverend James "Jimmy Joe" Robinson was born in Connellsville, Pennsylvania, of which he said, "The town was a place where we Blacks accepted sitting upstairs in the theatre. Our special place to swim was the river, because we weren't allowed in the public swimming pools. We accepted our treatment because our parents told us to do so. They were afraid that, if we did not accept the discrimination, we would be harmed."

When Robinson entered the University of Pittsburgh in 1945, he was Pitt's first Black football player. "There were not many Black students at Pitt then, so you had to be very careful where you went in Oakland. You were not welcome in grooming and eating establishments. You couldn't go to Scotty's Diner." Even though he was a star football player, he was not permitted to stay in the dorms at Pitt and lived at the Centre Avenue YMCA. When the team traveled, he was unable to stay in hotels with the White players. "When the football team played at West Virginia University, I was shocked to find I was hung in effigy. That was horrible and a bit frightening, but somehow, it did not hit home that, despite my sports stardom, I was still considered to be a *nigger*!"

---

30 I challenge some young, energetic scholar to further investigate Nick Flournoy so his contributions to the civil rights movement can receive the recognition they so much deserve

Robison continued to describe life for Blacks in Pittsburgh. "In Pittsburgh, you had to be careful; you had to accept the fact that you were a second-class citizen. You had to be very careful about where you went. There were no laws that said that Whites had to serve you. I never questioned our treatment, never asked why we could not go to high school dances. I had no racial consciousness." I watched Jimmy Joe's eyes grow moist as he remembered this with obvious, deep pain.

Robinson left Pittsburgh after graduation from Pitt. He returned in the 1960s to a world where Blacks were beginning to reject discrimination. His life changed when he went to a conference in Camden, New Jersey where Leroy Jones and Ron Karenga spoke. "They spoke about strange concepts, such as 'The Motherland.' Karenga said that we had to reject our slave names and adopt *African names.* I was confused. I said that something is wrong. If these folks were telling the truth, I have been duped all of my life. When I returned to my hotel room, I cried. I was so angry about all the pain I had suffered in high school and at Pitt. I was angry with all White folks. I was angry with myself. I changed; I became proud of who I was, developing a pride about being a descendant of Africans. That conference turned me all the way around."

Robinson later participated in demonstrations led by the Student Nonviolent Coordinating Committee in Greenwood, Mississippi. The demonstrators were told by police that they would be arrested if they crossed a line. He and others stepped across the line, and were promptly arrested; Robinson spent a week in jail. "When I got out, I was angry. When I got back to Pittsburgh, I was a different person. I was never the same."

He was beaten by Pittsburgh police during the protest against the construction of Three Rivers Stadium. "Our crime was trying to get Blacks into unions. The demonstration against the construction of the US Steel Building in downtown Pittsburgh was especially dangerous. They dropped things on us from high on the construction site, and some workers were carrying guns."

Robinson spoke about the anger Blacks experienced when Martin Luther King was murdered. "He was a messiah, and was going to lead us into the Promised Land. The presence of the National Guard and the police in the Northside communities only added to the anger."

When asked whether he had ever feared for his life, Robinson replied, "No, I was never afraid. I was young and dumb. The young men from the community protected me. What I was doing was too important to allow fear to stop me. I wanted my son to grow up being proud of his identity. I am pleased that my children have been taught that there is a pride in being Black. They learned that it was fine to have thick lips, curly hair, and Black skin. I could now tell them that you are alright, you are somebody special."

Did Blacks make progress during the movement? Robinson thought for a moment, and then replied, "Yes, some Blacks have made tremendous progress, but as a race, NO! When you look at 25% of Black males being on probation or parole, when you look at the high Black infant mortality rate, when you realize that we have made few gains between the 1960s and the 1990s, you have to say that we are still way behind."

Was it worth the effort? "Yes. As I recall my conversion and awakening, I know that God called me to the church to do justice. It is something in me. God has pushed me to deal with injustice. I had an obligation. I would do it all again, if God did the pushing. Unfortunately, racism did not end. Some of the White folks involved in the movement returned to the institutions that caused the racist problems in the first place. The problem is still there and we are still dealing with it. I'm just glad that your project is giving me the opportunity to say some things that I haven't talked about in years. This project is important, and you are doing it at the right time. How would I like to be remembered? Just as someone who made a contribution to his people and the world."

Robinson was an ever-present figure at demonstrations all over Pittsburgh. One of his lasting contributions was establishing The Bidwell Training Center.

Bill Strickland
Bidwell Cultural and Training Center, Director

I met Bill Strickland during the early days when Bidwell Cultural and Training Center was being established. He had been chosen to head the Center because of his education, demeanor, and reputation as a potter. Located in a blighted area on the Northside of Pittsburgh, the Center's mission was to provide training and cultural activities for residents in that neighborhood.

Born in Pittsburgh, Strickland recalls that Pittsburgh was like two different cities—one Black, one White—cohabitating in the same time and almost the same space; yet virtually separate. "When I was young, some friends and I were rebuffed and arrested for swimming in Dormont pool. We were charged with trespassing. This was a common charge police lodged against Blacks who sought to utilize facilities in White communities. The police were noted for using this charade in order to enforce the northern Jim Crow customs that were treated as if they were laws."

Bidwell Cultural and Training Center grew out of the turmoil of the civil rights movement and became world-famous under Bill's leadership. Rev. Robinson, one of the founders of the Center, was unable to head the newly forming organization, because of his responsibilities to Bidwell Presbyterian Church and his deep involvement in civil rights activities. Robinson asked Strickland to head Bidwell. Strickland, a ceramic artist at the time he "inherited" Bidwell, created Manchester Craftsmen's Guild, which shares the same impressive building. "I raised the millions of dollars needed to construct the facility," Bill said. "It took 16 years of planting seeds with corporations and foundation leaders before I had enough credibility to raise the funds for a state-of-the-art center." Eventually Bidwell/Manchester Craftsmen's Center obtained certification as a private educational institution providing training in areas such as the culinary arts, photography, and horticultural sciences. Strickland's recruitment of corporate leaders differentiated Bidwell from most other human service organizations and is responsible, in part, for the huge success of his organization. Strickland was free to do that cultivation, serve on boards, and travel extensively because he was fortunate to have recruited Jesse Fife as the second in command. Over the years Bill and I have been involved in many far-ranging activities.[31]

At some point, Strickland trained as an airline pilot. When asked why he did not leave Bidwell in order to pursue this glamorous career, Strickland replied, "I did pursue it for a while; then I got laid off. At about the same time we began a capital campaign for Bidwell. I thought it would be irresponsible to leave at that point. I decided to stay here and that decision was a wise one." Bidwell Cultural and Training Center and The Manchester Craftsmen's Guild have enjoyed phenomenal growth and now have international chapters.

---

31 Through my involvement in the struggles and triumphs of Bidwell, I also met Jesse Fife, the Center's long-time Associate Director, who deserves recognition for his significant impact on Pittsburgh's art, cultural and political scene.

Recalling the days of the movement, Strickland said, "That was a time when Blacks, as a community, came together in order to effect change. The bourgeoisie and the street people came together for a common goal. There had been nothing like it then, and there is nothing like it now. People risked their lives for the movement. When we demonstrated against the construction of the U.S. Steel Building, the construction workers dropped metal objects off the top girders. They could have killed someone."

Asked why the movement had ended, Strickland offered, "People got disappointed. Things did not change as rapidly or as much as they had expected. We were prepared, from the movement point of view, but we were less prepared from the leadership aspect. We were not strong on institution building. When it was all over, we had done little to change White institutions and little to strengthen our own institutions. When you examine the issue closely, you will find that we really did not make that much progress. Many of our successes were rolled back by White society. Affirmative action was not completely successful. Civil rights are still not guaranteed for all Blacks. The employment and economic gaps are still there. Many Whites did not take the riots of 1968 seriously. White folks on Mount Washington were actually entertained by Black people burning down The Hill. The National Guard and the police did nothing to stop the riot; they only contained it."

Was it worth it? "Yes! It was an issue of the quality of life. Would I do it again? Absolutely! I really didn't have a choice. My greatest accomplishment was the construction of the Bidwell/Manchester Craftsmen's Guild. My greatest disappointment was that I was not able to make us independent of public funds. No nation was ever built on grants. We must move the race forward." Strickland wishes to be remembered "primarily for the arts."

Allies in the Catholic Church

While not a civil rights organization, the diocese had several priests and nuns who were involved in direct action. They also were the sponsors of Black Catholic Ministries and other programs that assisted us in the movement. I can't find anyone who remembers the name, but they were also leaders in a non-denominational, church-sponsored group that used its significant dollars to fight racism and discrimination. If a group did business with this group and was found to discriminate, the group would cease spending money with them.

Monsignor Charles Owen Rice

Monsignor Charles Own Rice cut quite a figure, tall, resplendent in dark glasses, black suit, and a Panama, straw hat. I met him in the mid-1960s, and we seemed drawn to one another from the very beginning. My former wife was a Catholic, and it might be possible that I met him at one of the services at his church, Holy Rosary in Homewood. When my first son, Shawn, was born, my wife wanted him to be baptized in the Catholic Church. The priest who was to preside over the christening refused to allow my Jewish friend, who was to be Shawn's godfather, to participate. I called Father Rice who said, "Ralph, my boy, no need to worry. Call the priest back in two days." I did, and the ceremony went on as planned.

Monsignor Rice was born in New York City in 1908 and arrived in Pittsburgh in 1920. Eventually he served at various venues in the Pittsburgh area, including St. Agnes in Bloomfield, The House of Hospitality on Wylie Avenue, and The Orphans Asylum. For ten years he served as the resident priest at a soup kitchen on Tannehill Street in the lower Hill District. It was at this assignment that he became sensitized to racism and this changed his life forever. "After all," he said, "we were in a Black community."

Father Rice often referred to himself as "just a humble parish priest," but he was anything but that. He was a White man who fought with great vigor and dignity in a battle that was not his. He was greatly respected by Blacks who accepted him as a man who had a mission to help the downtrodden. Of course, he angered several Whites who opposed his using funds from the Catholic Church to help "rabble rousers."

In 1966, he was assigned as the priest at Holy Rosary Catholic Church in Homewood, one of Pittsburgh's largest Black communities. "I asked for that assignment," he said, with a twinkle in his eyes. "I wanted to be where the action was." His first action in Homewood was to support the jitney drivers in their battle with the city, the cab companies, and the bus company, all of which wanted to put these men out of business. Jitneys were illegal taxis that came into existence because White-owned cab companies' refused to serve the Black community. Despite complaints to the Public Utilities Commission that controlled the licensing of cab companies, Blacks could neither receive service from nor be hired by the Yellow Cab and People's Cab companies. Father Rice recognized this blatant travesty. "The husband of one of my parishioners was arrested for operating a jitney. I called Attorney Byrd Brown and got the man released. After all, in my mind, and in the minds of my church members, the man was guilty of nothing but earning a living by providing a service that Whites refused to provide."

Father Rice was also known as "the labor priest," a role that often found him at odds with the unions. He stated that Whites formed unions to protect themselves against Blacks competing for lucrative trade jobs. He supported organized labor, as a principle, but not when it came to their racist practices.

As one can imagine, Father Rice's' support of Black causes did not always sit well with White Catholics. "I convinced the Diocese to give Bouie Hayden some money for a just cause." Hayden was an outspoken Black leader, often rough, sometimes vulgar, always in the faces of Whites. He was both hated and feared by many in the White community. "When news of the grant surfaced, I was hung in effigy and thousands of Whites left the Pittsburgh Diocese. I could have handled the grant in an under-the-table manner and gotten away with giving Bouie money, but I wanted to be above-board."

Father Rice wrote about equality in his weekly column in *The Pittsburgh Catholic*. He was not a one-dimensional protestor. He could often be seen demonstrating over issues related to peace, justice, and the inhumanity of war. Among those with whom he marched were Harry Bellefonte, Sidney Poitier, and Stokely Carmichael. Recalling the protests against the Viet Nam War, Father Rice said, proudly, "We were effective. We stopped the war and got rid of a president." He marched in New York with Dr. Martin Luther King. "Cops were on every roof," he recalled. "White children and nuns marched right beside us. One of the officers told me that someone might come from the crowd and try to harm King. I took hold of King's arm and never let go for the entire march." God and Father Rice protected King from harm, at least that time.

When Dr. King was murdered, "Some of us Whites—clergy and laypeople—met at The Smithfield Street Church in downtown Pittsburgh. We held a quiet demonstration, but decided not to take our protest to the street. That was for Black folks to do. We realized how deep their anger and sadness must be at the loss of this great man."

When asked whether he had ever feared for his life or priesthood, Rice seemed surprised by the question. "I was doing the right thing! What was there to fear? Oh, certainly there were the usual threats, some nasty things were done and said during marches, and the FBI told me that The National Association for the Advancement of White People was going to blow up the church, but I was not afraid."

Was it worth it? "Yes, yes, yes; people got jobs; we got people out of jail, we fought for a just and fair system; we stopped the war and got rid of a president. I put my prestige on the line, and I am happy that I did. If you run into an injustice, you must go after those who caused it; go as high and as hard as you have to in order to solve the injustice."

When asked how he wanted to remembered, Father Rice, the self-proclaimed "humble parish priest" replied, "I fought for justice and got no personal gain from it." Amen, Brother, Amen!

Father Donald McIlvane
Priest of Saint Richard's and Corpus Christy Churches
Convener of the Pittsburgh Area Council on Race and Religion
Catholic Interracial Council, Member
Pittsburgh Chapter of the NAACP, Member
United Negro Protest Committee, Member

Father Donald McIlvane was a short, fearless man who asked no quarter and gave none. A White Catholic priest, he was a familiar figure at demonstrations and negotiations. He was an outspoken advocate of peace and justice and often risked the displeasure of his peers and the leaders of the Catholic church, many of whom could not agree with his "militant" stance against racism.

My first meeting with Father McIllvane was not positive. I was the newly-appointed director of The Hill District Community Action Program, part of the national "war on poverty." Father McIlvane was the advisor for a predominantly White group that was confronting organizations they perceived as detrimental to poor and Black folks. I resented these Whites telling me what my organization must do. I tried to be polite at first, but grew more and more resentful of their audacity, until I told them to get the hell out of my face! Later, Father McIllvane and I became allies.

Father McIlvane described racial conditions in Pittsburgh this way: "It's hardly Heaven today, but it was really *BAD* then. I am proud to say that I was a small part of the push for improving employment for Blacks. Members of my parish often talked with me about the discrimination they suffered. I would go to negotiations of the NAACP and UNPC strengthened by the experiences of my Black parishioners." In addition to employment problems, McIlvane also worked on the blatant housing discrimination in Pittsburgh.

He joined the marches in Selma, Alabama, knowing he would be the object of the virulent hatred of those Southerners who considered White civil rights workers to be traitors and called them "*nigger* lovers." Before McIlvane went to Selma, a young Black civil rights worker came to see him. As was the case with many of those who participated in the Poor People's March, the young man was dressed like a farmer. "He told me, if I couldn't turn the other cheek, I shouldn't go to Selma."

Recalling the demonstrations in which he was involved, McIlvane said, "They were well-organized and disciplined. We demonstrated against Gimbel's department store, Duquesne Light Company, and others. Often Whites were not very friendly towards demonstrators. At the Three Rivers Stadium construction demonstration, the police were out to harm Black folks. I was proud to be a part of the action."

For the most part, the Catholic Church supported his efforts. "Bishop Wright gave me his full support. Of course, things may have been very different had I been stationed in Mount Lebanon instead of The Hill. Things did get a little hairy once. I gave some money to Bouie Hayden. THAT certainly pissed off many White Catholics who said that they would never again give any more money to the church."

When asked why he became involved. Father McIlvane sat erect and said, "Because I am Catholic and an American. I had no choice but to confront the problems faced by the members of my church. Irish pugnaciousness made me a little better fighter. The Catholic Church was opposed to racism. While I believed in and loved my country, I wanted it to change. I wanted laws passed to fight discrimination."

Was he concerned about his safety? "Never. Others were more concerned for me. During the riots of 1968 after King's murder, Herbert Bean [a prominent Black Hill District businessman] told me to stay by his side. 'Everybody don't know you. All they'll see is your White skin. This is not a good time for a White to be walking the streets of The Hill.' I can't condone violence, but there was a lot of rightful anger that Blacks were expressing. For the first time, many Whites had to accept that Black anger was righteous."

When asked how he felt about Black leaders considering him to be a leader as well, McIlvane said, "That makes me very proud. Still, we haven't done enough to address racism in the delivery of health care. Far too many Whites resent Black progress. Far too many Whites feel that Blacks have been handed too much."

Was it worth the effort? "Oh yes. I was part of something of consequence, a small part of history. I have a feeling of satisfaction." How would he like to be remembered? "As a man who worked for all people, especially African-Americans."

John Hannigan
Director of Social Concerns at the Catholic Diocese of Pittsburgh
Founding member of the Diocese Race and Reconciliation Group
Investigator for the Mayor's Commission on Human Relations
The E.T. Williams Community Center, Board Member
Kingsley Association, Board Member

I met John Hannigan when we both worked at the University of Pittsburgh. In 1966, John organized focus and sensitivity groups around issues of race, providing training for Black staff, students, and faculty free of charge. During one session, he took Black folks and some corporate folks to the top of the Cathedral of Learning. "The Whites practically ran out of the building in order to get away from the Blacks," he laughed.

"I remember that I met you, Ralph, when you were an assistant dean at Pitt. I had this bright idea of bringing in some professional trainers from Cleveland to work with Blacks from Pittsburgh in a series of sessions dealing with racism. Was I naïve! I thought that the White trainers were better prepared to lead than the Black folks. I invited a number of Blacks based on where I thought they fell on the political spectrum. Ha! I thought you were a nice middle-class, middle-of-the road, Black man. I was so shocked to find out how militant you were. I made the same discovery about Sister Martin DePores, whom I had considered to be a sweet, quiet nun. She mentally beat up the White trainers, and you threatened to 'kick the ass' of one of the trainers if he said another word to you. I was told that, when the man tried to say something to you after your threat, Sister DePores advised him to shut up, because you really would kick his ass. I also found out that all the Blacks, regardless of their politics, came together as a group to protect the most vulnerable Blacks against the White trainers. After the first day, the lead trainer said that he felt almost like he was not the real trainer. You piped up and said, 'That's because you ain't.' I learned a great deal then about Blacks and the movement. It helped me later as I became more involved." Both John and I are very old warriors now, but when either of us asks for a favor, the other responds without regard to the cost of the favor. Though John is White, I call him "my brother by another mother." I truly love this man.

Hannigan was employed by the Mayor's Commission on Human Relations. His position at the Commission came about as a placement from the School of Social Work at Pitt. Hannigan said, "I guess they liked what I was doing because they hired me at the end of my placement. I stayed there for six years." During his tenure, he witnessed first-hand what racism was doing to Blacks. "I remember Dr. Oswald Nikons being turned down when he tried to purchase a home in a White community. During that time, I was an investigator for the Mayor's Commission, and I tried to determine the source of trouble in racist situations. I traveled around Pittsburgh in an interracial group that monitored situations where racist actions had taken place. I was always treated well in Black communities, but the group was treated poorly in White communities. Whites did not like the members of our group being comfortable with one another. I was viewed as a traitor by the White community. I remember speaking once to a group of 160 Whites about racism. By the end of my talk, all but three of them had left.

Later Hannigan used his position as Director of Social Concerns at the Diocese of Pittsburgh to push for social equality. He was one of the founding members of the Diocese Race and Reconciliation Group. At John's request, I joined the faculty of the Diocese Committee on Racism. The purpose of the group was to help the Catholic Church in Pittsburgh rid itself of racism. He served on the Board of two Black organizations for which I subsequently worked. John was one of my saviors on those Boards, and helped me to fight for equality. While he really did not need to involve himself in a movement to change the lives of Blacks, involved he was! John was a very religious Catholic, who as a White could have stayed above the fray. But he felt that racism was a sin and was compelled to do all he could to combat this evil.

John expressed disappointment that we failed to end the rampant police brutality by White cops against Black people. "The Police Trial Board was a farce," he said.

Would he do it again? "No question about it! The ideal for me is that you serve, and society is bettered by what you do. I would urge all people to move towards a more just society. I was doing the Lord's work."

How would he like to be remembered? "For my sense of humor, and as someone who enjoyed life and made some contributions to a just cause."

Black Catholic Ministries

Black Catholic Ministries was established by the Catholic Diocese. There may have been others who ran the organization but I knew only Bob Pitts. He worked hand-in-hand with other civil rights organizations in Pittsburgh and Wilkinsburg.

Robert L. Pitts
Black Catholic Ministries, Executive Director
Wilkinsburg Chapter of the Pittsburgh NAACP, President
1st Black Mayor of the Borough of Wilkinsburg (Elected in 1983)

When I first met Robert Pitts, he greeted me (as he did everyone) with the words, "Hello, family." I thought that was pretty neat. We worked together on many projects and, of course, I regularly had him on my radio and TV shows.

Bob came to Pittsburgh from Cleveland in 1971 to set up the Black Catholic Ministries' office. The Catholic Church had declared that racism was a mortal sin and established Black Catholic Ministries to combat racism at every level of the church. Pittsburgh was the Ministries' second office in the country. Recalling his early days in Pittsburgh, Pitts said, "As head of the Black Catholic Ministries, I forced the Catholic church to face racism in its own ranks.[32] I was also active in the Pittsburgh NAACP and was often a member of negotiating and strategy teams dealing with the rampant racism in Pittsburgh. I remember being involved in demonstrations, direct action, or negotiations against the University of Pittsburgh, Duquesne Light Company, United States Steel, construction sites, department stores, Volkswagen Automobile Corporation, and Warner Cable Company. Duquesne Light Company had one of the worst minority hiring records in the city. They were very uncooperative in our face-to-face negotiations, so other methods were necessary in order to assure their cooperation. We got people to call the company every couple of minutes so that Duquesne's phone lines were tied up for days. We had people go to its office and pay their bills in pennies, nickels and dimes. We had folks turn off all the lights in their homes from 7 to 9 P.M. Finally, after this intense pressure, we got an agreement with them."

Speaking with me in 1991, Pitts said, "We've not made as much progress as we should have. We still have never had a Black mayor in the city of Pittsburgh; we still have only two Blacks, out of nine positions on City Council; we still don't have enough Black political leaders." When asked if the efforts had been worth the trouble, despite his disappointment with our progress, Pitts replied, "Oh yes, yes, but I am looking for the young folks to step up and take our places. I don't know about *you,* Ralph, but I am *tired!*

How would he like to be remembered? "I have to admit that I smile when folks still call me 'Mister Mayor.' That's a good feeling. I am fortunate. I want to be remembered as just Bob Pitts."

Black Muslim Allies

This group, also known as The Nation of Islam, was based on the Muslim religion. In reality, it was a mixture of both religious and political ideologies. The titular national leader was Elijah Mohammed. However, the most famous leader was a firebrand who went by the name of Malcolm X. His rising popularity led to jealousy from many members of the organization. The group rejected integration as a means of Black equality and advocated for Black political and economic independence.

---

32 Author's Note; When I became a faculty member in the Diocese's Ecumenical Council on Racism, I asked a priest if it was true that the Catholic Church had declared that racism was a sin. When he said yes, I asked why more priests did not use the altar to speak out against this particular sin. I expected some sort of religious or esoteric answer. I was floored when he said without hesitation, "Ralph, we could get away with preaching about racism every so often. But, if we did that on a frequent basis, we would soon be speaking to an empty church."

Although the Black Muslims did not share the same philosophy as other civil rights organizations in Pittsburgh, they deserve mention because they had in common the goals of equality and financial independence. The group believed that integration was a failed strategy and that White America did not want Blacks to be integrated into *their* society. Rather, they said Blacks should be given their own portion of the United States where they could be in control of their own destinies. They further advocated that Blacks must cease to be a nation of beggars and consumers and should build their own economic entities. The land they sought was to be located in the Southern part of the United States, in farming country. Once the land was secured, they believed that Blacks should grow their own crops, raise their own livestock, process the end goods in their own plants, and distribute it to stores in trucks owned by Blacks. They also argued for the establishment of a Black school system, no longer depending upon the oppressor to properly educate their children. They pointed to the Jewish community as an example of a people who, while sending their children to public schools, also provided culture-specific schools in their own communities.

Minister Robert X
Leader of the Homewood Mosque of the Nation of Islam

Minister Robert X was Pittsburgh's version of Malcolm X. I met him in the 1960s when I was doing research on the Nation of Islam. He also appeared frequently on *Black Horizons*. I became close with Robert and his family and spoke with them often at the restaurant they operated in Homewood.

Minister X was nearly as articulate as Malcolm X. He inspired many people to give up self-destructive behavior such as drugs, alcohol, smoking and fornication. Many a young thug was turned around by hearing him speak. Neither he nor his group participated in marches or demonstrations. They focused their attention on economic development and had a grocery store, a mosque and a restaurant in the Homewood area. When the movement was in full swing, the store and restaurant were frequented by Muslims and non-Muslims alike. The mosque welcomed visitors, but non-Muslims expressed discomfort with the practice of having women and men sit separately during religious services. Many non-Muslims adopted Muslim names and greeted one another in Arabic. However, most fell short of actual conversion. Minister Robert X tried to recruit me to join the Black Muslims. I was tempted to do so, but simply could not accept the disparate treatment of Muslim women.

Despite difficulties with recruitment, the Pittsburgh Black Muslim community did show that Blacks could achieve a measure of success without dependence on the White community. Unfortunately, not much remains of the experiment except for the local Mosque.

CHAPTER 10

Allied Community-Based Organizations

The Urban League of Pittsburgh

Although the Urban League of Pittsburgh is often thought of as a civil rights organization, it was not. I heard this fact emphatically conveyed by Whitney Young, the national leader, when I attended a mandatory training program at the National League's Headquarters. Young informed his audience that the Urban League was a **social service** organization, providing training programs to prepare Blacks for entering into mainstream America. League offices were specifically prohibited from engaging in direct action activities like picketing, demonstrating, and boycotting. Under my breath, I muttered, "That's a damn shame! They *ought* to be side-by-side with the rest of us 'radicals'." Young overheard me, asked me to repeat myself. I asserted that the League did the movement a disservice by setting itself apart at a time when we needed to present a united front against racism. He was more than a little pissed! "Who are you again?" When I answered, he said, "Oh, yes. I've already heard about you from my Director of Public Information."

Later in the day, that very same Director of Public Information, proudly distributed a press release in which he denounced Reverend Martin Luther King's remarks opposing the Viet Nam War. After reading the press release, I couldn't refrain from asking, "Sir, excuse me, but did you hear Dr. King's remarks or read the text of his speech?" He said he had not. "Sir," I continued, "how could you respond to something you neither heard nor read? Just what were you addressing and how could you do so without knowledge of Dr. King's remarks?"

"Reporters called me, read Dr. King's remarks to me, and asked for a comment."

"Did they read you the entire document?" He didn't know.

I said I was ashamed (furious actually) that a supposed leadership organization had opposed Dr. King without fully knowing what was said. I suggested he should recall his comments until he had fully read and comprehended King's remarks. Naturally, the "incident" was reported to his boss and mine. When I returned to Pittsburgh, Mr. Edmunds called me to his office, looked over the rims of his glasses, and said, "Damn, Ralph. I can't send you anywhere without you getting into trouble. Whitney Young called and informed me about your challenging him and his PR director." I apologized for embarrassing him, but I stood by my remarks.

107

Arthur J. Edmunds
Urban League of Pittsburgh, Chief Executive Officer

As head of the Urban League, Arthur Edmunds took many barbs from young, militant Blacks who considered the League to be a middle-class organization out of touch with "ordinary Black folks." He walked a tightrope between militant activists and conservative corporate leaders who could take away their financial support should the Urban League speak out too vehemently against injustice. Much of the criticism was valid.[33]

My relationship with Art was that of boss and employee until, seeing the handwriting on the wall, I left the Urban League after a year. I also knew and got along very well with Art's second wife, Gladys, who owned a travel agency. Through this connection, Art and I became friends and remained so until his death in November 2008.

Art was born in Detroit, Michigan and moved to Pittsburgh on July 4, 1960, (his birthday) to take charge of the Pittsburgh Urban League. "I had intended to stay about five to ten years, but wound up heading the organization for 28 years. When I arrived, about a dozen organizations had staff working in the area of race relations; yet racism persisted. In the year I arrived, *The Pittsburgh Courier* had just published a series on the conditions of Black employment. One statistic still stands out in my head; 20% of city government employees were Black. When I looked more closely, 99% of those employees were garbage collectors. Employment for Blacks was bleak. You could stand downtown and watch the people leave as the offices closed and see almost no Blacks. This was despite the fact that the City had already passed fair employment laws."

He continued, "My wife wanted a new house, but none were available in Black communities. We asked a Black realtor for help. He said that he had the perfect house for us but, because it was in a White community, we would have to look at the house at night!"

"Because racism and discrimination were so bad in Pittsburgh, Blacks often gave it more power than it had. One day I told a senior staff member that I needed to open a bank account. She told me that I would probably need a reference. This turned out not to be true, but the sad thing was that she actually believed it. Blacks accepted their fate, more or less, but there was always resentment and isolated protests about the unfair treatment."

"Early in my tenure, I was curious about the number of Blacks that were in policy-making positions in human service organizations. I sent a survey to several Community Chest agencies, and some of those agencies called the Community Chest headquarters to ask why we wanted the information. The implication was we were doing something wrong. On another occasion, a group of outstanding Blacks, including Eric Springer, Dave Epperson, and Wendell Freeland, held a meeting with the Pittsburgh Housing Authority. We wanted to know why there were no Blacks in high positions. The executive asked if there were any Blacks who were *qualified* for such positions."

For more than 25 years, the names of Arthur Edmunds and the Pittsburgh Urban League were synonymous. Under his leadership, the League played a vital role in the civil rights movement. "For the most part," Edmunds explained, "our role was to provide technical assistance. We were the first

---

33 In all fairness, the Pittsburgh branch of the Urban League changed dramatically when Esther Bush took over in the waning days of the movement.

organization called to fill the jobs created by the protests. We qualified people for the new positions as they opened up. During the demonstration against Equitable Gas, one official said they had tried to get qualified Blacks from the Urban League, but had been unsuccessful. I was able to tell Jim McCoy that the man was lying. The man threatened to report me to the United Way. We had set up a 'good guy, bad guy' situation that was quite effective. The bad guys were those militants who demonstrated and frightened the White folks. We were considered the good guys because we were not participants in the demonstrations. Companies would run to us for help, so that they wouldn't have to deal with the trouble makers. What these companies did not realize was that we were very much involved in the strategy. We knew who was going to be targeted, so we just sat back and waited for the 'militants' to scare the companies in our direction. Even some Black folks did not understand and accused the Urban League of being too docile."

"We had a reputation for good training programs and placed some very highly trained Blacks in key positions. Sometimes companies even lured away my own employees. They figured that, if a person worked at the Urban League, they were well trained and probably not at all militant.[34] So, when other organizations in the movement suggested that companies contact the Urban League, they couldn't claim our trainees were unqualified. I saw the League using social work and training in education, employment and housing as the way to equality. I got many invitations to join private industry, but I had a commitment to the League. In that capacity, I could play a major role in the movement."

The only time Edmunds felt afraid was "during the riots of 1968. I lived near East Hills and was downtown trying to get the city to do something. I received threats that the rioters were going to burn down my house. A friend was on my roof with a rifle, ready to protect us. That was frightening, but it didn't happen. I was concerned because I had seen some senseless acts during the riots. There was a fruit market on Frankstown Avenue, near where I lived. The news media reported that it was destroyed by the rioters. Later, we found out that the place had been torched by its owner. Some places were looted, vandalized, or destroyed. The riots had negative effects; the burned-out businesses never returned. The riots did cause some changes in Black employment, but lately most companies have gone back to business as usual. We made some progress since the riots, but we're not moving very rapidly towards equality."

Was it worth the effort? "Oh, yes! I would not have been able to sleep at night had I not been involved. Would I do it again? YES! I am disappointed that business has not given its full support to equal employment opportunity. Our own community is not making certain that Black families remain strong."

How would he like to be remembered? "He did his best."

---

34 What Edmunds said was certainly true for me. I was employed as the Director of Public Information and Research at the League when I was lured away by H.J. Heinz Corporation. The Heinz director of human resources told me he had purposefully "raided" the League because he knew they had highly trained Black employees.

K. Leroy Irvis, Attorney

Urban League of Pittsburgh, Member

Elected to the Pennsylvania House of Representatives in 1958; 1st Black selected as Speaker of the House in the Commonwealth (as of 2021 the only Black to hold the position)

Appointed to the University of Pittsburgh Board of Trustees in 1970

K. Leroy Irvis was an eloquent speaker whose booming voice commanded immediate attention. He used this gift in his work with many organizations and during his tenure in the Pennsylvania House of Representatives. It seems fitting, however, to recount his phenomenal success by linking him to the Urban League of Pittsburgh, where it all began.

I met K. Leroy around 1968 when I visited his Centre Avenue office in The Hill with a proposal to establish a Black Cultural Museum. I was hoping he could help me secure Commonwealth of Pennsylvania funds, and although that did not come about, we grew closer because of our interests in civil rights and art. (Irvis was an accomplished wood sculptor.)

Irvis was known as "K. Leroy Irvis" or KLI by close friends and family. He first became actively involved in the civil rights movement by picketing downtown department stores in 1947, long before the actual beginning of the movement. "On one occasion," he said. "I was meeting with the mayor, who was not very impressed with my demands. I led him to the window, pointed to a bus parked on the street, and said that at a given signal, the bus would depart and a mass picketing would take place downtown. That time the mayor angrily conceded. I was less successful with the issue of Black clerks and organized a demonstration against Kaufmann's department store. My public demonstrations did not meet with the approval of my boss at the Urban League of Pittsburgh. I was far too militant." Irvis was promptly dismissed from the League.

Irvis was very instrumental in the establishment of Community College of Allegheny County. While the institution is considered a county project, Irvis used his clout as a State legislator to make certain that state funding was available to establish and continue the college. Without his tireless efforts, the Community College of Allegheny County would not exist. One of the outstanding provisions of the college is that any Allegheny County resident is permitted to attend. The tuition of the college is kept as low as possible so that it is affordable to nearly everyone.

In February 2007, Dr. Elmer Haymon and I led an effort to construct a science building on the main campus of the Community College and name it after K. Leroy Irvis. We persuaded Dr. Stuart Sutin (then president of CCAC) and John Dziak (president of the teacher's union) to use the need for a new science facility and the popularity of the recently-deceased Irvis, to raise money for a new science center. Ground was broken for the K. Leroy Irvis Science Center in 2009 and was opened for classes in the summer of 2013. Key to the completion of the project was the steadfast support of Katherine Irvis, the widow of my long-time hero.

Irvis, as a result of his relationship with William Strickland, Jr., moved the state legislature to provide funds for Bidwell Center, making it possible for the center to survive some very lean years.

By providing highly respected leadership in Pennsylvania government, K. Leroy Irvis opened the doors to state representation, through which many Blacks later walked. His leadership, whether on the picket lines or in government, made him a pioneer in the field of civil rights.

Ronald Davenport, Attorney
Urban League of Pittsburgh, Member
1st Black Professor & 1st Black Dean, Duquesne University, School of Law
Principal owner and later sole owner of Sheridan Broadcasting
Member of the NAACP Legal Defense Fund; Head of a Legal Defense fund in Mississippi[35]
A Principal in ARCHO, a not-for-profit housing corporation

It seems appropriate to list Ronald Davenport next to K. Leroy Irvis. During the April 1968 riots, Irvis was burned out of his apartment/office on Centre Avenue, and at Ron's invitation, stayed in his home for almost a year. Davenport was born in Philadelphia and did not move to Pittsburgh until the summer of 1963 when he was hired as the first Black Assistant Professor at Duquesne University. Initially, he spent time getting to know other Black attorneys in Pittsburgh and became friends with Irvis, Byrd Brown, Henry Smith, and Wendell Freeland.

I had met Ron Davenport at various functions, but he became my boss when he acquired ownership of WAMO, an AM/FM radio station which broadcast my program. I spoke with him often in that capacity, and even offered to buy WAMO-AM, when it was not making money, but the offer was turned down. Many Blacks thought Ron was unapproachable and aloof, but I never experienced any superior attitude during our many conversations. When I mentioned that I was planning to interview Ron for this oral history project, someone said, "Good luck with that! Davenport is not going to let you interview him. He's too important to talk to people like you." Fortunately, I had not consulted this negative person before Ron had already agreed to meet at my office for an interview.

He says that he met with no overt discrimination when he moved to Pittsburgh. "However, when I was taken to one of Pittsburgh's private dining clubs, there was some question as to whether I was going to be served in the main dining room."

In 1963, he became active with the Urban League of Pittsburgh and eventually became its president. In a role he described as "mostly intellectual," Davenport did most of his civil rights activities behind the scenes, working with other Black attorneys to change laws and protect demonstrators. "I didn't try to be the voice of the Black community; others were quite capable and better suited for that role than I was."

"In 1964, I realized that not all Pittsburgh civil rights leaders were working together, so I invited several of them to the Duquesne law school to discuss the issue. I was impressed with the leadership of the Poverty Program. Unlike other cities, Pittsburgh's program was controlled by a Black man, David Hill. It was one of the most significant programs in the country. Not only did it provide employment for many Black professional and para-professionals, many of the professionals were veterans of the civil rights movement. They brought their experiences to bear on the Poverty Program."

Along with a colleague, Matt Holden, Davenport formed a little-known organization called the Ad Hoc Committee and invited Byrd Brown, K. Leroy Irvis, and other Black leaders to plan a strategy for changing the world. One of their accomplishments was to control millions of dollars that came into Pittsburgh under the Poverty Program. "We made certain that the money got to the people. We made certain that average and poor people were on the Board. They were able to make decisions rather

35 The NAACP Legal Defense Fund had hired Thurgood Marshal and other Black attorneys to argue the landmark case *Brown* v. *The Board of Education of Topeka, Kansas.* It was also the organization that paid many of the fines and bail bonds for those jailed during demonstrations throughout the United States

than being pawns of the politicians. I believe there wasn't a program in any other city that involved as many Black people and gave them so much control."[36] They were responsible for hiring Dave Hill, and subsequently David Epperson[37], to head this program that became one of the most important efforts to change conditions that robbed Blacks of dignity and opportunity.

By 1970, Davenport was appointed Dean of the Duquesne University School of Law. When asked if he experienced discrimination, he said with a twinkle in his eye, "There may have been some White folks who had a problem with my being there, but *I* had absolutely no trouble being there. When you're in a position like that, you must have a sense of confidence in who you are. You see, I was a Black man not only physically, but intellectually as well."

Davenport had decided that a high level of political activity was essential to Black success in Pennsylvania. As a result, he, C. Delores Tucker, and Reverend Leroy Patrick formed the Negro Democratic Committee, later to become the Black Democratic Committee. In Pittsburgh and in Pennsylvania, the Committee worked for the inclusion of Blacks in Democratic politics and for attention to issues of importance to African Americans. He would like to be remembered as "someone who did the best with what I had."

Wendell Freeland, Attorney
Urban League of Pittsburgh, Board Member and President

Although World War II ended before he saw combat, Wendell Freeland had been a member of the Tuskegee Airmen. He was not among the first groups who were trained to become fighter pilots, but was trained as a bombardier. Those chosen for that position had to prove they were among the most intelligent men to be included in the US air force. Wendell was, in fact, an intellectual giant.

Wendell was so light-skinned that some of us joked that he was the whitest Black man we had ever seen. He was also a natty dresser and frequently wore a bowtie. I believe I met Wendell when he appeared on *Black Horizons*. Although he and I called one another "friend," the truth is we had a friendly, respectful relationship. Wendell was older and belonged to prestigious groups of which I was not a member. I admired his wry sense of humor. He called me for help when one of his clients needed an appraisal of their art work.

Wendell was among those who helped to integrate Highland Park swimming pool. He was arrested when in military uniform for refusing to obey racist policies of the US Armed Forces. Sadly, serving our country did not translate into equal treatment. Racist policies had supposedly ended in 1949 by Presidential Executive Order, but the discriminatory practices continued for many years. Life for Blacks

---

36 I can attest to the accuracy of Davenport's assertion because I was the assistant coordinator to one Poverty Program on the South Side of Pittsburgh and the head of the Hill District program.

37 David Epperson later became Dean of the University of Pittsburgh, School of Social Work.

in Pittsburgh and across the country was made better by Wendell Freeland, who departed at age 88—far too soon.

William Russell Robinson
Urban League of Pittsburgh
Member of Pittsburgh City Council
Representative in the Pennsylvania State House
Member of Allegheny County Council

William Robinson and I became friends when we both worked for the Urban League of Pittsburgh. He and I had many conversations about civil rights, justice, and politics. Although Bill did not remain long at the League, it was during this time he decided to enter politics. I believe his employment at the Urban League helped him formulate his plans for the future. Despite early losses to better known candidates, he became known for his resilience. Opponents who had defeated him often wrote him off as finished, only to be surprised when Bill showed up in another elected role. Some considered him flamboyant, because he always wore a bright red flower in the lapel of his suits. He was an articulate, well-read man, and a master at the political game.

Robinson was born in Pittsburgh in 1942. His mother was a maid; his father was a porter. Remembering the days prior to the civil rights movement, Robinson remarked, "Pittsburgh was a hard place for Blacks to succeed. If you could succeed here, you could succeed anywhere. I remember when there were no Blacks driving buses or street cars for the Pittsburgh Railway Company, what eventually became the Allegheny County Port Authority. You could ride a bus or trolley anywhere in the area, but you would not see a Black driver. Once I took a trolley to West View Park; the further away I got from the city, the more isolated I felt. West View Park was okay inside, but Blacks ran into hostility in the stores and other public places just outside the park's fences."

"Once I was stopped by the police. I can't even remember why, probably for DWB [Driving While Black]. One of the officers was Black and told the White officers I was a member of City Council. One of the White cops said, 'I don't give a damn who he is.' My impulse was to protest, but remembering what often happened to Black men in this situation, I remained silent while the Black officer made it clear that he was, in no way, going to support the actions of the White officers."

Robinson explained the lack of organized protest against the blatant racist treatment of Pittsburgh Blacks, "Blacks had gotten used to second class citizenship. They expected to be turned down for jobs, harassed by police, having access to only substandard housing. They continued to moan, primarily to one another, but did not believe that anything positive would be done about their situation."

Robinson continued, "I called about a job opening for a management trainee. I had just graduated from Ohio State University. I reported for the interview dressed in a suit and tie. The interviewer gave me this strange look. It was as if I was not the same person who called about the interview. He let me know that this job opportunity was not for me. The company did not hire Blacks and had no hesitation about saying so."

In the mid-1960s, Robinson was a member of *Job Call*, a television program on KDKA television. He made certain that all the job opportunities featured were open to Blacks. "I did not want folks to go through what I had experienced when I first started applying for jobs." Robinson's appearance on *Job*

Call made him the first Black to be regularly featured on a television show on any station in Pittsburgh. The year was 1967 or 1968. KDKA later brought in its first Black anchor person, Vic Miles.

Robinson became part of a very rare all-Black television crew for KDKA TV. Residents and organizations in Homewood had organized Harambee, the Black community's first arts festival. Festival organizers made it clear to KDKA and other stations that no all-White television crews were welcome. Roy Morrow hastily assembled a crew that included Robinson who was the interviewer for the coverage of the festival.[38]

Robinson's first step in embracing the civil rights movement was to abandon the all too common "Quo Vadis" hairstyle. In this style, hair was cropped close and vigorously combed toward the front of the head resulting in a short, wavy "do." Black men had been taught that long, kinky hair was unattractive. Lower socio-economic class men, athletes, and entertainers often had their hair "conked" (chemically straightened) or "processed" (straightened and then waved in a very flamboyant style). The latter two styles were considered inappropriate for Black men who were seeking middle class status. Consequently, many men adopted this close-cropped hair style worn by white men in the movie *Quo Vadis*, supposedly about ancient Rome. Robinson abandoned the style and let his hair grow long into an "Afro."[39]

At the time of his newly-awakened Black pride, Robinson was a new employee at the Urban League of Pittsburgh, along with another radical—me. Bill and I felt strongly that the League should be more relevant to Blacks who did not have the education and experience to benefit from the League's job and education programs. Bill, Stuart Strothers (another employee who shared that view), and I often acted in concert to force the League to change.

Robinson recalled, "I wanted the League to be more proactive, so I interrupted a board meeting to suggest how board members might become more involved. Leon Haley, the Deputy Director, tried to dissuade me, and Ron Davenport, who was the board president, was not at all supportive of my actions. I felt compelled to say the administration had not taken the plight of the average Black person very seriously. We were not doing all that we could do to assist *all* Black people. I tried to get other Blacks involved, but soon found myself nearly alone. The administration said that I was the ring leader of a group of League troublemakers and was summarily dismissed. I am not sorry about what I did, because much of what the Urban League does today can be traced back to my demonstration in the board room." Robinson indicated that despite his termination, his relationships with Art Edmonds, Ron Davenport, Leon Haley and Wendell Freeland are fine.

"I remember that, when the riots of 1968 broke out in The Hill and Homewood, I was in my East Liberty apartment, crying and afraid. I felt unsafe. I went to a gun shop and bought a gun. This feeling compelled me to become even more involved. I decided that politics was the arena for me. I began by running for, and losing, a seat on City Council. Eventually, I won that seat and later successfully ran for the State Legislature. I felt politics speaks to power. Politics is the straight line; a small group makes decisions that affect thousands of people. I felt that this is where I should be, if I wanted to make significant changes."

Was he ever afraid for his life or his job? "Having been fired once sort of takes the fear out of job loss. You find that you can survive and continue to lead a meaningful life. I never worried about losing

---

38 Roy Morrow had been an intern on WQED's *Black Horizons,* where he had participated in a special training program designed to have more Black professionals employed by all-White stations in Pittsburgh.

39 Interestingly, no such hair style was found in Africa at the time. Later, Africans would embrace the style, as well

another job. If I had been, I would never have entered politics. I have lost political races a number of times, but I always came right back. I never feared for my life. I did feel personally hurt when Martin Luther King was murdered. That took the steam out of our engine. We have yet to recover from that loss. Some Blacks did act out of fear during the movement; some of them stayed home, did not participate in anything because they were afraid of losing their jobs."

As to progress made during, or as a result of, the movement, Robinson offered, "Progress is a 'yes and no' issue. No, to the extent that we have not reached racial equality; there are still racists in high places. We still cannot move freely in this society. On the other hand, we have come a long way since slavery. We have overcome the color barrier in some cases, but not in others. We have made some political progress, but many Blacks still exist in poverty. I can look back at the good, the bad, and the ugly and say that Bill Robinson understood how to use his success to get better results for Black people. I can go to my grave knowing that I did my best for my people. I hope to be remembered 'as a person who loved his people so much that, in the quiet of the night, I cried for them.'"

Goldia Dargan
Urban League of Pittsburgh, Education Counselor

I first meet Goldia Dargan when I returned to Pittsburgh after the army and was trying to accumulate the money I would need to attend the University of Pittsburgh. After explaining my situation, I received a call from Goldia letting me know I had been awarded enough scholarship funds to cover about half my tuition. To supplement these funds, I looked for work, confident that as a successful military veteran I would find a job. I had forgotten just how racist Pittsburgh was. Unable to acquire sufficient funds to start college, I decided I needed to return the Urban League scholarship money. When I met with Goldia, she did not reach out for the check. Instead she gave me a stare that could peel paint off a wall and said in a low menacing voice, "What are you going to do about college if you return the money?" Improvising, I said I'd get a job and continue saving till I had enough money for college. "Bullshit," she spat. "What you really are going to do is find some little, insignificant job; buy some junker car; get in debt; find a cute young lady and get involved; she'll get pregnant; you'll marry her and begin to raise a child. You will never go to college, and you will live a life of quiet desperation. You will never have a good life or make contributions to help your people! That would be such a waste, and I'm not about to allow that to happen."

I was so stunned, I was unable to come up with one of my signature, smart-ass responses. Goldia continued, "You just keep that check and keep your behind in that chair. I will be back." With that she stood, glared at me again, and left the room. In short order she returned, thrust out her hand, and said, "Here is an Urban League check in the amount you need to pay your first year's tuition. It's a special loan program, and you are expected to repay it as soon as you graduate. Now get your behind over to Pitt; pay your tuition, and bring me back proof that you've given Pitt all the money they require." And that was the no-nonsense tour de force that was Goldia Dargan. Barely able to say "thank you," I left feeling blessed. I think I was in love!

Sometime later, Goldia asked if I could give her a ride to the bus station, because she was leaving Pittsburgh. I protested and threatened to leave school if she abandoned the city. She just laughed and said she was certain I'd stay in school and have a good life. My third job after graduating from Pitt was with the Urban League, and I was sure I could locate Goldia, something I had failed to do in my previous attempts. I also tried to repay the loan, but never received the necessary paperwork. Finally, I asked Turk, the Urban League comptroller, where I could find information about my scholarship loan. In the file room, I could find no record of the loan, even when I checked folders in case my paperwork had been misfiled. Frustrated, I spoke again with Turk and after hearing the year of the loan, he consulted past ledgers. "Ralph," he said, "this is really weird. We didn't have a loan program in that year. But I do recall something about Goldia being upset that some young man was going to waste his life, and she had to get him some scholarship money." We stared at each other, realizing that Goldia had used her own money to give me the "loan."

As Goldia had predicted, life was good to me. I earned a doctorate, became a professional photographer, had a career in broadcasting, and good positions in industry, social service, and education. I opened an interest-bearing account and started "A Gift from Goldia" program. Whenever I was able to help someone and they felt a need to repay me, I told them about Goldia and asked them to pass on her story and help others. Like a pebble tossed into a lake, the ripples of Goldia's kindness and generosity have expanded for more than 50 years.

Through discussions with Phyllis Goode and Margaret Albert, I learned mine was not the only life that Goldia changed for the better. Frustrated that the Urban League did not have sufficient funds to help all those who needed money for college, Goldia had the idea of creating the Negro Emergency Education Drive (NEED). Feeling she did not have the name recognition or clout to pull off a drive to raise millions of dollars for scholarship aid, she had approached two prominent Pittsburgh women[40] to adopt the cause. NEED was a huge success, but Goldia's name was never associated with it.

In the 1980s, I was working at the Kingsley Association and asked Phyllis Goode, who served on the organization's board, to look for Goldia when she attended National Urban League functions. At Christmas time in 1987, Phyllis called to ask if she could bring a friend to see my African art collection. Upon opening my door, I was met by Phyllis, another tall, handsome woman, and a young boy about 10 years of age. I invited them in to tour my collection, but Phyllis said, "Ralph, this is Goldia!" Finally, I had the chance to ask the question that had been haunting me for the past 26 years. "Why, Goldia? You didn't know me. You didn't know what I'd make of myself. Why would you take such a chance?" She just smiled and denied her amazing act of kindness.

"Don't pretend you don't know what I'm talking about. Turk told me the truth. I've been looking for you all these years to ask why you'd give your own money to a perfect stranger."

"If I did give you the money, and I'm not saying I did, the money was well spent! I know about your accomplishments; about your radio shows and television show; about your civil rights work; about your career at Pitt and doctorate."

I asked Goldia if she liked my art collection and if any one piece in particular had appealed to her. "Oh, yes. That wooden sculpture of a kneeling antelope; it's one of the most beautiful pieces I've ever seen." I excused myself and returned cradling the sculpture, one of the finest examples of Bamana Chi-Wara helmet dance masks I had ever seen. "Here," I said, "please accept this as a small token of my admiration." She reached out, held the sculpture, and stroked it gently. Then she tried to give it back, saying she couldn't possibly accept such a gift. "Goldia, this is one of my most precious material

---

40 Goldia Dargan along with Marion Jordan and Florence Reizenstein established NEED, which awarded scholarships to thousands of Black students during its years of operation.

possessions. You can't refuse it. It's from our Motherland and in the tradition of our ancestors, I will be shamed if you refuse my gift. The harmony of the ancestors will be disrupted. You simply must accept it on behalf of the ancestors." Thank god she accepted the gift, as did Phyllis to whom I gave a piece of African art as a thank you for bringing Goldia to me.

Phyllis called me later to gloat about the stunned look on my face when I realized Goldia was standing in front of me. Then she said, "You don't have to tell me, but was that piece as expensive as I think it was? Did your heart stop when she asked for it?"

"Well, in the first place, she didn't ask for it. She simply said she liked it. Remember, all the things I've accomplished are a result of her selfless gift. If she had asked for the entire collection, I would have hired a truck and had it delivered to her."

A short time later, I received a thank you note from Goldia saying she loved the sculpture and it would help to light the dark places in which she walked. Damn it! There should be no dark places for this remarkable woman who brought light into the lives of so many young Black men and women.

Urban Youth Action (UYA)

This group was not classified as a civil rights group, but it did fight racism and discrimination by working with industry and government in order to provide opportunities for Black youth. The group activities were run by the youth themselves with the guidance and training provided by dedicated adults.

Bernard F. Jones
Urban Youth Action, Founder
Allegheny Conference on Community Development, 1st Black Assistant Director
Poise Foundation, Founder

Bernard Jones was born and reared by his mother in a public housing project in Pittsburgh's Hill District. "My mother insisted that there were greater things for me to do. Failure was simply not an option. She said she had brought me this far by herself, and she wanted me to take my kids even further. Sure, I was raised in the 'projects,' but I saw outstanding leadership there; much of it coming from Black women."

I met Bernie when he and the members of Urban Youth Action presented me with my first award for my work as the host/producer of *Black Horizons*. I was impressed with this man, and we soon became friends. He and I went to the Million Man March together. At the march I learned Bernie was having trouble with diabetes. I cried when he died.

Bernie was one of my heroes; he claimed I was one of his. He called me "The Warrior," and once said, when I was complaining about some prominent Black folks who would not help me battle a viciously racist group of White women, "Look, Ralph, we all know that you are a warrior and that you will fight anyone; but you can't expect all of us to join your battles, especially when you are fighting the wives of some of the most powerful White men in Pittsburgh. Some of the folks you are pissed at depend upon donations from those men to run their organizations; can't you see that?" Sure I could see that, but I figured a true warrior did not shrink from his/her duty to protect the village. These folks had sold out and I never forgave them.

Jones said that he received many negative messages from Whites about Blacks. "They treated us like children. They treated us like we were 3rd or 4th class citizens. When Blacks were served drinks at West View Amusement Park, they came in paper cups; Whites received theirs in glasses. Wow! I hadn't thought about that for years. I guess that bothered me more than I thought. The image burned itself into my brain. Whites told us that the best jobs we could get were the ones in the steel mills, or operating an elevator in Gimbel's department store. My mother said that she would kill me before she would allow me to work in a steel mill. I believed her!"

"One day I was walking home from downtown and was stopped four times by White cops. They kept asking me what I was doing. All I was doing was walking home. I was pissed off." In another incident, while Jones was still living in the projects, some White girls were allegedly attacked by a Black boy. White cops picked up Jones as he was walking home and stood him in front of the White girls for identification. All the girls stated that Jones was not the culprit, but the cops kept trying to convince the girls to identify Jones. Apparently, the only link to the crime was his first name. When Jones' mother showed up at the police station to get her son, she told the cops, "If you ever pick up my boy for something he didn't do, I will kill you." The cops did not say a word.

In addition to his work with Urban Youth Action, Bernie established The Poise Foundation, still the only Black-controlled and operated foundation in the tri-state area. Mainstream, White-controlled foundations offered little support to Black organizations. Without grants from The Poise Foundation, some of the most important small Black organizations would not have survived. Fortunately for new Black organizations, Bernie sometimes awarded funds because he "saw something of promise." For example, "Bernie frequently listened to and watched my radio and television shows. When I was the host of *Black Talk* on WCXJ radio, I frequently championed some neighborhood that needed funds for an important project. At one time I began repeatedly devoting on-air time to a group from Homewood asking for financial support. One morning Bernie called and said, "Hey Ralph, I am so tired of hearing you talk about that group. To get you to shut your mouth, I am going to meet with the director of the program and see if Poise can fund the project. If I give them the money, will you please *shut up*; at least about *that* group? Deal?" Bernie visited the group, liked what he saw, and gave them the funds they needed. Bernie was very good at helping new groups leverage their money in order to attract funds from White-controlled foundations.

Until the time of his death, Bernard F. Jones and The Poise Foundation were one and the same. However, the work of the foundation was helped immeasurably by Ed Guy.

Jones recalled that, for the most part, Blacks accepted the poor treatment heaped upon them on a daily basis. He explained, "While Black folks seemed to accept their ill-fate, beneath the surface was a growing, quiet anger." This anger reared its head during the urban riots of the 1960s. As Assistant Director of The Allegheny Conference on Community Development, he advocated strongly for the inclusion of Blacks in county planning initiatives.

C. Richard Gillcrese
Urban Youth Action, Executive Director

Richard Gillcrese was a confidant of Bernard Jones, and a role model and mentor to countless young Black Pittsburghers. I met Richard through Bernie when I was helping with some UYA projects. We worked together on other causes and frequently saw each other at various civil rights meetings. I was impressed by his dedication.

Gillcrese was born in The Hill in 1944. He said, "I grew up all over The Hill because my family moved so often. I remember all of the homes and businesses that Blacks owned in The Hill. Folks were doing pretty well; then came this thing called Urban Renewal, that was supposed to *help* us. Instead, what they did was destroy businesses and homes and chase Blacks out of The Hill."

"When I left The Hill and went downtown, I found out that I could not try on clothes and had to have a co-signer in order to put money in the bank. I remember I used to get on a bus to go to my grandmother's house in Swissvale. White folks would look at me funny and would say things like 'get out of the way, *nigger!*' Blacks accepted the treatment on the surface, but inside a seething resentment was building behind closed doors."

"As a child, I attended Camp James Weldon Johnson. The camp was started so that Black kids could have that experience, because we couldn't go to the White folks' camps. I was inspired by what I learned about how Blacks had made major contributions to America and the world. At 14 or 15 I joined the picket lines. I was at the demonstration against Duquesne Light and a bunch of other places. During the riots of '68, I worked with Tim Stevens to try to keep Black kids from being harmed. In 1966, I became involved with UYA Urban Youth Action, and Bernie Jones became my mentor. I loved my years at UYA because they trained young folks how to fully participate in all that was going on."

Operation Dig

Nate Smith
Operation Dig, Founder
Black Construction Coalition, Founding Member
Operation Push, Founding Member
Named one of the 100 Most Influential Blacks in America by *Ebony* magazine
Named one of the most influential Black men in the country by *Jet* magazine.
Board Member of numerous state organizations

Nate Smith, a former boxer, was one of the most menacing members of the civil rights movement in Pittsburgh. His shining, bald head, dark skin, and dark piercing eyes struck fear in the hearts of many an opponent. Smith always seemed ready to explode into violence and had an "in your face" confrontational style. He never backed down and seemed not to know the meaning of fear. He did, however, say that during the march to Three Rivers Stadium he wondered if death was near.

I met Nate when the movement was going strong, and he appeared on my radio and television shows. We were colleagues more than friends. That changed around 1981 after the movement had waned. I was in Harrisburg seeking funding for programs of the Kingsley Association, an agency I directed.

During a visit to the Office of Community Affairs, I noticed Nate's name and telephone number posted prominently on a bulletin board, but didn't think much about it. I filled out an application and left to await a decision. One day as I was cutting grass at my home, Nate drove by and told me I was not going to get the grant. When I asked how he knew that, he replied, "Man, you know I serve on the board, and they voted not to give you the money."

I was so angry, I wrote a very nasty letter to the governor asking how they could turn me down while giving money to Nate, who served on their board. I knew, of course, that they would tell Nate of my protest, and sure enough, Nate's reaction came very soon. Nate and I lived on the same street and again I was in my yard gardening when Nate drove up and told me the State folks gave him a copy of my negative letter and urged him to "do something about it."

Nate knew I was spoiling for a fight and said, "Man, we ain't gonna fight. That's what they want us to do. I've known you for a long time and have always admired your work. I figure you just don't understand what this money thing is all about. I think you owe me an apology, but we ain't gonna fight about that. I have always loved you, my brother."

With that he drove off. I was stunned by his refusal to fight. A while later I invited Nate to lunch. When he sat down, I extended my hand and said, "I apologize. I checked out the situation and found that the money I was after was part of a slush fund the governor uses to reward those who had worked to get him elected. You were one of the important supporters in the Black community. I worked against his election so, obviously, I was not entitled to any of the money. I am sorry." Nate accepted my apology, we became good friends, and remained so until he died.

Ribbon Cutting Ceremony – Mayor Richard Caliguiri (left) with Joseph Rhodes, Roland Matthews, C. Delores Tucker, Nate Smith, Ewari Ellis, Clyde Jackson and Harvey Adams

Nate started Operation Dig after seeing a construction project in The Hill where only Whites were employed. He confronted the manager about the absence of Black workers, but his protest fell on deaf ears. He returned to the construction site with a group of men and shut it down. Smith said that millions of dollars were being paid out to White folks who operated heavy equipment, but no dollars were going to Blacks. One of the union officials said, "Okay Nate, give me X number of Blacks and have them report to work. We couldn't find any Blacks who had the experience to fill the damn jobs. That's when we started to train Blacks as heavy-equipment operators through an apprenticeship program run by Operation Dig." Smith then took on other unions and forced them to accept similar apprenticeship programs. He served notice that he would no longer accept construction projects in the Black community that excluded Black workers. Given the deep racism in Pittsburgh, Smith said, "Sometimes the construction workers tried to hurt us. When we asked them to stop working so that we could get jobs for Blacks, they ignored us. It was a little extreme, but I had to show folks how quick a pound of sand in a gas tank stopped a construction vehicle."

Smith also teamed up with Reverend Jessie Jackson in Operation Push to force construction unions across the country to adopt non-discriminatory practices. "The Pittsburgh Plan" became a national model, and Nate became a nationally known figure in the attack on Unions that barred Blacks from membership. Smith was instrumental in establishing The Black Construction Coalition.

Nate recounted his encounters with racism as a very young man. "My father worked as a janitor for a local roller skating rink, which excluded Blacks. One day Dad was sick; I went to the rink to clean for him. When I got to the building, I got on the elevator to ride to the top floor. The elevator operator yelled, 'Colored people didn't ride the elevator. Take the stairs'." Nate, who was 12 years old, refused to get off. His father was upset because Nate had

FIGURE 10.1

BLACK CONSTRUCTION COALITION
LEADERS & MEMBERS

- Dr. Lloyd Bell, University of Pittsburgh
- Ron Davenport, Duquesne University
- Clyde Jackson, United Black Front
- Dr. Norman Johnson, Carnegie Mellon University
- Nate Smith, Operation Dig
- James "Swampman" Williams, Operation Dig

caused "problems." "Dad also worked at a theatre in the all-White Dormont area. I told the theatre manager that I had come to see my father and to watch the movie. He said I couldn't come in; Negroes weren't permitted. Then he says, 'You can't be Mr. Smith's son, because he's White'." As is often the case, a White person could not tell the difference between a light-skinned Black person and a White person. They use only skin color to determine race, completely ignoring other pertinent visual clues.

When Smith was 12 years old, he lied about his age and enlisted in the Navy. "I became a boxer and was the champ of the division. When I knocked out my first White boy, I was scared they would come after me. They didn't and that was the first time I realized that you could knock out a White boy and get away with it! I had thought that they would *lynch* a Black man just for *hitting* a White boy, and here I was *knocking White boys out!* When I found out that you could get away with it, I knocked out every White boy I met. I also had thought that White men were invincible," Smith laughed. "I *loved* knocking out White boys!"

"When I came back from the Navy, I found that Blacks were being treated like slaves on a plantation. I came back from the South and found out that we had 'South' up here! They had so little respect for Black folks; they would pay you $10 to vote for a specific person." He saw some respect begin to come to Blacks "when we shut downtown down during one of our demonstrations. The natives were restless, and folks didn't know what to do with us."

As a result of his civil rights work, Nate became friends with a number of influential people including Reverend Jessie Jackson, Edgar Kaufmann, Elsie Hillman, and Cardinal Wright. "I got to travel around the world and meet some famous people like the Pope, Reagan, Nixon, Bush, and Arafat."

Smith first met Cardinal Wright when both appeared on a panel on a television show. "When we were introduced, I reached out to shake hands, and he pulled back and would not shake. I didn't say anything, but at the end of the show, when he reached out to shake hands, I refused. If he wouldn't shake hands when we were off-camera, I sure wasn't going to shake his hand on television. I told him I felt he was a racist. He apologized and explained that he had injured his shoulder and was in a lot of pain. 'When you reached out your hand, I saw your power and was afraid I would be hurt. When we were in the studio, I could brace myself on the desk, so I felt safe.' I believed him, and we became good friends. When he went to Rome to be appointed a cardinal, he invited my wife and me and paid our way. Before the ceremony, Bishop Wright called and told us to wear the African outfits we had brought with us. Ordinary people weren't allowed in to the ceremony so he had us pretend to be African dignitaries. There we were; sitting right in the front row. When they crowned him a cardinal, Bishop Wright knelt to kiss the Pope's feet. As he did that he turned his head and *winked* at me. That's how I got to meet the Pope.

"I also met Yasser Arafat and exchanged watches. I needed to know what time it was at home, no matter where I was in the world. So I had this special watch with two faces. Arafat saw it and liked it, so I took it off my wrist and gave it to him. I guess he was impressed, because he took off his watch and gave it to me. It was a goddamn Rolex!"

Smith felt that, no matter how famous people become, we are all the same. He had no respect for a handful of "elite Niggers!" "They rose on our backs and became rich. No matter how high they rise, they're still Black and will die Black!" Smith did express appreciation for many Black and White leaders including Byrd Brown, Swampman Williams, Dave Epperson, James McCoy, Matthew Moore, Alma Fox, Frankie Pace, Frankie Mae Jeter, and Moe Coleman, a White man who helped him start Operation Dig. "He helped thousands of people. He had a plum job and didn't have to do anything. As a White person, racism wasn't hurting him, but he still helped thousands of Blacks."

When asked if he ever feared for his life, Smith replied, "No, I never feared for myself. I was afraid about what might happen to my family and the people I cared about, but I was never afraid of nobody. I made folks fear me!" Smith admitted that sometimes he underestimated the danger. After the demonstration following the murder of Martin Luther King Jr., Smith got on a microphone to urge the marchers to follow him back downtown to shut it down. "Harvey Adams wrestled me to the ground and said he couldn't let me do that. The cops were waiting for me. If I went downtown, some of them were going to kill me. He saved my life."

Responding to the question as to whether progress was made, Smith replied, "We lost a lot, but we did make some progress. You're interviewing me; that's progress. I don't have no regrets; I would do it all over again, if I had to. If I wasn't involved in the movement there is no way a guy like me would have met all the famous people I did. Regrets? Never. I feel good!"

Smith reflected on conditions for Blacks today. "We didn't demand enough! We never really got a piece of the pie; we got the crust! We don't have the kind of leadership we had then. Folks in high places forgot how they got there. In some ways I think we are worse off than we were during the movement; too many common folks got left behind!"

Smith concluded with advice for people today. "Believe in yourself. If you are not happy, be happy! You asked me how I want to be remembered. I want to be remembered as *Nate Smith!* Watch the movie."

James "Swampman" Williams
Operation Dig, Co-Founder
Black Construction Coalition, Member

I met James "Swampman" Williams as a guest on my television show. Williams was a big man, standing well over six feet and weighing more than 250 pounds. When some racist organizations ignored the leaders of the movement or tried to harm demonstrators, Williams' imposing presence convinced them of the error of their ways. He was part of a small, powerful group of young men who often accompanied Northside leaders to negotiations and on demonstrations to make certain no one was harmed. He was a frequent member of negotiating teams. Although his imposing demeanor could be intimidating, he had a wonderful sense of humor and was very funny.

When Williams arrived in Pittsburgh in 1952, he knew nothing about racism and differences in treatment because of color. That changed when he went into the military service and saw that Blacks were treated unfairly. He became aware of the civil rights movement in 1963, when Reverend Cicero Martin asked him to help in the Northside efforts to end racial discrimination. Rev. Martin told Williams that he should accompany a group that was going to the March on Washington. Williams went and "spent the day with Martin Luther King and those cats. There was some White dudes at the march from Alabama and Mississippi carrying KKK signs and throwing tomatoes at us. I was getting ready to kick some ass, but I was stopped by this older Black man, who said 'Hold on young fellow; we didn't come here to fight.' When I came back to Pittsburgh, I was still mad!"

"I joined the movement in Pittsburgh because I seen all this construction going on in my neighborhood. I asked Mr. Scott what these White folks was making. Mr. Scott said $50 to $80 a day for even the low paying jobs. So I said that we Blacks ought to be making that kind of money, especially on jobs in our own community. I contacted Obie Sims and George Wright to discuss this situation and started raising hell over here in Manchester. Then came along Nate Smith, and we all put Operation Dig together. We began to get good construction jobs for Blacks."

When asked about his particular role in the movement, Williams smiled and said, "I was a strong arm guy. I liked to start trouble. Dave Craig [Pittsburgh Public Safety Director] called me a demagogue, meaning I liked to take the law into my own hands. I thought it was comical. When we were going to visit a construction site, I would get my guys pretty wound up with wine and whiskey. Let's just say I took all the *fear* out of them and put a little *life* in them. We would roll up on a construction job, and I would say 'Hey man, how many brothers you got working on this job?' Then a ruckus would break out, and we would just close the job down, especially if it was in our community. We really wanted to see some Black faces at that time."

Swampman mused for a second, and continued, "At the end, I realized that we were still dealing with the Man who controlled the game. Operation Dig had a lot of success in getting brothers good paying jobs. We were getting the brothers "B" books, which is an international operator's book. With a "B" book you were supposed to be able to work anywhere in the world. We said to the Man, 'Listen, when we get these books, we can get our own jobs anywhere in the city, the county, or the world. Right?' The Man said, 'Not really; you see we just got together and revised the whole system. Now we have a referral system, and there are about 3,000 ahead of you.' That showed us that we were stepping into another guy's ballgame. He makes the rules; he changes them. If he don't like *them* changes, he changes them again. He is always changing the rules to fit himself, because it is *his game.* It's just like at my house. I make the rules, and I change the rules; if I don't like the new rules, I just change them again. When you try to take something away from the Man, he's always out to get you."

Williams continued to reflect on the movement and all the hatred. "I was never a bigot. Mom was a Christian; she never taught us bigotry. It was not in me. When we were raising all that hell, it was just like being in a gang fight. Other people called it a race riot, but to me it was just a gang fight. It was just that the other gang had White guys on it. I had *fun* at it! I was not mad. I didn't hate the White man. I was just saying, 'Hey I want some of the brothers to work.' Hell, there was nothing in it for me." Williams laughed and said, "I didn't want to work *myself!* Really!"

When asked how it felt to be considered a leader in an important movement, Williams replied "Hey, the first time I appeared on television, I broke my neck getting home so that I could see me."

Would he do it again? "Yes; if the times was the same. But everything we did then, as a people, we would have to upgrade." Was it worth it? Williams thought, for a moment, then said "For me, personally? NAW! I got a lot of respect. I got all the fame a cat could ask for. But I still live in a three-room apartment. It don't bother me. Don't get me wrong, it was an experience in my life that was well worth it. I'd do it again, if I had to, but I'm looking to do better things now. The way I look at it, we are on an economic surge from the grass roots up. You look around at everybody. Like the Bible says, 'before the glory comes the humiliation.' We are at the end of times. I can see it. God is moving throughout the world. We did not accomplish our dreams. As a race, we never owned businesses; we never created businesses from the bottom up. Our young people never seem to go nowhere. They don't know about the better side of life. We need to get us some businesses. We need to take these kids some places. I want to own 10,000 car washes and detail shops. Then I would take some of that money and send some poor kids to college. I would like to lead them out of the ghetto."

The Black Construction Coalition

This little-remembered organization concentrated on creating employment opportunities for Blacks in the very lucrative construction industry. They negotiated with unions and companies that were constructing buildings in Pittsburgh. Figure 10.1 lists leaders and members of the Coalition identified in the records available to me.

Halfway Art Gallery

Ed "Ewari" Ellis
Halfway Art Gallery, Founder and Artist
United Black Front, Founding Member

At the time I met Ed Ewari Ellis, I was Executive Director of The Hill Community Action Program, an arm of the so-called War on Poverty. My office was located near the New Granada Theater on Centre Avenue. One day I noticed a group of White Catholic priests shading their eyes and peering into an empty commercial space across the street. Curious, I felt compelled to ask if they needed any help. That's how I came to meet Ewari Ellis and learn about the Halfway Art Gallery. Its purpose was to exhibit and sell works of art created by Black males who were in prison or recently released. The Gallery soon began to sell other items, including books, African clothing, and African art. The only other person who seemed to serve in an official capacity was Carol, Ewari's wife, who became more involved as the Gallery took on the air of a boutique.

Ellis was a menacing fellow, tall, strongly built, with broad shoulders, a full beard, and huge "Fro" on which was perched a colorful African-style hat. He also wore African-style shirts called Dashikis. When we shook hands, I knew from the grip that he was trying to intimidate me. As his grip grew tighter, so did mine. We stared into each other's eyes. Finally he said, "Tough little son-of-a-bitch, aren't you?" I just smiled and pretended that he had not hurt my throbbing hand. Later, Ewari appeared on my television show. We developed a strong friendship based on mutual respect.

Ellis was born in Homestead, a suburb of Pittsburgh. "On the surface, things seemed fine for Blacks in Pittsburgh. Of course I knew that something was not right, because my father educated me on how to behave as a Black person. I had to stay in my place and get along with Whites. We kids resented being told that we had to sit in the balcony at the theater in Homestead. We took out our anger by throwing food and other stuff down on the White patrons. The theatre owners responded by reversing the seating pattern and making us sit on the main floor, while the White kids had to sit in the balcony. My dad told me that Blacks could not be foremen in the mills and held the lowest-paying jobs. There were segregated lunch counters in the five-and-dime stores. We accepted that sort of thing before the civil rights movement."

Ellis became involved in the movement when a friend asked him to accompany him to the 1963 March on Washington. "I knew Martin Luther King was going to speak, but I was more interested in hearing and seeing Marlon Brando, who was also at the march. On the evening after the march, I heard Malcolm X on the radio. He was asking whether march participants thought they had really done something significant by participating in the largest parade ever financed

**Ewari Ellis (far right) with other members
of the self-defense team**

by the White establishment. He said that, if we wanted better lives, we should not integrate, but should develop our own."

When Ellis established Halfway Art Gallery in 1955, it was right in the middle of all the action taking place in The Hill as the civil rights movement was gaining momentum. It was only natural for Ewari to become deeply involved in the movement and emerge as a powerful, outspoken leader. He was a demonstrator and a very skilled negotiator, often using his menacing demeanor to extract promises from corporate America. He was so involved in civil rights activities that many people forgot that he was also an accomplished artist working in oils and pastels. Many organizations purchased his artwork as status symbols.

Ellis knew many of the other Pittsburgh leaders. He thought that Nick Flournoy was one of the best organizers in the movement and that Byrd Brown was the most dynamic. He was also impressed with Harvey Adams, who used his position on the police force to keep White officers in check. "But the most unsung hero, as far as I'm concerned," said Ellis, "was a woman named Texas Jackson. She was a rough, loud woman, who came to nearly every demonstration and was involved in many negotiations. 'Tex' would say things at meetings that others were too afraid to express. She allowed us to play the game of 'good cop, bad cop.' White folks were so afraid of her that they often made concessions just so they wouldn't have to deal with her. She died without getting any of the recognition she deserved." Ellis mused for a moment and said, "There will be some folks who get credit for great leadership and vision, but we should remember that we stand on the shoulders of giants who came before us."

"At some point," he continued, "probably after King's murder, I walked away from CORE, The Black United Front, and other mainstream civil rights organizations. I joined the Black Panther Party, because I believed that we had to focus on Black Nationalism, not integration. My focus moved from equal opportunity to Black liberation. King was assassinated by some poor White cracker in Tennessee. The racist crackers will always assassinate the one identified as our leader. What we must do is pull together as a people. We have to have a movement of the masses; then they can't stop the movement by killing just one person. Even in our anger, we got together at Ebenezer Church the next day to talk about how to control what was going to happen in Pittsburgh as a result of King's assassination. One of the things that grew out of that meeting was the United Black Front, headed by my buddy Clyde Jackson. It was started later in 1968. We decided that Whites had to play a supportive role in the UBF. This was a change, because Whites had gotten used to having leadership roles in our movement. We told them that the best thing they could do was to go back to their own community and raise money to fight racism. Some of them insisted on having a role in the UBF, but we did not allow that. It was time for us to take care of business ourselves. And that is exactly what we did."

The UBF was instrumental in helping the Black Construction Coalition and Operation Dig as well as starting Wylie Industries, a black-owned nail factory. "We were militant and proud of it. Many Black folks got good positions because of us, whether they will admit it or not."

Recalling a business establishment that suddenly appeared on Centre Avenue right after the riots, Ellis said, "We welcomed the brothers who were running the Black Bazaar and Books for Freedom. We thought they were bringing culture to The Hill. They were CIA/FBI stooges, put here to spy on us, and play the old 'divide and conquer' game. They even hired some local Blacks to spy on the movement. Some brothers and sisters sold out for a low-paying job or a small amount of money. The planting of CIA and FBI agents in our midst caused a great deal of paranoia among the members of the movement."

Ewari was an adaptable leader. When wearing African-style clothing fell into disfavor, he put aside his Dashiki and donned a suit. When I asked about his change in style, Ewari responded, "It ain't gone man, I just took it off my back and put it in my mind."

Was he ever afraid during the movement? "Sure," he responded. "I had to move my family several times, because of the threats. I wish I had a nickel for every time I was called a "Nigger." We had a fire at my home on Stanton Avenue. When I gave the address, the person who answered the phone at the fire station asked if it was Ewari Ellis's home. I said 'yes,' and the police arrived before the fire department. They were looking for firearms. They arrested me, but had to let me go because they found nothing. My friends in the movement spent a lot of time hiding from authorities. They wanted to kill us the same way they killed many Black Panthers across the country. The cops hated us. When they arrested a Black person, we would show up with 200 people. Attorney Wendell Freeland helped us get a bunch of folks released from the trumped-up charges."

Ewari made frequent appearances on *Black Horizons*. "I remember that the White folks who controlled the station didn't give you a budget, Ralph. When we were taping, you didn't have any money for editing, so, if we made a mistake or some mechanical glitch happened, you would get pissed and say 'Ahh shit, we have to start the whole damn show all over again.' That was so funny because the White folks must have thought that you were some middle-class brother who never swore. You know yourself that the show caused the FBI to be suspicious of *YOU!* I bet they had a file on you." My old friend was correct. Many years later I saw my FBI dossier.

Ellis accused the United States Government of introducing cheap drugs into the Black Community as a way to "fuck up our lives. It worked; a lot of young brothers got strung out on dope and lost their interest in Black folks. It gave the cops a convenient excuse to raid and intimidate the community. The drug squads were worse than street thugs. We no longer had control of our own community. Because of the drug element, churches stopped being involved in the struggle. The war on drugs is a sham excuse to come down hard on Black folks. Anyone with any sense knows that Black folks don't bring drugs into the country. We don't own the planes or the boats. We aren't the major distributors. But the vast majority of folks arrested for drugs are young Black males who have been set up by the narcs. The government could stop the drugs tomorrow, if they wanted to. Some of the White cops use the drugs as an excuse to pull guns and push Black folks around. They then go on television and show dope and guns, so White folks go for the hype and really believe that Black folks control the dope and use it more than Whites. We know that ain't hardly true. Things have gotten so bad in many Black communities that, between the cop goon squads and the gang banging drug dealers, folks are afraid to go out of their homes. What we need is a new movement to stop the drugs. We need to force the government to get drugs the hell out of our communities."

When I started this oral history project, I had lost track of Ellis and no matter how hard I tried, no information about Ellis came my way. Then as fate would have it, I was talking with Haruma, an African art dealer who had sold Ewari many pieces over the years. During the conversation, he seemed disturbed about something, and when I asked what was bothering him, he said in broken English, 'Mr. Proctor, you remember Ewari? Last week I was walking down the street in Washington, D.C.; I see this man I think I know him. When he come closer, I see it is Mr. Ellis. We hug and talk a little bit. He give me his address and telephone number. When Ewari walk away, I cry. You remember how Mr. Ellis was always a BIG man, big shoulders, big arms. He so big, everybody afraid! Mr. Ewari not big anymore. He look

Terrible. He is very small, skinny, look almost dead! No teeth, his hair have dreds, long strings of hair. I think he very sick. I am afraid for him."

As soon as Haruna left, I called the number he had given me and left a message. Within a few days Ewari called. "Man, Ralph, things ain't like they was in the old days. I'm sick; my diabetes is kicking my ass. I don't have no spare money, so you will have to help me out. All I need is bus fare and a few dollars for spending money." After I sent him a money order, I told a couple of mutual friends what I had done. One of them said, "Man, you can kiss that money goodbye. Ewari is strung out on dope. He'll probably spend your money and never show up." He advised me to give up and complete the project without Ewari.

Unfortunately, Ellis did fail to show on the appointed date. I called Ewari and said I simply could not finish this important story without his input. I told him that I was going to send him a non-refundable, round-trip bus ticket and would have a couple of hundred dollars for him, *when I saw him!* A few days later, Ewari rolled into my office in a wheelchair. As Haruna had indicated, Ewari looked absolutely terrible, a shell of his former powerful self. Despite all that the interview went very well and we had a great time reliving the past.

Ewari stayed in town, for a while, with relatives. One day he called and asked if he could come in to talk to me about something very important. When he arrived, he said that the interview had helped him remember who he was during the movement. "Man, I was an important cat! I'm gonna clean myself up and get back to my painting. I've been praying, and I asked the Lord where he wanted me to go, so I need to get some money from you because the answer was go to Wheeling."

"Wheeling?" God told you to go to *Wheeling?"*

Ewari laughed and said, "Yeah, man, that's what I thought. When I got that message I said 'God are you sure you were talking to ME?' After we both stopped laughing, Ewari explained that he was going to do as God had directed, but he had no money. Then he unwrapped a cloth to reveal about five pieces of African Art.

"Ewari, I can't buy the last pieces of your collection. According to our African ancestors, I would be wrong to reap benefit from the misfortune of a friend. I just can't do it!"

Ewari said that he understood, but this was all he had that was worth any decent money. I took out my check book and wrote him a check. He thanked me and asked if I would keep the pieces for him until he returned. I told him to take them to Wheeling with him. He then asked if he could bring several paintings by so that I could put them on display at my next exhibition at Kingsley Association. I agreed, and a few days later Ewari returned with several paintings. He told me to send any proceeds to him in Wheeling. That was the last time I saw my friend, the Warrior, alive. Ewari died in 1994.

Ewari's death passed unnoticed by many. Perhaps those who loved him did not have time to let the larger community know of his passing. Perhaps many who took their individual accomplishments as a sign of their own power had never heard of Ewari's role in the movement. Perhaps many had already forgotten him. Whatever the case, Ewari's funeral was not well attended by those who once called him "Brother."

When it was time to carry Ed "Ewari" Ellis to his final resting place, there were only five pallbearers. The funeral director asked for a sixth volunteer. I wanted to jump up, but waited to make certain that the family did not have someone in mind. When there was no response, I volunteered. I placed an African cross in his casket to accompany him on his journey to the next life. As we carried my old friend to his grave, I promised him that I would make certain that others knew about his role in the movement. I am doing that now.

During the interview, Ellis said, "Thanks, Ralph, for finding me and bringing me back to Pittsburgh. I am proud to do this, because now my children will realize that I really was involved in the most important movement of my time. Folks will see this tape, and I will be remembered."

I had asked Ewari if it had been worth the effort. "Oh HELL yes! Definitely, for my life, for my children, it has been important. I will be known as a Black man who was involved and who made mistakes, but I was there! My children will be better off and have a better sense of responsibility, because their father was in the movement. I am prepared for the other side. It has been fantastic! The Creator has blessed me with my children and my art. I had my first grandson recently. I wish I had gotten a formal education, but I did the best with what I had."

Ellis sent this message to his children: "When you see this tape, I hope you will feel the same sense of pride and strength that I felt as an African-American who was involved. Have faith, because I believe that when the people demand it, a prophet will appear." In addition to being remembered for his involvement in the movement, Ewari wanted to be remembered as an artist who created things of beauty.

The Pittsburgh Courier

Frank Bolden
War Correspondent
The Pittsburgh Courier, Reporter

Frank Bolden used the printed word as his method of achieving Black equality. Employed by *The Pittsburgh Courier* for 27 years, he used his column to push back against discrimination on all fronts. During World War II, Bolden was one of only two Black war correspondents. His printed words let the nation know how Black soldiers were being treated overseas. Later, Bolden became a well-known expert in Pittsburgh Black history.

Frank Bolden

Frank is one of those individuals who seemed to have always been in my life. He appeared as a guest on my radio and television shows and was a major source of information as I pursued my research into the civil rights movement in Pittsburgh. On more than one occasion, when I went to his house to speak with him, he had a pile of newspapers and other documents at his feet that related to the subject we were going to discuss. He could retrieve *anything* from his peculiar filing system, which consisted mainly of piles of papers and documents that took over one or more of the rooms of his house. I am also a great admirer of his wife, Nancy.

Bolden came to Pittsburgh in 1933 and found it to be much the same as southern cities in terms of its treatment of Blacks. As he recalled, "When I was an undergraduate at the University of Pittsburgh, they recruited another Colored lad so that I would have someone to talk to in Biology class. Such was the life of Blacks who attended Pitt in the 1930s. Things were pretty bad for Negroes in Pittsburgh.

Black students at Pitt could not find places to live in Oakland, where the University is located. Many of them stayed at the Centre Avenue YMCA, or in private homes in The Hill. There was no room in the inn as far as staying in Oakland was concerned. What few jobs Negroes got sometimes depended on what hue they were. Light-skinned Black women worked in powder rooms in department stores and hotels. Dark-skinned folks worked in the post office. Blacks were treated better in Washington, D.C., and Philadelphia."

Bolden graduated from the University of Pittsburgh in 1934 and told me, "After I received my degree I walked across the grass on Pitt's campus and went to see the superintendent of the public school system. The man examined my transcript and remarked that he was very impressed with my academic accomplishments. He looked up and said, 'Too bad you're not White. I would hire you right now, but we don't hire Coloreds to teach in our schools.' He thought he was being kind when he offered to make a call to one of his friends in another school district outside of Pittsburgh. He said he was certain that he could find a job for me, but not in Pittsburgh. The fact that he did not hesitate to tell me these things, to my face, shows you how powerless we were in this town!"

When I asked what he had done about the racist situation, Bolden replied, "Since I wanted to stay in Pittsburgh, I decided that I had better pursue another career. That led to my career as a journalist. In those days, if Colored folks had a burning need to teach, they went somewhere else. There was no sense in protesting. Who was going to help you?"

Bolden recalled speaking to Mayor David L. Lawrence about the fact that Blacks were barred from swimming at the city-owned Highland Park swimming pool. The mayor informed him that Blacks did not need to swim there because they had access to pools at Ammon Recreation Center and Kennard Field. Both pools were located in public housing projects. The Mayor also told Richard Jones, who was a law partner of Homer S. Brown, "If you people keep pushing on the park issue, I will see that you never become a judge." Such threats were commonplace during the early days before the Pittsburgh civil rights movement.

Ammon Swimming Pool, Hill District

"Most Blacks in Pittsburgh accepted their fate," Bolden said. "As a result, most of the progress was made, at least initially, because of people like Robert Vann and Reverend Leroy Patrick who came here from out of town. Most of the Colored leaders were class conscious, and too many leaders failed to secure the support of the people who lived in the public housing projects. You can't be a leader unless you have the support of all the people."

Bolden explained that Pittsburgh was considered to be "Up South," because of its exclusion of Blacks from meaningful participation in any aspect of daily life.

"Light-skinned Colored folks had it a little better, because they looked like White folks. More Black folks with Ph.D.s worked in the Post Office than in colleges or universities. Things were so bad that people were impressed by Colored folks who had jobs as 'Negro Aviators.' You know, Ralph," he said with a laugh, "the Black folks who operated the elevators in the downtown department stores."

"Don't get me wrong," he continued. "There were some Colored folks who had money, but those folks did not work for White folks. They had come to Pittsburgh in the early days and set up their own businesses. There were doctors, lawyers, printers, jewelers, drug store owners and people who owned small hotels, bars and nightclubs, and even a Proctor hair salon or doll hospital in the lower Hill, near Downtown.

It's sort of funny. Whites excluded Blacks from *their* world, but they sure included themselves in ours! They came to The Hill for entertainment. You could walk into the Hurricane Club or the Crawford Grill and find more White folks enjoying the music than you would find Colored folks. This was a common sight until after the riots of 1968. That scared White folks, and they stopped coming to The Hill. When they stopped coming, so did the money.

Another source of Black wealth was the numbers barons. They lived a very different life from the rest of us. They went on hunting trips and ocean cruises; had fancy cars. In fact, Tennie Harris, the renowned *Courier* photographer, was known for his fine cars. What folks didn't know was they were given to him by his brother, "Woogie," who was one of the Colored numbers kings.

There was Woogie Harris, Gus Greenlee and Mr. Robinson, who owned the Grill. They were the banks of the Black community. They sponsored the teams in the Negro Baseball League. You know Pittsburgh was the only city

William "Woogie" Harris, numbers baron (right)

to have *two Negro League teams*. We had the Pittsburgh Crawfords and the Homestead Grays. The Crawfords were named after the Crawford Grill that Mr. Robinson owned. Both the teams were financed by the numbers barons. Woogie was instrumental in giving Lena Horne her push to stardom. There are photos around here that show Woogie and a very young Lena Horne out dancing and having a good time. We probably will never know the extent to which these guys bankrolled other folks and businesses, too."

Edna McKenzie, Ph.D.
Chair, Department of Black and Minority Studies, Community College of Allegheny County (CCAC)
Association for the Study of African American Life and History, Member
Pennsylvania Historical and Museum Commission, Member

Although Edna McKenzie did not rise to fame as a civil rights leader, she was well known for her strong advocacy. As a reporter for *The Pittsburgh Courier*, she worked to rally support for the rights of Blacks. I first met Edna when she enrolled in my Black history course at the University Of Pittsburgh.

She was an older student who was contemplating a mid-life career change. Subsequently she completed a Ph.D. at the University of Pittsburgh and became a nationally recognized authority on African-American history. When she retired as a Professor Emerita from CCAC, she urged me to apply for her job, in spite of my insistence that I had no interest in working for CCAC or anyone else. She persisted, and I continue to teach at CCAC.

Dr. McKenzie, was not one to bite her tongue when she witnessed unfair treatment of Blacks. On one occasion, she was attending a meeting of the Pittsburgh Historical Society to consider how the organization could correct its history of ignoring issues important to Blacks and having no Black staff members. Although the Society had recently hired its first professional Black staff, it was still in some difficulty with the foundation community and the IRS.

As Dr. McKenzie and I entered the building, we greeted the new Black staff person. McKenzie asked him to do something for her, but the gentleman informed McKenzie and me that he would have to talk to us later because he was on his way to pick up some donuts for the meeting. "Come on, Ralph," Edna said. "We are going to pay a visit to the executive director." The executive director had barely greeted us, when McKenzie launched her protest. "How **dare** you?" She spat out the words. "You invite us here to discuss your historical lack of interest in Black folks, and we're greeted by the *only* Black professional on your staff, and he was scurrying off to buy *donuts!* That is insulting to all of us. Why would you denigrate the man by making him fetch and carry. I am appalled! What the hell were you thinking? Don't you *ever* demean him like that again." The director apologized, saying he had not given the issue any thought. Big mistake! Edna immediately launched another attack. "That's the problem with you folks. You *never* seem to consider the implications of your actions towards Blacks." She extracted a promise from the executive director that the Black professional would never be treated in such a degrading manner again.

Throughout her second career as a historian, McKenzie was a highly regarded educator who served on a variety of city, state, and national commissions and committees responsible for addressing issues of importance to Blacks.

The Multicultural Arts Initiative

The Multicultural Arts Initiative grew out of The Pittsburgh Foundation's interest in supporting the Black arts community. I credit Janet Saurbaugh, a program officer at the Foundation, with helping to launch the Initiative.

Janet Saurbaugh
The Pittsburgh Foundation, Program Officer[41]

I had read a newspaper article that The Pittsburgh Foundation was starting a program to support multi-cultural arts organizations. At the time, I had started to promote African art in the Pittsburgh public school system. I sent a letter indicating my interest in applying for a $55,000 grant to expand it. Having known Janet before she joined The Foundation staff, I was confident that my letter would receive a fair hearing.

---

41 Janet later moved to the Heinz Foundation where she worked with Phyllis Goode, the first Chairperson of Multicultural Arts Initiative.

Shortly thereafter, Janet and I spoke on the phone. "Ralph," she said, "I can't give you that much money. We don't even have that much money in our yearly budget."

Of course, this made me angry, and I fired back, "If you don't have that much money, you need to quit perpetuating the myth about supporting the African American arts community. You're just like every other organization in Pittsburgh; you profess an interest in Black art, but it's just lip service."

Alarmed by my vehement statement, Janet said it was her understanding that The Carnegie Museum of Art and other cultural organizations were interested in various forms of Black art.

"That's Bull. I've dealt with all of them and have found nothing to support the truth of your statement. But don't take my word for it. Call them; visit them; ask them to show you what they've done." When I ended our phone call, I was certain that was the last I would ever hear from Janet.

To my surprise, not long afterward, she called and said she had followed up on my suggestion. To *her* surprise, she found that none of the White-controlled cultural organizations could show that they had supported any form of Black art. She concluded the conversation saying she intended to ask the upper administration of The Pittsburgh Foundation to commit substantial funds to the new initiative.

Soon the Multicultural Arts Initiative awarded its first grants, but Blacks were not pleased. Over lunch, Janet asked me to help her understand why this was so. "Janet, The Foundation made a major miscalculation. You gave almost no funds to Black organizations. The money went to White organizations so they could do Black programming. Not only have those organizations done nothing for Black arts, they have no Blacks in their administration or Boards." Again Janet followed up and changes were made in the next round of grants.

Many years later, Janet confessed that I had scared her. Perhaps that's why she never asked me to assist with forming the Initiative.

Phyllis Moorman Goode
Member of many Boards of Directors including The Pittsburgh Foundation and Kingsley Association

I met Phyllis Moorman when I was introduced to her by a friend who lived around the corner from me. She was a very attractive young woman who owned the first Ford Mustang I had ever seen. Unfortunately, I was already dating someone when I met Phyllis. She later married Robert Goode, and the three of us became good friends.

Goode established her own reputation as an advocate for civil rights. A woman of small stature with an engaging smile and equally engaging personality, Ms. Goode was widely accepted by the White community. Her acceptance led to offers to serve in organizations that did not normally admit Blacks. Wherever she was, she used her position to advocate for Black equality. When Kingsley Association, a youth-service agency with a long history of racial discrimination, began its search for a new executive director in the 1970s, they did so without considering any Black candidates. Goode, who was on the Board of Managers, stopped the process, even though the Board had already extended an offer of employment to yet another White male. Goode told the Board that their actions were unacceptable and forced them to re-open the search. A Black was subsequently hired for the position. She has served on numerous Boards, always advocating for equality. She was the first chairperson of the Multicultural Arts Initiative of The Pittsburgh Foundation and The Howard Heinz Endowment. She was one of the first Blacks to serve on the distribution committee of The Pittsburgh Foundation.

The United Black Front

Unfortunately, few records remain of this early effort to bring together members of many of the groups fighting racial discrimination in Pittsburgh.

Clyde Jackson
United Black Front, Leader

I met Clyde when I attended my first meeting of the United Black Front. The organization was located on Wylie Avenue near Kirkpatrick Street in the Hill District, near the headquarters of the NAACP. Clyde was very close to Ewari Ellis, who helped Clyde with organizing and fund raising. Clyde presided over some pretty raucous meetings as folks jockeyed for the top spots in their respective organizations and

FIGURE 10.2

UNITED BLACK FRONT LEADERS/MEMBERS

- Phil Carter, Director of DIGIT, a Black think tank
- Ewari Ellis, Director of the Halfway Art Gallery
- Nick Flournoy, Leader of Forever Action Together
- Dr. Norman Johnson, leader of a Carnegie-Mellon University-based remedial program for Blacks and other minorities who had been admitted on a provisional basis.
- Vic Miles, Black news anchor on KDKA-TV
- Nate Smith, Leader of Operation DIG
- Sala Udin, Head of House of the Crossroads, a drug-treatment program in The Hill

The United Black Front. Soon, Clyde devoted much of his attention to Wylie Industries, a Black-owned nail factory located in the Strip District. Clyde died rather early in the movement, and both Wylie Industries and the UBF suffered as a result.

Lloyd Bell, Ph.D.
Black Construction Coalition, Member
University of Pittsburgh, Assistant Vice President

Lloyd Bell was the first Black I knew who had earned a Ph.D. Like many other young Blacks, I was very impressed with him and he inspired me to work on my own doctoral degree. Because we were both very strong-willed individuals, we had our moments of conflict when we both worked at the University of Pittsburgh. I was once told by a White member of Pitt's administration that, because of Lloyd's and my constantly pushing for the rights of Blacks, Lloyd was the most hated Black in the history of Pitt and I was the second. Eventually, we became very good friends and remained so until his untimely death. Lloyd died while in a nursing home recovering from a fall that left him paralyzed from the waist down.

Lloyd Bell was born in Cambridge, MA, and came to Pittsburgh in 1962 to finish his Ph.D. at Duquesne University. He lived on Ivy Street in Shadyside, which was Pittsburgh's answer to New York's Greenwich Village. Bell recalled, "I came here to go to school. I stayed away from Black folks for a year." Soon, however, Bell began to experience racial discrimination. He went into a store and was not served. When he asked a clerk to wait on him the man just walked away. "The neighbors on Ivy Street told one another that my roommates and I were football players, even though we carried briefcases. They said that our being football stars made us acceptable neighbors. The neighbors reported us to the police, claiming that we were using pot and playing loud music. Both charges were lies."

After graduation, Bell began to meet Blacks who were involved in the movement. "Community Action Pittsburgh was jumping. It was Pittsburgh's poverty program and was controlled by Blacks. I met Norman Johnson. I met Dave Epperson, who was the second Black man to run the agency. Folks were getting jobs without degrees. I had never seen anything like it. Blacks were controlling millions of dollars. I met Mary Lou Smith, the fiery Black leader from Beltzhoover, and Clyde Jackson of the United Black Front. I met Mobutu, Byrd Brown, Swampman Williams, Reverend Eberhart. One day Ewari Ellis showed up without an appointment and asked me what I was all about. We formed a strong and lasting friendship. It was time to join the movement. My first membership was in the Black Construction Coalition. Coming together with all the leaders was a spiritual revival for us. The connections I made then still hold today.

"While I was meeting all these really cool folks, Black students were raising hell at Pitt. They took over the University computing center and made demands concerning improving conditions for Blacks. One of their demands led to Chancellor Wesley Posvar hiring me as an Assistant Vice President. At first, the Black students didn't trust me. Posvar tried to use me against the students. That sent me on a rampage. I began to push the University to make its resources available to the community.

"At the construction site for the U.S. Steel Building, the unions had hired 'goons' dressed as construction workers to intimidate the marchers. One day my car was stolen from a public parking lot. When the car was 'recovered' and turned over to me at the pound, I got in, started the car and drove off. The first time I hit the brakes, the car *accelerated!* A sense of reality set in. What I was doing was dangerous! As you know, I had a private psychology practice that consisted almost exclusively of Black clients. One day a well-dressed White woman came into my private office and said, 'You will be in trouble if you continue doing what you are doing. Your life is in danger.' In the South, you expected this. I did not expect this to happen in Pittsburgh. Our lives, our careers were in danger. Loud-mouth Lloyd, soft-spoken Ralph, we were both in danger." I found myself laughing at that statement. I think it was the first and, probably the only time, anyone referred to me as soft-spoken.

Was it worth it? "Hell yes; it was a spiritual experience. I met and became friends with some of the finest, most dedicated Black folks in Pittsburgh. When I see the African chair you gave me, it was worth it! I'm disappointed that there are fewer Blacks at Pitt today than there were in 1968. But still, it was worth it."

How does he wish to be remembered? "As a person who had a passion for Black folks."

The United Movement for Progress

Charles "Bouie" Haden
The United Movement for Progress, Founder

Although Charles "Bouie" Haden appeared on *Black Horizons*, I did not know him well. Hayden did not have much formal education, but owned a small grocery store in Homewood that served as the headquarters of the United Movement for Progress. He was a rather large man who sported a large salt-and pepper Afro hairstyle. His tactic was direct confrontation of anyone—Black or White—who he thought was obstructing Black people's progress. He was not above cursing people out and his conversations were often laced with profanity. Because of these behaviors, Hayden was one of the movement's most controversial leaders. Many, including some established leaders of the movement had trouble acknowledging him as a leader. Despite these objections, Hayden forced people to deal with him and his organization.

Hayden founded the United Movement for Progress because he felt that some of the mainstream civil rights organizations were moving too meekly, too slowly. He was opposed to Planned Parenthood, accusing them of trying to limit the growth of the Black community by decreasing the birth rate. He published a newspaper, *The Thrust*, that he used to advocate for equal rights. Because of his in-your-face militancy, Hayden was often the target of death threats.

One of Hayden's ardent supporters was Father Charles Owens Rice, the pastor of Holy Cross Church, located not far from Hayden's grocery store. When Rice gave money to Hayden's organization, there was a backlash among many Whites who vowed never to give any more money to the Catholic Church.[42] During the riots of April, 1968, Haden, Nick Flournoy, and others put on orange sweatshirts and patrolled the Homewood area. They were trying to keep Black youth from doing anything that would put them in harm's way. Their message to the youth was "cool it!"

Although The United Movement for Progress had few followers, Hayden's vocal outbursts forced other Black groups to move more rapidly. The organization might have grown when the movement became more militant, but Hayden died in 1974. His funeral was held at Holy Cross; those in attendance reported that there were 60 cars in the funeral procession.

The Congress of Racial Equality (CORE)

It has proven a difficult to find people who were are part of the Pittsburgh chapter of The Congress of Racial Equality. This is surprising, given that CORE was one of the important national organizations and had strong chapters around the country. In Pittsburgh, however, the organization participated in a few meetings and demonstrations, but did not have much of an impact. Few even remember that the organization existed. Both Ewari Ellis, Director of Halfway Art Gallery, and Nick Flournoy, Leader of Forever Action Together, were involved in the short-lived group. The leader of the group was Bill Coles, who left Pittsburgh before he had much of a chance to recruit many members. I believe that he left to assume a position as a professor at an Ivy League university, and I was unable to locate him for this project.

The Black Panthers

Many people do not know that there was a Black Panther presence in Pittsburgh. Their headquarters were located at 574 Brushton Avenue in Homewood-Brushton. Harold Wright, a spokesperson for the group, was quoted in the April 18, 1970, edition of *The Pittsburgh Courier*:

> The National Committee to Combat Fascism, which is the organizing and political wing
> of the Panther Party, calls upon all the people of Homewood and every other Black

---

42 Whites were far more likely to "accept" mild-mannered, soft-spoken Blacks and had problems with activists like Hayden, Nick Flournoy, Harvey Adams, Nate Smith, and other more "militant" leaders. They even had problems with Byrd Brown because he was far from being a shrinking violet. Many claimed that I was "too militant" on *Black Horizons*. I thought I was rather mild-mannered under the circumstances.

community, to put an end to this wanton murder and brutality of our people. We cannot, under any circumstances, allow these atrocities to be perpetrated unpunished by the racist pig police who infest and occupy our community.

Wright was reading from an official manifesto of the Panther Party as a way of addressing the recent and historical killings of Black men by police in Pittsburgh.

The Courier also quoted Wright's comments on Pittsburgh public schools:

There will be a meeting called, very shortly, of every Black student in the city schools. The National Committee to Combat Fascism will organize the Black students, and teach them how to defend themselves, and protect themselves against the bigoted students and racist pigs, and the byword of these students hereafter is going to be: 'Arm yourselves or harm yourselves.'

I examined issues of *The Pittsburgh Courier* from 1970 to 2002 and could find no other mention of the Black Panthers in Pittsburgh. A couple of people told me there had been a shoot-out between the Pittsburgh Panthers and the police, but I was unable to verify this incident. Many people with whom I spoke said that so-called Black Panther offices around the country were actually "fronts" established by various law enforcement agencies. The purpose was to trick Blacks into joining so that a surveillance system could be set up and members could be imprisoned. I have no definitive evidence of this theory. I can only say that a Panther Party office was set up in Homewood in 1970 and then seems to have simply vanished.

The East Liberty-Homewood League for Community Improvement

The East Liberty-Homewood League for Community Improvement was formed in 1950 to fight discrimination in those neighborhoods. The group successfully won a fight to allow Blacks to swim in the Peabody High School pool during the summer months. They also succeeded in getting a Black clerk hired at the Thorofare Super Market on Frankstown Avenue in Homewood.

FIGURE 10.3

EAST LIBERTY-HOMEWOOD LEAGUE FOR COMMUNITY IMPROVEMENT

Leaders
- James Jordan, President
- Gains Bradford
- Moses Edwards
- Fred Gladney
- Fulton Johnson
- Jennie Marshall
- Louis Mason
- Russell Shelton

Members
- Lucille Carter
- Elenor Davis
- Lafayette Davis
- Isaac Groom
- Henry McCullough,
- Mansfeld Sales
- Roger Talieferro

CHAPTER 11

VOICES FROM THE FIRING LINE

Allied Community Activists

Every movement has heroes who do not claim to work with any particular group; they are known by their deeds. The individuals in this Chapter seemed ever-present at demonstrations, mass meetings, and negotiations, yet are not clearly attached to any one specific group. Often these individuals worked with multiple groups, including the NAACP, the United Negro Protest Committee, The Urban League, The Black Construction Coalition, Operation Dig, and many other groups.

Before turning to specific individuals, I want to mention the role of women during the movement. During my research, I noticed few women on the list of potential interviewees. I called Alma Speed Fox, former Executive Director of the Pittsburgh NAACP and arguably the most famous surviving member of the movement, and asked, "Where were the women?" Fox laughed and said, "In the back room, making sandwiches. But I'm only partly joking. At the beginning of the movement, most women played an important, but often behind the scene, supporting role. This was a time of transition. For the first time in the history of this country, Black males were in positions of leadership. Many Black women encouraged men to take charge. Many women played key roles that were largely hidden from view. Therefore, the Black men got the publicity and notoriety."

Unfortunately, as leaders emerged, some of the men were in direct competition with women. Sometimes the competition was friendly, sometimes it was vicious. Some men felt that Black women had been complicit in relegating Black men to secondary roles in the Black community. These men involved themselves in actions designed to keep Black women out of leadership roles. What is tragic about this view is that it played into the hands of the "massah," who devised elaborate "divide and conquer" schemes to create an environment where Blacks distrusted one another.[43] At any rate, competition between men and women for important leadership roles in the movement was quite evident.

---

43 The divide and conquer techniques had been perfected by the Portuguese in their conquest of vast areas of Africa and was transferred to the "New World" in an attempt to control slaves. Gender was one basis for the "divide." The document, "How to Make a Slave," contains a letter supposedly written by Willie Lynch, a white West Indian plantation owner. The letter detailed a plan for controlling slaves for a thousand years. This chilling document explores the depravity of the slave system and attempts to explain why even today descendants of slaves are distrustful of one another. My research indicates that the document was not written by a slave owner, but rather by a Black Think Tank using a fictitious device to raise awareness of brainwashing and psychological control. Despite the question of authenticity, the issues explored are real, and I recommend this document as reading for all Black people. https://thechallengernews.com/2019/10/willie-lynch-letter-the-making-of-a-slave/

Unfortunately, the names of many women who helped to plan and execute the movement are lost to history. I offer the following tributes in honor of the many women who served as dedicated and valiant "foot soldiers" in the war on discrimination. I am proud to count these remarkable women as colleagues, friends, and mentors.

Pauline Hall
Committed Community Activist

Pauline Hall came to Pittsburgh in 1936. "At that time, life for Blacks was the absolute pits!" She had moved from Washington, D.C. where many Blacks held fairly well-paying government jobs and could enjoy a reasonably good life. "Some Blacks in Pittsburgh did live pretty well. They lived on 'Bes Row;' those were the better off Black folks—doctors, lawyers, school teachers—who lived on Sugar Top."[44] Hall was poking a little fun at them. "Pittsburgh was weird," she continued. "Homewood folks thought they were the best. But they seldom left their own community. I lived there, too. We came to The Hill to dine and dance all night." When asked if these all-night sessions included any consumption of alcoholic beverages, she smiled, winked, and said, "I was young then. I have to say that I sure had a good time!"

Asked why she became involved, Hall replied, "I don't know what got into me. I was living high on the hog, working a good job. I guess I just had to do something! I became involved in the movement as soon as I heard about it. I was at every meeting, every protest—Heinz, Point State Park, Three Rivers Stadium, and US Steel. I was so upset about the police beating us at Three Rivers, I never went to one event there. The worst was US Steel. Harvey Adams tried to get me to go home, but I wasn't going nowhere. I still get goose bumps thinking about those creeps at US Steel dropping stuff down to hurt us. Most of us thought that nothing was going to happen during either demonstration. Boy, were we wrong. We forgot that we were 'Up South' in Pittsburgh. These showed me how ugly Pittsburgh really was."

"After the demonstrations, I went to the jail to make sure the women who had been arrested were being treated right. We had the right to be treated like human beings, and I was going to make sure that we were. There was even a bomb threat at Central Baptist Church. We were a little worried because we knew that those bastards would bomb churches."

Was it worth it? "Yes! It was great! It put me right where I belonged. Would I do it again? YES! Right this minute! If they started it again, right now, I would be right there! We have not progressed as we should have. Jim [McCoy] must be looking down on us, shaking his head and wondering why we did not go on, why we stopped working in the movement."

I had such a good time during the interview with Mrs. Hall, we made arrangements to continue the interview after she returned from a visit to the hospital to see about a growth on her jaw. As we parted, this most charming lady smiled and said, "You're sure you want to come back and hear me run my mouth again?" Unfortunately, the growth was malignant. Mrs. Hall never came home from the hospital. That was indeed a personal and professional loss. I bet she is looking down, wondering when we are going to get started again.

---

44 Sugar Top was a well-kept community, located in what was referred to as "The Upper Hill." The predominantly Black community included a small number of Whites who were not afraid to live in close proximity to Blacks. The "Sugar" tag was a reference to the "sweet life" that well-off Blacks were believed to live.

Margaret Dobbins Milliones
Founder, Pittsburgh Black Women's Forum
Among the Founders of the Black Action Society, University of Pittsburgh
Member, Pittsburgh Board of Public Education
Member, Pittsburgh Chapter, NAACP

Margaret Dobbins Milliones earned her spurs as an active, vocal participant in the southern civil rights movement during the 1960s. She remained active when she moved to Pittsburgh and married Jake Milliones, a very militant activist who became a member of Pittsburgh City Council.

I met Margaret when she was staying at the home of Bob Lavelle, a key activist in Pittsburgh's NAACP chapter. She was a rather plain-looking woman on the outside, but radiated inner beauty; she was wise beyond her years. She was a confidant for many of the "young Turks" of the Pittsburgh movement, including me.

Margaret and I rapidly developed a strong, loving friendship. She was my conscience and had a gentle way of allowing me to see the error of my thoughts, before I made a fool of myself. One time, I was berating another member of the Pittsburgh movement for his lack of courage and commitment. Margaret listened for a moment, then asked, "Ralph, have you always been as advanced as you are?" I knew I was in trouble, because that question was sort of like "have you stopped beating your wife?" I tried to get my foot out of my mouth by responding with, "I am not advanced. I am just a plain ole brother, trying to make some sense of all this!" Margaret did not buy it. "Come on, Ralph. We all think you are a bright star in the movement, but I wonder if you have always been at this stage of development, or did people forgive your mistakes and allow you a chance to grow?" Damn it, she had me trapped! I stammered, "You're right; folks did mentor me and give me a chance to develop." "Well then" she said: "Can't you give the Brother the same chance you were given?" Of course I responded affirmatively. I would have promised anything to get Margaret off my case.

We often traded war stories about our days in the southern civil rights movement. As a veteran of the Southern movement, Margaret knew the scars I carried from that experience. She helped me deal with the nightmares, and, in my most militant days, helped me to become a wiser, gentler human being.

Margaret was an excellent orator, and we participated in a number of events in Pittsburgh, often appearing on the same program, delivering talks about the movement. She had a magnificent way with words, and I regret that I didn't think to record her thoughts for posterity. She fought especially hard for education equality for Pittsburgh's Black youth. In recognition of her service to students, Herron Hill Junior High School was renamed Margaret Milliones Middle School in her honor.

Sadly, my friend died of a massive stroke all too soon. As I filed past her body at the church funeral, I wanted to scream, "Margaret, get the hell up from there. The battle isn't over. We have far too much work left to do." I wish they would have sung "We Shall Overcome," the old spiritual Margaret and I sang many times. She would have enjoyed hearing it one more time. I would have started the song myself, but my heart was too heavy.

Mal Goode
Local Radio Broadcaster
1st Black to become a national correspondent on the ABC
television network

Family Portrait with Mal Goode

Mal Goode was a member of a prominent Black Pittsburgh family. Some family members owned pharmacies; one of his sisters was known as Mary Dee, a popular local disc jockey; another sister, Ruth White, established the Sickle Cell Anemia Society. Goode was born in Virginia and came to Pittsburgh in 1908 or 1909. At first the family lived in Sewickley, then in Homestead. His father worked in the Homestead Steel Mills. Goode worked for 12 years in those same mills.

Goode recalled that Blacks and Whites lived peacefully, side-by-side in Homestead. "Despite the fact that Blacks worked in the mills, everything was not equal. Blacks got about $8-$12 an hour; Whites earned about $25. Blacks were discriminated against in *all* walks of life. I never had a Black school teacher during my years of public education. In the movie theaters in Homestead, Blacks sat on one side of the theatre; Whites on the other. There was one Black in the Homestead post office and one Black mail carrier. It was *unthinkable* to expect to see Blacks in any other capacity; most Blacks worked in the mills." Goode remembered that, because even Black college graduates could not expect to get a good position, "I hid my college class ring when I applied for jobs. I was told that if White folks knew you were educated you had almost no chance of getting the kind of jobs usually reserved for Blacks. Conditions in those days would break your will. I don't think that things have changed that much since 1932. Black ministers spoke out in church against the unfair treatment, but what could you do?"

Despite facing debilitating racism, Goode said that he was not deterred "because at home, I was taught the importance of getting an education; no Cs, Ds or Fs were allowed. My father knew Andrew Carnegie, who told him to make certain that his kids got an education. Many Blacks were not so lucky; they did give up. They lost their self-respect. They said that there was no sense trying because the doors were closed."

Goode recalled that, in the late 1940s, some Black clergy in the area were protesting racial discrimination, but he could not recall specific incidents. Pressure was increasing concerning racist activities, but most Blacks were not a part of the pressure. Most of the protest was being handled by the NAACP. The pressure increased around 1954 as a result of the Supreme Court decision (*Brown v. the Board of Education of Topeka, Kansas*) that effectively nullified the "separate but equal" doctrine. Then in 1955 there was the Montgomery bus boycott. Goode remembered with great pride the 1954 Democratic National Convention, during which Fannie Lou Hamer expressed that, in regards to racism, she was "sick and tired of being sick and tired."

Goode got into Broadcasting after a heart attack left him unable to perform strenuous physical labor. "I took a job with *The Pittsburgh Courier*. In 1950, I bought a station wagon and spent three months touring the South." During his travels he helped *The Courier* build its national circulation. Goode hosted a radio show in 1949 on KQV called *The Courier Speaks*. The show lasted one year. Subsequently, he worked for WHOD radio in Homestead. "I teamed up with my sister, Mary Dee. She was already famous as a disc jockey. I did a news show from 3:00 to 3:05 p.m. and 8:00 to 8:15 in the morning. I knew Jackie Robinson and had him on my show. In those early days, my radio show consisted largely of reading the newspaper to the audience so that listeners could know what was going on in the whole world. I wanted Pittsburgh Blacks to know that Blacks elsewhere were getting jobs and making progress. I wanted them to be encouraged that things could get better. After all, if we were getting jobs in other cities, we could do the same." Goode thought that the appointment of Homer Brown as a judge made Blacks proud.

On one occasion, Goode was allowed to read a Pepsi commercial on WTAE-TV during a sports broadcast. Normally this would have been done by Bob Prince, the voice of the Pirates, but Prince was absent. Goode never got a chance at a repeat performance, because a listener called in and asked, "Was that a Nigger you had on the air, instead of Bob Prince?" The station manager told Goode that "if there was one call, there are probably hundreds of people out there who feel the same."

After brief stints with other Pittsburgh radio stations, Goode was hired in 1962 by ABC as the first Black national newscaster. Jackie Robinson played a role in this turn of events. Robinson had appeared on an ABC program and had remarked that there were no Blacks on the station. In 1961, Robinson had come to Pittsburgh to speak at a Jewish organization function. Goode drove Robinson to the airport after the talk. "It was during that drive that Robinson told me that ABC was looking for a Black reporter and suggested that I apply." Goode called about the position in May; in July he was one of eight finalists; he was hired in August. "It sent tingles up my spine as I realized what this could mean to Blacks in this country."

"My first assignment was to interview the Ambassador of Iran. Five weeks later, on October 25th, the world was shown surveillance photographs of Russian missiles in Cuba and the Cuban Missile Crisis burst on the international scene. I was assigned to cover the crisis. The White reporter to whom this coverage would ordinarily be assigned was on a hunting trip and could not be located. No one else was available, so they assigned the story to me. I appeared 17 times on national television covering this story. I was so proud, and I believe that Blacks in Pittsburgh were also proud." Goode was correct: the Pittsburgh Black community celebrated Goode's success as if it was their own. Goode spent eleven years with ABC.

New Black reporters sought Goode out and asked for his advice. He mentored the next two generations of broadcast journalists, including Ed Bradley.

Was it all worth the effort? Goode responded: "Sure! One of the joys of my life was seeing a large number of Blacks get jobs on national television, and I played a role in that happening. I would suggest that those who have risen in this country maintain a sense of calmness, because you did not do it by yourself. How would I like to be remembered? I tried to do the best I could, with the talent that God gave me, to open doors and encourage others and inspire them, because we are a *Great* people."

Charles Greenlee, M.D.

Charles Greenlee came to Pittsburgh in 1932 and found living here not much different from living in Mississippi. "We had to sit in the balcony at theatres. I was from the South, where we had to ride in the back of the bus. My family simply would not ride on those buses. Banks did not make loans to Black people, regardless of the amount of money they had or their social status. My brother, Gus, was a numbers baron. He had enough money so that he could protect me against racism. He and "Woogie"

Harris financed the Negro Baseball League's Pittsburgh Crawfords and the Homestead Grays. They also helped finance many Black businesses that were turned down by these racist banks."

After he returned from medical school and a stint in the United States Army, Greenlee set up practice in the Black community, where he stayed until he retired. He could have moved to an affluent neighborhood, but that was not his style. Dr. Charles Greenlee was my physician for more years than I can remember. During many of my appointments we would discuss the plight of Blacks. His wife, who worked as his receptionist, was always chastising me. "Listen, Ralph, you are a bad influence on him. He saves up all the corny jokes he heard since the last time you were here, because he knows you will crack up. I have sick people out there waiting to see Charles, and all they hear is you two in here laughing your asses off!" Hey, he *was* a good joke teller. Doc and his office staff also took delight in teasing one another, especially if it was at my expense. When Doc found his nurses talking to me, he'd say, "Listen, honey, I know Ralph is smooth and cute and all that, but don't become too interested in him; he is a hell of a lot older than he looks!" All of us really loved this good-hearted man.

Dr. Greenlee was a quiet giant, working behind the scenes, advising leaders, and providing monetary support. He railed against Planned Parenthood, proclaiming that it was practicing genocide on the Black community. His greatest contribution, however, was his challenge of The University of Pittsburgh School of Medicine's discriminatory admissions policies. At the time, only a specified number of Blacks (and women) were accepted for each year's class. If they had filled their quota of women or Blacks, no more would be admitted even if they more qualified than White applicants. When the University would not change that policy, Dr. Greenlee successfully challenged the University's right to receive federal funding. When the federal funds were stopped, the University lifted the discriminatory quota system. As a result of his persistence, Black people now enjoy a better opportunity to attend the University of Pittsburgh School of Medicine.

Greenlee and Bob Bolden made another important medical contribution to Pittsburgh Blacks. They wrote the proposal that resulted in the establishment of the Alma Illery Health Center that still serves the medical needs of the residents of the Homewood area.

Why did he become involved in the movement, when he could not benefit from it? "Because I am my father's son. In North Carolina, where I was born, White folks searched Black's homes anytime they wanted to, but not my Dad's. He would have killed them. He saved enough money to send me to college. He believed that Whites accepted educated Blacks. That was one of the few times he was wrong. If it was not for my family, I would have wound up working in J&L Steel Mill." He then drew a parallel between himself and Byrd Brown. "Byrd's family insulated him against racism, as well, but he still became a powerful leader."

When asked whether the struggle of the civil rights movement had been worth it, Dr. Greenlee responded with a very emphatic "NO." He felt that the efforts we all had put forth had not been rewarded with sufficient gains. He questioned whether we gained as much as we lost, as a result of integration. Of all the people interviewed for the oral history project, Greenlee was the only one to express this sentiment.

Greenlee felt that the movement failed because Whites retained economic control. "You notice that as soon as King spoke out against economic injustice, he was killed." Greenlee pointed out that the incarceration of Blacks increased dramatically when Whites found that fortunes could be made by building prisons. "It's all about money. We seem to have gone backwards economically. We controlled more money and had more businesses before integration. Organization without economics is a failed effort."[45]

Greenlee also felt that part of the failure was our own. "Most of us have not kept the faith. We would be better off if we went back to when we had our own businesses. It took hundreds of years of slavery to get us thinking the same way. We lost that during the civil rights movement. It was everybody for themselves. If we are to make some progress, we need to take White folks off the walls of our churches and put Black folks on them. How can you be free if you worship a White God?"

Morton "Moe" Coleman, Ph.D.
University of Pittsburgh, School of Social Work, Professor
Pittsburgh Board of Education, Member
Technical advisor to the Pittsburgh Poverty Program

Morton "Moe" Coleman spent his adult life working for the equality of all people. As a Jew, this battle was not really his; as a White man, he could have remained uninvolved. With quiet modesty, he worked behind-the-scenes as an advisor for business and government leaders. His calm, reasoned voice caused others to weigh his advice very heavily. Unlike many Whites, Coleman did not base his advice on what *he thought* Blacks deserved or needed. His advice came from Blacks from all walks of life who trusted him as a friend. He quietly opened doors through which many of us were able to walk. He served on many boards and organizations. Coleman never hesitated to speak out, privately or publicly, about the evils of racism.

"I remember Pittsburgh as a very segregated city. As a social worker for Hill House Association and Kingsley House, I saw the racism. Both were settlement houses meant to serve Blacks. Ironically, Kingsley House was initially a racist organization. It was established in 1863, but refused to serve Blacks until the 1950s. I found that out the hard way when I took an all-Black basketball team to Kingsley and was forced to beat a hasty retreat by Italian youth who did not want Blacks in their community. Funny, later I accepted a job at Kingsley House. I worked hard to help integrate the organization. Ralph, you are now the executive director of Kingsley. In 1950, they would not have even hired you to be a social worker. I guess things do change."

Moe was reading a report on economic conditions for Blacks in Allegheny County when it occurred to him that something was amiss. The data showed conditions to be relatively good. Coleman approached the author and suggested that the statistics didn't accurately represent the situation. He urged the author to look more closely at the same issues from the perspective of Blacks. A new, revised report showed that Blacks in Allegheny County were far worse off than had been originally thought. In fact, of 50 comparable U.S. cities, Pittsburgh was far worse in its treatment of Blacks and women.

Coleman observed that the civil rights movement in Pittsburgh was different from other major cities. "One of the problems was the way Blacks were forced to settle in Pittsburgh. In other cities, there was usually one Black community. In Pittsburgh there were several, so the movement had a distinctive neighborhood flavor. Each of these distinct communities developed their own leadership. This sometimes made it difficult to mount coordinated, city-wide efforts. Knowing this, members of

45 Despite his distrust of the "system," Greenlee felt that "President Johnson was the best president Black folks ever had." At the time Barack Obama had not been elected.

city government and the corporate community often tried to exploit the differences among leaders of the various neighborhoods. I saw that very clearly when I was working for the mayor."

"There were some bright spots" he continued. "The Pittsburgh Poverty Program, under the leadership of a Black attorney, Dave Washington, was significant in the advances made by Blacks in Pittsburgh. While it did not directly change corporate America, it did provide Blacks with the education and experience to take advantage of jobs that were opened up by the federal Equal Employment Opportunities Act. It created managerial opportunities in government and industry where few such opportunities existed. It broke down some barriers to better jobs for Blacks; developed its own patronage system; became one of the largest employers in Pittsburgh; provided jobs for people who had no degrees, and gave Blacks entry to board rooms of government and educational institutions. Another important aspect of the program was that it taught poor people to organize and make demands. Some Black middle class elite came out of the poverty program. It was an important training ground for poor and Black people, even if it did not eliminate poverty in America, as it was hoped."

When asked why he became involved in a movement, Moe replied, "Two things. I could not understand inequality and self-serving. My sense, as a Jew, is that if any group is oppressed, so are we. Fairness to Jews depends upon fairness to all groups in society." Responding to the question as to what happened to the strong Black/Jewish relationship that developed during the civil rights movement, Coleman said, "The split came over Affirmative Action. Blacks became angry with Jews who operated businesses in ghettos but failed to hire Blacks. Blacks also were surprised and angered when they discovered that some of the worst slum landlords in urban ghettos were Jews. Jews became angered by what they perceived as quotas in the Affirmative Action Program. Another problem was the issue of Israel. Blacks identified primarily with the Arabs who had been displaced by the Jews. If news came across the airways about some act by Israeli Jews, Blacks sided with the Arabs. Many Jews have anti-Black feelings, and many Blacks have anti-Jewish feelings."

Speaking about the civil rights movement, Colman remembered, "Everyone, Black or White, had a role to play if they chose to do so. Whites, while welcome, had to be reminded that they could not lead the movement. Many Whites were placatory of the system. You could not be that and still be an effective advocate. Byrd Brown was an excellent leader because he was comfortable on the street and in corporate headquarters. We did not make as much progress as we had hoped. One of the problems was the White backlash. When the movement moved from opportunity goals to results goals, many Whites became uncomfortable because they were going to have to compete with Blacks for jobs that once automatically went to them. Jobs in this region became more scarce as the world economy changed. We began to lose thousands of jobs in the steel industry and manufacturing. Now Whites realized that they were competing with Blacks for an increasingly smaller piece of the pie. We are probably more segregated today than we were in 1968; issues of class and racism have combined to form a formidable barrier to Black progress."

Was it worth it? "Oh, yeah!" came the enthusiastic response. "The 1960s were a real high! I would not have missed it for the world. We had good times. I would do it all over again, but would focus on insuring institutional changes. We could have permanently changed educational institutions. We could have tried to imbed certain things of permanence. We had to break down segregation, but perhaps we needed to place more emphasis on valuing one another's cultures. One of my greatest disappointments was the fact that the changes we made were not sustained. I would suggest that the struggle for equality never ends and would urge people to get out and do something."

How would Moe Coleman choose to be remembered? "He did his best." Indeed he did. I cannot claim that I am unbiased about this man because I am not. Moe has been my friend for as long as I can remember, and was there for my triumphs and tragedies. When I was down and felt I had no strength left to fight, Moe was there to help me discover some small pocket of strength I did not know I had. From the very beginning of this oral history project, Moe encouraged me and affirmed its worth, even when my own alma mater, the University of Pittsburgh, had no interest in it.

Thomas Kerr, Attorney
Carnegie Mellon University, Professor
American Civil Liberties Union, Board Member
Mayor's Commission on Human Relations, Member

Thomas Kerr was one of the White people who put his career in a prestigious Pittsburgh law firm on the line by becoming involved in a movement. Other members of his family also became involved, and he told me, "I listened with a profound sense of horror and anger as my son related how police surrounded his car, began breaking the windows, and threatened my son and his friends. The boys were simply driving near the scene of a demonstration. The police attacked their car when they saw that the boys had long hair. This brought home, with clarity, the many stories I had heard from Black people who spoke about unprovoked attacks from Pittsburgh's finest."

The law firm for which Kerr worked was afraid that clients might not be too pleased with Kerr's public posture in the area of Black equality. Nor were they pleased about his vocal, public opposition to the Viet Nam war. He was given a choice of ceasing his activities or leaving the firm. Kerr chose the latter, and became a law professor for Carnegie Mellon University.

When asked why he risked so much to become involved in a movement, Kerr replied, "I was a member of the First Unitarian Church in Shadyside. The church and the ACLU were looking into the unfair treatment of Blacks in Pittsburgh. The church put up its property to secure the bail for arrested demonstrators. Some individual members of the congregation also put their houses up to secure bails. I and other members of the ACLU became involved in monitoring the arrest and incarceration of demonstrators. Apparently the police were riding around at demonstrations attempting to intimidate demonstrators. I had no moral choice but to become involved."

"I also became involved in addressing problems of *de facto* school segregation. While southern U.S. school systems were segregated by virtue of Jim Crow laws, no such laws existed in Pittsburgh. But schools were, in fact, just as segregated as those below the Mason/Dixon Line, because of segregated housing practices. Students went to so-called 'neighborhood schools.' The problem, of course was that the neighborhoods were very segregated. The Pittsburgh Public School Board condoned the practice. Members of the board were appointed by the Judge of Common Pleas. While this group of 'elite' individuals determined the fate of thousands of Black kids, they sent *their* children to private schools. In the meantime, they used the public school system to train Blacks for the lowest positions in the steel mills. My daughter came home one day and reported that a White teacher had forced a Black youngster to stand in front of the class and eat a part of a paper airplane he had constructed. There were confrontations over a White teacher who seemed to take delight in paddling Black girls. Black teachers were barred from teaching in White schools. I had a friend, Bob Cook; he was Black and was a fine leader in the Head Start program. Cook was appointed, under pressure, as the principal of Frick Elementary School, in Oakland. The White parents mounted a strong protest against their children having a Black principal. The Board offered Cook little support. Cook retired over this situation and the district lost an excellent educator."

As further proof of racial discrimination in Pittsburgh, Kerr mentioned, "None of the three daily newspapers had any Blacks employed in any capacity except as janitors. The bus companies had no Black drivers. Most businesses and government offices refused to hire Blacks. As a result, there appeared to be a demonstration at noon nearly every day in Pittsburgh. During some of the demonstrations, Pittsburgh police harassed the marchers and were extremely pleased when they were able to arrest someone. Some of the most abusive officers did not wear badges at demonstrations in order to prevent marchers from identifying them."

"There were many examples of employees of picketed businesses harassing the demonstrators. Construction workers carried guns to construction sites. Some of them dropped hot rivets from lofty perches, as they tried to intimidate and harm the marchers. Employees of Duquesne Light Company dropped water-filled paper bags and condoms on people. The trouble did not stop once the companies began to hire Blacks. Some cases came before the Mayor's Human Relations Commission. In one case a young Black man who was hired by the carpenter's union returned to the union headquarters each night to find a hangman's noose in his locker. He quit. In another incident, each time a Black man who was hired by a large bank went to the bathroom, the employees gathered outside the stall and told loud, racist jokes."

"Pittsburgh trade unions were no friends of Blacks. They kept Blacks out of unions by claiming that Blacks were unqualified. The White union members passed on their memberships to sons, cousins and nephews. All the jobs building Three Rivers Stadium and The United States Steel building went to White-controlled unions.(See Chapter 18 for additional details.)

Kerr recalled that many college professors and students participated in the demonstrations. The University of Pittsburgh Chapter of the NAACP was at many of the demonstrations. Many students picketed the U.S. Steel construction site. A CMU professor lay in front of one of the construction trucks.

Did he fear for his life? "Yes. During one demonstration, a White cop pushed me out of the picket line and into the path of an oncoming truck on Grant Street. I received several death threats. One evening, we had the leader of the Pittsburgh Realty Board to our house for dinner. We were trying to get the realtors to stop discriminating against Blacks. While we were speaking, the phone rang. Our son, David, had been in a demonstration at the Pittsburgh Hilton. He got arrested and was beaten up by the police. My wife fainted dead away."

When asked whether progress had been made as a result of the movement, Kerr said, "There were relative advances, but we were not completely successful. There are new laws to protect against discrimination, but the problems continue. The problems abated for a time, only to rise again. Each generation must be willing to speak out. We must work against discrimination all the time. It must become an integral part of our lives."

Was it worth the effort? "Oh, absolutely! It was fun. This was *living*. This was action! It had many benefits on a personal basis as well. My son said to his friends and siblings, 'We can't use drugs, because if we get arrested, it will reflect on the work that Mom and Dad are doing'."

How does he wish to be remembered? "As a member of a family that worked together and shared the experience of fighting discrimination together." Kerr died in February of 2006. According to his obituary, published in the *Pittsburgh Post-Gazette*, the American Civil Liberties Union had conferred the title of "Mister Civil Liberties" on Kerr when he was honored in 1995. The title fit him. So does the honor bestowed on him by the Freedom Corner Monument Committee, which enshrined his name on its monument in The Hill District.

Philip B. Hallen
Maurice Falk Foundation, Executive Director
United Negro Protest Committee, Member
Pittsburgh Chapter of the NAACP, Member

Philip B. Hallen was a White man who dedicated his life to the elimination of racism. Although some were wary of him, I can say he was a true friend of the movement. Late in his life, Malcolm X concluded that Whiteness and Blackness were found in the heart, not on the skin. From that perspective, I have always been proud to call Phil Hallen "Brother."

Hallen used his position as Executive Director of the Maurice Falk Medical Fund to fund many seminars, conferences, and meetings addressing the issue of racism. He funded mental health initiatives, believing neither perpetrators nor victims of racism could enjoy mental health. He contributed funds to the PBS civil rights Documentary, *Eyes on The Prize*. Black people and organizations always knew that they could count on Hallen for moral and financial support. One of his most innovative and lasting contributions was supporting the creation of Freedom House Ambulance Service.

As a Jew who had a sense of what it was like to be a minority, Phil's first physical involvement came on the national level. Through the Falk Foundation, he purchased trucks filled with medical supplies, food, books, and other items needed by people who had been evicted for participating in Mississippi's voter registration movement. Hallen risked bodily harm by driving one of the vehicles himself.

Was he ever afraid? "No, not when I was working with Pittsburgh groups, but it was frightening to drive those trucks through Mississippi." He said that we had made some progress, but thought there needed to be an institution to conduct research in race relations. "Too many people relaxed after passage of civil rights legislation. They thought the battle was over, but it was just beginning. Some of the same problems we fought during the 1960s are still here today. Despite all the picketing, demonstrations, and legislation, we did not change many minds. Oh yes, we made progress, on some levels. Many individuals made tremendous strides, but life for the masses has not really changed that much."

Was it worth it? Hallen smiled and asked, "What else would I have been doing? I would certainly do it over again, but with more vigor and insight!"

Sala Udin
Founder and Director of a drug prevention and treatment program called Ille Elegba which means "the house of the crossroads" in the West African Yoruba language
Pittsburgh City Council, Member

Sala Udin was from a large family, many of whom were involved in important issues that impacted the Black community in Pittsburgh. Unfortunately, Sala left Pittsburgh during the height of civil rights activities and returned when the movement was in its decline as a mass movement.

Formerly known as Sam Howze, he adopted the name of Sala Udin Saif Salaam, which is Arabic for "seeker of wisdom, sword of truth." Later, he shortened his name to Sala Udin. Udin spent most of the civil rights years in Mississippi, where he was beaten and arrested. He was a trusted friend and assistant to City Council member Jake Milliones. In the 1990s, after he was elected to fill the late Milliones' City Council seat, Udin completed Milliones' dream to erect a monument to the Pittsburgh civil rights movement. The monument, "Freedom Corner," is located on Centre Avenue in the lower Hill district.

Glenn R. Mahone, Attorney
1st Black Attorney hired by Reed Smith law firm
1st Black partner, served two terms on the firm's Executive Committee

Glenn R. Mahone served as a US Army Combat Engineer Platoon Leader during the Vietnam War. In Pittsburgh, he was a well-known member of the legal community, respected for his quiet, dignified stewardship of many organizations. In his capacity as a partner in Reed Smith, he served as a mentor to many young Black attorneys.

Although I had known Glenn for many years, I did not include him in the 1st edition of this book. In part, I was not sure where he best fit as he was a ubiquitous figure in the civil rights movement. Among the many positions he held were:

- Founding Member of the Penn Hills Chapter of the NAACP
- Sheridan Broadcasting Corporation, Shareholder, President and Chief Operating Officer
- National Association of Broadcasters, Board Member
- Radio Advertising Bureau, Board Member
- Duquesne University, Trustee
- Westminster College, Trustee
- Urban League of Pittsburgh, Member/Chair
- Mathews International Corporation, Board Member
- Allegheny County Airport Authority, Chairman for 13 years
- Manchester/Bidwell Corporation, Board Member/Chair
- University of Pittsburgh School of Social Work, Member Board of Visitors
- Virginia State University, Rector (Chair) of Board of Visitors

Through his involvement in these many organizations, Glenn met and helped uncountable numbers of men and women who were also fighting for equality and justice. I have included Glenn here as a way of honoring not just him, but the thousands and thousands of unnamed warriors in the civil rights movement.

CHAPTER 12

VOICES FROM THE FIRING LINE

Government-Related Allies

The Pittsburgh Black Guardians

This group, established by Black officers in the Pittsburgh police force, was formed in opposition to the all-White Pittsburgh Fraternal Order of Police (FOP).

William "Muggsy" Moore
Appointed Pittsburgh's 1st Black Chief of Police

William "Muggsy" Moore was among the few Black officers on the Pittsburgh police force when he was hired in 1951. Bill was a frequent guest on my television program. I admired his tenacity and his willingness to risk his position with the police force in order to protect marchers against those who would hurt them. We soon became friends.

Moore recalled that discrimination and segregation were an everyday part of being Black

Police Officers with William "Mugsy" Moore (right), first Black Pittsburgh Police Chief

in Pittsburgh. "There was nowhere to go outside your own community where racism did not confront Blacks at every turn in the road. When Jackie Robinson played against the Pittsburgh Pirates, he had to get a room at the Centre Avenue YMCA, because no White-owned hotel would admit him. Black youth watched their parents being denied the opportunity to eat hot dogs at five-and-dime stores in downtown Pittsburgh. When a man went into Adam's Hat Shop on Fifth Avenue, he better know the exact size of the hat he wanted to buy, because once the hat was on his head, he was required to purchase it. Black men couldn't try on suits; Black women couldn't try on dresses. Of course, trying on swim suits was out of the question. Blacks couldn't swim in public pools in White communities. Of course, we were never hired as life guards at these pools. When Blacks integrated Highland Park Pool, some Blacks were injured by renegade White thugs. The city assigned police to help Blacks at the pool, but the Black swimmers were inside; the cops were outside. The White officers were assigned in pairs; the Black cops stood by themselves. One of the Black officers was attacked and injured by an angry crowd of White hoodlums."

"When I got out of the military service, I went to college at West Virginia University. I left after three years, because my mother became ill. I returned home to help take care of her. I got a job in the mill, which was normal for Blacks. I also put in several civil service applications. I applied for security positions, jobs at the post office, the Liquor Control Board, the fire department, and the police department. I became a cop because the police department was the first to offer me a job. Back then Black police were hidden. They were assigned to 'Night turn,' back beats at night. They could not ride in or drive squad cars. They were denied access to jobs in the Investigation Unit. A day job for a Black cop meant cleaning or painting the police station. We had no power."

In 1967, to fight the daily disrespect and discrimination, Black officers formed the Black Guardians. "The purpose of the organization was to advocate for Black officers and to protect the Black public. The White officers were distrustful and frightened by the Black officers coming together. Yet none of these White officers were concerned that Blacks were not elected as officers of the FOP. If Black officers were brought before the Police Trial Board, they were always found guilty. White officers who committed the same infractions never had charges filed against them. Many charges brought against White officers were for brutality against Blacks. Although most of those charges were justified, the White cops always walked away without even a slap on the wrist."

Moore also maintained that the White police establishment practiced psychological brutality against Blacks. "The police brass allowed speak-easys [illegal after-hours joints that served liquor], numbers, street prostitution, drugs, and gambling to flourish in the Black community. This kind of activity was not tolerated in White areas."

In 1986, Moore became the first and for many years the only Black Police Chief of the Pittsburgh Police Department. "Glen Cannon, the Public Safety Director, wanted me to be a figure-head, while he ran the department. I was not about to let that happen.. He excluded me from meetings dealing with the Police Department. I had a verbal confrontation with him in order to get him to back off. I spent a lot of time being angry. Here I was trying to help Black cops and Black people, and I was surrounded by racists in blue uniforms. The reputation of the Pittsburgh Police Department was so bad, I had a hard time convincing many Blacks that I was not like all the White cops or even some of the bad Black cops, who were just as oppressive as the bad White ones. When many Blacks looked at me they saw the blue uniform before they saw my Black skin!"[46]

Was it worth it? "Yes, yes! To have been a part of it and see the changes we made in the system made it well worth the effort. I would do it all over again. The movement will come again, because we have not yet achieved full equality. The so-called 'War on Drugs' really means a war on Blacks, an excuse to crack Black heads. You can't stop drugs by arresting street dealers. Drugs can only be stopped at our borders, and we are not doing that. We use catch phrases for political purposes, and all the while, the

---

46 This sentiment was expressed by many Black male and female officers with whom I spoke.

police department treats the White community differently." Moore wants to be remembered as a man who did the best he could for his fellow man, Black or White.

Herman Mitchell

Black Guardians, Founding Member and 1st President
Pittsburgh Police Department, Commander
Program to Aid Citizen Enterprise (PACE),[47] Board Member

I met Herman Mitchell when he was a young police officer assigned to The Hill. I admired his courage in addressing the evils of Pittsburgh's racist establishment. We soon became friends.

Throughout his tenure as a police officer, whether as a rookie or, eventually, a commander, Mitchell was a champion of the rights of Blacks. He participated in demonstrations and used his position to protect the marchers. He was at constant odds with his superiors on the police force because of his advocacy for Black officers.

Mitchell's first encounter with racism came when he was in the Army during the 1950s. "I went into a restaurant in Maryland, where a red-faced White woman screamed, 'We don't serve your kind here!'

Herman Mitchell, one of the early Black Police Officers

Things were more subtle in Pittsburgh when I returned from Korea in 1954. Most good jobs were closed to Blacks, but I was now married and tried everything I could in order to support my family. Ralph, don't laugh, but I sold typewriters and vacuum sweepers! I worked for H.J. Heinz and Kaufmann's. I was not able to get a job as a press operator, even though I had training in the profession. All the press operator jobs were union controlled, and the unions did not admit Blacks. I answered ad after ad, only to have doors slammed in my face; it was degrading, and I was really pissed off. I had put on a uniform and served my country well. All I was doing was trying to feed my family, and every door was shut in my face. Finally, I took the civil service exam and, two and a half years later, in 1958 I was hired as a Pittsburgh police officer. I wanted to be certain that Black folks did not get hurt by anyone. I marched in several demonstrations, because I wanted to protect demonstrators from rogue police who were intent on harming marchers."

Conditions on the force reflected the racism of Pittsburgh. "White officers resented my presence. I wanted to be a motorcycle cop, but apparently having one Black motorcycle cop [Karl Jackson] was enough for the department. Sure Blacks were being hired, but we were not treated the same as White officers. I'm positive that I and other Blacks would have risen rapidly through the ranks, had it not been for the color of our skin."

---

47 PACE made grants primarily to small Black not-for-profit organizations that would have never been funded by mainstream funders..

National Alliance of Postal Workers

Few Pittsburghers have heard of this group, probably because its focus was achieving equal rights for postal workers. For many years, the United States Postal Service was one the few employers of a large number of well-educated Black folks. In fact, I often heard colleagues say the post office employed more Black Ph.D.s than most universities.

Roland Saunders
National Alliance of Postal Workers, President
United Negro Protest Committee, Member
Program to Aid Citizen Enterprise, Board Member
Congress of Federal Organizations, President

Roland Saunders was born in Pittsburgh; his family lived at the junction of Watt Street and Webster Avenue. He and I attended the same elementary school. In those early years, he was more of a "tormentor" than a friend. He and his older brother took delight in playing "the dozens"[48] on me as I passed their home.

Roland recalls, "Black Pittsburghers were treated badly as far back as I can remember. As a youngster, I was not aware just how bad it was. As I look back on it now, it was really bad. I attended Watt Street School. All but one of the teachers was White. At Schenley High School there was a White guidance counselor, Mrs. Pittler. She was noted for advising Black students to go trade school and not even apply to college. One can only wonder how many Blacks lived in abject poverty and hopelessness because of the 'advising' of this racist woman and the many other so-called advisors who dashed the hopes of Black students all over America."

Saunders said, "Most Blacks simply accepted the bad treatment. There were no Jim Crow signs hanging around Pittsburgh, so most Blacks felt better off than southern Blacks and just didn't make any waves. People would talk about the racism in Pittsburgh, but did not confront the system. Racism was sort of tolerated. I worked for a restaurant, B&G Foods, but I couldn't go to the other side of the counter and get served. Mom said that I had to be twice as good as White folks to get ahead."

Saunders went on to explain that there was a difference between his generation and those who came before. The younger generation, whose school years spanned from about 1943 till 1956, did not as easily accept the discrimination, and many became active, militant civil rights workers. "I think our parents helped to raise our consciousness, and we eventually decided to confront the system."

"I jumped into the movement right after military service by joining the National Alliance of Postal Workers. I became the leader of the Black postal workers. I'd see supervisors walk past sleeping White workers, but write up a sleeping Black worker. I am not saying that the Black man's behavior was right, but if you are going to discipline Black folks, you better damn sure discipline the offending White ones as well. I was there for all the demonstrations—Duquesne Light, the Board of Education, all of them. The demonstration at the downtown U.S. Steel Building was a dangerous place. The construction workers came armed with handguns and tried to injure the marchers by dropping hot rivets and other objects on

---

48 "Dozens" was a verbal sparring game in which participants traded outrageously exaggerated insults about each other's mothers. The rules of the game included verbal signals to keep the game going or to end it. Far from being mean-spirited, the game was meant to help young Blacks to become tough in the face of verbal abuse.

them. They even tried to urinate on us. But I had no choice about protesting, unless I wanted to continue to be denied my rights. I was never denied because I was Roland Saunders, but I was constantly denied because I was a Black man. When I was involved in the movement, I never sought a job for myself. I was trying to end a condition, resolve a problem that could not keep occurring."

"I also became involved with the United Negro Protest Committee. It was the best thing I ever did, because I got to meet and work with Jim McCoy and Nate Smith. Jim developed a lot of leaders." Saunders also served for ten years on the Board of PACE (Program to Aid Citizen Enterprise). The program was started as a result of The United Way's funding patterns. Black leaders proved that small Black organizations had almost no chance of getting funds from mainstream funders. PACE solved the problem by getting funds from United Way and distributing them in a much more inclusive manner. Many well-established Black organizations owe their existence to the funding provided in their early days by PACE.

As a result of his civil rights activities, Saunders often received threatening phone calls. He laughed as he recalled that, in demonstrations, he was frequently standing next to Alma Fox, the feisty executive director of the Pittsburgh NAACP. "That was a dangerous place to be. Alma was always doing something wild. Through it all, I never really thought about my personal safety. There were times when we just could not seem to get all folks on the same page, like during the 1968 riots when some hot-headed young Blacks burned down the Mainway Super Market. They didn't know that the UNPC was getting ready to buy it and use it for the benefit of the community. What a shame!"

When asked about the important leaders of the movement, Saunders said, "Byrd Brown, James McCoy, Alma Fox, Matthew Moore, Reverend Patrick." Those names were no surprise, but the next part was a complete shock—"and you, Ralph. Your show, *Black Horizons*, was very important. Few regular media folks would allow us to tell our story, but you did; you kept folks informed about the issues. Besides, I think I remember you at a few demonstrations."

In the final analysis, was it worth it? "Oh, yeah! We can all look back, collectively, and be proud. We eliminated the 'White only' ads that were the norm in Pittsburgh newspapers. We busted up a bunch of discrimination practices; we got jobs and careers for Black folks. We did well. While I am disappointed that so many of us never became involved in any way, if I had to do it again, I would be right there. I might do some things a little smarter, but I wouldn't have missed it for a million dollars." Hopefully, I'll be remembered "as a person who dedicated his life to make life better for all of us."

The Congress of Federal Organizations (COFO)

This was an organization that started in Washington, D.C. and comprised employees of the Federal government. I do not know how many other chapters there were, but I recall a Pittsburgh chapter was started, did not become very active, and lasted for only a short time. Roland Saunders served as President and Alma Fox as Vice President.

The Mayor's Commission on Human Relations

Now called The Pittsburgh Commission on Human Relations, this organization was created to enforce the anti-discrimination laws passed by City of Pittsburgh government. We in the movement used the legal powers of the Commission to investigate organizations and individuals for discrimination based on race, gender, family status, age, religion, and sexual orientation. The commission has the power to fine those who commit discrimination, as well as prescribe other remedies such as awarding back pay and issuing cease-and-desist orders.

FIGURE 12,.1

MAYOR'S COMMISSION ON HUMAN RELATIONS

- Reverend Leroy Patrick, Commissioner
- Alma Speed Fox, Commissioner
- Ralph Proctor, Commissioner
- Attorney Byrd Brown, Solicitor

Additional Organizations

The Pennsylvania Commission on Human Relations was a state-wide, anti-discrimination group that investigated alleged discrimination against individuals from protected classes.

Equal Employment Opportunities Commission (EEOC) was the federal organization that investigated charges of employment discrimination.

Community Action Pittsburgh was popularly known as the "poverty program." Its purpose was to end poverty by changing the nature of American institutions by providing "maximum feasible participation" of the poor. Many civil rights veterans were employed by the program, thus the programs often challenged racial discrimination. When the country became involved in the Viet Nam War, this program was gutted and became a mere shadow of its former self.

Model Cities was another ill-defined federal program that entered the scene with a whimper, competed with and duplicated many of the services offered by Community Action Pittsburgh and had little, or no, impact on the lives of Black folks.

SECTION 3

FIGHTING THE JIM CROW CULTURE IN PITTSBURGH INSTITUTIONS

Demonstration at the Civic Arena

In the years from 1963 to 1968 so many protests occurred that it is difficult to account for all of them. This section offers glimpses into the types of actions that were taken to combat Jim Crow culture in the media, housing, education, employment, banking, health care, the criminal justice system, and retail/entertainment. I weave my own experiences with those of others to convey a sense of resistance. In a number of cases, I also draw upon accounts published in *The Pittsburgh Courier*.

Protest in Downtown Pittsburgh, including Vince Wilson, Father Donald McIlvane, Charles Kindle & Mathew Moore

CHAPTER 13

FIGHTING JIM CROW CULTURE

Fighting for the Right to Swim

"I always knew that Blacks were not permitted to swim in Kennywood Park. I never thought of that as being racism; I thought that was just the way things were."

– LOUIS "HOP" KENDRICK

For many years we were prohibited from swimming in the nicer public pools. We were forced to swim in pools located in or near public housing projects or a few public pools such as the County-owned pool in South Park. This pool was called "The Ink Well," because of the claim that Black swimmers dirtied the water. There was a pool in Kennywood Amusement park that refused to allow Blacks to swim. When Blacks attempted to swim in pools where they were not welcome, they were often beaten by mobs of angry Whites. In many cases the police stood by and watched the beatings without taking action to save the Black citizens or arresting the White thugs.

It may seem frivolous to begin writing about resistance to discrimination at a swimming pool. After all, a recreational activity is not as essential as housing, education, employment, or medical care. Yet many believe the civil rights movement in Pittsburgh began in 1931 when protests erupted over the banning of Blacks from the city's newly opened, public swimming pool in Highland Park. Thus, this event is worthy of attention, not only for its historical significance, but also for the length of time it took to achieve success.

The protest began with a group of outraged Black citizens who were then joined by the Pittsburgh Chapter of the NAACP, Twelfth Ward Civic League, and the Baptist Ministerial Alliance. The struggle at the Highland Park pool as well as others around the city was violent. Government officials did little to intervene and police officers often stood by while Blacks were harassed and beaten. The process of integrating Pittsburgh swimming pools took until 1952, and even that date can be debated.

The struggle was chronicled in headlines and articles published by *The Pittsburgh Courier*.

1931, August 8—DENY SEGREGATION AT HIGHLAND PARK POOL, BUT NEGROES ARE BEATEN WHILE COPS LOOK ON: Despite the assurance by the city's Public Works director that there would be no discrimination at the newly opened pool, the first group of Blacks was turned away under the guise that they needed to show health certificates. No such demands were made of White bathers. The Blacks returned the next day, allegedly under police protection. The group of four Blacks changed clothes and entered the pool area. When the Blacks entered the pool, the cops searched their clothes, and the swimmers were threatened by a mob of young thugs from the Larimer area. The Blacks asked the police for protection, but were ignored. The White thugs beat all of the Blacks as the police looked on. No arrests were made. The incident prompted a protest meeting by Black citizens calling themselves *The Twelfth Ward League*.

1931, August 29—Twelve Black youngsters swam successfully at the pool, under alleged police protection. When all but three of them left, a White cop suggested that the White youngsters "go get your gang. We can't afford to let these niggers run the town." Soon three car loads of White thugs began to beat the three Black youngsters and to hold them under water. The police did nothing. When the commotion attracted some Black folks who were attending a nearby picnic, things got even uglier. Some of the Blacks attempted to scale the fence around the pool. According to eye witnesses, the police drew their guns and threatened to shoot the Blacks. When Blacks yelled at the police, they attacked and beat the Black men and women. Eight Blacks were arrested. Not one White person was beaten or arrested. The Blacks were taken to jail. The NAACP paid their fines, and they were released. All this occurred despite the fact that Mayor Kline claimed, "the Highland Park Swimming Pool is for everybody. Go and swim anytime you want to. I will straighten out the whole situation and see that you get protection." Apparently the mayor forgot to inform the police and the Larimer area thugs.

1931, September 5—The mayor placed a Black police officer on the park pool staff, at the insistence of the Twelfth Ward Civic League and the NAACP.

1931, September 12—Park police were being moved from the pool since things appeared to be "quiet."

1934, June 24—City Police Instructed to "Protect" Negroes Who Go to Highland Park Swimming Pool.[49]

1934, August 18—A group of Black swimmers was beaten at the pool. The leader of the Black group had some of the White youth arrested and threatened legal action that would close the pool.

---

49 I spoke to many Black folks and some Whites, as well, who said that, despite rumors to the contrary, Blacks were still being routinely beaten by White thugs when they tried to use the pool.

1935, July 13—Police Look on as Whites Beat Youth at Pool: A 9-year-old Black youth was brutally beaten by a band of White "hoodlums" as police looked on. Police Inspector Kellie, from the Number 6 Police Station in East Liberty told Black citizens, "Why can't you people use the Washington Boulevard Pool? I don't approve of Colored and White people swimming together."[50]

1935, July 20—Cops Turn Backs as Whites Attack Girl Scouts at Pool: According to the story, the police turned their backs to the incident and some were even seen to be laughing. Police knew the White youth and refused to arrest any of them.

1939, September 2—Drive Girls from Highland Park Pool.

Discrimination against Black swimmers continued and the police provided no protection, despite the fact that every Pittsburgh mayor since 1931 had promised that the pool was for "everyone." In August 1945, a group of Black youngsters from Good Hope Baptist Church were driven from the pool; 14 years after the protests had begun. *The Pittsburgh Courier* continued to chronicle the persistent discrimination.

1950, April 29—Riot Case Finds Albert Guilty of Taking Negroes to Pool: In 1948, Nathan Albert, a Black man, took a mixed group of swimmers to Highland Park in order to protest the discrimination. He was arrested, charged with conspiring to start a riot, and found guilty two years later.

1951, June 30—Urban League Head Ejected from Highland Park Pool: Alexander J. Allen, Executive Director of the Pittsburgh Urban League, was escorted from the pool by a group of White thugs while the lifeguards stood by and did nothing. The police arrived but declined to arrest anyone because Allen had "not been denied admission." The Frontier Club, the NAACP, the Urban League, and other groups promised stronger action than that they had taken in the past.

1951, July 14—League Head, 2 Swim at Highland Park Pool: Allen, James Jordan, Jr., and Norman Johnson swam in the pool. They indicated that they were cursed at and insulted. A rock thrown from outside the pool hit Mr. Jordan in the ankle. "James Burgetet, executive director of the Centre Avenue YMCA, and P.L. Prattis, executive editor of *The Pittsburgh Courier*, who were outside the enclosure as observers, were surrounded, threatened and finally rejected by the young [White] hoodlums as "so old we wouldn't get any credit for whipping them."

1951, July 21—NAACP Sues to Close Highland Park Pool: Reacting to the July 14 incident, the Pittsburgh chapter of the NAACP decided it was time to take legal action. Richard F. Jones, president of the local chapter said, "The Legal Redress Committee

---

50 According to several Blacks with whom I spoke, the Washington Boulevard pool was old, small and dingy. It should have been torn down when the Highland Park pool was built a short distance away. Instead, it was designated by the City's Jim Crow customs as the "colored" pool. What is interesting and always the case, I could find no written evidence that such discriminatory policy was in place. Yet, it was clearly evident that Blacks and Whites alike knew that this was the acceptable place for Black folks to swim.

has conferred; drawn up legal papers….and has decided to bring suit for an injunction to close Highland Park Pool." In addition, the group pressed for the closure of the Washington Boulevard Pool as being small and dilapidated. At the request of the city, the hearing was postponed. The NAACP agreed to drop the suit if Blacks were guaranteed the right to swim where they wanted. Jones and the NAACP then urged Blacks to swim at the pool to test the promises.

1951, August 4—Many Swim Safely at Highland Park Pool. Among the swimmers were the Reverend Leroy Patrick and nine of the youth from his church. According to Rev. Patrick, "The Youth of my church and I were working hard one summer on a difficult project. I suggested that, as a reward, we all have a swimming party at Highland Park Pool. The kids gave me a strange look and informed me that we were not permitted to swim in the pool because they were 'colored.' I inquired further and found that the kids had told me the truth. The more I found out about the pool the more incensed I became. I went to City Council and informed them that my people would be swimming in Highland Park Pool, and I wanted the police to protect us from harm. When the day came for us to swim, the White kids who were working with us from East Liberty Presbyterian Church did not show up. Eight of my youngsters did, but a few of them claimed they had forgotten their trunks. After I gathered the required number of trunks we headed for the pool. We got out of the cars and linked arms. The police had surrounded the park. The closer we got to the pool, the harder it was to keep my little group going forward. We changed clothes and entered the pool area. The two of our group who could swim, headed for the deep end. I stayed in the part of the pool where I could stand up. You see, I *could not swim!* As soon as we entered the water, the Whites got out and yelled "NIGGER WATER, DIRTY WATER" and other racist remarks. My kids wanted to leave, but I made them stay for about an hour. When we left the pool, we just sort of sauntered to our cars. We really wanted to run, but we could not show any sign of fear. I then encouraged other Black groups to swim in the pool. We formed the Swimming Pool Committee of the NAACP. For 25 days various Black groups used the pool. No group would go more than once; the tension in the pool was just too great. The City government put tarps around the fence so no one could see in. We finally integrated the pool and most of the Whites never returned. I was so turned off by the experience that I did not return to the pool for many years."[51]

Others used the pool at about the same time, including three members of the NAACP Youth Council, headed by Melusena Carl. At times, White hoodlums watched Black swimmers and later attacked them on the street. Police said they would investigate. Attorney Jones urged Black citizens to continue using the pool. In the meantime, the NAACP asked the courts to continue monitoring the pool.

> 1951, August 11—Highland Park Pool "Under Test" Remainder of Summer: Attorney Jones and Attorney Henry R. Smith asked for a continuance of the lawsuit until September 17. The Legal Redress Committee also pressed the city administration to identify and prosecute the White hoodlums who had been beating Black folks. Some hoodlums were taken to juvenile court.[52]

---

51 I have used information gathered during an interview with Reverend Patrick in 1991 to elaborate on *The Pittsburgh Courier* headline.
52 Unfortunately, I was unable to find any documentation about what, if anything, happened to them.

In June of 1952, Attorney Henry Smith filed a lawsuit against Mayor David L. Lawrence for operating a segregated city pool system. Mayor Lawrence happened to be out of town when the court action was filed. His assistant capitulated to the demand for Blacks to be permitted to use the pool. It appears this marked a turning point in the fight to integrate swimming pools in and around the city. However, that can be debated as indicated by the following *Courier* headlines.

> 1953, May 23—Pressures Mounting against Parks' Bias. The story speaks to the discrimination practiced by both Kennywood and West View Parks. The pressure was coming from Reverend Leroy Patrick's NAACP Swimming Pool Committee. The protest was gaining wide support both in the Black and the White communities.

> 1953, July 25—Negroes Swim at Main South Park Pool Just Like at Highland: Previously, Blacks had been confined to Scully's Pool at the park. The change came as a result of a group of Blacks under the NAACP Swimming Pool Committee attempted to use the pool. The incident came close to a physical confrontation. The NAACP protested the incident and forced a change.

A June 7, 1952, article in The *Courier* indicates that Reverend Leroy Patrick had turned his attention to the issue of Black employment at the city pools. He sent an open letter to Mayor David Lawrence demanding Black lifeguards be hired for Highland Park Swimming Pool. As was the case with Jim Crow culture, there were two faces of discrimination. One was equal access to goods and services; the other was the right to employment. In the following chapters, both sides are explored across a range of social institutions.

CHAPTER 14

FIGHTING THE JIM CROW CULTURE

Media

The Jim Crow Culture prevailed in the three forms of media at the time—newspapers, radio, and television. As illustrated in the preceding Chapter's account of the Highland Park Swimming Pool protests, *The Pittsburgh Courier* was a vital source of information about and for the Black Community.

Fighting the Jim Crow Culture of Newspapers

During the time of the civil rights movement, Pittsburgh had three major newspapers—*The Pittsburgh Press*, *Pittsburgh Post-Gazette*, and *The Pittsburgh Sun-Telegraph*—all White-owned newspapers. Reading these, one would conclude that Blacks in Pittsburgh existed only as athletes, entertainers, or criminals. Articles about issues and events of interest to Black citizens were absent. No Blacks were employed as reporters, assignment editors, copy editors, society editors, or any other significant capacity. Want-ads and advertisements included wording like "White only" or "seeking white person to." Protests against this exclusion and discrimination during the 1950s and 1960s were simply ignored.

While not a civil rights organization itself, *The Pittsburgh Courier* played a vital role in the civil rights movement, not only locally but across the country. Started by Robert L. Vann, *The Courier* was a Black-owned, weekly newspaper that gave a voice to those who would otherwise have been silenced. In addition to publishing the Pittsburgh edition, *The Courier* also published a national edition as well as editions geared to Black events in many other cities. Because the story of *The Courier* has been covered extensively by other authors, my intention here is to acknowledge that it played an important role in combating racism.

Frank Bolden was a war correspondent who came to work at *The Courier* first as a reporter and then as editor. He demonstrated great courage in reporting on issues and events of importance to the Black community. At the same time, it is important to acknowledge the courage of the Black Pullman Porters who worked on the nation's railroads. In an attempt to kill the national reach of *The Courier*, White distributors refused to deliver the paper across the country. The Pullman porters carried

**Mal Goode (center), Mary Dee (cutting cake).
Next to her is Leonard Walk, owner of WAMO Radio**

supplies of the paper with them and dropped them off at predetermined spots at the nation's railroad stations. From there, the papers were picked up and distributed to establishments in Black communities.

At the height of its power, the best Black writers and noted intellectuals wrote for *The Pittsburgh Courier*. Actually, they had no choice; no White newspapers would hire them. Among the notable authors were Martin Delaney, Marcus Garvey, and J.A. Rogers. Sadly, *The Courier* suffered under integration, as the best writers were lured away to higher-paying jobs in the White papers. The same is to be said about the managerial talent. Furthermore, advertisers were no longer forced to buy advertising space in *The Courier*. After all, they said, we can reach Black buyers in the "other" papers as well. Black readership also fell off as Black folks spent more time reading White papers. As we moved towards integration, we often moved away from our own institutions.

Fighting the Jim Crow Culture of Radio

March 11, 1961 **Pittsburgh Courier** *Headline—Pittsburgh Group to Fight Radio-TV Bias: The people involved were the ever-present Reverend Leroy Patrick, The Greater Pittsburgh Improvement League, and the newly-formed Federation of Negro Artists and Models of Pittsburgh.*

Blacks were noticeably absent from radio except for insulting stereotypes like those depicted on the *Amos and Andy Show*. In the 1950s and 1960s, Black Pittsburghers were certain that we had a "Negro" station, and pointed proudly at WHOD (later WAMO). They were surprised to learn that the station was owned by a Jewish gentleman, Leonard Walk.

The station remained White-owned until it was purchased by Sheridan Broadcasting in the early 1970s. The corporation also purchased WYJZ-AM, the sister station to WAMO-FM. Sheridan Broadcasting remained the only company to have a radio station in Pittsburgh that was Black-owned until the late 1990s when the Homewood/Brushton Revitalization and Development Corporation started a station with the call letters WCXJ. It was located in a building owned by the Corporation in Homewood. Unfortunately, because the corporation knew little about operating a radio station, serious problems ensued, and the station closed its doors by 2000. The closing was a loss to the community that, for a while, had an alternative to the teen-oriented music featured on WAMO. I had the great pleasure of producing and hosting talk shows on both stations. Beginning in 1963 and continuing through 1998, Ron Davenport says he always felt that Blacks did not need special programs. Rather, all they needed was an opportunity to have a piece of the pie. It was that notion that led him, along with Arthur Edmunds, Glenn Mahone, Milton Washington, and others to explore the idea of buying a radio station. They decided to borrow $1.4 million dollars. "That was a great deal of money then, but I thought it was actually better to borrow more than less. You see, if you borrow $50,000 and have trouble repaying it, you have a problem. If you borrow a million dollars, rather than having a problem, you have a partner." The group purchased WAMO, a formerly White-owned station in Pittsburgh. Eventually, Davenport became the sole owner of The Sheridan Broadcasting Network and owned scores of Black stations around the country. Davenport said, "I became involved because I saw an opportunity to make a contribution while having a good career, as well. That gave me the financial wherewithal to become the owner of Sheridan Broadcasting Corporation that catered to Black communities across the country."[53]

Every radio station except WAMO became the target of negotiations and direct action by Pittsburgh civil rights organizations. Station managers claimed that their audiences did not want to see or hear "that stuff," meaning events and issues of interest to the Black community. With no Black assignment editors on their staff, the idea of covering positive stories about Blacks simply did not occur to them. By way of example, during the waning years of the civil rights movement, a local alternative newspaper ran a feature story called *Radio Wave Wars* about talk show hosts in Pittsburgh. When I asked the newspaper's editor why no Blacks were included in the article, he responded he was unaware of any Black talk show hosts in Pittsburgh. As I started to name some of the Black hosts, the editor said, "Well, the title of the show was incorrect. It should have been "KDKA and WTAE Radio wars." "Does that mean that you think there are no Black folks on either of those stations?" I then named several of my comrades who had shows on KDKA and WTAE. Finally he asked, "Do you think I did that on purpose? Well, I didn't; I just did not think of Black talk show hosts when I put the idea together." The editor's lack of awareness typifies the White broadcast community's ignorance (willful or not) of the role Blacks were playing in the media. Intent is not a prerequisite for determining whether racism and discrimination existed. "That is one of the main problems with folks like you." I continued. "You just don't *think about Blacks.* Furthermore, it does not matter whether you shoot me on purpose, or accidentally; the fact remains that I am still shot."

John Christian, who for years performed on WAMO radio as a disk jockey called "Sir Walter" knows full well about the intricate nature of racial bias on radio. When I first heard his voice on WAMO, I was

---

53 Unfortunately, many Blacks thought WAMO was a social service organization and that they should be able to have input into all aspects of the operation. No matter how many times I reminded folks this was a business, and they could exert some influence on a racist system by purchasing ads or forming businesses that complemented the radio station, I never convinced them. I was accused of "selling out," even though all but the last several months I was on the airwaves, I was not paid a cent. It was my way of contributing to the community.

very surprised to hear an English guy playing music on a Black-oriented radio station.[54] My reaction to "Sir Walter" was, "What the Hell is an English dude doing on Black radio?" Then I met this "English Dude"; he was *Black!* My eyes must have bugged out as John Christian extended his hand. He laughed and said, "Not exactly what you were expecting, huh?" That was an understatement!

It turns out that his accent was genuine. John was born in a small New England town where everyone had a broad English accent. "Hell," he said, "until I left home, I assumed that everyone spoke the way I did!" The accent was fortuitous as John made a small fortune advertising Budweiser beer on the radio as "Sir Walter Raleigh." "Man, Ralph, I was raking in big bucks; even paid for a new home with the beer commercial ads. Then the company decided to advertise on this growing thing called television. That was the end of my Budweiser career. They said they had decided to 'go in another direction.' Of course, when you are Black, you know that the new direction did not include you." The sad part is that the company never even explored the possibilities of using a Black man on a television beer commercial.

John's character was well-established on WAMO. His publicity shots included his visage sporting a black derby and a monocle perched on his nose. In 1969, when all media were responding to pressure from the civil rights movement, John left WAMO for WIIC-TV (the local NBC affiliate) to host *Black Impact*, the station's first Black-oriented show.

My own involvement in radio began in 1963 when Reverend Herbert Wilkerson invited me to appear on his call-in radio show, *NAACP on the Line.* Shortly after I started on the show, I joined the staff of the Pittsburgh Urban League. One day Arthur Edmunds, the League's Executive Director, called me into his office where Leon Haley, the Deputy Director, was also waiting. Edmunds began, "We know that you are the co-host of the NAACP show on WAMO. When people think of the show, they think of you. The show is real popular. We think the show is a little, well, *militant.* Now that you work for the Urban League we're afraid people might get the impression that the Urban League is also militant. We were wondering if you would consider giving up the show to avoid confusion."

I was stunned and angry; my response was fast and furious. "First, the show is not militant. Second, the show airs on Sunday evening, which is my own time. I will not even consider giving up the show. Is that an order?" Fortunately, the battle I was expecting didn't materialize. Neither mentioned the issue again, and I never felt that either held the decision against me.

Quite frankly, I was surprised to be called a militant as I had never categorized my belief system. In the 1990s, some organization, perhaps the Black Media Federation, put together a traveling exhibit dealing with Black media pioneers in Pittsburgh. One of the shows featured was *Black Horizons*, accompanied by a photo of me. I never saw the exhibition, but a friend said the label affixed to the *Black Horizons* section of the exhibition said something like "Ralph Proctor lent an air of militancy to the local airways." There was that word again. Several years later, I appeared with Chris Moore on the 20th anniversary show of *Black Horizons.* Moore asked "Ralph, have you always been so militant?"

"Me? I have never been militant."

Moore said, "Roll the tape!" I was stunned to see an old image of me appear. I was dressed in an African dashiki; wore a big Afro hair style; had a gold-colored chain draped around my neck and

---

54 Porky Chedwick, also White, was an extremely popular DJ on WAMO. Because he appeared live at dances called "sock hops," his Black followers knew he was White. Porky was a flamboyant character who spoke "jive" on the radio, billing himself as "Pork, the tork, your dadio of the radio, your platter-pushing pappa on WAMO." Both Black and White kids ate that up. At first I was offended by a White trying to sound Black, but once I met Porky, it was hard to be offended by someone who was obviously "way out."

dangling from the chain was a black, carved wooden clenched fist clutching a folded dollar bill. I sank into my chair as this strange apparition began to speak. "This is the first anniversary of *Black Horizons*. In that first year I understand that we have offended some people. For that I make no apologies. Now on with the show." When the lights came back up in the studio, everyone was laughing, and I was mortified.

Fighting the Jim Crow Culture of Television

Television was a particularly troublesome area during the era of the civil rights movement. There were no Black producers or assignment editors, which meant that Whites always decided what stories of the Black community would be covered. This resulted in television crews covering sports, entertainment, or crime. There were few Blacks as news anchors or reporters; Black on-air reporters were seen primarily early in the morning, late at night, or on weekends. Vic Miles and Kathy Milton were among the first Blacks to appear on Pittsburgh television in the 1960s. In 1967, William Russell Robinson was the first Black to be featured on a regular basis on a non-news show—*Job Talk*, sponsored by the H.J. Heinz Company. His job was limited to announcing job openings for which Blacks might apply.

The lack of Blacks as television producers in Pittsburgh came to an end in 1968 when WQED, the local PBS education station, created a weekly program addressing issues in the Black community. Sam Silberman, the director of local programming, was responsible for the show. Virginia Bartlett was the show's producer and host. I was among a small group of Black leaders who were invited to view and comment on the first airing of the show. The group was stunned to see a White female as producer/ host. After the viewing, Silberman and I had a heated conversation. I asked if he, as a Jew, would hire a Gentile to produce/host a series about Jewish life. He said that he would not. How then, did he reconcile that with his decisions about the show about Black folks?

After several minutes of arguing back and forth, Silberman promised to make changes as soon as new shows were taped. Indeed, after three shows, a Black female host appeared. My initial delight was short-lived, however, when I realized I knew her; she was an African who had indicated that she was a member of Liberia's ruling class of former United States slaves. She had not the faintest idea what it was like to be a member of an oppressed minority.

Another heated exchange ensued during which I accused Silberman of being out of touch with the Black community and the growing civil rights movement. At the conclusion of the conversation, I hung up, feeling that I had burned that professional bridge. Much to my surprise, Silberman called about a week later and declared, "I've decided that your arguments have merit. There *should* be a local Black person as the producer/host of the show. Congratulations, you have just inherited a television program."

"But I don't know a damn thing about producing a television show. I can't do that." Silberman reminded me about the freelance work I had done for WQED and the fact that I had co-hosted *NAACP On the Line* on WAMO. He was confident I could do the job and concluded with, "You complained. I listened. So put up or *shut up!*" Trapped by my own protests!

After accepting the challenge, I discovered the show had no budget. The station had two camera crews, an A Crew and a B Crew. The A Crew was responsible for taping the nationally popular and revenue-generating *Mister Roger's Neighborhood*. The B Crew was assigned to work on my lowly public affairs program. (Ironically, the B Crew became more skilled than the highly-regarded A Crew.) They made me feel welcome in a strange land; helped me develop my skills; hung around after the show, and had stimulating conversations with my guests. I credit them for a great deal of the show's success. One of the cameramen was an old high school classmate, Art Vogel. I'm sure his ready acceptance of me had paved the way for the positive reception I received. Although Art is White, his obviously genuine caring about justice and equality was a great asset.

Anyone who watched *Mister Roger's Neighborhood* could see the show had a very expensive set, complete with trolley tracks, trees, and all sorts of props. Since there was no budget for *Black Horizons*, the crew simply turned the *Mister Rogers'* set around, splashed colorful lights on the blank panels, put a few chairs on a platform in front of them; behold, *Black Horizons* was created.

Many welcomed this first "voice" of the Pittsburgh Black community. However, approval was not universal. In his June 28, 1969 *"Comment"* column of *The Pittsburgh Courier*, editor Carl Morris wrote, "*Black Horizons*, the weekly half-hour show on WQED-TV, is coming under attack in certain quarters of the Black community. The chief complaint seems to be that the program is too 'black nationalistic oriented'." Others applauded the "militant" voice of the show, even though I did not consider myself to be "militant."

Many people give me credit for being the first Black producer/host of a locally produced public affairs program. Actually, that honor goes to the host of *Say Brother*, produced in Boston. Nevertheless, *Black Horizons* caught on. As folks asked for tapes of the first few shows, I pleaded with them, "Please don't copy my show; it has taken this form only because we don't have any money." Despite my pleas, various incarnations of *Black Horizons* sprang up across the country.

In the second year of the show, Silberman secured a grant that would allow him to be hired on a full-time basis. I reminded him that I was still the only Black face on WQED and the only Black on *Black Horizons'* staff. I said, "If you gave me the station today, I couldn't get a program on the air, because there are no Blacks trained in any aspect of television at WQED." I insisted that the funds be used to set up a training program for other Blacks. To Silberman's credit, this was done. Were it not for the sensitivity of this Jewish man, the Jim Crow culture of television might have been prolonged. Sam played a vital role in the development of Black television, not only in Pittsburgh, but across the United States. Whenever I appeared on television and spoke about the early days of *Black Horizons*, I was quick to give credit to Sam. He was equally quick to discount his role.

Not too long after *Black Horizons* began, commercial television stations in Pittsburgh realized that they had been caught napping. Apparently none of them had even thought about a public affairs program aimed at the African-American community and hurriedly put together such programming to catch up with WQED. Because WQED did not rely on advertising income, it could afford to broadcast *Black Horizons* at 8:00 PM, while similar shows on commercial channels were relegated to non-prime time slots. Nevertheless, each station did move forward with hiring Black producers/hosts for public affairs shows:

KDKA TV (Channel 2, CBS). *Together* with Yvonne Forston and Joe Freeman
WTAE TV (Channel 4, ABC*), Black Chronicle* with Dee Thompson and Kathy Milton[55]
WIIC TV (Channel 11, NBC), *Black Impact* with John Christian
WPGH (Channel 53, Independent station, later FOX network), *The Other Side*

---

55 The station had recently hired both Thompson and Milton as on-air newscasters.

At long last television had several shows featuring music, entertainment, and stories relevant to the Black community. *Black Horizons*, despite changes in time slots, frequency, and hosts, remained on the air until 2016. Chris Moore, who came to the show from Arkansas, was the fourth producer/host. Thank God, he outlasted everyone else and was on the air for more than thirty years.

When I became involved with *Black Horizons*, I did not think it would create a conflict of interest with my civil rights activism. WQED's administration soon disabused me of this opinion. The precipitating incident involved an on-air "debate" between me and the local leader of the American Federation of Teachers. I felt strongly that the Union prevented the firing of several very racist teachers in the public school system. He disagreed and our discussion escalated into a shouting match. At the time, the Federal Communication Commission had rather strong rules about fairness on the airways. According to station management, I had violated the rules of fairness by representing the civil rights groups while being the host. The tape was withdrawn and destroyed without ever airing. At that point, I had to decide which role was more important, civil rights activist or television producer/host/talent. I reasoned that there were many capable folks who were active and effective in the movement, but at the time, *Black Horizons* was the only television voice of the movement in Pittsburgh. The station management and I reached a cold truce. I reluctantly agreed to tone down my active participation in public demonstrations so that I could remain neutral on the air in exchange for the station's ending its heavy-handed censorship.

In truth, I did continue my civil rights work, but at a reduced level. I made certain that when news media cameras were present, I was never photographed. I still regret missing the march when protesters were beaten by police as they attempted to cross the bridge leading to the construction site for Three Rivers Stadium.

Two years after *Black Horizons* began, I took a long look at what had been accomplished in Pittsburgh in the area of Black involvement in the electronic media. *Black Horizons* and similar programs continued to be the voices of the Black community. WQED TV, at my urging, had begun an internship that would eventually lead to many Blacks being trained in positions in the electronic media. However, WQED and other radio and television stations had done little to truly integrate Blacks into significant managerial positions. I approached WQED with this problem, with not much success. Finally, in exasperation, I filed a discrimination suit with the NAACP against the station. It was one of the most difficult things I had ever done. Just before filing the charges against WQED, I appeared as a guest on KDKA's *Together Show* and announced I would not return to the air "until stations had made significant strides with respect to the hiring, retention and promotion of Blacks." I had hoped to set an example for other Black "stars" to follow. To my surprise and disappointment, both hosts responded by saying, "Wow, we wish we had that kind of courage." No one followed my lead, and the hiring of Blacks in significant media positions remained a distant concern for all involved.

My self-imposed exile lasted from 1971 until 1987, when I returned to WAMO as a talk show host. Later that same year, I returned to television as a producer/host of another Black talk show called *From Our Perspective*.

Shortly after I returned to television, a very distinguished-looking, older Black lady approached me and said, "I know who you are. I used to watch *Black Horizons*. I also know you don't like a whole bunch of attention, so I'm not going to create a fuss. I just want to talk to you for a few moments." She gently took my hand as we walked down the street and continued, "I want to thank you for giving Black folks a voice. I know that you are a special man, and I know God has touched your life. I know you have not changed and I really like that. So, I just want you to know that there are folks who love you and pray for you. You're a good man, and I don't ever want you to change. You hear me?" I was so moved, a tear ran down my cheek. She reached up, wiped the tear away, placed an incredibly gentle, soft hand on my cheek, and without another word, walked out of my life, but not my soul. To this day, I do not know who she was, but I owe her my eternal thanks. Her words still linger in my heart and mind.

A Faint Glimmer of Hope

As the fortunes of Black television waxed and waned over the years, many Blacks came to expect little from White-owned television stations. Still, we felt things would change dramatically if we could own a station. In January 1991, Eddie Edwards, a Black man, was announced as the new owner of WPTT-22 television. Edwards, host of a public affairs program on the station, had apparently purchased the station from Sinclair Broadcasting, which also owned WPGH (Fox). Edwards promised things would improve and hopes rose that Blacks would now have good positions both in front of and behind the cameras. Unfortunately, rumors soon began circulating that there was something fishy about the deal.

Edwards was said to be a "front" for White-owned WPGH. In his April 13, 1999 column, Tony Norman, a Black reporter for the *Pittsburgh Post-Gazette* wrote, "Best known here for his 'ownership' of WPTT-22…[Edwards] engenders strong feelings of contempt and admiration on both sides of the city's racial divide." Norman goes on to talk about Edwards and Sinclair Broadcasting's joint attempt to duplicate the controversial "Pittsburgh thing" in other venues. However, The Reverend Jesse Jackson of Operation Push and the Rainbow Coalition challenged the plan. According to Norman, "Jackson's Rainbow/PUSH Coalition as well as several major media companies have filed objections with the FCC to deny Edwards four more stations. Outside Pittsburgh's insular black establishment, the move to block Edward's bid to 'buy' more stations has become a crusade to restore the integrity of the 'Minority Ownership' law."

The May 1, 1999, edition of *The Pittsburgh Courier* added to the story indicating that rumors were spreading that Edwards would no longer own the television station as soon as the FCC permitted broadcast companies to own more than one station in a local market. As I tried to sort through the facts of the situation, those who might have known the truth refused to comment, fearing retaliation.

In November 1999, Edwards announced he was selling the station back to Sinclair Broadcasting. The sale occurred in the wake of the FCC announcement that one broadcast company could legally own multiple stations in one market area. By selling WPPT to Edwards in 1991, Sinclair was able to regain control of the station which under former laws would have been impossible.

According to the newspapers, Edwards parlayed a $10 down payment into $16.8 million. If that is true, it certainly was a brilliant personal move. In a November 18, 1999, *Pittsburgh Post-Gazette* article, Edwards announced his intention to buy several radio stations and become a voice in Black communities across the nation. As of 2013, that had not happened. Edwards reportedly lives in Pittsburgh, but has disappeared from the public scene. Many had hoped that Edwards would reappear as the owner of both radio and television stations, as he had promised. Perhaps the whole truth of the situation will someday emerge. Whatever the truth might be, Blacks rode a roller coaster of hope, hopelessness, hope, and again at the end of the whole sorry affair, hopelessness.

CHAPTER 15

FIGHTING JIM CROW CULTURE

Housing

From the early days of Fort Pitt at the confluence of the Allegheny, Monongahela, and Ohio Rivers, Pittsburgh was a segregated community. Unlike many other Northern cities, Pittsburgh did not develop one major, contiguous Black enclave. Rather, as discussed in Chapter 3 (Figure 3.1), distinctive Black ghettoes existed in communities throughout the area. Embedded in the city's cultural memory was the demarcation of areas where it was acceptable for Blacks to live.

In most cases, regardless of the community, the housing provided for Blacks was woefully inadequate. The influx of large numbers of Blacks during the great

Slum Housing, Hill District, circa 1950s

migration from the south between 1917 and 1925 created a great need for housing. The pressure for more housing continued well into the 1950s. In response, many single-family dwellings were subdivided to accommodate three, four or five families. Basements and unfinished attics were converted to apartments. Even old bakeries, poultry stores, and horse stables were converted to housing. Southern Blacks who migrated to Pittsburgh indicated that many of the homes were worse than those they had left behind.

Because local affiliates of the national Multi-list Corporation controlled the sale and leasing of the vast majority of homes and apartments in the United States, the corporation played a dominant role in determining the housing options available to Blacks. After earning a master's degree in Real Estate and Insurance, Robert Lavelle faced discrimination in the job market. In response, he worked nights at *The*

Pittsburgh Courier and operated his own real estate firm during the day. Lavelle was determined to help Blacks find and purchase homes.

Having already been accepted into the Realty Board, Lavelle thought he would be able to join the Greater East End Multi-list Corporation, thereby giving him and his clients access to home ownership in White communities. Each time his membership application came up for a vote, he was told, "Sorry, Bob, you just didn't get enough votes." Finally, Lavelle grew angry and said, "I can't permit you to deny me the opportunity to earn a living." With those words, he sued the Greater Pittsburgh Multi-list Corporation in Federal Court, charging them with violation of the Sherman Anti-trust law. "Initially, members of the Multi-list Corporation thought that I would go through the Mayor's Commission on Human Relations. They thought that the worst thing the Commission would do was slap them on the wrist and fine them a hundred dollars. They didn't take me seriously."

The National NAACP took interest in Lavelle's suit and invited him to New York to discuss the case. "They wanted to see if they had a 'clean horse' to ride; that there were no skeletons in my closet that might discredit the case. I had five pre-trial conferences." In 1967, the first pre-trial conference began. Recalling those days Lavelle said:

> I knew things could get bad, but I didn't realize how bad. It's a good thing that I didn't know; I might have chickened out! I knew that they would try to stop the suit, but I had no idea that they would break into my bank account, that they would threaten my life, my wife's life, and the lives of my children. They would say "we know where your children go to school. Something might happen to them." They described my car and said that, if I did not stop, my car might be blown up. They sent me used toilet paper in the mail. They sent examiners from the State Board of Realtors to investigate my business in an attempt to take away my real estate license. They even paid a local unscrupulous Black man to tell lies about me in court. Fortunately, he lost *his* license for illegal activities before he could tell his lies in court. It was a stressful time.

Fortunately for Blacks in this country, Lavelle did not back down. Eighteen months later, he won the case. When the story was picked up by the national media, the Multi-list members finally gave up and voted him into the organization. Now he had access to any house sold on the open market. His hard-earned victory was not just important locally. Now other Black realtors throughout the country could join other such groups. This brave, quiet, unassuming man made it possible for Blacks to buy houses in any community anywhere in the land.

Despite the hard-won battle, all of Lavelle's troubles were not over. One day he received a call from a White woman who wanted him to handle the sale of her home in the all-White Stanton Heights neighborhood. Lavelle said, "I was very pleased to gain access to this previously-closed, very desirable community. We were driving through the area looking for her. When I looked up, I saw a crowd of Whites. One woman yelled, 'That must be *Him!*' Realizing we were in danger, I turned around and drove away, while the crowd continued to yell obscenities at us. Later I learned that I had been set up. The woman who phoned me had had a fight with her neighbors. In retaliation, she offered me the 'opportunity' to sell her home. Then she went around the neighborhood bragging that she was selling her home to colored folks. Upon hearing this, the neighbors set up an ambush for me."

In addition to this type of racist harassment, Lavelle also encountered problems when insurance companies used "red-lining" to refuse to insure homes in "high risk" Black communities. If Blacks were permitted to buy insurance, the rates were much higher than for Whites. At that time, no Black insurance agents were employed by any major insurance company.

Another obstacle was the difficulty Blacks encountered when applying for mortgages, especially when trying to buy homes in White communities. Lavelle's first attempt to sell a home brought him face-to-face with the discriminatory lending practices of major banks:

> I located a house in the middle Hill. I had a buyer who had one third of the money to put down on the house. That was more than enough to qualify for the loan, but Mellon Bank told me that they did not make mortgages in that area.

> I went to Mellon again, about a different house. This time my client had 50% of the money needed for the loan. I made an appointment over the telephone to see about the mortgage. When I showed up, the loan officer saw me approaching and, over the intercom, told the secretary to inform me that I would not be getting the mortgage. The man then came out of his office and said, "What makes you think that you can walk in here and get a loan?"

> That made me realize that if I was going to sell houses, Blacks would have to have their own money to lend.

Lavelle was able to make this happen when he acquired Dwelling House Savings and Loan. As he explained:

> The business was a Mutual State chartered association owned by the people who saved there. At the time they were mostly Irish and Europeans. When I acquired it, it only had assets of $67,000 and was about to be liquidated. They took me in as a director, because I presented a plan to save the charter. I insisted that Attorney Henry Smith also be named as a director.

Lavelle moved the Savings and Loan office into his real estate office and held an open house to raise enough funds to keep Pennsylvania from liquidating the firm. This succeeded. Corporate Pittsburgh saw the need to support a Hill District financial entity. Harold Tweedy, chairman of First Federal Savings and Loan, helped and advised, and the Edgar Kaufmann Foundation deposited the last amount needed to obtain federal insurance of accounts in 1970. This helped ease the fears of small, individual depositors. Now Robert Lavelle was able to sell homes anywhere in the country and to provide the mortgages.

Despite Lavelle's efforts, the housing market remained an arena of inequity. The Jim Crow culture continued to exert its influence. For example, many White folks believed that Blacks moving into the community would cause it to deteriorate and, in turn, decrease the value of their property. Whites bolstered their prejudices by pointing to conditions in some poor inner-city communities as proof that, "Niggers don't take care of property." Unscrupulous realtors played on these fears for their own advantage by using a tactic called "block busting." Realtors would go from door to door telling residents that Blacks were going to take over their neighborhood. If this alone did not start a stampede toward the suburbs, they would purchase one house at well above fair market value from a homeowner who feared the coming "hordes" of Blacks and knew the offer was far greater than the fair market value.

After buying the first property, realtors hired Blacks to pose as prospective homebuyers. These shills drove old dilapidated cars into the neighborhood and behaved in a loud and obnoxious fashion. While the "buyers" were making their presence known, the realtors were busy visiting other neighbors, pointing to the Blacks, and asking whether the residents wished to live in a community with "that kind of person."

The next step was approaching a resident and offering to buy their home at a reasonable price. They would later return and offer a lower price. When residents pointed out this price disparity or said the first seller had made a profit, the realtor countered with, "Yeah, but that was *before* Blacks started moving in." Even though Blacks had not actually moved into the community, the White homeowners' fears were becoming a reality.

Soon, "FOR SALE" signs appeared on lawn after lawn and realtors snapped up houses at bargain prices and resold them to Blacks, who for the first time in their lives had access to quality housing—albeit at greatly inflated prices. As each house sold, the desire of the Whites to exit increased and almost overnight neighborhoods such as Homewood-Brushton, Wilkinsburg and Penn Hills changed from White to Black enclaves. Contrary to popular fiction, when Blacks moved into these communities the property values actually *increased* to the benefit of speculators.

During the 1960s, I was speaking to a group of fearful White folks who had called a meeting to discuss the fact that Blacks were moving into the neighborhood. During the discussion, one woman declared, "You know, when one Black person moves into the neighborhood, they just take over the neighborhood." I asked, "If one moves in, and the rest of you don't move, how will we take over your neighborhood?" There was dead silence. It was as if no one had ever contemplated the idea of simply staying put.

Another approach for discouraging Blacks from moving to White neighborhoods was "steering." *Steering* was a two-sided strategy realtors used to perpetuate *de facto* segregation. On one side, Whites were discouraged from moving into Black areas. The experience of a co-worker illustrates this version of steering. In 1963, Tony came to Pittsburgh to join a research team in the biochemistry department of the University of Pittsburgh School of Medicine. He contacted a realtor for assistance in finding an apartment. As they were driving through Wilkinsburg, Tony spotted a for-rent sign posted by the realtor's agency and insisted that the agent show him the apartment. Reluctantly, the realtor complied and when Tony wanted to rent the apartment, the realtor said, "There are Colored people in this area." Tony asked, "What are Colored people and why should that make a difference." Upon hearing the agent's explanation, Tony became angry and rented the apartment, where he lived without incident for many years.

The other side was steering Blacks away from White communities by showing them only what was available in Black or mixed communities. If Blacks insisted upon seeing homes in White areas, they would be shown either run-down homes or homes that were far beyond the prospective buyer's price, while claiming that all the houses in White areas were just as expensive. Even after WHITES ONLY signs were no longer legal, "For Sale" and "For Rent" signs would seldom be openly posted in "off-limits" neighborhoods. If a rental was advertised, when Blacks applied suddenly the unit had just been rented and nothing else was available. Prospective renters might be shown run-down slum units and told that was the only housing available in the area. Or, if the housing was decent, they would be required to pay far more than Whites in order to move in. Even in Black neighborhoods, the limited supply of decent housing meant they might have to pay more than they would for comparable housing in White communities.

The passage of anti-discrimination housing laws in the 1950s did not bring an end to discriminatory practices. The April 4, 1953 edition of The *Pittsburgh Courier* announced that The Reverend S. Amos Brakeen, pastor of the Shiloh Baptist Church, had been named to head an NAACP committee which would work to end discrimination in the use of public accommodations in the Pittsburgh District. The Young Adult Chapter of the NAACP as well as other fair housing groups worked with the Mayor's Commission on Human Relations to unmask and challenge discriminatory housing practices. In addition to Black-led civil rights groups, several White-led groups joined the battle against segregated housing, including CHOOSE (Clearing House for Open Occupancy Selection) and SHARE, a group working in the South Hills area of Pittsburgh. Between 1963 and 1968, these groups fought to break down the barriers that prevented Blacks from renting or owning homes in traditionally all-White neighborhoods.

The Young Adult Chapter of the NAACP established an effective process to document housing discrimination and thereby successfully bring law suits against offending landlords and real estate agents. First, a team of Whites would go to apartments, private homes, and realty companies to inquire about a property. Sometimes we went into action as a result of a complaint being formally filed; other times, we would be alerted by someone who had been subjected to discrimination even though they had not filed a complaint. Once the White test team gained entrance to the house or apartment, they would pretend to be well qualified renters or home buyers. While talking with the owner/realtor, the couple took copious notes on:

- the cost of the unit,
- extra fees,
- any special conditions and prohibitions related to the rental/purchase,
- the name of the individual who showed the unit, and
- whether the person was an owner or an agent.

After thanking the folks involved, the team said they needed a bit of time to make a decision, and then rendezvoused with a Black test team waiting nearby. Precautions were taken to make certain the team members who called for an appointment could not be identified as Black by controlling for speech pattern, place of employment, telephone number, and current place of residence, using addresses in White communities.

During the Black team's visit, they might be told the place had been removed from the market, was under contract, or there was a mistake in the listing such as a wrong address, a misstated rental or purchase price. Sometimes the Black team would be told about additional fees that had not been mentioned in the original ad. For example, the White team might have been told the upfront fees were the first month's rent and a security deposit, while upfront fees for the Black team might include the first and last months' rent, a security deposit, a breakage fee, extra money to cover the cost of running the air conditioner, and a credit check fee. Thus, a White couple might need a total of $1,000 in order to rent an apartment, but the Black couple might need $3,000 or $4,000. During the viewing, the Black team took copious notes and soon afterwards, the two test teams met to compare notes. If there were differences, a complaint form was filled out and filed with the Human Relations Commission. We won the vast majority of our cases. This strategy was used very effectively not only in the area of housing, but also with retail establishments such as bars, restaurants, skating rinks, dance facilities, and beauty salons.

On one occasion in 1965, a CHOOSE volunteer accompanied my wife and me when we went to see an apartment in Squirrel Hill, a predominantly Jewish community that had a reputation for racial discrimination. Fortunately, in this case, nothing negative occurred, and later I became close to the landlord and his family. He told me that he had been offended by the presence of the CHOOSE representative and resented the assumption that he would discriminate against Blacks. As we spent time talking on many occasions, he later understood. If only other landlords would have been as open-minded.[56]

Very different outcomes occurred when I went to see apartments in later years. In one case, I responded to an ad about an apartment, and the landlord suggested that I come over to sign the lease. A White woman answered the door and nearly fainted when I introduced myself. Upon recovering from her shock, she announced that the apartment "had just been rented." Suspecting discrimination, I had a White friend check out the complex. As we suspected, the apartment was still available to White folks. I sued and won the case.

In another instance, I wanted to see an apartment in Penn Hills. Apparently the realtor assumed I was White and assured me he was able to keep Blacks out of his rental units, because he said, "I can always tell when a caller is a Nigger." Apparently, his language detection skills were not as good as he thought. I was shown the apartment, but suddenly it was no longer available. I called the agency shortly after a White friend had visited the same apartment. Once again, I was told the place had already been rented. I filed a discrimination suit with the Pennsylvania Human Relations Commission. The issue was investigated and the Commission found in my favor. The Commission issued an order that the agency could not rent, sell, lease or otherwise encumber any of the many units in the complex until I "was satisfied." It was very gratifying to prove my case, but in the interim, I had rented another apartment. Deciding that the realty agency needed a lesson, it took me some time to be "satisfied." On a weekly basis, I looked at other apartments, but for some strange reason, none seemed quite right. After about four months, I finally said "Sorry, none of your units are acceptable." Their discrimination had turned into a very costly proposition.

In the 1990s, housing discrimination still continued; it simply went underground. At the time, I was serving as a commissioner on the Pittsburgh Human Relations Commission along with my friend and mentor, Alma Speed Fox. The Commission received a complaint from several White women who were employed at a major apartment leasing corporation. The women were greatly disturbed that the company manager had instructed them not to rent to women with children, certain Eastern groups, and

56 Tensions between Jewish landlords and Black tenants had a long history in the Hill District. The first generation of Whites to live in The Hill consisted of well-to-do gentry who moved in the late 1800s to places like Shadyside, the near-Northside, and Point Breeze. When they left, they sold their stores and houses to a second wave of immigrants that included Italians, eastern Europeans, and Jews. When these Jewish residents later moved from The Hill, they kept their properties and many became slum landlords. When Blacks began to demonstrate against crowded, substandard, over-priced housing, they often found themselves picketing members of the Jewish community. This was problematic because, in many instances, Jews and Blacks were allies as they fought anti-Semitism and racism together.

Blacks. The case was assigned to a Commission staff member, Yancy Miles, who verified the women's claims. I was then assigned to preside over the case. The company's initial, dismissive attitude changed when Miles brought in one of the best U.S Department of Housing and Urban Development attorneys. Because the realty firm had hesitated at the monetary fine suggested by Miles and me, the attorney said that the "bullet-proof" case would become his if they rejected the offered settlement. He then presented newspaper articles featuring some of the cases he had settled. In every instance, his cases cost the discriminating party several million dollars. The representatives of the discriminating firm quickly accepted the settlement offered by the Pittsburgh Human Relations Commission.

So far, I have been discussing discrimination as it played out against individual, would-be renters, and potential home buyers. Over decades (even centuries) the accumulating discrimination against individuals affected whole communities. In the mid-1950s, however, the city of Pittsburgh initiated a massive "urban renewal" project that succeeded in destroying one of the most vibrant, economically viable Black communities in the country.[57]

Community Death through Urban "Renewal"

By the early 1950s, many areas of The Hill were in need of refurbishing. Housing stock was aging; many absentee landlords were not maintaining their properties and neither were tenants. Even so, this multi-racial, multi-ethnic community enjoyed an all-too-rare culture of tolerance. Small businesses and entertainment venues were patronized by community residents and visitors. So, while The Hill could use help to upgrade its housing and infrastructure, the underlying social and cultural fabric of this small "United Nations" was well worth preserving.

Enter the plan for urban renewal. Robert Pease, a graduate of Carnegie Institute of Technology (now Carnegie Mellon University) played a key role as architect and driving force behind the plan. First as a staff member and later as the Executive Director of Pittsburgh Urban Redevelopment Authority, Pease was instrumental in guiding what have subsequently become textbook cases of failed urban planning.

Urban "Renewal" of The Hill began quietly enough. Residents thought they had no reason to fear the process. Robert Pease had promised: (1) one new dwelling would be built for each one demolished; (2) dilapidated housing would be replaced with new, affordably priced units; and (3) residents would be provided with good, temporary housing so they could easily return to their beloved community at the completion of the project. According to *The Hill District History* published by the Carnegie Library of Pittsburgh:

> In September 1955, the Federal Government approved the Lower Hill Redevelopment Plan, making available $17.4 million in loans and grants. Ninety five acres were slated for clearing, with the demolition of the first 1,300 structures to be razed set for June 1956. Redevelopment displaced 8,000 residents; 1,239 Black families and 312 White families. Of these numbers, 35% went to public housing communities, 31% to private residences, 8% bought homes. About 90 families refused to move and ended up in substandard

---

57 As I work on this edition of *Voices*, the news media has been reporting on the 100 year anniversary of the cataclysmic destruction of a wealthy, self-sustaining Black community in Tulsa, Oklahoma. Although the specifics in the Tulsa and Pittsburgh situations differed, underlying fear, jealousy, and racism wantonly destroyed both Black communities.

housing. Of those who were relocated, few received any relocation compensation, with minimum compensation relief coming from the federal government.[58]

When Robert Pease's promises are evaluated against this picture of "renewal," it raises the specter of a racist assault, not just on isolated individuals, but on an entire community.

Promise 1—One New Dwelling for Each One Demolished

One could argue, as Pease undoubtedly did, that this promise was kept—especially if only the letter, not the spirit, of the federal urban redevelopment law is considered. Beneath this surface analysis, however, lies a grimmer picture. Many so-called "single-family" units housed two, three, or even four families. Owners, who had sub-divided large, old homes into small apartments, rarely reported this practice, because they had not obtained the necessary zoning variance to make the units legal. The officials of urban renewal were well aware of the fact that, if one house was built for each house that was demolished, the process would leave many families homeless. To prevent the displacement of all families living in the lower Hill, three or more new units would have been needed.

Promise 2—New Affordable Housing

As demolition of existing houses proceeded, little systematic follow-up was done to account for the relocation of all displaced Black families. Using *The Hill District History* figures, approximately 434 families moved to public housing projects. If the unofficial number of displaced families is considered, as many as 1,300 families may have entered public housing. If a family had more than three children, the City offered no assistance in finding new homes.

Located on Bedford Avenue in the Middle Hill was a middle-class Black community called Whiteside Road. The smallish, single-family dwellings were beautiful, quite unlike anything else in the area. The community was very well maintained by its Black residents. The City used eminent domain to condemn this neighborhood, replace it with a public housing project, and had the audacity to call it Whiteside Road.

Ironically, many Lower Hill residents made too much money to qualify for public housing, but too little for market rate rentals. Consequently, this pushed many families into substandard housing scattered throughout Pittsburgh neighborhoods. The exodus from the Lower Hill caused overcrowding in many other parts of the city, including the Middle and Upper Hill, Homewood, East Liberty, Beltzhoover, the West End, Sheridan, and the Northside.

"Redevelopment" of The Lower Hill

As indicated in *The Hill District History*, 95 acres were targeted for demolition and redevelopment. Given the promises for new, affordable housing, one might reasonably assume that a residential

---

58 The numbers cited in *The Hill District History* match figures I compiled by analyzing the records of the Urban Redevelopment Authority's own records.

community for displaced Black families was intended for the site. Instead, the site became home to three major complexes.

First, the city built Washington Plaza, a high-rise apartment complex, consisting of 594 <u>high-rent</u> units and upscale retail shops. A fence surrounded the complex and had a guarded entrance to control access. The shops were for the exclusive use of Washington Plaza residents and bus service was provided for residents who wished to frequent the downtown area. The high-rise was constructed so that the wall facing what remained of The Hill had no windows. Not only was the housing unaffordable, the complex literally turned its back side to the former neighborhood. Traffic corridors to the downtown shopping area were disrupted and nothing was done to attract new retailers to The Hill.

Second, the city built Chatham Center, an elaborate hotel complex complete with a very expensive restaurant, a movie theatre, a public parking lot, and a high-rent office complex. Third came the Civic Arena, a sports and events complex with an elaborate dome that could be opened to allow attendees a view of the sky and the downtown skyline. The portion of the building into which the roof folded conveniently created a visual barrier between downtown and The Hill.

While the residents of The Hill were promised revitalization of <u>their</u> neighborhood, what they got was a flawed plan—developed by and for Whites. As the new, high-end complexes rose from the rubble of demolition, at least 1,551 families and 431 small businesses had been displaced. Blacks lost much more than their close-knit community. They lost economic and political power as well. Black-owned businesses in the lower Hill had included pharmacies, jewelers, cleaners, grocery stores, bars, and nightclubs. These provided employment for many Blacks, including locally and nationally known musicians who played at the Crawford Grill Number 1, the Hurricane Club, and the Savoy. Urban renewal forced the closing of all these businesses. Because life outside of the Lower Hill was filled with racism and restrictive covenants against Blacks, many of these businesses were unable to relocate to other communities. This had a devastating impact on Black economic power.

Charitably, one might say that urban redevelopment as a government function was in its infancy and the mistakes made in The Hill offered lessons (albeit bitter ones) from which the urban planners learned. For example, planning had proceeded without the involvement of local residents and community leaders. The dangers of this miscalculation were duly noted as Pittsburgh's redevelopment attention moved on to East Liberty.

Urban Redevelopment Lessons Learned?

The East Liberty section of the city had a central shopping district that once was called "Pittsburgh's second downtown." It was home to furniture, department, and jewelry stores, pharmacies, several floral shops, five elegant movie theatres, several restaurants, bars, realtors, a prominent Cadillac dealership, branches of every major Pittsburgh bank, a number of magnificent old churches, and a variety of other businesses and landmarks. Moderately priced housing lined Frankstown Avenue along with several bars and nightclubs which somewhat compensated for the loss of similar establishments in the Lower Hill. Stretching out from the central shopping district were additional small stores, bars, restaurants, and nightclubs as well as residential units. The Ellsworth Avenue Bridge connected vehicle and pedestrian traffic to Shadyside, a very affluent neighborhood. Highland Park, another affluent community, was also adjacent to East Liberty. Despite this wealth of assets, East Liberty, like The Hill, was in need of refurbishing. Enter the Urban Redevelopment Authority.

Because city officials had been so severely criticized about the redevelopment of The Hill and because a large majority of East Liberty residents and business owners were white, meetings were held to share the new vision for the neighborhood. Officials were welcomed with a mixture of distrust and gratitude. Polished presentations and glitzy flip charts convinced residents and business owners that, *this time*, the Urban Redevelopment Authority had conceived a plan that would revitalize the community and save it from further decline.[59]

Unfortunately, the plan contained a fatal flaw—construction of a road that would completely encircle the heart of East Liberty. Rather than traveling through the heart of the business district, commuters could now speed around it. The multi-lane road effectively isolated the businesses from the affluent Highland Park neighborhood. Demolition of the Ellsworth Avenue Bridge severed the main access route from the affluent Shadyside neighborhood.

The convenience of on-street parking adjacent to shoppers' destinations was replaced by consolidated, metered parking lots that increased walking distances, a major nuisance when loaded down with purchases. Robert Pease suggested that merchants remedy this problem by building a second entrance that faced the traffic circle. During this time, suburban malls with free parking were becoming shopping destinations around Pittsburgh.

The Blacks who had just recently relocated from The Hill found themselves facing a new wave of displacement. As the economic heart of East Liberty dwindled from lack of customers, storefronts became vacant. Housing was left to deteriorate. Crime increased. And those who could, left for safer, cleaner neighborhoods.

As the urban renewal juggernaut plowed its way through Pittsburgh's Black communities, impoverished Black residents were again left behind with substandard housing in a fragmented, often hostile, neighborhood. The supply of homes and apartments into which Blacks were permitted to move dried up. Realtors

Urban Renewal, the beginning of the end

---

59 Often, such meetings are purported to be public hearings where those who will be most affected by proposed developments can provide input, have their concerns addressed, and participate in decision-making. Yet, even today, the planners and government representatives come prepared with fully conceptualized plans, beautiful computer-rendered schematics, and promises of progress. Audience questions are deflected with responses like, "Excellent question. As you can see here (click on PowerPoint diagram), we have…" Whether the design element genuinely answers the questions takes second place to "selling" the experts' vision.

reaped a financial windfall by controlling the for-sale and rental stock. They knew that Blacks, who were being displaced by urban "renewal," would need to find places to live. They also knew where Blacks were permitted to live. They were aware that no one was going to build new units to accommodate Blacks except, of course, public housing complexes. These realtors snatched up available for-sale units and made a small fortune from subdividing the units. Sometimes these units were unbelievably small. Because Blacks were desperate for decent housing, they accepted inflated rents that were far above market rate. The overcrowding of these units often led to their rapid deterioration.

For those who lacked the financial resources to pursue rentals or ownership in the private market, public housing projects were often the only alternative. Although the projects were allegedly integrated, for the most part, the integration resembled a checkerboard. There were several "courts" in each project, each with a set number of apartments. Blacks lived in some courts; Whites in others, and might never cross paths. Further, the projects were built on hilltops with few access roads. This served to isolate lower income Blacks from middle to upper class communities. The effects of "urban renewal" continue today as residents of public housing projects and other blighted communities battle poverty, drugs, and violence. Jim Crow culture is remarkably persistent.

Building demolished during urban renewal

CHAPTER 16

FIGHTING JIM CROW CULTURE

Cemeteries

One might think that death brought an end to the indignities of discrimination. Sadly, this was not the case as the nation's cemeteries were as segregated as housing. In the South, the law prohibited burying Blacks next to Whites. No laws prevented Blacks from being buried in White northern cemeteries, but Jim Crow customs did the job just as well.

Around 1968, a friend of mine died in a small West Virginia town. His sister, my girlfriend, asked me to accompany her to the funeral. I was a bit apprehensive, given the fact that I knew hers was the only Black family in a White church. At first I thought I had been too suspicious, too judgmental. After all, the White minister was giving Mickey a good send-off. He spoke with eloquence about the special person Mickey was; how everyone loved Mickey; how sad it was that he had gone to his reward, which was surely in heaven.

I chided myself, "Ralph, maybe you are wrong about this situation; maybe they did love Mickey." At the conclusion of the ceremony I rode in the family car to the cemetery. A fancy wrought iron gate marked the entrance to the cemetery, but the procession kept moving. "Hey," I said, "we just missed the entrance." Everyone remained silent, even after I repeated my statement. Shortly, the lead car turned onto a dirt road next to a small, one story house that looked abandoned. Chickens were running through grass long overdue for a cutting. Slowly, the situation dawned on me. We had just entered the colored-only graveyard. The chickens were scratching on the graves of Black folks.

"Don't say anything, Ralph, please! You will only hurt Mom." I did not wish to add to the family's grief, so I remained in the vehicle as my friend was buried in that God-forsaken place. It still hurts that the family of my friend accepted this humiliation without protest. I was so angry; I wanted to return to that church and knock it to the ground. The journey back to town was made in complete silence. Jim Crow had won again!

I faced this same humiliation in 1980 when my mother died and again ten years later when my father passed. Both were buried in segregated Pittsburgh cemeteries, and like my long ago girlfriend, I kept silent. In the case of Mom, who I loved more than life, I did not protest out of respect for my father. Neither he nor my other relatives understood why I fought so hard against racism. It did not seem kind to force my views on my family when they were grieving Mom's death. When my father died, I said nothing because, in life, he would not have appreciated my protest. Like so many others, I kept silent while my hatred for the system burned like a fire in my soul.

Pittsburgh has two "public" graveyards—Allegheny Cemetery and Homewood Cemetery. For many years, the latter was restricted to rich, White folks. The grounds are dotted with magnificent grave stones and mausoleums bearing the names of the most famous of Pittsburgh's elite. When Blacks were finally permitted to be buried in Homewood, their graves were placed in a flat area where markers had to be flush with the ground. No one actually said that Blacks couldn't be buried in the area with above ground monuments, but the initial costs and annual maintenance expenses were prohibitive.

I tried to determine when the quiet Jim Crow discrimination against Blacks in Homewood Cemetery ended, but failed to find a definitive answer. I spoke to the administrative offices of Homewood Cemetery and Allegheny Cemetery and, of course, no one would admit to knowing anything about the process. Nor were any official records to be had. I checked random editions of *The Pittsburgh Press*, *Pittsburgh Post-Gazette* and *Pittsburgh Sun-Telegraph* from 1921 to 2000 and found no mention of segregated cemeteries. I searched *The Pittsburgh Courier* from 1920 to 1980, and even there I found relatively few articles:

> September 22, 1951—CEMETERIES HAVE GHETTOS FOR DEAD." The article, written by Alma A. Polk, "… indicated that there were special sections for Negroes in Homewood, Allegheny, Greenwood, Duncan Heights, Uniondale, Highwood, Mount Lebanon, Braddock, and Monongahela cemeteries." Polk quoted Daniel A. Cain of East Liberty as saying, "I have never seen a white funeral in any of the colored sections, and that includes even the veterans' plot." John Crunkleton, a funeral director from the Northside, said most of his funerals were in Uniondale and Highwood Cemeteries, where "They have strictly 'colored' sections for the single and double-grave spaces."

> November 7, 1959--Pittsburghers Speak Up Column. *The Courier* posed the question: "Do you think that Negroes should push for non-segregated cemeteries, or should they sponsor their own?" Of the thirteen people interviewed, three were in favor of separate cemeteries, and ten preferred the graveyards to be integrated.

> April 27, 1996—Burying Racism. In her commentary, Bernice Powell Jackson wrote that Blacks continued to be buried in segregated cemeteries, even at that late date.

CHAPTER 17

FIGHTING JIM CROW CULTURE

Education

Public Education

For many years, it was a felony in the South for Blacks to be caught with a book in their hands. Whites who taught Blacks to read could also be punished. While no such laws existed in the North, educating Blacks was not even considered until well into the 1800s. In Pennsylvania, the Acts of 1802 and 1804, provided for free education for poor children, but did not apply to Black children. It was assumed that Blacks would not be attending school with White children, yet no provisions were made to educate Black youngsters separately. At first, Black citizens made no move for inclusion in public schools. Instead, they made plans to educate their own children. In 1818, the first school for Black children was opened, but soon failed for lack of funds. In 1832, Blacks met in the African Methodist Church to organize the Pittsburgh African Methodist Episcopal Church. The organization opened one school, but it, too, failed for lack of funds.[60]

FIGURE 17.1

OFFICERS OF PITTSBURGH AFRICAN METHODIST EPISCOPAL CHURCH

- John B. Vashon
- Louis Woodson
- A.O. Lewis.

By 1853, Pittsburgh had opened four free public schools. No Blacks were permitted to attend; all the teachers were White. On December 18, 1853, Blacks sent a letter to the Director of the Second Ward School asking that Black children be permitted to attend a school located at First Street between Wood and Smithfield Street in the downtown section of Pittsburgh. The school would be operated by Blacks, but the Board of Education was asked to pay the salary for the teacher. This very modest request was completely ignored.

---

60 The information about the history of public education is drawn from my doctoral dissertation research, now published as *Racial Discrimination against Black Teachers and Professionals in the Pittsburgh Public School System, 1834-1973* (Oakmont, PA: Learning Moments Press, 2021).

In January 1837, Charles Avery, Samuel Church, and Alex Laughlin sent a letter to the Board of Education stating that the laws regarding free, mandatory public education were intended for Black as well as White children. If Black children were barred from attending school with White children, then the Board of Education should consider setting up separate schools or providing funds to pay for the teacher in the school already operated by Blacks.

Finally, in 1837, the Board agreed to the requests of Black citizens and established two "Colored" schools. The first was located on the Northside in the Robinson Street Baptist Church. The following year a second school was opened in a small Black church located on Litenberg Alley. Over the next few years, the schools were relocated in various Black churches until 1867, when they were combined in the newly constructed school on Miller Street in The Hill District.

In 1854, the Pennsylvania legislature passed a law requiring that all Pennsylvania school districts establish separate schools for Negro and Mulatto children. As long as Pittsburgh's "colored" school operated, some Blacks were hired to teach at salaries lower than those of their White counterparts. In 1874, the Pittsburgh Board of Education petitioned the State for permission to close the "colored" school, because its costs placed a financial burden on the district. In 1881, the school was closed when the State rescinded the mandated separate "colored" school system. Black students were then permitted to attend schools located in the ward where they lived.[61] At that point, the Board of Education stopped hiring Black teachers and the blatant discrimination continued until 1937.

From the time the "colored" school was closed until 1937, minutes of the Pittsburgh Board of Education meetings made no mention of educating Blacks or hiring Black teachers. Blacks seeking positions as teachers in Pittsburgh were told, quite openly, that the Board had no intention of hiring them. While Pittsburgh prohibited the employment of Black teachers, many other Northern cities began to hire Black teachers.[62] Despite this seemingly hopeless situation, Blacks continued to pursue their dreams of becoming teachers. They went to college, received their degrees, and promptly left Pittsburgh for jobs in more hospitable cities. However, pressure was increasing for the Board of Education to cease its blatantly racist hiring policies.

The Pittsburgh Courier, under the leadership of owner Robert L. Vann, mounted a relentless public campaign. State Legislator Homer S. Brown, Attorney Richard Jones, and others lobbied the Board behind the scenes. Then Brown held state legislative hearings into the Board's hiring practices. Under this constant pressure, the Board relented, and the February 2, 1935, issue of *The Courier* announced, "35 Apply for Jobs as City Teachers." On March 9, 1935, *The Courier* reported that nine Blacks had qualified to take the teacher's exam. Despite these first, tentative steps, no Blacks were hired, and it appeared that none would be.

Because the Board failed to act in a decisive manner, a second round of hearing was launched by Brown who chaired Pennsylvania's Legislative Committee. In recalling the hearings, Brown explained the strategy he and Attorney Jones had used. Rather than arguing from a moral or civil rights stance, they argued that such practices, if proven, were a violation of Article 10 of Pennsylvania's constitution, which

61 Although it appeared that schools in the North were integrated many years prior to desegregation in the South, beneath the surface many northern Blacks did, in fact, attend segregated schools. After 1898, Blacks were free to attend any school in their neighborhood, but since the neighborhoods were segregated, the schools remained segregated as well.
62 Among the cities hiring Black professionals were Gary and Indianapolis, Indiana; Cleveland, Ohio; Philadelphia, Pennsylvania; and Washington, D.C. In addition, Black teachers could find employment in many southern cities.

provided for the operation of a public education system. Since Blacks are part of the "public," their exclusion from the teaching ranks was a violation of Commonwealth laws. The hearings, which began in April 1937 and ended in the same year, found the Pittsburgh Board of Education guilty of discrimination in the hiring of Black teachers.

Despite its new, forced hiring practices, the Board continued a pattern of discrimination. Initially, Black teachers, assistant principals, principals, and office staff were assigned only to elementary and junior high schools in the Black enclave of The Hill District. The first Blacks hired were either music or physical education teachers; the next field to open to Black teachers was home economics. Not until much later were Blacks hired as administrators at the central Board office. Despite some progress, choice assignments still went to Whites, and Black teachers found the paths to promotions and pay raises blocked. In the 1960s and 1970s, the Board became the target of many demonstrations by civil rights groups. Pittsburgh did not get a Black superintendent until well into the 1990s even though, for many years, black students outnumbered Whites.

I must say that the Black teachers at Vann Elementary and Herron Hill Junior High were excellent and taught their students far more than what was in the textbooks. When the Pittsburgh School system was integrated, all of these fine teachers were transferred to White schools. Conversely, the very best Black teachers were not replaced by the very best White teachers. In fact, the NAACP complained that the only White teachers to be assigned to Herron Hill were those who could not find a way to avoid the transfer. Under integration, the Black community lost an invaluable resource.

Discrimination in the hiring, assignment, and promotion of Black teachers, administrators, and clerical staff is one side of Pittsburgh's Jim Crow culture in the area of education. The other side is treatment of Black students in "integrated" schools. When ordered to integrate the Pittsburgh public school system, the Board used bussing as a strategy to fulfill the mandate. Interestingly, it was always Black youngsters who were bussed to White schools. In only one instance were White students bussed into a predominantly Black neighborhood where an elite school was located at the periphery of the community. Many Black residents were upset because they felt that Black youngsters had a harder time getting into this local school than White youngsters.

In Chapter 3, I mentioned some of the discrimination I experienced as a student at Schenley High School. To those I add the following anecdote as an exemplar of the unfair treatment to which Black students were subjected:

> In reaction to the complaints of Black students, the administration rigged the next election for student government. White candidates had been told of their participation weeks ahead. I found out I was to be the Black candidate 10 minutes before the election speeches were to be held in the auditorium. I barely reached the stage before my name was called. The White candidates had had a chance to wear dress clothes for their presentations. I was dressed in a sweat shirt and jeans. The other candidates and the principal acted as if they smelled something rotten as I approached the podium.

> Since I had been offered as a weak appeasement to Black students, I had little to lose. My impromptu speech had everyone but those on the stage laughing. To the administration's consternation, I won the election for president of the student government. I was not the

first Black student to serve as president, but I was the "wrong kind of Negro"—too dark and right from the ghetto. The previous Black president had been light-skinned, came from an upper crust family, and lived in the rich neighborhood of Schenley Heights. Even worse, I insisted on representing the student body rather than serving as a "mouthpiece" for the principal. Because of my comments at student government meetings, the administration took the unprecedented step of not publishing minutes of the meetings.

One day, Mr. Kohut, my homeroom teacher, asked me to hang back for a minute so he could speak to me about the administration's concerns. They were upset with my stance as a vocal advocate for students. If I did not "straighten up," all of the awards I was supposed to receive at graduation—including my scholarships—would go to Robert Taylor, who had been the administration's preferred candidate for student government president.

With a heavy heart, I explained what had happened to my parents. I felt they had to be involved in my decision, because I didn't want to disappoint them. They had been very proud when I graduated from elementary school and junior high with highest honors and many accolades including being class valedictorian. Mom and Dad said, "Son, you do what you think is right, and we will still be proud of you." No, I was proud of them!

When I told Mr. Kohut of my decision, he put his hand on my shoulder and said, "I thought that is what you'd do. I want you to know that I'm as proud of you as your parents are." The die was cast! I continued to be a thorn in the side of the administration. And true their threat, I sat on the stage at graduation and saw all my awards go to Robert, except for two scholarships they had to announce, because I had won them on my own. I shook Mr. McCormick's hand with all the strength I could muster, stared him down, and vowed to get even.

A few years later, I sat on a Board of a poverty program that Mr. McCormick approached for some funding for his school. I reminded him of my graduation from Schenley. Certain that whatever funds he received would not serve Black students, Mr. McCormick's requests were not approved during the years I served on the board.

Later, as a member of Pittsburgh's Young Adult Chapter of the NAACP, I was involved in examining treatment of Black students in the city's school system. We determined that Blacks were suspended from school at twice the rate of Whites for the same offense. In particular, Black males were suspended at a rate *five times greater* than White male students for the same offense. We learned that many White teachers assigned to predominantly Black schools seemed to believe that Black children were incapable of learning, so why waste time even trying. This resulted in a self-fulfilling prophecy as teachers didn't teach, students didn't learn and as they failed, many dropped out of school. The Pittsburgh Chapter of the NAACP contended that the system treated young Black males so badly many of them were turned off to education by the third grade.

I attended three public schools: Robert L. Vann Elementary School on Watt Street in The Hill, Herron Hill Junior High School in the Upper Hill, and Schenley High in Oakland. I could fill another book with stories about the ill treatment Black students experienced, particularly at Schenley. Many of the individuals presented in Section 2 of *Voices* recounted experiences of racism at the hands of White teachers, so I will not repeat those. Suffice it to say, as we progressed from elementary to high school, prejudicial treatment intensified. My friends and I agreed that White kids who seemed to be cool in elementary school started treating us badly once we entered into junior high school. When students graduated from Herron Hill and went to Schenley High School, they entered a predominantly White world. About 70% of the student body was White; there was not one single Black teacher or administrator in the school. Although White kids associated with Blacks inside the school buildings, they pretended that they did not know us when we were outside. This hurt a great deal, so my friends and I retaliated by refusing to speak to White students while on school grounds. In addition to this social form of discriminations was the advice of teachers and counselors that we should attend trade schools, even though the labor unions would not admit Blacks. Black students were discouraged from taking classes that would prepare them for college.

Higher Education

Common sense would suggest that racism was not prevalent in higher education where so many highly intelligent individuals worked. Sadly, that was not the case. Discrimination was entrenched toward students, faculty, and staff. I share some of my experiences, only as examples of prejudice encountered by so many who dared to enter the "ivory tower." My focus is on the University of Pittsburgh, because I was most familiar with that institution. Similar discrimination was practiced in other Pittsburgh area colleges and universities. During the course of the civil rights movement, Chatham College, Carnegie Mellon University, Duquesne University, Carlow College, and Allegheny Community College were among those targeted for demonstrations, sit-ins, take-overs, and negotiations.

At the University of Pittsburgh I had no Black professors; the only Black teachers were graduate assistants or interns. There were no Black administrators. The only Black employees I saw during my undergraduate days (1961 to 1965) were the two elevator operators in the Cathedral of Learning, cafeteria workers, and janitors. Of course, there were some athletes, but often I was the only dark face in a sea of white students in a 200-seat auditorium.

The few of us Black students sought comfort by congregating in one corner in the "Tuck Shop," a snack shop in the Cathedral of Learning basement. Because we were free to sit anywhere we wanted, some Whites including writers for the *Pitt News* wanted to know why we were self-segregating. Apparently they couldn't comprehend that we wanted to combat the isolation we were experiencing by spending time with those who were sharing the same experiences.

During my undergraduate days I was befriended by a White professor, or so I thought until the day he called and asked for my help with a "problem." It seems his television had died and he was looking for a "good deal" on a new one. I had a friend who owned a furniture and appliance store where I thought I could get him a new set at cost. This offer was met with dead silence. Then he said, "That was not exactly what I had in mind."

"Oh? What then?"

"Well, you know. I thought you could get one by using your connections."

"Wait," I said with dawning understanding and anger. "Are you talking about my *stealing* a television?"

"No! Of course not," he replied with shock. "I would never have you do something like that! I just thought that your connections could get me a 'slightly warm' television."

My so-called friend assumed my "ghetto connections" gave me access to people who stole for a living. He saw nothing wrong with exploiting these imagined connections. After all I was a Negro.

The friendship finally ended when I asked him for a small favor that would have cost him nothing, and he responded with a stern lecture laced with racist overtones. I was happy to be rid of him, but it still hurt that he was simply using me to prove how liberal he was. It hurts even more to admit I was so enamored by the thought of having a White professor as a friend, my ego overrode my good sense.

Acts of Resistance

Upon returning to Pittsburgh in 1960, I joined a very active Young Adult Chapter of the Pittsburgh Branch of the NAACP, participating in many demonstrations and discrimination investigations. As mentioned in Chapter 5, I was challenged by Dorothy Williams to start a student chapter of the NAACP at the University of Pittsburgh. I accepted the challenge and as President of Pitt's Chapter, joined with members of other organizations to protest the many racist practices we were discovering. Discrimination was pervasive in the hiring, promotion, and retention of faculty, administrators, and staff. The School of Medicine had a quota system for admitting Blacks and women. The April 4, 1964 edition of *The Pittsburgh Courier* carried a story with the headline "PITT NAACP BIAS PROBE COMPLETED." The article reported bias in the membership policy of the University Club. Of course, the NAACP chapter brought an end to the practice.

Organizing the University of Pittsburgh chapter of the NAACP was a bit of a challenge, especially since a young Jewish woman and I constantly battled for leadership. She was coming from a community that was accustomed to being the leaders. I was coming from a community that was just beginning to assume leadership of our own organizations. I finally said, "Joy, there's no way I'm going to allow a White person to lead this chapter." When she persisted, I finally said if she didn't back down, I would ask her to leave the organization. When I spoke with Blacks who led other groups, they expressed the same frustration with Whites wanting to lead interracial groups. Accustomed to leadership roles, many White liberals didn't understand why we felt it so important to lead Black and interracial organizations. Those who understood willingly took non-leadership roles to help the civil rights movement. Others got angry and left.

I was involved in so many protests that I was labeled "a troublesome militant" by many of Pitt's administrators. The more I exposed discrimination at Pitt, the greater the risk of retaliation by the University administration. How surprising when one of my scholarships was "lost!" In a counter move, I secured another scholarship, so when the financial aid department told me that they had "accidentally" given my scholarship to another Black student, I smiled, pulled the paperwork for the new scholarship award out of my pocket, and presented it. Their "mistake" had made not one dent in my financial situation.

Joining the World of Academia

While an undergraduate, I had many conversations with a White professor about the culturally biased and fairly irrelevant education I was receiving. In 1968, years after those conversations, I had a good, fairly well-paying job as head of the Poverty Program in The Hill. One day the professor called and asked, "Ralph, do you remember those conversations about the irrelevance of Pitt's education system? Well, I've just taken a job as a dean at Pitt, and I want you to come to work for me." That's how I became the first Black Assistant Dean in the history of the University of Pittsburgh.

As an assistant dean, I was able to continue fighting for equal rights. Together, the dean and I accomplished his goal of changing the face of undergraduate education at Pitt. We established the New Careers Program, revised the University Community Education Program, and made it possible for more minorities and women to attend Pitt. Professionally, this experience was very satisfying. On a personal level, however, it sadly turned out that my boss held a number of prejudiced stereotypes. One day we were discussing my future at Pitt. I said I wanted to get a doctoral degree in his field, which was philosophy. He said something like, "Well, you know a degree in philosophy takes a lot of work. It is a very *academic* program." His words stung! Racism ran deep at this so-called liberal, educational institution. I began to pay much more attention to my boss' behavior. He was, indeed, a liberal racist.

One day he came into my office to ask my help with a personal problem. Once again I let my ego over-ride my protective defenses and asked how I could help. His daughters were being terrorized by a neighborhood dog that frequently chased them home from school. He rejected my suggestion to call the police saying he had already tried that and they could do nothing unless an actual physical attack took place. To my suggestion of contacting the city's animal control department, he responded, "Been there, done that" with no help in sight. He had tried, to no avail, speaking to the dog's owner. When I had no other solutions to offer, he said, "I thought you could have someone 'take care' of the dog." Yes, this liberal college dean/professor wanted to put out a contract on the dog and assumed I had criminal friends who would kill it. Needless to say, I rejected his request to solve the dog problem as well as his assessment that I wouldn't be able to handle the rigors of a doctoral problem.

I met with the dean of the School of Education and learned I could earn a doctorate by take two trimesters of classes. My life and work experience, including being a college administrator and teacher, would count for the remaining credits required for the degree. They would also provide already-compiled data that could be used for my dissertation. How could I resist such a sweetheart deal? Easy! It felt as though these folks thought I did not have the intellectual capacity to earn a degree in the normal way. So instead, I enrolled in a very rigorous graduate program in the History Department. Maybe my sensitivity to perceived insults wasn't such a good thing. I could have had a doctorate in one and one-half years, rather than the five long, hard years it took to complete the history degree.

Teaching Black Culture and Black History

For many years Pittsburgh Blacks who attended any institution of higher learning could not study their own history. While Blacks who attended Black colleges and universities were proudly learning about the glories of ancient Africa and the contributions of African Americans, we northerners were being deprived of any such information on the college level.

During my time as Assistant Dean, I enrolled in an evening course on African-American Anthropology taught by a White professor named Art Tuden. I attended the course and loved the new information I was learning. As a result of taking the course and my developing friendship with Art, I wound up teaching a course called "African-American Anthropology." In the same year, I was offered the opportunity to teach Introduction to Social Work. I found that I loved teaching, but my primary responsibility was still as Assistant Dean in the College of Arts and Sciences. It was as a result of that position that I became the first Black to teach African American history at Pitt.

In 1968, the history department, under Dr. Samuel Hayes, made a commitment to hire its first Black instructor who would teach a new course on African-American history. I was working in my office when the phone rang. A Black student was irate about the cancellation of the African-American History course. I promised to look into his complaint and went back to what I was doing. In short order, the phone rang again; it was another student complaining about the cancelled class. After several more calls, I called Dr. Hayes who said the Black professor who had agreed to teach the course decided he did not wish to come to Pittsburgh. "I have no one else in the department who is qualified to teach the course," Dr. Hayes explained. Just as I was about to thank him and hang up, he asked, "What did you say your name is?" When I responded, Ralph Proctor, he said, "Are you the same person who has that show on WQED? What's it called—*Black Horizons*?" When I confirmed this, he continued, "I have been watching your show and it's obvious you know something about African-American History. Why don't you teach the course?"

I was stunned and asked if I could call him back. Hurriedly, I called several friends, all of whom advised me to take the challenge. I did so and, as they say, "the rest is history." I started reading and writing at a fevered pitch. I spent that first term barely one lesson ahead of my students. After teaching for about a year, it was obvious that there was not enough time, in one term, to teach the totality of the Black experience. I divided the course into two parts. According to my research at the time, we were among the first mainstream, White-controlled higher education institutions to take this step.

When I began teaching, the civil rights movement was at the height of its power and influence. I expected my African-American history classes to be filled with Black students. Surprisingly, of more than 200 students in the class, 75 percent were White! It was five years later that the population changed and more Blacks than Whites signed up for the class.

I wanted to be the best possible teacher. I envisioned my classes as being fun, informational sessions, after which students would hang around and engage in heavy philosophical discussions. At the end of my first class, the bell rang, and 200 students dashed for the auditorium exits. In a nano-second, I was standing alone with a bewildered look on my face. What had gone wrong?

I worked even harder on my second lecture, and before lecturing, invited students to stay after class and engage in some give-and-take discussions. The bell rang and the mass exodus was like a herd of stampeding African elephants. I was devastated. I was obviously a failure as a college professor.

The third time, I stopped a student and asked, "Why do they run as soon as the bell rings?" She gave me a strange look and replied, "You really don't know?" In response to my befuddled silence she said, "Mr. Proctor, just look at you! You are a powerful man with broad shoulders, wearing a dashiki [African shirt], with that big 'fro' hair style, and a carved black fist dangling from a gold chain around your neck. You have a very commanding presence. Most of these kids, including me, have never seen a Black instructor. There you stand looking all menacing, telling the kids in that deep resonant voice that bounces off the walls, what White people have done to Black people over the past. Come on now, these are White kids. To put it briefly, they're scared shitless of you!"

I was dumbfounded, but began checking out her theory. One student said, "Hell man, I'm Black and you scare the shit out of *me* when you talk about your experiences in the civil rights movement. If I was White, I would stay as far away from you as I could!"

All this information was overwhelming; I wanted to be as good a teacher as Art Tuden, yet I was failing miserably. I decided to sit in on one of Art's classes to see if I could find the source of his magic. Even though he was a tough instructor with high expectations, his classes filled to capacity. Students got angry with other students who took too long to complete exams, chiding them that they were cutting into Tuden's lecture time. So what was his magic? Laughter! Art used humor to engage his students in some very tough content.

Well, no one had ever accused me of being humorous. What to do? I spent the week before my next class in a systematic exploration of stand-up comedians. I watched every single one who appeared on television and listened over and over again to record albums featuring comedy routines. Finally, it was time to debut the newly minted, humorous Ralph Proctor.

The students piled into class, and I began to review information from the previous classes. Only, this time, I used humor and told a few lame jokes. Soon the air was filled with laughter. When the bell rang, students stayed and talked among themselves; some even asked me questions. Soon the advisors were telling me that my course was among the most popular at Pitt. I was elated.

In my second term, I entered the classroom on the first day of class. A young White woman sat near the front of the room, and I was delighted that she had decided to enroll in the second half of the course. I said "Good evening. How are you?" She turned bright crimson, but claimed she was okay when I asked if she was alright. I apologized for embarrassing her, but she claimed she wasn't embarrassed. Then it hit me. "You're afraid of me, aren't you?"

"You better believe it!"

"I don't understand. You took the first half of the course and now you are taking the second half. Did I frighten you in the first part of the course?"

"Yes, you did!"

"So why did you sign up for the second half?"

"Oh. I signed up for the class, because you are such a good instructor; the best I ever had. But you scare the shit out of me. I live in the nurse's residence about six blocks away. The first day of class was a beautiful summer evening, so I walked to your class. You kept yelling at me about what Whites had done to your people. You scared the shit out of me! By the end of class my knees were shaking so badly I could hardly walk. I had to call my boyfriend to come pick me up and drive me back to the dorm. I had him do that every time the class met, otherwise I would have never been able to finish the course."

I laughed and promised I would not yell during class. "So, did you make the same arrangement with your boyfriend?"

"No. I broke up with him. He said something racist. Before your course, I wouldn't have known it. I guess it's your fault we broke up."

I promised that, if I frightened her as badly in the present term, I would personally drive her to her dorm. She said, "Well, I hope your car is close by, because this conversation has me totally freaked! Just look at my hands." They were indeed shaking very badly. I drove her to her dorm that evening. Soon she was making the journey by herself.

As I said, when I began teaching at Pitt, it was the height of the civil rights movement. I soon learned that, despite my strong indications to the contrary, some of my students began to view me as some sort of folk hero. I discouraged this view for a number of reasons. The most important was that I was no hero. I was just an ordinary man doing what he believed in. Second, when folks put you on a pedestal, they sometimes have unrealistic expectations of you. This became apparent one day fairly early in my teaching career.

As I was gathering my notes at the end of a lecture, Freda, an old friend from the southern movement, bounded down the steps and leaped into my arms. We embraced, silently exchanged a few gentle kisses, wept a bit, spoke a few words, and then she was gone. As I was composing myself, I noticed two students and a man I didn't know standing nearby. All were White. When I asked if they wanted something, one of the women said, "I am so disappointed in you. I thought you were the coolest, most powerful man I had ever met. I was so thrilled, I brought my husband to meet you, and what do we see? Some White woman in your arms!"

When I recovered from my shock, I was furious. "I don't know who the hell you are and why it's any of your business who I embrace. I have no time or tolerance for your misguided hero worship! You're no different from the racists in the South who could not stand the thought of my touching, let alone loving, a white woman. I don't owe you any damned explanation, but I want you to know just how bigoted your remarks are. I went on to say:

> The woman in my arms was Freda, who I met during the southern movement. She ate the same food, slept on the same mats, and endured the same pain and humiliation Blacks endured.
>
> During one of the marches, a White mob that included local law enforcement officers attacked us. I was trying to protect another marcher, lost my footing, and fell. The rednecks were on me immediately, and I was having one hell of a time trying to get to my feet while protecting my head. Out of the corner of my eye, I saw this flash of White skin and thought, "Damn, they really are trying to kill me." It turns out, it was Freda. She had run between the cops and dived onto my body to protect me. I knew immediately that she was in mortal danger, which gave me super strength. I picked her up and kicked one of my attackers in the balls. He screamed so loud that the other fuckers froze. That gave me time to get Freda out of danger. I yelled, "What the hell were you doing, woman! You could have been killed! You know that they would not hesitate to kill you, a White woman, protecting a Black man! You know the rules. They hate me because I'm a Nigger. They hate you more, because you are a nigger lover. They'd rather kill you than me. What the hell got into you?"
>
> Freda was shaking like a leaf; tears cut through the sweat pouring down her face. She said, "I don't know. You are always helping everyone else, protecting the women and the children. Now there you were, on the ground. I had never seen you off your feet. Everyone was frozen! Nobody was moving to protect you, so I had to do something!"

I said, 'Girl, you are one crazy White woman. I love you for your courage, but if you ever do something like that again, I will personally kick your ass!" Shortly after that I left the South and came home. I haven't seen my hero in eight years.

I concluded this explanation by telling the student, "For your information, she came here tonight to say goodbye. She's leaving for Africa, because she can no longer live in a country that treats Blacks so badly. She said she won't return until Blacks are treated right. I expect that I will never see her again. My heart is breaking. As far as I'm concerned you can get your racist ass out of my class." With that, I walked away to mourn the loss of my good friend. I never saw Freda again.

I had been at Pitt for five years (1968 to 1973) when my boss decided to leave Pitt. He became upset when I said I wasn't resigning my position just because he was moving on. Apparently he had told some amorphous "them," that I would leave along with him. "Tell *them*," I said, "you're not the Pharaoh and I'm not killing myself because you're stepping down." He was livid. Despite my refusal to resign, another Black man was brought in to replace me. The dean who replaced my boss let the discriminatory cat out of the bag. The dean's office was configured to have a White male as Dean; a White male as Associate Dean; a White female as Assistant Dean, and a Black male as Assistant Dean. I immediately sued in Federal Court. I lost the case as witnesses lied about the situation. In the interim, Pitt eliminated my position, as part of the all-too-familiar "reorganization."[63]

A new position was created with a different title and slightly altered responsibilities. My "replacement" stopped by to chat with me soon after he set up his office. I tried to be helpful and keep my own feelings from influencing his adjustment to the university. Less than two weeks later, he returned to my office. "I'm quitting," he announced. "This job is so obviously a sham. It was created for a Negro as nothing more than window dressing. I earned my Ph.D. just like these other administrators. I'm insulted. I'm not about to be a 'House Nigger!' In case they can't figure it out, I'm going to tell them exactly what they can do with this job." He shook my hand and stomped out of my office. I wish I could have been a fly on the wall of the Dean's office. Later, one of the secretaries told me it had been quite a scene. I, too, left Pitt completely disgusted with "liberal" educators.

In 1968, the year I began teaching Black history at Pitt, the Community College of Allegheny County (CCAC) offered its first course on African American History at its Northside Campus. The evening course was taught by William Russell Robinson, the first Black to teach such a course at CCAC. Soon, other colleges and universities in the tri-state area followed, but only after considerable outside pressure.

Sadly, discrimination at CCAC was pretty much the same as at Pitt. This was ironic, given that K. Leroy Irvis, the first Black man elected as Speaker of the House of Representatives of the Pennsylvania legislature, had played an influential role in securing funding to start the institution. CCAC was intended to be open to all county residents and tuition was to be kept low to make it accessible to economically disadvantaged students. The main Allegheny Campus, located in a predominantly Black neighborhood, was often referred to, by many White staff and faculty, as the "nigger," "colored" or "inner city" campus. When the college opened its doors in 1966, most of the staff and faculty hired were White. From its beginning, the atmosphere has been unwelcoming to Blacks. Black leaders were

---

63 During the height of the Civil Rights movement, organizations reorganized to rid themselves of troublesome Blacks like me. Proving this to be a discriminatory process was very difficult.

appalled that a college—created by government and supported by tax revenues—openly practiced racial discrimination. The college soon became a target for demonstrations and civil rights negotiations.[64]

Children in Hill District School

---

64 In 2006, a new president came to CCAC, Dr, Stuart Sutin under whom significant changes were changes were made towards equality. First, a new soon-to-be-constructed science building would be named in honor of K. Leroy Irvis. The idea for the naming of the building came from the late Dr. Elmer Haymon, Jr and me. Under Dr. Sutin, I was fortunate to be asked to establish a new division, called the Office of Institutional Equity and Inclusion. I served as the first Vice President and Chief Diversity Officer of the new division.

In 2008, CCAC hired its first African-American president, Dr. Alex Johnson. He was followed by the Black president Dr. Quintin Bullock, who immediately started changing the culture of CCAC by hiring more Black administrators and creating a new initiative committed to bringing about a college-wide focus on diversity, equity and anti-racism. I am happy to report that I have worked on the new initiatives and significant changes are being made as I prepare this new edition of *Voices*.

CHAPTER 18

FIGHTING JIM CROW CULTURE

Employment

I recall one of the early efforts in civil rights in Pittsburgh. Mal Goode and the Greater Pittsburgh Improvement League tried to seek equal employment opportunities for Blacks by negotiating with the old Frank & Seders' department store way back in the late 1940s.

In Pittsburgh, in order to get the few good jobs available to Blacks, you had to be a certain hue. I was too dark to be an elevator operator. I'm not kidding; they told me this at Gimbel's Department store in downtown. CHARLES KINDLE

* * *

Eleven powerful local organizations were preparing for an "immediate action campaign" against the "Big Five" Pittsburgh department stores that employ Blacks only as stock clerks, janitors and elevator operators.[65] Among the organizations involved in the protest were: the NAACP, the Urban League, the Committee against Discrimination in Industry, the American Federation of Labor, the PAC, CIO, the Department of Civil Liberties of IBPOE, the Committee against Discrimination in Pittsburgh Department Stores, and the Allegheny County FEPC. The number of people involved in the action was estimated at 3,000. Thousands of handbills were printed with the help of the Elks Civil Liberties Department and were distributed throughout the downtown area. The flyers urged fair-minded people to call or write to the stores and cancel their charge accounts. Article in December 7, 1946 edition of *The Pittsburgh Courier*

* * *

---

65 Although the article did not name the "Big Five" stores, it is likely they were referring to Kaufmann's, Gimbels, Frank & Seder, Joseph Horne's and Rosenbaum's. I remember quite clearly that I never saw Black sales clerks in any of these stores until well into the 1950s and 1960s. That was the overt, illegal racism. Indicative of the Jim Crow culture was the tacit understanding that White customers would always be served before Black customers. I will carry to my grave the bitter memories of my mother waiting patiently for her turn, only to be brushed aside once again if a White person approached the sales clerk. When I tried to voice my outrage, Mom, who did not wish to "cause trouble," tried to shut me up by placing her hand over my mouth.

In The Hill, we had the Centre Avenue YMCA; we weren't permitted at the other YMCAs. My father was the chairman of the Board. That's probably why Frank and I became the first Negroes (we were Negroes then) hired as Counselors-in-Training at the Y's Camp Kon-o-Kwee. The next year the camp director came to me and said, "Byrd, you are the best Counselor-in-Training we ever hired. We are going to promote all the other trainees to full counselors, except you and Frank. I feel really bad about that, but the parents, especially those from the Northside would not appreciate having a Negro counselor. That was my last camping experience, and my dad resigned from the Board.
BYRD BROWN

* * *

Isaly's, a dairy company with stores in many neighborhoods, claimed they could not hire Blacks to scoop ice cream, because Black folks' hair broke off and melted the ice cream. Many Isaly's stores were picketed until they were forced to hire Blacks. Of course, they initially hired Blacks only in areas where there were many Black customers.
BYRD BROWN

* * *

Isaly's rationale for not hiring Blacks would be ridiculous, if it weren't emblematic of Pittsburgh's long history of employment discrimination. In the 19th century, most Pittsburgh Blacks worked in unskilled jobs in the steel mills or as common laborers, seamen, coachmen, waiters, whitewashers, servants, barbers, housekeepers, and washerwomen. Between 1910 and 1930, the majority of Black women worked as barbers, hairdressers, cleaners, servants, and untrained nurses; most Black men worked as domestics or in manufacturing as unskilled laborers. Blacks also worked as chauffeurs, porters, ditch diggers, hod carriers, and waiters. Blacks were encouraged to attend trade schools instead of college; yet labor unions would not admit them after they learned the appropriate trades.

Black workers did not worry about promotions or raises. They worried about keeping the jobs they had and accepted ill treatment to hold on to even the lowest of jobs. Despite the fact that Blacks spent more per capita on goods in downtown stores, no Blacks were hired in department stores until 1947 when they had jobs as stock boys, cleaners, and elevator operators. Black clerks weren't hired until much later. No Blacks sold shoes until the 1960s. Public utility companies employed Blacks only as janitors.

Byrd Brown recounts the time when shoe stores never hired a Black person. "Naturally, they did not want us in such a sensitive position because it involved grabbing and fooling around with White folk's feet. As a representative of the Black community, I always took the position that I would not meet with underlings from any company; I'd speak only with the top brass. The shoe store management (all were owned by two companies) sent Jesse Owens, a public relations person, to represent them. I guess they thought we'd be impressed with negotiating with this Black former Olympic hero.[66] I knew Mr. Owens; I had been at his home. I said, "Jesse, it's not appropriate for me to meet with you instead of the president,

---

66 Jesse Owens achieved international fame when he beat Hitler's supposedly superior Nazis in foot races in the Olympic games.

because you lack the authority to make major decisions." He understood and wasn't offended. He did not want to be put into that position, but it was his job.

There were no Blacks in the Pittsburgh judicial system. In 1950, Homer S. Brown was the first Black appointed as a judge. Until 1941, Blacks were not permitted to try out for the Pittsburgh Pirates. Until 1946, the Pittsburgh trolley company simply declared "it was not their policy to hire Black drivers." There were no Black bank tellers, let alone bank officers.

An article in the December 8, 1945, edition of *The Pittsburgh Courier* announced that Attorney Homer S. Brown, a long-time activist, legislator, NAACP leader, and jurist, had led a successful fight to secure a local Fair Employment Practice law in Pittsburgh. Also involved in the fight were R. Maurice Moss, executive director of the Pittsburgh Urban League; Alma Illery, and Florence Reizenstein, treasurer for The Allegheny County Committee for a Permanent FEPC and well-known pioneering civil rights activist. Despite this legal victory, Jim Crow culture continued to exert discriminatory practices as Blacks tried to move into professional positions.

I offer the following personal experience as an example of the humiliation faced by so many Blacks as they sought employment. When I returned home after my time in the military, I was accepted as a student by the University of Pittsburgh. Between the G.I. bill and a scholarship from the Urban League of Pittsburgh, most of my college expenses would be covered. But I needed to earn money to cover my living expenses. To assist with my job search, I made an appointment with the Commonwealth of Pennsylvania Department of Employment Security.

At the "unemployment office" I was given a series of tests to determine my aptitudes, skills, and knowledge. When I met with an employment counselor to review the results, he said, "Wow, you sure knocked these tests out. You did better than the vast majority of the people we tested around the country. In fact, your worst score puts you in the top five percent of the population. That's amazing!" Perhaps he expected me to be pleased by this praise, but given my experiences with racism, I thought it likely he was surprised a Black man could do so well. When I raised this issue, he denied any such bias, proceeded to refer me to a potential employer, and scheduled an appointment for the next day. When I arrived, I was ushered into the manager's office where we chatted for a few minutes before he said, "You have the job, and you can start tomorrow. But I need to ask, why are you dressed the way you are?" I looked down at my dark blue suit, white shirt, pale blue tie, highly polished shoes, and matching hat. "This is the way you are supposed to dress for a job interview, isn't it?"

"Sure, sure, but didn't the guy at the unemployment office tell you that you already had the job?"

"No," I replied. The guy looked at me strangely and asked, "Did he tell you what the job was?"

"All he said was I'm more than qualified for the position."

The manager was getting more uncomfortable by the minute. After what seemed like an eternity, he looked at me and said, "Damn that jerk anyhow. Listen, kid, I really am impressed with you. I wish I had another job to offer, but I don't. Ralph, this job is a stock clerk. That's why I wondered why you were dressed in a suit."

Holding back tears of rage, I left and never returned. Welcome home to racist Pittsburgh!

Banks discriminated against Blacks in both their lending practices and in hiring policies. As head of the University of Pittsburgh Chapter of the NAACP, I engaged in investigations and demonstrations against many organizations, including Mellon Bank. To test the fairness of Mellon Bank's hiring practices, my friend Skip and I applied for management trainee positions, even though neither of us really wanted such jobs. (Skip was headed to Medical School. I was not certain where my future lay in the racist environment of Pittsburgh, but banking was not anywhere on my list of possibilities.) After initial interviews at Pitt, we both passed a series of all-day interviews held at Mellon headquarters. Skip received a job offer; I received a form-letter rejection. I responded to the pro-forma dismissal by revealing the test that Skip and I had conducted and accused Mellon Bank of discrimination. I was then offered a job as a bank auditor/examiner, a position for which I had not applied and for which I had no qualifications. I was about to turn down the job when I received calls from Joe Hines and Robert Goode, the first and second Blacks to be hired by Mellon Bank. Both urged me to accept the job offer. Mellon officials were counting on my turning down the offer, thereby giving them an opportunity to claim (1) the test I had conducted was a publicity stunt intended merely to embarrass the bank, and (2) that Blacks were interested not in working, but only in protesting. Reluctantly, I accepted the job.

Mellon Bank was not a welcoming environment. As the first Black hired as a bank examiner, I knew I would be under close scrutiny. I was assigned to a team that conducted audits of Mellon Bank branches throughout the Pittsburgh area. None of the branches had Black employees, and many were located in neighborhood where few, if any, Blacks lived. Swissvale was one such neighborhood with a well-deserved reputation as a racist community. The NAACP and the Mayor's Commission on Human Relations were both involved in a number of complaints about unfair treatment Blacks received in this community when they applied for jobs or housing.

Having worked hard to prove myself, I was permitted to take turns as the head of the travelling team. I entered the Swissvale branch and was greeted by the manager who asked, "What can I do for you, Boy?" Presenting him with my identification, I replied, "I am Ralph Proctor, and 'Boy' is not in my title. However 'head of the audit team' is." The man turned bright crimson as he tried to explain away the "Boy" remark. It was too late. I found so many things wrong with this bank, my boss called from the main branch and said if I did not allow the manager to make some corrections, he would lose his job. I responded that I was simply following standard audit procedures. If he wanted the manager to correct some items, that was his right as my supervisor, but I was not about to change one word. I think they let him off, but I am certain that the manager was a bit more careful with the use of the word "Boy" after that.

On another occasion, my team drove in two cars to audit a branch serving the well-to-do, White community of Mount Lebanon, a frequent target of demonstrations. Having arrived before the rest of the team my group sat in my car chatting. At the sound of tapping on the window, I looked up to see a Mount Lebanon Police Officer, who said, "We got a call at the station that there were some suspicious men parked in the lot in front of the bank. They said it looked as if you gentlemen were 'casing' the bank."

The other members of the team started laughing. One said, "We're Mellon Bank auditors, and Ralph is the head of the crew." I showed the officer my identification, and he joined my companions in a good ole' laugh fest. The officer noticed that I was not amused, and said, "I can see that you don't think this is funny, but I'm not laughing at you. I am enjoying this, because I have to go into the bank and tell them that they called the cops on the *auditors*. I can't wait to see the manager's face. I hope I can keep a straight face. It would almost be worth taking the day off so that I can see what the hell happens at *this* audit." He walked away, still laughing. When he got inside, we could see him speaking to the manager and then he started laughing again. The cop had a good time; my team had a good time; the bank manager had the worst three days of his life!

I hated my job at Mellon, but had to continue. I had to prove that a Black man could do the job. I had to take the close scrutiny with a smile; had to be careful about my every move. Screw ups on my part would be used as an excuse to discriminate against other Blacks. I bit my lip on those occasions when I otherwise would have punched someone in the face.

I was, of course, given the worst tasks to perform. One of the most undesirable auditing tasks was a job called "Miscellaneous," which consisted of reviewing all the odds and ends that fell into no particular single category. Realizing that this was another attempt to force me to quit, I decided to make a game of the task, which really required more manual dexterity than brains. I felt up to the challenge since I had once scored at the 98th percentile when given a manual dexterity test. Whenever I was given the Miscellaneous assignment, I simply smiled and went off to do my job. During one of these audits, my two immediate supervisors called me into their office. One said, "Ralph, Joe and I have been watching your performance, and we are concerned because you always finish 'Miscellaneous' faster than anyone ever has. We think you might be missing something. Why don't you sit here with us? One of the main jobs in 'Miscellaneous' is checking mortgages and loan documents to make certain they are accurate. In order to do that, you have to check the following things very carefully."

The two supervisors then slowly turned each page of a mortgage and pointed out what I was supposed to check. Apparently satisfied with themselves, they smiled at one another and waited for me to acknowledge that I had forgotten something. I turned the document around and replied, "Yes, I do check all of those items, but I discovered that the mortgage could still be invalid unless you also check the following." I then pointed out about ten other parts of the document that no one ever checked. When I finished, both men turned beet-red, and Joe said, "Damn, Ralph, we never thought about those things, but you are right." They never questioned me again.

About one year into the job, around Christmastime 1965, we were auditing another bank in a small suburban community. Once again I was called into an inner office. I thought, "Damn, now what?" I was invited to sit down. The crew chief said, "We just got a call from headquarters and our boss wanted you to know that we all think that you are the best auditor we ever hired! How is *that* for a fantastic Christmas present?"

I smiled and said, "Thank you, and I have a present for you also." They grinned and said "What?" Without changing my expression, I said, "I QUIT! I only took this damned job to prove a Black man could do this job that you hold in such high regard. Now that you have admitted that a *Black* man is your best auditor, my job is done. Please make sure that you send my last check before Christmas." The looks on their faces was almost worth all the indignities I had suffered. Without saying another word or waiting for them to reply, I rose, walked out of the office, grabbed my coat, and headed out the door. I waved to some of the other audit team members and wished them a merry Christmas. Free at last, free at last; thank God almighty, I was free at last. According to Robert Goode, my successful tenure as an audit/examiner helped to open Mellon Bank's doors for Blacks in that and other positions.

I make no claim that my own small efforts of resistance brought about sweeping changes. Credit for that goes to the thousands of demonstrators who picketed everything from retail stores to giant corporations. One example of such protests took place around 1947 or 1948. As Robert Lavelle described it:

Some friends and I were discussing the fact that Silverman's Drug Store and Kaplan's Grocery, both located on The Hill's Herron Avenue, had many Black customers. We tried to convince the business owners that, because the establishment made most of their money from Blacks, they should employ Blacks. When they dismissed our request, we decided to picket both stores. We showed up, with signs in hand, on a Saturday night. Sadly everybody ignored their picket lines, even Black folks. We tried talking to them; told them that we were doing this for **them.** None of us needed jobs. They just ignored us! We had picketed but for a short time when the store owners called the police who came and threatened to arrest us. I protested and indicated that we were within our constitutional rights to picket and that they had no right to arrest us. My friends got a little scared and convinced me that we should end our protest. We left, but I tried to convince them that we could not be arrested for peaceful assembly. I wanted to return and picket again. Unfortunately, the police bluff worked, and my friends wanted nothing more to do with the incident. Later Silverman's hired and trained Blacks."

Lavelle refused to take credit for Silverman's change of heart, but I think he and his friends played a significant role. So often, those who protested, demonstrated, picketed, and boycotted establishments that practiced discriminatory hiring policies humbly downplayed their contributions to the civil rights movement. Yet, through persistent efforts changes were made. Credit also goes to the hundreds of thousands of other men and women who worked twice as hard to prove Blacks were capable of doing the same work as Whites. Sick and tired of Whites always questioning whether Blacks were "qualified" for employment, Byrd Brown offered as good a measure of equality as any when he appeared as a guest on a radio talk show:

I remember the shocked look on a White talk show host's face when he asked me when I would be satisfied with the progress made in this country with respect to discrimination. I replied 'When the number of dumb Black folks that have jobs equals the number of dumb White folks that have jobs.' For some reason I was never invited to appear on that show again.

Fighting for Construction Jobs

City and county leaders, under intense pressure from civil rights organizations, agreed to set aside a certain portion of construction funds for Blacks. Supposedly Blacks were to receive 25% of funds for any project spending government funds. In *no* case did the percentage of funds *ever* reach that benchmark. The companies used a variety of tricks to circumvent the law. They were quite successful, even with such projects as the construction of Three Rivers Stadium, which was largely financed by public funds.

Two of the most violent demonstrations occurred in response to discriminatory hiring practices and the awarding of construction contracts. One occurred on the Manchester Bridge which led to the site where the Three Rivers Stadium was being built as the new home of the Pittsburgh Steelers and Pittsburgh Pirates. The other took place at the site where United States Steel was building its new headquarters.

Three Rivers Stadium Demonstration—Black Monday—August 25, 1969

Writing on August 30, *Pittsburgh Courier* reporter Diane Perry wrote a follow up on the demonstration that had been held on Monday, August 25. Under the headline, "GOLDEN TRIANGLE IS HIT BY COP BRUTALITY, MASS ARRESTS: Thousands See Blacks Clubbed," Perry described the scene:

> A sense of calm prevailed in this embattled city, Wednesday, after a week's activities which included the macing of Attorney Byrd Brown, president of the Pittsburgh Chapter of the National Association of Colored People; women and children knocked to the ground, prodded and beaten by city police using clubs; people forbidden the right to collect in one of our public parks, mass arrests and mass convictions. The entrance at the foot of the Manchester Bridge which leads to the construction site at Three Rivers Stadium was crowded early Wednesday morning with demonstrators as it had been since Monday.
>
> The demonstrators were gathered again, in full force. Over 300 members of The Black Construction Coalition of Pittsburgh and their leaders were marching again at press time to protest the discrimination practiced against Black men by the building-craft unions.
>
> The police force was still very much in evidence, but there were a visual number of Black policemen to escort the demonstrators on their march.

Byrd Brown explained the events that led to the confrontation:

> After many failed negotiations between the City, the NAACP and The United Negro Protest Committee, it was obvious that we would never reach agreement about the construction jobs at Three Rivers Stadium which would soon be the home of the Pittsburgh Steelers and The Pittsburgh Pirates. We were negotiating about thousands of jobs for Blacks and millions of dollars. We called a mass rally to shut down the site. We were going to march peacefully across the Manchester Bridge and shut down the construction of the stadium. The police had other ideas. It was a police riot.

Brown went on to describe the scene:

> We had 300 people arrested and 300 people hospitalized. We thought we were going to die. As the thousand or so marchers started across the bridge, we were met by hundreds of heavily armed police, complete with mace, helmets, and big, ugly riot clubs. It was like a scene out of Mississippi.
>
> The cops were determined that we were not going to march. We were equally determined that we were. The police attacked the unarmed, peaceful marchers. They beat the marchers and sprayed them with mace. I was maced and couldn't see; somebody took my arm and led me off the bridge. Later, many of the marchers told me they were convinced the cops were going to pick them up and throw them off the bridge.

We made our way across the bridge, and I asked folks to assemble in the park on the Northside. I was pissed! I told the folks that we were marching again tomorrow and said, "I'm not telling you to come unarmed. If the cops are going to beat us, we are going to do some beating ourselves. If they beat us again, we will beat the hell out of them. We are going to shut that site down!

The crowd roared its approval, ready to do battle, ready to meet violence with violence. Because of the utter stupidity of the official who gave the order to attack the marchers, the Pittsburgh civil rights movement was very close to getting really ugly. Fortunately, the mayor called for a meeting and promised that this would not happen again. It's a good thing, because some cops were going to get hurt. We were going to bring our own "enforcers."

Others who recalled the events of that day included:

Roland Saunders: The police met the group as they attempted to reach the construction site. In order to get to the site, which was located on the Northside, we had to cross the Manchester Bridge. Before we could cross the bridge, we were met by a large force of armed policemen who attacked us without any provocation. I really believed the police were going to throw us into the river! The police action only made the marchers angrier and filled them with even more resolve.

Hop Kendrick, of the NAACP: We were met on the bridge by violent police who savagely beat the peaceful marchers. The cops were too close for us to back up, and I couldn't swim. I was not afraid, but I was sure I was going to die!"

Delores Stanton: Those cops did not wear badges; we could not identify them later. You know I'm chicken. When the cops started beating us, I ran again."

Dr. Lloyd Bell: I was not in town when this incident took place. I got a call saying, "You have to come back. Black folks are PISSED. They are talking about violence! They are saying they are coming back tomorrow and, this time, they are going to be armed." One minister cried. He was praying but, on the other hand, he was talking about folks protecting themselves by any means necessary. Folks are serious. If something was not done, Pittsburgh police were about to find that Black folks, in Pittsburgh, were not pacifists.

Canon Junius Carter: As the police goons tried to break up the demonstration by viciously beating the demonstrators, I was reminded of Mississippi. Present in the crowd that had retreated to a park on the Northside were several angry young men who were prepared to meet violence with violence. I spoke to several folks of all ages who came back the next day, armed and ready for battle. Fortunately, when the group assembled, several Black officers accompanied the group. Among the officers were William Moore and Harvey Adams. Their intention was to protect the marchers.

U.S. Steel Headquarters

Members of the civil rights fraternity were frustrated by the failure of a major corporation to negotiate in good faith. Demonstrators shut down work on the construction site by blocking ladders and otherwise preventing the construction workers from doing their jobs. On the second day of the demonstration, the construction workers went to the construction site very early in the morning and positioned themselves high on the steel framework of the building. When the demonstrators arrived, the construction workers began to throw hot rivets down at the marchers. Some even tried to urinate on the men and women below. Fortunately, no one was injured.

As Attorney Thomas Kerr describes it:

> When a massive demonstration was held at the U.S. Steel construction site, the police were out in force, trying to break up the demonstration. Before 9 a.m., they had arrested 286 people. There was no mechanism for processing these demonstrators quickly. Each demonstrator was brought before the magistrate, one at a time. People were staying in jail far too long for such a minor offense. We called Mayor Tom Flaherty, who got the fines reduced and the marchers processed more rapidly. The reduction in fines was a good thing, because many churches were paying the fines from church treasuries. Despite the mayor's intervention, most of the marchers were still in jail when the noon hour arrived. The system, despite holding folks so long, had made no provisions to feed people. Among those arrested were nine nuns. We went out and bought 260 lunches and forced the police to feed the arrested demonstrators.

The Fight Continues

Even as late as 2001, the fight for equity in the construction industry continued. In that year, Three Rivers Stadium was deemed no longer suitable and construction began on the construction of two separate arenas—one for the Pittsburgh Steelers and one for the Pittsburgh Pirates. The old promises of Black participation were dusted off again. Preliminary reports issued by the Stadium Authority indicated that the 25% goal had been reached. Careful examination of their report forced the Authority to admit that the construction firms had, once again, used trickery to inflate the numbers. The true figure was less than 10%.

As Byrd Brown later observed:

> The funny thing about this whole construction business is that, at the beginning of the country, all construction was done by Blacks. Once the industry became unionized and high-paying, we were pushed out. The same goes for the waiter industry. In fact, all the food industry was controlled by Blacks because cooking was low labor that was considered fit only for Negroes and colored folks. Now they have pushed us out of the catering and restaurant business. The unions had NO Black folks. For a while, we got some jobs, but under the Nixon and Reagan presidencies, we lost ground. It's partly our fault; we haven't been diligent enough.

CHAPTER 19

FIGHTING THE JIM CROW CULTURE

Health Care

In February 2007, CNN aired a program during which one White and two Black panelists discussed why Blacks died in disproportionate numbers from certain diseases. The panelists discussed the fact that Blacks did not avail themselves of medical treatment as readily as Whites, largely because they did not trust the system to provide proper care. The White panelist expressed surprise and asked why Blacks distrust the medical community. In unison, the Black panelists replied, "the Tuskegee experiment." They said Whites might be surprised how much this is discussed at all levels in the Black community.

While there is some disagreement about the exact details, most scholars agree that this government-sponsored experiment began in the 1940s in Tuskegee, AL. The government wanted to study the long-term effects of syphilis, and depending on the source, the US Department of Health either injected some rural, uneducated Black men with the disease or recruited men who were already suffering from the disease. While there is strong disagreement as to how the men contracted the disease, it is undisputed that they were never told that they had a fatal disease. Rather, they were told the government was trying to help them manage a malady called "bad blood." The victims believed they were getting better, because the open sores soon disappeared, a belief the researchers used to prove their intention to help. In reality, this signaled the end-stage of the disease, and an agonizing death would soon follow. The experimenters failed to treat Blacks people, even after penicillin was proven to cure the disease. This was in violation of a law requiring that all people known to have syphilis must receive penicillin.

Because the government hid the facts of the disease from the men, they in turn infected unsuspecting women. The researchers did not treat the women, reasoning that this would let the men know the truth about their condition and demand treatment. This would thwart the researchers' goal of studying the effects of the disease to the point of the death. When each experimental subjects died, his body was subjected to an extensive autopsy.

Officials controlling the experiment not only directly withheld penicillin, they also made certain that the men received no treatment from other sources. Ironically, a Black physician, Dr. William Hinton, was one of the scientists who perfected the treatment for the disease. The Tuskegee Experiment would have continued until all the men died, if a reporter had not discovered and revealed the experiment in a New York newspaper article. In the end, it was discovered that of the 339 men in the study, 28 died directly from syphilis; 200 died of related causes; 40 wives were infected, and 19 children were born with the disease. Suspicion of government health services and the medical community persists today, as evidenced by the Black community's reluctance to accept vaccination for COVID-19.[67]

The intentionality and scale of racism exemplified by the Tuskegee Experiment is beyond comprehension of those with any compassion and moral compass. Yet, on a daily basis, Blacks have been and continue to be subjected to racist policies and practices. A few examples drawn from my own experience and those I interviewed illustrate the point.

Mercy Hospital, which is right next to The Hill, did not want to serve Black folks. When a Black person came there for treatment, they were put outside on the "porch" regardless of their illness or condition. The "porch" was where the hospital employees kept drunks and dope addicts. HARVEY ADAMS, POLICE OFFICER AND BLACK GUARDIAN

The University's Presbyterian Hospital had a strange blood transfusion policy under which Blacks could receive only two pints of "White blood," while Whites could receive unlimited pints of "Black blood." When asked for an explanation, a hospital official vehemently denied any racist notion that "Black" blood was inferior. In fact, they believed "White blood" was weak and too much of it would harm a Black person. White people were permitted unlimited pints of superior "Black blood" that would actually improve White's health. The absurdity of this convoluted, self-serving justification was mind-boggling. RECORDS OF PITT CHAPTER NAACP

* * *

I was about 9 years old, when I saw a scene that still haunts me. Sitting on a small porch attached to a candy store/numbers joint was a Black woman. She had been stabbed in the chest, and the hilt of the knife protruded from the bloody wound. Her assailant must have hit a major artery. "Shit, look at that. She ain't gonna last long, spurting out blood like that!" Another person asked, "Did somebody call the cops?"

"It don't make no damn difference. Y'all know damn well that they don't hurry to pick up Colored folks. You bet your sweet ass she will be dead long before them sons of bitches show up!"

Right before my eyes, she was dying. Her eyes rolled back in her head, leaving only the whites visible. She moaned softly, her breath sounded like she was breathing under water. She became incontinent and urinated on herself. The smell of blood, urine, and defecation filled the air.

---

67 Thomas Parran, Jr., former Surgeon General of the United States came to the University of Pittsburgh to help establish its Graduate School of Public Health, where he served as dean from 1948 to 1958. The building housing the School of Public Health was named in his honor. On June 29, 2018, the University's Board of Trustees unanimously voted to remove Parran's name from the building, because the Tuskegee Experiment (and another in Guatemala) were conducted while he was the US Surgeon General.

"Damn, where the hell is the cops?"

"Don't make no difference now, she gonna die right there. Somebody get a sheet or something to cover her up!"

No one moved. The woman let out one last moan and cried out, "JESUS, JESUS!" Then she stopped breathing. In the distance I could hear the faint wail of a siren. AUTHOR'S RECOLLECTION

Hospitals refused to train Blacks as nurses. Many hospitals would not hire Black nurses or doctors. Of course, there were no Blacks in the administrative staffs of any Pittsburgh hospital. Not only did they discriminate against professionals, they also segregated Blacks as patients and were reported to civil rights groups for treating Black patients poorly. FRANK BOLDEN, EDITOR, *THE PITTSBURGH COURIER*

Inherent in the Jim Crow culture was an acceptance of the fact that many Blacks died while waiting for transportation to local hospitals. When faced with serious illness or injury, Blacks faced discrimination both inside and outside of hospitals.

In response to pervasive racism in health care and the police department which provided emergency transportation to hospitals, the United Negro Protest Committee founded Freedom House Ambulance Services, a bold and innovative initiative. The Service began in 1968 when organizers provided 300 hours of intensive training in life-saving first aid measures to long-term, unemployed men, many of whom had not finished high school.

Naysayers clucked their tongues and said, "No way this can work." Some spread unsubstantiated allegations that some program participants were pimps and drug users. But thanks to the men who took a risk to become involved and the support of several key White supporters, Freedom House Ambulance succeeded.

Phil Hallen, head of the Falk Foundation provided funding and helped to convince Presbyterian Hospital to serve as Freedom House's base of operations. Moe Coleman arranged for training funds through a City-based, federally-funded program for training the unemployed. Coleman also convinced several well-known physicians to help with the training. An estimated 2,000 Black lives were saved each year when Blacks received timely and appropriate pre-hospital care. According to a February 28, 2007, article in the *Pittsburgh Post-Gazette* Freedom House paramedics became legends and heroes. People even offered to pay their restaurant tabs.

Initially, Freedom House services were confined to The Hill, as the White community mistrusted this Black operated service. Eventually, however, Freedom House gained not only a local, but national, reputation for the quality of its service. Freedom House was born out of racism and racism killed it. I am convinced that Freedom House embarrassed Mayor Peter F. Flaherty, and smarting over that, he retaliated by terminating the contract with Freedom House and starting his own City of Pittsburgh paramedic service. The Freedom House staff that had already proved their ability by answering more than 45,000 emergencies was forced to take new written academic tests. I am further convinced that Flaherty and his cohorts knew that the men, who had little formal education, could not pass the test. They were right.

Although a few Freedom House employees passed muster, the new City of Pittsburgh paramedic service had virtually an all-White staff. Racism killed a gem created by Blacks in response to racism.[68]

The Fight Continues

More than 70 years have passed since Freedom House Ambulance Service was established in an effort to bring quality pre-hospital care to the Black community and the Pitt Chapter of the NAACP brought an end to the absurd blood transfusion policies at Presbyterian Hospital. Yet, as so many leaders of the movement lamented, the changes that were made did not go far enough, and in many cases, were rolled back. The illusion of inclusion that perpetuates the Jim Crow culture has once again been pierced by the widespread news coverage of disparities in response to the COVID-19 pandemic. Across the country, Black communities were among the last to receive adequate supplies for testing and vaccinations. Hospitals serving Black communities had fewer beds and supplies needed for the intensive treatment of those afflicted by the virus. And, under the ever-present shadow of Tuskegee, Black citizens expressed reluctance to receive the vaccine even when it was offered.

---

68 For additional information about the history of Freedom House, see Matthew L. Edwards, "Race, Policing, and History — Remembering the Freedom House Ambulance Service." https://www.nejm.org/doi/full/10.1056/NEJMp2035467. In the article, Edwards points out that "Freedom House became the pilot course for EMS training for the U.S. Department of Transportation and the Federal Interagency Committee on Emergency Medical Service." It is a tragedy that this innovative program that had an impact far beyond Pittsburgh was usurped by a racist power structure.

CHAPTER 20

FIGHTING THE JIM CROW CULTURE

Government

Without adequate representation in government, it was virtually impossible for Blacks to access the power structures that controlled civic life. In Pittsburgh, there was a noticeable absence of Blacks in the upper echelons of city and county government.

The lack of Black representatives on the 9-member city council was a constant source of anger and embarrassment for Black residents. The situation arose from the fact that council members were elected on an at-large, city-wide basis. Although Council was supposed to represent the concerns of all Pittsburgh residents, Whites did not truly understand issues of concern to Black voters and, therefore, were in no position to address them. Under this system, it was unlikely that more than one Black would serve on council. (Figure 20.1 lists the few Black councilmen who had eventually been elected under the city-wide system.)

A step toward remedying this lack of representation was the passage of a referendum that allowed for redrawing district lines. This resulted in two Black and seven White districts, which meant the White majority's position could always prevail.

In addition to battling for more representation on city-council, civil rights leaders met on a constant basis with the city's mayor to secure better jobs and higher positions for Blacks in the city bureaucracy. The City-County Building and the mayor's office were frequent targets for demonstrations. This was still true in 2014 when the first edition of *Voices* was published. The majority of department heads and top administrative positions in city government remain the exclusive realm of Whites.

FIGURE 20.1

EARLY BLACK
CITY-COUNCILMEN

- Louis Mason, Jr.
- James Jordon
- James Bulls

County government was no better and was also the target for frequent demonstrations and negotiations by civil rights groups. Not until the election of Bill Robinson in 2004 was there a Black on the County Council. Blacks in Pittsburgh and Allegheny County struggled under city and county government administrations that did not represent them, provided little opportunity for input, and provided almost no opportunities for meaningful employment.

As of 2020, no Black person has been elected mayor in the city of Pittsburgh.[69] In 1987, Blacks did have a real chance to elect prominent attorney and former civil rights leader, Byrd Brown. Brown entered reluctantly, at the urging of a group who had formed to field a Black candidate. This seemed like the best opportunity Blacks would ever have to win the seat. The race was going to be tightly contested, with three prominent White male contenders likely to split the vote. By analyzing previous elections, the group determined that if Brown got 90% of the Black vote, he needed only 5% of the White vote to win. Brown was easily the most qualified candidate ever to run for the office. He won many of the campaign debates by a wide margin. Yet he lost the election. I conducted an informal survey to find out why more Whites had not voted for Brown. Many admitted that he was the better candidate; they even conceded Brown had fared better in the debates and his plans for Pittsburgh's future made more sense than the plans offered by the other candidates. Still they could not bring themselves to vote for a Black man. Others felt that casting a vote for Brown would be a wasted vote since they believed that he had no chance of winning.

However, the most disturbing reason for Brown's loss lies at the feet of Blacks who did not vote for him. The reasons are both disgusting and revealing. Many said, "I just don't like him." Some, who expressed this sentiment, admitted that their negative feelings stemmed from Brown being financially well off. The fact that he lived well, drove an expensive sports car, and owned a boat simply did not sit well with many jealous folks. Many Black women refused to vote for Brown because his wife was White. One woman told me, "I am not going to vote for your friend because, if he is elected, I can't stand the fact that I will look up at the television and see a White first-lady." I responded with, "My sister, do you think that by voting for a White candidate, you will look up and see a *Black* first lady?" At any rate, Brown could have easily won, had Blacks turned out in large numbers and supported him. The African American community shot itself in the foot by not electing Brown. The truth of the matter is that in any city where a Black person has been elected mayor, the lives of Black folks have improved dramatically. Instead Pittsburgh Blacks now live in a city that remains one of the most racist cities in the United States.

Demonstration in City Council Chambers

---

69 In 2021, Ed Gainey was elected mayor of Pittsburgh, making him the first Black to hold the position since the city's founding over 260 years ago..

CHAPTER 21

FIGHTING THE JIM CROW CULTURE

Criminal Justice

Racial Profiling and Police Brutality

There was a time when I often trained Pittsburgh police in community relations. I recall that, during one training session, one of the police officers became so upset during a heated verbal exchange, he reached for his gun. Fortunately for me, the police were required to leave their weapons at the front desk of the academy; otherwise, I would have been dead. AUTHOR'S RECOLLECTION.

The police instigated the riot and blamed it on Blacks so that they would have an excuse to kill Blacks. The police were the KKK of the North. They were ready to "spank" Blacks anytime they needed to. They knew that the criminal justice system would permit them to get away with anything they wanted to do to Blacks. The so-called Police Review Board is a joke. They never punished White cops for killing or beating Blacks. During their alleged "reviews," no matter how blatantly racist the cop's actions were the Board always found that the police used "just the right force." HARVEY ADAMS

These two anecdotes point to the "street level" dimension of racism within the criminal justice system. As activist and politician William Robinson told me, he like many other Pittsburgh Blacks expected to be stopped by police because he was Black. Black men were often beaten and/ or killed in confrontations resulting from illegal stops by racist cops.[70] The situation got so bad that the Black Guardians passed out printed information advising Black men how to conduct themselves when

---

70 When I was doing research for my doctoral dissertation, I decided to explore the relationship between Blacks and the Pittsburgh police department. I was stunned to discover scores of cases, dating back to 1915 and continuing to 1980, where innocent Blacks had been beaten or killed by police. Some of the cases seemed to clearly illustrate that cops never were punished for beating or killing Black men, women and children. In none of the cases I reviewed did I find even one officer who was punished, or fired for killing Black folks.

they were pulled over. Parents, too, taught their children (particularly sons) "how to act" when they were stopped by police. Harvey Adams, founding member of the Black Guardians, expressed deep concern about Black-on-Black crime. "It robs you of your dignity. It robs you of your reputation. We pay a high price when we attack one another. We fall on one another out of our frustration. It is easier to attack another Black because we are right there, crowded in unsanitary conditions. It is easier to find a Black person than it is to hunt for a White one."

> *When I was Director of the Pittsburgh NAACP, the Pittsburgh Police Department was only 3.5 percent Black. "You don't get that kind of number merely by chance. That kind of statistic is an indication of a persistent pattern of discrimination. We fought hard to try to change that."* Tim Stevens

Fighting Back

The Pittsburgh Courier provides a record of several early efforts to resist racism in the police:

April 10, 1954, Headline—Mayor Hears Protests: A lively meeting was held at Bethel AME Church in The Hill, which according to the paper, "represented the greatest mass demonstration of concerted action Negro citizens have ever shown." Thousands of Blacks attended the meeting and protested the treatment of Blacks in Pittsburgh, including police brutality. Mayor David Lawrence was "amazed' by the protest and said, "I am opposed to the oppression of anybody, but the right approach to the problem is NOT a mass meeting." In other words, Blacks should "behave."

June 18, 1955, Headline—Leaders Ask, "When Will City's Negro Officers be Upgraded?" Black civic leaders were pressuring the City to promote Black police officers.

January 21, 1961, Headline—GPIL Tells Mayor, "We Want Police Inspector, Other City Jobs Now. The Greater Pittsburgh Improvement League (GPIL) presented a solid phalanx, representing a cross-section of the city's 'New Look' leadership, as it stepped up its drive for jobs." Among the prominent Blacks involved in a series of meetings with the mayor were those listed in Figure 21.1.

FIGURE 21.1

PARTICIPANTS IN PROTEST FOR CITY JOBS

- Manford Sales, Outgoing President of the GPIL
- Vivian Moore, Secretary; Tavern Owners Association of Pittsburgh
- Leonard Brown, Retired police officer; president of the Business and Professional Association of Pittsburgh
- Reverend J. G. Harris, Pastor of Bethel AME Church
- Reverend James Cayce, Pastor of Ebenezer Baptist Church and member of the State FEPC
- Reverend Leroy Patrick, Pastor of Bethesda Presbyterian Church

As a result of a class action lawsuit, the Pittsburgh Police Department was placed under the control of the federal government and entered into a consent decree to address discriminatory practices. The decree stipulated that a Citizens Review Board would be established to investigate charges of police brutality and make their findings known. Another provision of the decree called for the hiring of one Black person and one female for each White male hired, until the race and gender representation balanced out. The consent order, signed by City officials, remained in effect until 2005. Unfortunately, after the decree was lifted, the Pittsburgh Police Department returned to its old habits; few women or minorities have been in the academy graduating classes since 2005.[71]

During an interview with Harvey Adams, I asked why he chose to enter law enforcement, especially given the racist nature of Pittsburgh police force. "We really had limited options if we wanted to make a decent living," he said. "Not everyone was suited for or wanted to work in the mills. I worked for the Welfare Department for a while, at $3,000 per year. The police department paid $3,600. In those days, that $600 meant I could buy a house. My decision was based on money. Once I got into it, I realized the possible positive impact I could have. I went from a patrol officer to the Community Relations Division. All the while, I was noting the awesome power the police had; and most police were ***bad!***" Because of discrimination, Blacks were not admitted to most White-owned night clubs. If Blacks went into a bar, the cops would come, beat, and arrest them. So, many Blacks avoided the White places and frequented illegal, after-hours joints. Then the police showed up to collect 'payments.' Let's face it. The Klan cops of Pittsburgh enforced the unwritten segregation and racist policies of the Pittsburgh leadership."

"You know, some of the Black cops were just as oppressive towards Blacks as the White cops were. Some of us decided that we had enough of the blatant racism against Black police officers. We formed The Black Guardians to protect us and help us deal with a racist police force and administration. We fought to stop the practice of Black cops always being passed over when it came to promotions. Our actions resulted in better opportunities for Black officers. One of my proudest moments came when Bill Moore sat his big frame in the chief's chair and filled it.[72] Our actions also opened doors for White females to become police officers. Even though their opportunities came as a result of the actions of Black folks, these White female cops were often as bad as the White men. The Black Guardians set up the first Black Drum and Bugle corps, the Thunder Herd. We stood up for the Black community. I was in Korea; I faced guns, mortars; Korea was not as frightening as when I stood up to those White, racist cops. Remember that, at this time, White cops were killing one Black man a month, and getting away with it! The judges, the courts, the magistrates were all in on this." Adams maintained that the 1968 riots resulted from Blacks being up in arms about the denial of their rights.

In the December 28, 1946 edition of *The Pittsburgh Courier*, an article (headlined "There is no Santa in Fight to Enforce Equal Rights Law") complained that the courts were not anxious to enforce the provisions of the 1887 Pennsylvania civil rights law. The reporter contended the courts had a poor record of enforcing the law which called for fines against violators. There had been only one conviction under the law since amended penalties had been added to the law in 1935. The Jim Crow culture prevented Blacks from entering the legal system and their appointment/election as judges. There were

---

71 In May 2008, Jeanne Clark, member of the Police Review Board; Tim Stevens, President of the Black Political Empowerment Project, and Esther Bush, CEO of the Urban League of Greater Pittsburgh were members of a task force trying to address the issue of the "Whitening" of the Pittsburgh police force.

72 William Moore was the first Black police chief in the history of Pittsburgh.

Early Black Police Officers: Prince Bruce ("Big Blue"), Ollie Mason & Fred Clark

no Blacks in the Pittsburgh judicial system until the appointment of Judge Homer S. Brown in 1950. He and his son Byrd Brown became dominant forces in the fight against many facets of Jim Crow culture. Among the attorneys fighting racism inside and outside of the judicial system were Thomas Kerr, Judge Henry Smith, and Ron Davenport.

The FBI always contacted Rev. Herbert Wilkerson, Executive Director of the Pittsburgh NAACP, trying to elicit reports on activities in the movement. On one particular call they told him communists were trying to prove they were involved in the movements and taking pictures for propaganda purposes. They cautioned Wilkerson to be wary of who marched next to him during demonstrations, because someone was trying to take pictures of him standing near communist party members. He suspects this warning was meant to have him view the FBI in a more positive light. One of my own encounters with the agency had a different twist on the communist party angle.

When I returned to Pittsburgh after my time in the army, I applied and was admitted to the University of Pittsburgh. I stayed with my parents while I looked for an appropriate bachelor pad. One day I noticed a copy of *The Daily Worker* on the mantle and asked my Dad, "Is this yours? Do you know what it is?" When I explained that it was the official newspaper of the United States Communist party, he exclaimed, "What the hell is a damn communist newspaper doing coming here? It sure as hell ain't mine."

"Dad, I suspect that it was sent by the FBI as an excuse to speak with me. So, when they call, just tell them that my name is the same as yours and that it was intended for me."

"What you talking about? Why would the FBI want to talk to you?" I explained that leaders of the southern movement had taught me how to deal with tricks like this that the FBI used to force folks to become informants. I was not afraid, because I wasn't a communist and had never even attended a communist meeting.

About a week later an FBI agent called my father who did as I had instructed him. The agent then called me and suggested that I come downtown to discuss my "communist leanings." I told him that I did not trust the FBI and was not about to come downtown and disappear from the Earth. By now I was working for Pitt and suggested that the agent meet me at noon in the cafeteria at Falk Hall on the university's campus. On the appointed day, I went to the cafeteria and sat in the middle of the room. If I was going to disappear, there were going to be thousands of witnesses to the event.

Soon, two White men approached. I just sat there, looking like hundreds of other folks dressed in white lab coats. How did they know who I was? Simple, they had photographs of me and thousands of other

K. Leroy Irvis & Police Commander

folks who participated in the southern marches and demonstrations. I knew that somewhere there was a dossier on me. I made a mental note to apply for it under the Federal Freedom of Information Act.

After introducing themselves, they sat and began the conversation by saying that they wanted to talk about my involvement in the Communist Party. Not in the mood to play their game, I quickly cut to the chase. "Listen, please don't insult my intelligence. You know damn well that I'm not at all interested in communism."

"Then why have you been receiving *The Daily Worker*?"

"Come on now, you and I know I didn't subscribe to any communist newspaper. We further know that the FBI sent the paper to me. I'm not stupid; I know that the United States army would not give me a top secret clearance and permit me to work on highly classified atomic missiles if anything in my background check had revealed anything abnormal. Being a member of the communist party in 1959 would have been suspicious. So listen up, I only have one hour for lunch and you are wasting my time. *What the Hell is it that you want?"*

Finally one of them said, "We understand that you were in the civil rights movement down South; we figured that you would probably be involved in the movement up here."

"Oh, you understand that I was involved. You know damn well that I was involved. You took enough damn pictures of all of us marchers to know what I looked like when you called me. So again, what is it you want?"

Having failed to intimidate me, they finally confessed. "Well, since you will probably be involved in the Pittsburgh movement, we thought you might be willing to keep us informed about significant events."

"Oh, I get it; you want me to be a squealer, a rat, a stool pigeon, or as you call it, an informant. Why on earth would you want me to be an informant?"

"Well, if you let us know in advance about demonstrations, we can be there to protect you and the other demonstrators."

"You mean the same way you protected us down South, when we were attacked and beaten? No thanks. I can damn sure protect my own ass better than you did. Not once did your picture-taking friends lift a finger to help children and women who were being beaten by vicious rednecks."

They claimed that they did not have the power to protect us down there, but up here they had more power.

"Oh. Okay. The University Pittsburgh Chapter of the NAACP is going to picket the Cathedral of Learning on Pitt's campus the next Wednesday."

In a very weary voice, the agent replied, "Yes, Mr. Proctor, we already know that; we read it in yesterday's morning paper."

"Damn! You mean I was late again?" The FBI soon gave up trying to get useful ammunition from this informant, but they did continue to monitor my telephone line for many years to follow.

I know this for a fact. Many years ago, in the waning years of the movement, I decided to use the Freedom of Information Act to demand my dossier. The FBI put me through all kinds of hoops before finally sending me six of the report's nine pages, claiming that three were withheld for "national security" reasons. What bullshit. How could anyone as unimportant as I was have anything on paper that was so sensitive that I could not be allowed to see it? Of the six pages I received, three of them had been almost totally redacted by someone who crossed out nearly every line with a thick, black, permanent marker. Of the three remaining pages, I could only see one complete sentence. That sentence was "subject is familiar with the Student Non-Violent Coordinating Committee." One of these days I am going to ask for the file again and see if I can get all nine pages. Who knows, maybe they will have added some more pages.

The Fight Continues

As I prepare the third edition of this book, the illusion of inclusion is once again being stripped away. In 1995, businessman Johnny Gammage was killed by police during a routine traffic stop in a

Richard Jones, Pioneering Civil Rights Attorney

community just outside of Pittsburgh. This abuse of police power gained some notoriety because Gammage was the cousin of Pittsburgh Steeler Ray Seals. Yet, none of the officers involved in the incident were found guilty of involuntary manslaughter let alone murder. Twenty-six years later, citizens across the country watched the horrific image of a Minneapolis police suffocating George Floyd in the exact same manner as Gammage had been killed. During those intervening years, the deaths of innocent Black men and women at the hands of police ignited the "Black Lives Matter" movement. Floyd's death was so visible that massive demonstrations broke out across the country (even the world). The illusion of equal treatment under the law could no longer be sustained.[73] In April 2021, a jury found police officer Derek Chauvin guilty of second degree manslaughter in the death of George Floyd. On June 25, Chauvin was sentenced to 22.5 years in prison. Despite this legal victory, many more cases of deaths similar to that of Floyd have come to light with no legal consequences imposed upon the perpetrators.

Wendell Freeland, Pioneering Civil Rights Attorney (center), William P. Young & Republican Gubernatorial Candidate William Scranton, 1963 (right)

---

73 For more detailed lists of Black deaths at the hands of police, see, for example: Renee Atar, *In Memoriam: I Can't Breathe,* https://www.reneeater.com/on-monuments-blog/tag/list+of+unarmed+black+people+killed+by+police; Alia Chughtai, *Know Their Names: Black People Killed by Police in the US.* https://interactive.aljazeera.com/aje/2020/know-their-names/index.html.

CHAPTER 22

FIGHTING JIM CROW CULTURE

Public Accommodations

If Blacks lived, played, and worked in areas with large Black populations, they were less likely to encounter discrimination. In enclaves like The Hill District, Blacks essentially created a duplicate, parallel world to serve their needs. Interestingly, many Whites also lived, shopped and sought entertainment in the Black communities, especially in a Lower Hill District area around Logan Street. In this community Blacks and Whites, regardless of ethnic background, lived in apparent racial harmony.[74] However, when Blacks ventured out into parts of Homewood-Bruston, East Liberty, Shadyside, Downtown, the South Side, the Northside, Oakland, or other neighborhoods, Jim Crow culture made it clear they were not welcome.

The long fought battle for equal access to publicly owned swimming pools was mirrored by efforts in other recreational, entertainment, and retail venues. According to an April 4, 1953 article in *The Pittsburgh Courier,* The Reverend S. Amos Brakeen, pastor of the Shiloh Baptist Church, was named to head an NAACP committee which would work to end the discrimination in the use of public accommodations in the Pittsburgh District. This coincided with the civil rights movement that began to coalesce during the 1950s. Pittsburgh's civil rights organizations mounted monumental efforts to wipe out racial discrimination well into the 1960s and 1970s. Despite those organizations' most brave and valiant efforts, Pittsburgh is not yet free of the subtle forces of Jim Crow culture into the 21st century.

Retail Establishments

Despite spending many dollars in department stores, Blacks were not afforded any measure of respect. When Blacks shopped in downtown department stores, they knew they had to wait until all Whites had been served. If Blacks were in the process of being served and a White person came to the check-out counter, the clerk would turn to the newly arrived White customer before finishing the transaction with the Black customer. Black women could not try on dresses in Pittsburgh department stores. If a Black man tried on a hat, he was forced to buy it.

---

74 Disruption of this harmonious co-existence was one of the great tragedies of the misguided urban "renewal" of The Hill District.

Beauty salons and barbershops refused to serve Black clients. While Robert Goode was a student at Westminster College in New Wilmington, PA, he worked with the University of Pittsburgh NAACP Chapter to challenge this practice among barbers who claimed they weren't discriminating because of race. They simply had no "training" in cutting the tightly curled hair of African Americans. Robert had hair with a texture very similar to Whites, so if they refused to serve him, it was easily established that the refusal was based on race, not on hair texture.

Entertainment Venues

A headline in the May 23, 1953 edition of *The Pittsburgh Courier* announced, "Pressures Mounting against Parks' Bias." The story speaks to the discrimination practiced by both Kennywood and West View Parks. The pressure was coming from Reverend Leroy Patrick's NAACP Swimming Pool Committee. The protest was gaining wide support both in the Black and the White communities.

Both Kennywood and West View were segregated. Kennywood, while allowing Blacks access to rides and concession stands, did not employ Blacks as ride operators, cafeteria workers (except in the kitchen), lifeguards, or any other capacity. It would not permit Blacks to swim in the pool. When the park lost a suit over the issue of the pool, the owners, at first, seemed to accept the idea of Blacks and Whites swimming together. However, shortly after the pool was integrated, the owners closed the pool, demolished it, and built a parking lot on the site.[75] Public schools with large Black populations were not allowed to hold their annual picnics at the facility. All such picnics were held at West View Park, which was nevertheless still segregated and hired no Black employees.

Blacks were not permitted in West View Park's "Danceland" facility. The owners claimed Danceland was a private club, and therefore, exempt from discrimination laws. The Young Adult Chapter of the NAACP tested this assertion by sending separate teams of Blacks and Whites to join the so-called "private club." All the Whites were granted membership; all the Blacks were turned away. On the basis of this evidence, the NAACP chapter obtained a desegregation order. Once the order was in place, a group of us returned to check compliance. With our newly-acquired membership cards in hand, we were admitted, and quickly became objects of intense gawking. As part of the test, we were obliged to participate in whatever activities were under way, which in this case, meant dancing the *polka* to the accompaniment of accordion music. Soon we were on the floor doing a damn good imitation of a *soul* polka. Some of the other patrons were particularly upset with our group. One of our members, Linda Kittle (one of playwright August Wilson's sisters), was extremely light-skinned and could easily be mistaken for a White woman. Thus, in the eyes of some of those in attendance, not only had we had the unmitigated gall to invade *their* Danceland, we were dancing with a White woman.

Fraternal organizations like the American Legion, Elks, Masons, and Shriners were segregated into Black and White branches. In response to being excluded from White social clubs, Blacks started what became the famous Loendi Club. Over the years, many of Pittsburgh's well-to-do Blacks held membership in the posh club, which served as the venue for a variety of social events including weddings, receptions,

---

75 Kennywood Park was not the only organization to respond in this fashion. When legislation was passed requiring public pools to admit Black people, many of them across the country were closed. For additional information, see Heather McGhee, *The Soul of Us, What Racism Costs Everyone and How We can Prosper Together* (Random House, 2021).

dances, and fraternal and sorority club meetings. The Young Adult Chapter of the NAACP held meetings at the Loendi Club which attracted many young, Black, and single professionals. While young adults may have come to socialize, many learned about and became involved in the civil rights movement through the club. Many of the members left Pittsburgh and became leaders in other cities. Many alumni who chose to stay in Pittsburgh assumed leadership roles in a variety of other organizations.

As mentioned by a number of the individuals presented in Section 2 of *Voices*, theaters in White neighborhoods would not sell tickets to Blacks. Or if they did, Blacks had to sit in the upper balcony. Bowling alleys and roller skating rinks were segregated. On November 2, 1946, *The Pittsburgh Courier* reported on a suit filed with Alderman Harry Fitzgerald against the Lexington Roller Rink in East Liberty for refusing to let Black teenagers roller skate at a school party. The resolution of the case is not known. However, as late as 1970, *The Courier* continued to report on open discrimination by skating rinks operated by Whites. On January 3, 1970, the paper announced that a group of Black youth was denied admittance to the Homestead Community Center. The United Black Protest Committee had to sue the Center before it would admit Blacks to skating parties. Several other skating rinks also denied Black youth entry, such as the Ardmore Skating Rink located just beyond the city limits.

George Barbour reported in the June 10, 1956, edition of *The Pittsburgh Courier* that nine Black youths who worked as vendors for Forbes Field were attacked by a group of White thugs, while members of the Pittsburgh Police force stood by and did nothing. The attacks stopped only after White vendors told the owners of the Pirates baseball team and the Steelers football team that they would refuse to work unless the club management did something about the attacks on the Black youth.

Restaurants and Bars

Eating establishments of all types refused service to Blacks. For example, five-and-dime stores (the precursors to today's dollar stores) had lunch counters where Blacks could buy food, but had to eat it outside. Several headlines from The Pittsburgh Courier illustrate early efforts to challenge such discrimination:

> April 7, 1945. A group of Black teenagers from a club called "The Eunettes" filed a civil rights suit against Isaly's Dairy Company for telling them they had to eat their ice cream outside. The incident took place in the company's main facility on the Boulevard of the Allies in Oakland. The suit was filed with Harry Fitzgerald, a well-known pioneer in advancing Black rights from his post as magistrate and alderman. Isaly's was let off with a stern tongue lashing.

> November 7, 1946—Civil Rights Cases Hit Courts. The article described several cases coming before Allegheny County courts and local aldermen. In one case, a Black deputy constable tried to serve a warrant against a White waitress who had refused service to Black customers. The woman refused to accompany the Black constable, saying, "You can't arrest me. You're colored." The alderman had to go to a police station and convince the sergeant to send a White police officer to the restaurant to make the arrest.[76]

---

76 In my research, I spoke to several of the early Black Pittsburgh police officers. They all complained that they were not permitted, initially,

December 21, 1946. Walter Wilson, with the aid of the NAACP, successfully brought suit against a White man, Psaras, for refusing to serve him in a Pittsburgh restaurant. The case was tried in Allegheny Court under the Pennsylvania civil rights law of 1887. Wilson received a post card saying, "You lousy Nigger. If you don't withdraw that case, you will be lynched."

In the 1960s, challenges to this Jim Crow culture mounted, and it would be impossible to recount all of the bars, restaurants, and nightclubs that were targeted for demonstrations. The Young Adult Chapter of the NAACP received complaints about establishments in East Liberty, Shadyside, Oakland, Squirrel Hill, Oakmont, Mount Lebanon, and small towns on the outskirts of Pittsburgh. For example, a complaint was made that bars in Oakdale were refusing to serve Black soldiers stationed at the nearby Nike Missile site. Two of the offending bars had been served notice by the Pennsylvania Human Relations Commission to cease this discrimination. The Young Adult Chapter of the NAACP activated its testing teams. One team was deployed to a bar with décor straight out of the old West. Tables were covered with the same kind of checkered tablecloths featured on the *Gunsmoke* television show. Steer horns adorned several of the walls, and a larger-than-life-size photograph of the bar owner dressed as the famous gunfighter from *Have Gun, Will Travel* graced another wall. When the test team entered the bar, the owner and his employees turned their backs and disappeared into the back room. Soon, the bar's phone rang and a short time later the owner re-emerged and, with much fanfare, pulled a western-style holster from under the bar, took out a shiny revolver, removed the bullets, slowly reloaded them, and then placed the gun on the counter. When his attempt at intimidation failed, he served the team warm beer at inflated prices. When the teams left the bar, local police followed them in another attempt at intimidation, which also failed. Neither the bar owner nor the police realized that one of the testers was a city magistrate who was carrying a gun, so the intimidation didn't work. When the two NAACP teams met to compare notes, they determined that someone in the bar visited by the second team recognized a team member and called to warn the owner of the Western bar. The year? 1965.

Hotels

Nowhere was discrimination more rampant than in the area of public accommodations. Blacks, for many years, were unable to stay in downtown hotels. In addition, the employment records of these hotels were abysmal. Many negotiations were held with hotels about both these issues.

Black entertainers, appearing before White audiences, sought rooms in the Center Avenue YMCA in The Hill District, Dearings Restaurant/Hotel, and a handful of other Black-owned hotels, because they knew that they could not stay in downtown hotels. Star Black athletes did not protest when they were not permitted to stay in the dorms at local colleges.

Until the civil rights movement of the 1960s and 1970s, Blacks had no place to turn for help. Under the leadership of Herbert "Coop" Ivey, the Young Adult Chapter of the NAACP tested discrimination, not only in housing but also a wide range of public accommodation. As a result of their investigations, sufficient evidence of discrimination was gathered to bring successful law suits against many Pittsburgh businesses.

---

to arrest White folks.

This brief account of resistance to Jim Crow culture highlights only some of the many protests and demonstrations of companies throughout the Pittsburgh area, including:

- Utilities companies including Duquesne Light and Equitable Gas
- Governments including The City of Pittsburgh and Allegheny County, the Pittsburgh Police Department, the Pittsburgh Fire Department
- Educational Institutions including Community College of Allegheny County, University of Pittsburgh, Pittsburgh Board of Public Education;
- Grocery Stores including Atlantic and Pacific Tea Company (A&P) and Kroger's Supermarket, New Diamond Meat Market, Meadow Gold Dairies, Braun Baking Company, Sealtest Company
- Department Stores including Kaufmann's, Gimbels, Joseph Horne's, Sears Roebuck, Thom McAn, and all the other shoes stores located on Fifth Avenue in downtown Pittsburgh
- Corporations including Mine Safety Appliance Company, United States Steel, Union Switch & Signal
- Recreational Facilities and Entertainment Venues including West View Park, Kennywood Park, Highland Park swimming pool, Lexington Roller Rink, Corrigan's Swimming Pool in South Park, the swimming pool in North Park, the Civic Arena, Three Rivers Stadium
- Real estate and housing organizations including Greater Pittsburgh Multi-List Corporation, Allegheny County Housing Authority, the Pittsburgh Housing Authority
- Restaurants including Paluchi's Bar in Oakdale, the Brass Rail Restaurant, Stouffer's Restaurant
- Media Outlets including *The Pittsburgh Press* and *The Pittsburgh Post-Gazette*, KDKA-TV, WIIC TV, WTAE TV, WQED TV
- Unions including every trade union in Pittsburgh, the American Federation of Teachers
- Hotels including the Hilton, Webster Hall, and Penn Sheraton hotels
- Hospitals including Presbyterian Hospital, Braddock Hospital, St. Francis Hospital, Montefiore Hospital, Mercy Hospital
- Sports and cultural institutions including the Pittsburgh Pirates, the Pittsburgh Steelers, Carnegie Museum and Library

Nat King Cole & Marla Cole with Owl Cab driver Leo Dodson; The Owl Cab Company, the only Black-owned taxi company in Pittsburgh, circa 1947

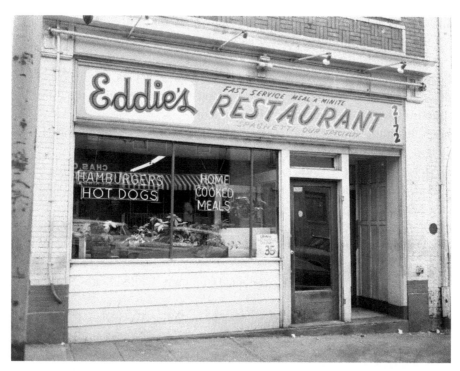

Wylie Avenue esblishment made famous in plays of August Wilson

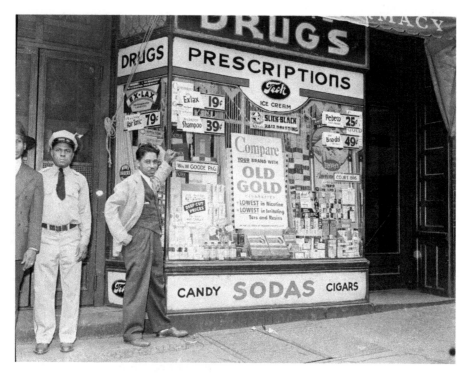

William Goode, drug store

SECTION 4

WANING OF THE MOVEMENT

The 1960s were a time of hope; hope that the United States would finally allow Blacks to participate in the American Dream; hope that Blacks would finally be judged by the content of their hearts rather than the color of their skin; hope that we could all participate in the age of equality. Unfortunately, the 1960s were also a time of despair for Black America: despair brought on by a failed War on Poverty; despair brought on by continued incidents of police brutality against Black citizens; despair brought on by a realization that, for most Black citizens, there would be no participation in the American Dream.

In a 1968 speech, Dr. Martin Luther King prophesied that we, his people, would reach the promised land, but "I may not get there with you ..."

**Rev. Cornell Talley shaking hands with the Rev. Dr. Martin Luther King, Jr.,
at podium in Central Baptist Church, c. 1958**

CHAPTER 23

The Death of Dr. Martin Luther King and the Pittsburgh Riots of 1968

Children gathered around memorial to Dr. Martin Luther King, Jr.

The Terrible News: King is Dead!

I was sitting in an Oakland restaurant having dinner with a special friend when I just barely caught the words playing on the television over the bar. "Martin Luther King, Jr., was *shot!*" King's premonitions came true on April 4, 1968 in Memphis, Tennessee, where he had been working with Black refuse workers to confront racism. With the death of King came the death of innocence. Blacks were deeply angered and profoundly saddened.

On Friday, April 5, 1968, a meeting was called at Ebenezer Baptist Church, one of Pittsburgh's main "civil rights" churches where the congregation was involved in the movement. As I entered the dimly lit church, I was met with an eerie quiet. People filed in slowly, greeting one another in hushed tones; some embraced; some quietly wept; I was numb. In the wake of the shocking death of Rev. King, members of the movement—militant, moderate, conservative—came together in shared grief. Posturing, one-upmanship, contentious conversations were set aside as everyone confronted the sobering question, "What do we do now?"

The potential for a cataclysmic riot was quite real. Many of those gathered at Ebenezer church knew that, when riots had occurred in other cities, more Blacks than Whites died, and the businesses in the Black community never recovered. We wanted to avoid such tragic loss in Pittsburgh. Someone suggested that, while we decide how to honor our fallen leader, we had to head off what would surely be a violent, deadly confrontation of the system. While many agreed, others—especially the younger members—vented their pent-up anger. They wanted to strike back and the consequences be damned. The angry ones wanted to make America suffer for all of the past transgressions against Blacks, including the killing of King. As one angry, young Black man shouted: "Why the fuck should we be the only ones who ain't violent. Man, they just killed KING. That sure the fuck ain't no nonviolent act. Fuck nonviolence! What the fuck has that gotten all you old fucks? Get off your damn knees and meet them where they are; an eye for an eye. Fuck peace! The man only respects power. Let's show some balls and some power." Not surprisingly, reactions to those impassioned speeches were split along age lines.

In the end, it was decided that steps would be taken to minimize the potential violence. Some men were dispatched to The Hill to ask bar owners to close early or remain completely closed. All of the bars complied with this request. Someone indicated that the manager of the nearby liquor store could not close without permission from a state official. Consequently, State Representative K. Leroy Irvis retired to the church office to call the Governor and request that he order the liquor store to close. Others contacted the Pittsburgh Board of Public Education to request that the public schools in Black communities close early so that students could be safe from the potential violence. The school board complied. By then, Representative Irvis reported that he had been unable to reach the Governor, but would continue to try. The group decided to end the meeting and to reconvene later in the day to hear Irvis' report and make further plans.

A Stupid Statement Leads to Trouble

The first item of business at the afternoon meeting was Representative Irvis' report that he had spoken with the Lieutenant Governor, who rejected the request to close the liquor store. His refusal made clear, not only his lack of respect for Black leadership, but also his desire to maintain the lucrative flow of cash into the state-controlled liquor business.[77] In a monumentally stupid error of judgment, the Lieutenant Governor stated that the state-owned liquor store would be closed only if there was trouble.

A voice rang out from the back of the church, "Shit, if that's all it takes to shut the motherfucker down, they *got* that!" Before any of the "old heads" could react, a group of defiant, young Black males broke away from the meeting and headed toward the liquor store. Realizing the potential danger, one of the older leaders placed a call to Number Two Police Station and asked that the young men be intercepted

---

77 Although liquor stores in Black communities did not carry the expensive brands of alcohol available in well-to-do neighborhoods, the volume of sales per capita in low- to moderate-income communities more than compensated for the lack of high-end sales. As psychologists have explained, poor people, regardless of color, are far more likely to use alcohol to narcotize themselves against the pain of an oppressive existence.

and held until the leaders of the group could come and get them. Their request was turned down with statement, "We can't arrest them unless they *do* something illegal." The police were then told that they should make their presence known by stationing officers in front of the liquor store. This simple, logical request was also turned aside. The riot was on—ignited by two insensitive White individuals and fueled by angry Black males. The young men went to the liquor store and kicked in the plate glass window as the police stood by and watched. The store had been closed by the "trouble" requested by the state government. After the group successfully closed the liquor store, they fanned out up and down Centre Avenue as rapidly as possible. Opportunists took advantage of the situation and looted the liquor store. Word spread rapidly that the police were doing nothing to stop the damage to or looting of stores.

Efforts to honor Rev. King continued. Byrd Brown and other civil rights leaders organized a march both to protest his murder and to honor the fallen King. Thousands of people responded to the call and gathered at Freedom Corner at Crawford and Centre Avenues. The marchers were met by riot police intent on keeping them out of the downtown area. They claimed they were stopping the march in order to protect Brown who was alleged to be targeted for assassination. The scene was tense. According to Alma Fox, Executive Director of the Pittsburgh NAACP, a red-faced cop repeatedly attempted to reach over the police in the front line, so that he could strike Brown with a riot club. A Black officer named Slaughter stretched his more-than-six foot tall frame and blocked the officer's attempts to injure Brown. "Since he couldn't hit me in the head, he kept moving until he could reach between the lines of police and poke me in the ribs," Brown recalled. Brown then said to the police, "We are going to march. Your attempt to stop us is illegal. We are no longer non-violent because of your actions on the bridge. We have ten thousand people; you have 300 cops. You can't stop us." The crowd surged forward. A group of about 25 Black men rushed the police line; for a moment or two both sides pushed against the other line. Alma Fox, who was standing beside Byrd Brown, said, "I don't know how it happened, but suddenly I was on my knees. I looked up and could see that the police had assumed a stance where each one's foot was touching the foot of the officer on each side. This caused their legs to be spread apart. I saw all this room and quickly crawled between one of the cop's legs. Once I was behind the police, I stood up and yelled, 'Come on, come on; I got through, so can you.' Four or five police grabbed me, picked me up, carried me to a paddy wagon, and threw me in. Somehow, during the tussle, the heel on my boot managed to contact the jaw of one of the cops. The crowd began shouting, 'Let the sister *go,* let the sister *GO!*' The public safety director, realizing that the situation was about to get completely out of control came over to the paddy wagon and asked me to get out. I refused and said, 'I'm not going anywhere. This is *my* wagon now! Your cops threw me in here and I am *staying* until we can march!'"

Byrd Brown then came over and told Fox that the public safety director had given permission for the march to continue. She left the wagon, resumed her place at the head of the line, and led the thousands of Black folks on a march through downtown Pittsburgh to Point State Park. As the marchers prayed and sang, Alma Fox recalls, "We looked back, towards The Hill. In the distance, we could see dark, black smoke billowing into the sky. The Hill was burning!"

Meanwhile the riot continued. I was later informed by White officers that the police were under orders to allow the riot to run its course. The police had set up a defensive perimeter around The Hill and had orders to shoot if rioters attempted to burn and loot stores in adjacent communities. The police watched as The Hill burned. To a lesser extent, the same scenario was taking place in the Homewood-Brushton community and the Northside.

In an interview conducted after the riots, K. Leroy Irvis told Laurence Glasco, "The mob was organized. It wasn't just a mob."[78] From my own observations, I would say that Irvis' observation was correct, but not complete. Several groups were moving through The Hill. Some appeared to be organized; others were not. Some folks were simply taking advantage of the chaos to settle old scores or steal merchandise Some of the arson was organized with specific places targeted either for burning or protection. In some instances, a bystander spontaneously emerged from a crowd to protect a threatened establishment. It is likely the full extent and details of the looting and burning will never be known. What is known, however, is that the riots could have been much worse.

Many Black leaders in the three major Black communities worked to keep the violence down (Figure 23.1). Not one life—Black or White—was lost as a direct result of hostile actions. Some police officers helped as well. Among the group who risked ostracism and job loss were Herman Mitchell, William "Mugsy" Moore (who eventually became the first Black chief of police in the history of Pittsburgh), and Harvey Adams (who had helped to form the Black Guardians).

One incident, in which Adams helped to prevent loss of civilian and police lives, occurred at the Number 2 Police Station in The Hill. As Adams described it, "This idiot came into the station and tried to get the cops to go outside and kill some *niggers*. He was drunk! I had to stop him. I pulled my gun and placed the business end on his nose and said, 'If you move, you lose. You are making me real nervous. That's not good, because I'm afraid that you might hurt me; I can't let that happen. Make no mistake about it; I will kill you if I have to. I'm your worst nightmare. I'm not going to let you shoot any Black folks, and I sure the fuck am not going to let you shoot me! I suggest you holster your gun and get the hell out of here before it's too late.' I was serious, Ralph. I *was* scared! But I was not about to let him hurt me or anyone else." I asked what the other officers were doing. Adams replied, "They were scared, too. Everyone wanted to go home to their families at the end of the shift. That fool was jeopardizing them as well. They just stood and watched the whole thing. I really didn't want to do it, but I had no choice. Sometimes you have to meet their animal conduct with your own animal fury. The man finally holstered his gun and left."

Adams also averted bloodshed in another confrontation when Richard Gilcrese of Urban Youth Action and some young Black men were preparing to attack Number 2 Police Station and free innocent Black men who had been roughed up and jailed. Adams was in the station at the time and heard the commotion. "I looked outside at the crowd of angry, chanting Black men. Inside the police were preparing for battle with every weapon in their arsenal. They had positioned themselves so that they

FIGURE 23.1
BLACK LEADERS WORKING TO STEM VIOLENCE

Leaders in the Hill included:

- Lloyd Bell
- Byrd Brown
- Vince Edwards
- Ewari Ellis
- Charles Harris
- K. Leroy Irvis
- Norman Johnson
- James McCoy
- Matthew Moore, Sr.
- Nate Smith

Leaders in Homewood included:

- Cannon Junius Carter
- Nick Flournoy
- Bouie Hayden

Leaders in the Northside included:

- Rev. Jimmy Joe Robinson
- Swampman Williams

---

78 Quoted by Alyssa Ribeiro in her Master's thesis, *A Period of Turmoil-Pittsburgh's April 1968 Riots and Their Aftermath.*

could unleash deadly, rapid gunfire at any group attempting to take over the station. The unarmed Black men did not stand a chance."

Adams went outside and told the group that he understood their frustration and admired their courage, but if they tried to enter the station there would be a massacre. "Pick a battleground when you have a chance to inflict damage on your enemy. You can't do that here. They're inside waiting to shoot you down. Don't let your enemy pick your battleground." To me, Adams said, "Ralph, I knew I couldn't stop them by telling them what they were doing was wrong. They felt they had the moral high ground and were ready to die. I had to appeal to their common sense. Thank God, it worked. Gilcrese later admitted that his actions were unwise, but stated that the folks were sick and tired of being mistreated by police."

In spite of his anger and this incident, Gilcrese was one of the young Blacks who tried to help during the riot in The Hill. "Ralph," he told me, "during the riots, I worked with Tim Stevens to keep Black kids from being harmed. I was afraid, but I was also pissed off. I saw the police and the National Guard shut down The Hill. They were like some obscene, fascist occupying force. Most of the young folks were really offended by Whites in uniform taking over our community. We often faced them down, yelling and screaming, daring them to '*do something!*' We were HOT! Their presence was the ultimate insult! I saw the looting and, at first, I asked myself why 'they' were tearing down the stores."

Adams was credited with saving firebrand Nate Smith who was about to lead a group of fired-up young Blacks to confront the police. Speaking of the incident, Adams said:

> The White cops hated Nate and looked for chances to hurt him. They said that if he led marchers back downtown, in defiance of the public safety director's orders, he was just another criminal, and they had a duty to stop him. They were just going to gun the brother down like a dog. I couldn't let that happen. I said "Nate, man, let's cool down for a minute. If you march downtown, they are going to shoot you." Nate was mad as hell and fired up. He wasn't interested in hearing any words. I had no choice. It was either physically stop him, or see him die. You remember that Nate was a powerful son-of-a-bitch who would fight any damn body, but I had to stop him, so I tackled his ass and held him down until he promised that he would not, on that date, march to his own death.

Later, when I asked Smith about the situation, he said: "Yeah, I was hot. Nobody was going to tell us when and where we could march. I didn't give a damn what Craig [the public safety director] said. We were marching. Harvey said some shit about the cops waiting to gun me down. I didn't give a damn. I wasn't gonna let no cops tell me what to do. I fired up the troops and said, 'Let's roll!' All of a sudden, Harvey jumped me and held me down. I was ready to kick his ass! Then I listened; he was trying to save my life. So, I told him that I was cool. The brother did save my life."

According to an April 13th article in *The Pittsburgh Courier*, Bouie Hayden and Nick Flournoy had volunteered to put together a group to help "cool it" in Homewood. In a meeting that included Police Superintendent James Slusser, the group asked for some sort of visible symbol, such as red shirts, that would identify them as peace keepers. Slusser said he did not want to turn Homewood over to "hoodlums and the criminal element and those who fomented riots." Some members of the Black group stormed out of the meeting in anger, but returned to reach agreement. Hayden responded to Slusser's insult, by saying, 'We are all criminals with police records, but we can stop this riot." *The Courier* says that, eventually, 20 grass roots folks were deputized to patrol the street and help youth "cool it."

Despite such efforts to quell violence, the riot continued full-blown into the next day. The word was out. Take vengeance against those who had cheated or harmed the Black community. Despite the police barricade around The Hill, I made my way past it to protect my parents and sisters who still lived there. One morning, I found my father sitting in a second floor window, armed with a rifle. Dad said, "Anybody who strikes a match around *my* house, damn sure better have a cigarette in his mouth." Tim Steven had a similar experience. "My family had a home at the corner of Francis and Wylie Avenues. My brother, my father, and I took turns guarding the home. We were afraid that some fool would burn the small, White-owned grocery store that was next door."

In addition to assuring my family's safety, I also wanted to help to maintain calm. While at The Halfway Art Gallery, I saw a young man rush in to say they were getting ready to burn the paint store on Centre Avenue. I said, "You can't burn that, because K. Leroy Irvis lives above the store." One of the men replied, "Who the fuck is that? I ain't never heard of him." When I explained that Irvis was our representative in Harrisburg, another man said, "Well he sure in hell ain't done nothing for us, 'cause I ain't never heard his name!"

Irvis himself recounted the incident. "The whole scene was wild. Blacks in Pittsburgh were actually rioting. I helped as best I could by trying to keep the young folks from getting into needless confrontations with the police and National Guardsmen. I was warned that some thugs were going to burn the store, and I was able to get my belongings out in time. I watched through the rearview mirror as the building went up in smoke. I went to live with another attorney, Ron Davenport, for a while. He said that he was happy to help me out. I'm trying to remember how I got word that the paint store was going to be torched." I said, "Think carefully." Irvis looked at me and asked, "Were you there?" "Yep," I replied." "Ah then, it was you! Things are a bit blurry, but I do remember you being there. That was a scary moment."

Another store destroyed during the riots was Mainway Super Market. I stood on the steps of a hardware store across from the market and watched as a not-too experienced arsonist tried to burn the market by throwing a Molotov cocktail against the cinder-block walls. After several unsuccessful attempts, another man appeared on the scene, slapped the would-be arsonist upside his head in disgust, and then showed him how to burn the market by throwing the incendiary device through a plate glass window. As the flames licked skyward, a little, old, demure Black lady who had been standing next to me, said, "Son, I don't usually think that violence is right, but they should have burned them sons of bitches out a long time ago." Unbeknownst to the arsonists, the United Negro Protest Committee was in negotiations to purchase the store and train Blacks to run it. A potential benefit to the community went up in flames.

"Hop" Kendrick remembered the burning of the Mainway Market with sadness. "I remember that the market was burned on Sunday. Many of the looters were dressed in their finest 'church' clothes; many of them had palm fronds, shaped like crosses. I will never forget the sight of those 'Christian' folks, all dressed up, looting the store. I was sickened by that sad, sad sight. I won't ever be able to forget it."

Another store targeted for arson was a meat market with a reputation for selling horsemeat to residents while claiming it was beef. The owner was also known for reselling out-of-date meat. He would go to markets in the Jewish community of Squirrel Hill; buy all the outdated meat; bring it back to The Hill; repackage it, and sell it as fresh meat. I knew this to be true, because one time a group of us followed him to a Squirrel Hill and watched as he loaded outdated meat into his van. One of the store's employees described how the meat was washed in a solution of baking soda and water, then was re-packaged, and sold to Black folks. This was one of the first stores to be torched. Further down Centre Avenue, close to downtown, several other stores were torched and looted. Among those burned were Fireman's Drug Store and Wolf's Shoe Store. In fact, many of the burned businesses belonged to members of the Jewish community.[79]

Some of the looters did not profit personally. One enterprising young man set up an impromptu shoe store on a corner in The Hill. As people with families, young children, or older people came by, he would invite them to sit on a looted bench and try on shoes. He had the foresight to loot a shoe size measuring device. He accepted no pay for his illegal activities. I watched him in utter amazement. When he had given away all of his looted shoes, I asked what he did for a living. He replied that he was unemployed. I walked away, shaking my head as I wondered how many other youth were wasting considerable talent because racists would not give them a chance.

Much of the food looted from grocery stores was distributed to needy families. At the time of the riots, I worked for H.J. Heinz Company, the giant food manufacturing corporation. With the help of my boss, Harry Carroll, I convinced Heinz to donate hundreds of cases of food for distribution in the riot areas. Volunteers gave the food to needy people; then distributed the remaining food to social service agencies. Ironically, many volunteers reported that it had been more difficult to distribute the food than anticipated. At some destinations, they discovered families had no space for any additional food. Refrigerators, cupboards, and pantries were bursting at the seams. Some families had helped themselves during the looting; others received food from looters. Someone noted, "Now ain't that a bitch. For the first time in my life, ain't no hungry babies in The Hill, and it took a goddamn riot to accomplish that."

While it is certain that arsonists burned many business establishments, it is equally certain that they were blamed for far more fires than they actually set. Some folks bragged about taking vengeance against racists who had treated Blacks unfairly. Many folks bragged openly about what they had "taken out." From these accounts, a fairly accurate list of what had fallen to rioters was pieced together. The remaining places, the ones outside the riot areas, had been torched by White owners who wanted to cash in on their insurance or saw an opportunity to move their business out of Black areas. Canon Junius Carter from Holy Cross Lutheran Church in Homewood said, "While the rioters did burn down some of the businesses in Homewood, we know for a fact that some of the businesses were burned by the owners themselves. They all collected big insurance settlements by blaming the fires on Black folks."

Not all stores were burned or looted. Black-owned businesses were not destroyed. Many of them posted signs saying "BLACK OWNED" or "SOUL BROTHER." Some White-owned businesses were protected, such as Gordon's Shoe Store whose owners had long-standing reputations for helping members of The Hill community, even extending credit to many customers. After the riots, they left The Hill, saying they were afraid. Someone stationed folks outside of a small, Italian-owned hat-cleaning business to say "hands off!" The proprietors also sold freshly popped popcorn that was better and cheaper than that sold at the New Grenada or Roosevelt Theatres. Unfortunately, they too left shortly after the riots. This was often the case in other urban riot areas; owners of stores that were not damaged still left out of fear. As a result, riot-torn areas never returned to normal.

---

79 The burning of Jewish stores and the later picketing of Jewish-owned real estate companies became very contentious issues between Blacks and Jews. In fact, the problem led progressive members of the Black and Jewish communities to form dialogue groups to address the issue.

A Lack of Accurate News Coverage: Lies and No Video

News coverage of the riots was spotty. No members of the media had been permitted in Ebenezer Church, as the leaders tried to keep the meetings a secret. When the rioting began, station managers were not willing to risk injury to their staffs. In fact, no news reporters were in The Hill on the first day of rioting. Not even the weekly, Black-owned *Pittsburgh Courier* was there. When the riot started on April 5th, the *Courier's* next edition had already gone to press. By the time the next edition came out on April 13th, the riot was old news.

White-owned newspapers were not there on the first or second day, so "news" they printed was gathered from second hand sources within the Black communities. In truth, it wasn't safe for White reporters to be in The Hill before the governor sent in the National Guard. Naturally, the accuracy of the information was not necessarily reliable. I recall reading some newspaper accounts and wondering "Where the fuck did they get that bullshit?"

When one local station sent a newscaster/commentator to cover the second day of rioting, a group of young Black militants told him, "You better get your narrow, bigoted, White ass out of here. You ain't welcome in our community." The reporter paid no attention and started to walk down the street, saying, "I'm a news reporter. I can go anywhere I damn well please." When I happened upon the scene, the angry group had already surrounded the reporter and his crew. I suggested that the reporter—who had a reputation for making disparaging remarks about Blacks during his commentaries—might place discretion ahead of foolhardiness and beat a hasty retreat. Wisely, he did so.

Saul Berliner, a reporter for *The Cumberland News* in Maryland, had a similar experience. "I was trying to cover the riot when I was approached by three young Black men who wanted to know what I was doing in The Hill. When I didn't leave, they began to hit me. I cursed them and told them that I was trying to do my job." That apparently angered them, and they continued to hit him. One of the men hit him with a large object. They left him alone after several minutes, and he went to a hospital where he received several stitches to his head and face.

WQED planned to cover an event being held in the basement of a church on the Northside of Pittsburgh. I warned the producer that it was a very bad time to send an all-White news crew into any Pittsburgh Black ghetto. My offer to go with the crew and take along a Black cameraman was ignored. A group of young Black men heard about the White crew being in the church, trapped them in the basement, and began to beat them. Fortunately, no one was seriously injured, and there was no major damage done to the equipment. (From that point on WQED began to develop Black crew members.) The lack of first hand news coverage resulted in fragmented, and often unverifiable, information as is illustrated by accounts of the National Guard's arrival.

Police in riot gear protecting Washington Plaza in Lower Hill during riots of 1968

**Police arrest demonstrators during
riot in Pittsburgh, 1968**

Fix Bayonets! Occupied By the Army

By the second day of the riots, the governor called up National Guard units from towns around Pittsburgh and deployed them to the riot areas. Seeing young soldiers in full combat dress was surreal. Everywhere in The Hill, there were cops in riot gear and soldiers brandishing rifles. Some of the soldiers rode on the backs of jeeps, their hands on fully-automatic machine guns. The soldiers set up a camp in the lower Hill in a large open area above the Civic Arena.[80] The huge statue of Saint Benedict the Moor faced downtown and gazed on the sad scene. Black residents were doubly angry—at the arrival of the National Guard and the fact that most guardsmen were White. Shouting matches broke out between bayonet-fixed, scared guardsmen and angry, young Black militants. Fortunately, the verbal confrontations did not escalate, because lurking not far away were armed men, waiting silently to retaliate against anyone who shot Blacks.

Newscasts and newspapers showed the photos of the National Guard staging and bivouac areas set up in the Black communities. The size of the force is a subject of controversy. Most said it was "about 1500." However, according to the *Cumberland News*, Lt. Colonel William Bedling said he had "3,500 men in action or in reserve around the Negro area," meaning The Hill.

Conflicting stories circulated about the guardsmen's purpose and whether their weapons

**Crowd gathered at Point Park
after demonstration, 1968**

were loaded. I spoke with one man with the 28th Signal Battalion from nearby Midland, Pennsylvania who said:

> When we were ordered to report for duty, I wondered what it was about. We were not a combat unit; we were sort of like a bunch of Boy Scouts. I don't remember exactly what we were told, but I got the impression that there were some problems with people rioting and setting fires. Our purpose was to take care of property. There was no mention that we were to take action against people; we were just supposed to keep people from burning any more property. We didn't march down the streets or anything like that; we were just to stand at the entrances to various streets. I was stationed at a corner of

---

80 Just above the Civic Arena was a large area where nothing had been built during the urban "renewal." Some say that the area was supposed to be a parking lot. Hill district residents spoke about the area in terms of it being a buffer or no-man's zone that protected the new occupants of the lower Hill from contact with the Black residents.

Wylie Avenue near the Civic Arena. Most of us were not issued any ammunition. We were supposed to establish a presence by standing there with fixed bayonets. I do recall that one guy did 'put a bead' [aim] at some man who was running down the street, but when he 'bore down' on the man, he was ordered not to shoot.

The truth is that one guy in each platoon was issued one clip of ammunition. He had permission to fire in order to

**Demonstration Assembling at
Freedom Corner, circa 1968**

protect himself or his unit. No one knew that we didn't have ammo, so we were pretty effective at making people think about our presence. No one really confronted us or threw anything at us.

I asked how he and the others felt about the fact that most of them had no ammunition. His answer was short and simple. "BAD! But, we weren't the first Guard unit to arrive. Things were pretty much under control by the time we got there. We did hear there was a little trouble back in Midland, and that things were really bad in Aliquippa, which is very close to Midland. We were in Pittsburgh for only a couple of days; then they sent us home."

Even newspapers around this area could not resolve the issue as to whether the guardsmen had been armed. *The Progress* that covered small Pennsylvania communities reported on April 11, 1968, that the Guard was told "they could fire their weapons only on orders. They were not allowed to load their weapons, but in each platoon three snipers were permitted to load their weapons. Colonel Coat would not say if the same orders were given to all the soldiers. He stated, 'You can understand that we don't want to tell people what they need to know to take advantage of us'." According to *The Progress*, the soldiers were told, "Men, you are going to take a lot of verbal abuse. But you are going to just take it. If you are physically assaulted, you can protect yourself, but do not load until you get the word."

The *Valley Independent* serving Monessen said there were 1,095 Guardsmen deployed in Pittsburgh. They also reported that there were 1,300 arrests and 517 fires during the riot. According to their report, "Company C officers said that their unit was equipped with ammunition, contrary to reports that The Hill was patrolled by unarmed soldiers." The same officers reported, "We had some people yell at us; that was about it. For the most part we found people to be very courteous." Soldiers said that some of The Hill District residents even offered them coffee.

On the day that the riots began, Lloyd Bell, an Assistant Vice Chancellor at the University of Pittsburgh and head of a department that provided technical assistance to inner-city neighborhoods, recounted the following incident. He and a White friend, John Hannigan, went to the university's athletic complex intending to relieve the riot-related tension by working out. When an armed soldier barred his entrance, Bell became incensed and angrily identified himself. The soldier replied that he didn't care who Bell was; his orders were to keep *all* unauthorized people out. At this point Hannigan distracted the guard so that Bell could look in to see what was going on. Sprawled across the floor of the gym were hundreds of soldiers armed with machine-guns, bazookas, and other weapons. Bell headed straight to Chancellor Posvar's office, where he screamed, "How could you let the army use this University to house troops that are to be sent against Black residents, who were unarmed. We're supposed to be about education, not death." The chancellor sadly informed Bell that he had received a call from the governor who ordered that the facility be turned over to the Pennsylvania National Guard, and that he was to say nothing to anyone about the situation. "Although, when my anger died down, I realized that Posvar felt he had no choice in the situation, things were forever changed between us," Bell later told me.

The stories about who did and did not have ammunition may never be fully known. During my research, I was informed that there were trucks full of ammunition that could be distributed very quickly. Also, even though I served in a non-combat, guided-missile unit when I was stationed in Korea, many of us had ammo stashed away, just in case we ever needed to protect ourselves. I wonder how many guardsmen may have done the same thing.

John Brewer, Jr., was away at college in North Carolina when the riot "jumped off." "After they closed the campus, I hopped a bus and headed home. My bus was turned away from Richmond, Virginia, because of riots in D.C. Folks were firebombing, breaking store windows, and stealing (or, as we called it back in the day, 'liberating goods from the man.'). We ran into scenes of violence all along the bus route. My normal eight hour trip from Durham to Pittsburgh took 16 hours. We arrived at the bus station in Pittsburgh and immediately ran into trouble. No Yellow Cab would pick us up. Public transportation to Homewood was not available. Police were profiling Blacks who were dressed like me, in military jackets, Afros, and the kind of hat Che and Castro wore. I got stopped and questioned three times. Telephone service was not available. Faced with the choice of staying downtown and being harassed by police or trying to get home, I began walking to Oakland, using every alley I could find. Once I got to Oakland, I was able to get a ride to Homewood. I walked down Homewood Avenue to the underpass near Finance and Homewood Avenue where I ran into a jeep loaded with soldiers who had a machine gun mounted on top of the vehicle. The National Guard was blocking all streets into Homewood. I backtracked and walked along the railroad tracks until I got to my folks' home on Oakwood Avenue— total time from Downtown to home, 3 hours." Brewer continued:

> I was involved with Harambee Center on Homewood Avenue. We had secret meetings about the riots and police oppression. I saw a group of so-called militants throwing rocks at armored military vehicles. Many of us listened over and over again to revolutionary albums like Malcolm X's album, *Ballot or the Bullet.*

> At one point I was asked to accompany some brothers from Homewood and The Hill to the airport to pick up the famous revolutionary poet, Leroy Jones. While waiting for Jones to arrive, I went to the men's room. I had a 'Fro and was wearing, jeans, a "Castro" hat, and an old military jacket with the words 'Is God Dead?' on the back. Two White men sporting crew cuts, black suits, and plain ties appeared so suddenly, it was

like they emerged from the walls or the mirrors. I was barely finished at a urinal when they converged on me, lightning fast. "Against the wall, PUNK! Don't move," they shouted. They grabbed my arms and pinned me against the wall. I was used to being confronted by 'pigs' in the South, who put a gun in your face and spat tobacco on your shoes while saying 'Hey, *nigger*, what you doing here?'

I kept repeating to myself 'just be cool.' The two took a pamphlet about the Cuban revolution out of my jacket pocket. "What's this?" one of them asked. Trying to joke my way out of the situation, I said, "It's a book about revolution." They hesitated, then asked what I was doing at the airport.

"I was planning to overthrow the baggage department. Have you ever tried to get your luggage on time from these people?" They were not amused, but said nothing more and left the men's room. About ten minutes later, we were on our way to Schenley High School where Jones was speaking. We all laughed as our car moved through traffic exchanging stories about police harassment.

I had many conversations with Byrd Brown, Alma Fox, Reverend Jimmy Joe Robinson, Matthew Moore, "Hop" Kendrick, William Moore, Harvey Adams, Herman Mitchell, and others about the behavior of the Pittsburgh police during the riots. Apparently, police were unhappy with their orders to form a ring around the riot areas and prevent folks from entering or leaving. Only if rioters attempted to leave the area was the use of fatal force permitted. They would have preferred a more general "shoot-to-kill" order.

Allegheny County police detective Louis 'Hop' Kendrick recounted, "I was returning to our headquarters, in Downtown, the day after King was murdered. As I entered the building, I could hear people singing. At first I couldn't make out the words. As I got closer to the squad room, I could hear the words very clearly; the White police officers were singing a tune from the *Wizard of Oz,* that folks sang when the witch got killed. They were singing 'Thank God, the Coon is Dead!'"

Alyssa Ribeiro in her thesis, *A Period of Turmoil – Pittsburgh's 1968 Riots and their Aftermath,* offered the following conclusion, "…the handling of the riots instilled resentment among the city police that only aggravated already tense relations with the community." She further stated, "The biggest decision that local officials had to make during the riots involved what level of force to use."

Some factions among the police advocated using the maximum force possible to quell the disorder. Others, including Public Safety Director David Craig and Morton Coleman, who worked in the mayor's office, opposed such extreme measures. Some merchants from The Hill District were pressuring the police to start shooting looters. Fortunately, the urgings of the rogue police were ignored. Had they not been, a bloodbath would have ensued.

Although most leaders of the Pittsburgh movement embraced non-violence, they would not have allowed themselves and others to be shot down. Some Blacks—already angry about beatings during earlier demonstrations—armed themselves against police. In addition, young Black adults, who had been gang members just a few years prior to the riots, were quite willing to return violence with violence. There had been persistent rumors that heavily-armed Black men from out-of-town had infiltrated The Hill and fully intended to protect Black residents from police brutality. I am firmly convinced that had the

Pittsburgh police used deadly force, major headlines may well have been, "HUNDREDS OF RESIDENTS, NATIONAL GUARDSMEN AND POLICE KILLED DURING RIOTS." Thank God, that did not come about, but we came dangerously close!

A Clandestine Visit by "The Man"

After the riots, a new store called "Black Bazaar and Books for Freedom" opened on Centre Avenue across from the Hill House auditorium. Strolling through the community taking photographs of the riot's aftermath, I thought it was a strange time to open a new store; after all, the smoke had barely cleared. Entering the store, I was greeted by the owners, both of whom were strangers. Afterwards, I stopped in at The Halfway Art Gallery as well as the offices of the NAACP, The United Black Front, and The United Negro Protest Committee. No one in any of the organizations knew the owners. Ewari Ellis, director of The Halfway Art Gallery, suggested that I do some investigation.

The next day, I returned to the store on the pretext of buying some African art. When the owners became quite friendly and talkative, I got the feeling that I was being "pumped" for information about the cause of the riots. They were really not very sophisticated at the "questioning game." Ordinarily, I would have been offended and walked away after calling the jive folks a few choice names. In this case, however, I was willing to put up with the clumsy interrogation, because I was trying to get some information myself. Although they were from out of town, they claimed a prominent, militant, civil rights leader had encouraged them to open the store.

Just as I was leaving, a Black woman emerged from a back room. She was the girlfriend of the civil rights leader just mentioned by the bookstore's owners. Seeing my surprised look, the woman signaled me to remain silent, and then said, "Ralph, why don't you take me to lunch?" After we settled into a table at The Crawford Grill, the woman told me the owners had hired her without knowing of her relationship with the civil rights leader. Her boyfriend asked her to stay at the store and try to find out more about the men. After lunch, I dropped the women at the store and the stopped to tell Ewari Ellis about the situation.

No sooner had I arrived home, when the phone rang. The caller was none other than the FBI agent who had tried to recruit me as an informant at Pitt. I knew that the FBI had been tapping my phone, but I didn't think I was important enough for them to shadow me. The caller knew that I had taken the woman to lunch at the Grill and wanted to know what we had talked about. That's when I knew that I hadn't been tailed, but the bookstore owners had reported my whereabouts to the FBI.

Returning to The Hill the next day, I again reported what had happened to Ellis, who told me that the bookstore owners were being "checked out." In short order, the two strangers had been traced to the CIA and the FBI. When this information surfaced, some of the younger men wanted to burn the store to the ground. The old heads told the young people to chill, because as long as the bookstore proprietors remained in Pittsburgh, their movements could be tracked. I continued to frequent the store, as did other civil rights workers. Everyone was pumping everyone else for information.

A week or so later, the woman who worked at the store called, and at my suggestion, we met rather than talk on the phone. The bookstore owners had allowed the woman to leave early on Friday evening, claiming that they "had to go somewhere." When she arrived at the store on Saturday morning, it was empty except for the showcases. The "owners" had simply disappeared, never to be seen again.

The Aftermath

In the days following the riots, I spoke to many city officials, police officers, and White and Black citizens. In addition, I listened to many callers to talk shows, including my own. Many were angry and confused by the riots. They asked questions like: "Why would the Negroes burn down their own homes and stores?" "Why are they so angry?" Or they made statements like: "I know it was just the thugs and criminals who participated in the riots. We know that the vast majority of the law-abiding Negroes think the riots were wrong."

Whites just did not understand the intensity of long-simmering, pent-up anger and frustration. The April 13, 1968, edition of *The Pittsburgh Courier* had an interesting statement in an article called "'THE MAN'S' GONE; ARSON, LOOTING, GROWING IN HILL DISTRICT—HOMEWOOD." It was a rebellion against all authority in which police officials said that they caught numerous Whites with Molotov cocktails in their hands." The article also explained the frustration many Blacks felt towards the city leadership. "The Negro leadership and even the grassroots breed had communicated the seriousness of the situation to the officials of government and the pillars of Pittsburgh industry and commerce here repeatedly, but nothing was done."

Blacks who had not personally engaged in arson or looting could nevertheless understand why their fellow citizens were rioting.

A month before the riots broke out, in its March 9, 1968, edition, *The Pittsburgh Courier* editors urged the City of Pittsburgh to form a committee to investigate conditions that led to riots in other cities. The article went on to say, "Pittsburgh can form such a committee now, before riots may occur here. Mayor Barr should appoint such a commission on urban problems which would address itself to the task of eliminating the artificial barriers which hold the Negro in a secondary role." The editors' plea, like those from so many other leaders of Pittsburgh's civil right movement was ignored.

The April 20th edition of *The Pittsburgh Courier* carried the headline, "BLACKS QUIT BARR'S RIOT TASK FORCE; NAACP HEAD RAPS CITY CIVIL DISORDER PROBE." At first glance, it appeared that Mayor Barr had responded, albeit belatedly, to the call for an investigation into the riots. He had appointed well-known, extremely qualified, and highly respected Black leaders to serve on the investigating Task Force. Why then was *The Courier* announcing that the following members had quit:

- Eric Springer, Chairman of the Human Relations Commission
- David Epperson, Director of the Mayor's Commission on Human Resources
- Louis Mason, member of City Council
- David Washington, executive director of the Mayor's Commission on Human Resources

Typical of the arrogance so often exhibited by government leaders, the mayor had never bothered to actually extend an invitation to serve on the Task Force.

The riots in Pittsburgh differed from those in other cities in the sense that no lives were lost. But the scars remained. When the smoke cleared, vacant charred ruins awaited demolition. White merchants fled, leaving Black communities bereft of supermarkets and a host of other retail businesses. Community residents forced to shop in other areas were not welcomed with open arms. Dr. Martin Luther King, Jr. was dead and, for all intents and purposes, so was the civil rights movement as it had been known.

Blacks said, "No more of this non-violence stuff. If they killed the prince of peace, they do not want peace." With the deaths of the two mightiest warriors of the movement, King and Malcolm X, Blacks now moved from concerns about integration to focusing on issues of Black Power. Many Whites feared the new militancy.

CHAPTER 24

Beyond 1968—
The Fight Continued

T he civil rights movement, *as we knew it* changed with the murder of Martin Luther King, Jr., in 1968. Many still pushed for equality. However, it was as if, when King drew his last breath, so did the formal movement he headed—or at least it was taking slower, labored breaths. Many Blacks were disenchanted. We thought that the murder of King was proof that this country was never going to accept Blacks as equals. If they killed this man, who preached peace and tolerance, the rest of us were readily disposable. Many who had accepted integration began to speak of self-determination and self-segregation. Many began to revisit the idea of complete separation from White society. Many were depressed and heart-broken. We ushered in the Black Power movement that revisited some of the beliefs of Marcus Garvey and Malcolm X. Many felt that integration had been a flawed idea from the beginning. Militancy increased as Blacks sought, once again, to define themselves. People in the power structure became alarmed at this new militancy. Black males became more menacing than ever before. At least, that was the feeling expressed by many in power, as well as ordinary White folks.

In the aftermath of the 1968 riots, there was a surge in civil rights activities. What follows are descriptions of several key events reported in *The Pittsburgh Courier*.

> March 15: The NAACP, Forever Action Together, The United Negro Protest Committee, and other rights groups demanded that the city fathers immediately promote a Black police officer as the first Black Police Superintendent.
>
> April 5—Headline: BLACK COPS URGE CHANGES IN POLICE DEPARTMENT. The Guardians, an organization of Black Police officers, joined with the NAACP and other civil rights organizations in demanding changes be made within the police department, including the naming of a Black Assistant Superintendent.
>
> May, 24: The Pittsburgh NAACP demanded the removal of the White dean of Pitt's School of Social Work. Allegedly, Dr. William McCullogh referred to Dr. Lloyd Bell, a Black Pitt administrator, as "this Boy!" Unfortunately, the article does not address the outcome. However, it does show that protests were continuing subsequent to the murder of King.

July 19—Headline: UNPC Schedules More Job Talks. The following companies were targeted for protests—Mellon Bank, the Aluminum Company of America (Alcoa), Koppers, Westinghouse Air Brake, U.S. Steel, Pittsburgh Plate Glass, United Parcel Service (UPS), and Kaufmann's, Gimbel's and Joseph Horne's department stores.

August: Demonstrations at construction site of Three Rivers Stadium and U.S. Steel Headquarters. (See Chapter 18 for more detailed account.)

September 6—Headline: UNPC, Mellon in Job Dispute. According to James McCoy and Matthew Moore of The United Negro Protest Committee, Mellon had refused to negotiate in good faith and will be the target of direct action.

September 20: The NAACP, The United Negro Protest Committee, and OIC (Opportunities Industrialization Center) charged that Pittsburgh Plate Glass was remiss in hiring Blacks. A meeting was held with PPG officials and both sides looked forward to fruitful negotiations.

October 4—Headline: Mellon Faces Picketing; PPG Under Attack. Members of the UNPC claimed that neither organization had lived up to promises made about Black employment.

October 18: Charles Harris, former member of the United Protest Committee and the NAACP, formed a new civil rights organization called The Greater Pittsburgh Direct Action Coalition. Harris was upset at an agreement reached between the UNPC and Mellon Bank. Harris said that the negotiating team disavowed any knowledge of the agreement. Harris said that the group would enlist the assistance of all "militant" groups in Pittsburgh.

November, 22: Gulf Oil Corporation, RCA, and the Main La France Accounting Company received letters of protest from the newly-formed Direct Action Coalition. President Charles Harris requested an immediate meeting with all the companies to discuss their hiring policies with regard to Blacks.

December 6: The United Black Protest Committee entered into negotiations with Sears to address discrimination in that company. At the same time, the NAACP was filing charges against the Pittsburgh Police for alleged police harassment of pickets who were demonstrating at the Sears stores. Both Alma Fox, NAACP executive director, and Alma Clark of the UBPC were arrested for "littering" during a demonstration at Sear's East Liberty store. Both women were passing out flyers about the selective buying campaign that was a part of the action against Sears. Obviously, relationships between the police and the civil rights community remained strained. James McCoy said that during the demonstration he was nearly hit by a police car as he was standing near the curb marshalling pickets. McCoy said that the act was deliberate.

December 6: The Direct Action Coalition sent a letter to Gulf Oil stating "We don't want your free drinks. We want jobs." For years, Gulf Oil had been spending thousands of dollars paying for cocktail parties of Black organizations in Pittsburgh and elsewhere. It was a commonly-known fact among Black groups that, if you were going to have a cocktail sip function, Gulf Oil would gladly pay for it. At the same time, Gulf had a deplorable record with respect to hiring Blacks. DAC pointed out that of the 1,100 Gulf Oil employees at its Pittsburgh headquarters, only 85 were Black, and 71 of those were employed in low-paying jobs such as cleaning, repair, message service, and mimeographing. Harris called Gulf's hiring practices "pitiful." Interestingly, some groups headed by "people-of-color" became upset with the Direct Action Coalition for "killing the goose that laid the golden egg"; forcing them to pay for their own drinks. The DAC made eleven demands of Gulf, including the immediate hiring of a Black man at corporate headquarters to assist the Equal Employment Opportunity Compliance Officer in executing Gulf Oil's corporate EEO policy.[81]

December 20: The Direct Action Coalition continued to bring pressure on the accounting firm of Main LaFrance and The Radio Corporation of America regarding Black employment. Main LaFrance did not employ even one Black, and RCA's record was deplorable.

Thus ended 1969, marked by name changes for Black civil rights organizations, a split in the leadership, and continued tension between members of the civil rights groups and Pittsburgh Police. What is evident is that, despite the internal changes, the civil rights groups continued to put pressure on Pittsburgh companies to hire more Blacks and to hire them in the upper echelons of the companies.

1970 Events

January 10. The year began with the Direct Action Coalition forcing the resignation of Everett Utterback, a Black man who was both the legal counsel and the deputy director of the Pittsburgh Housing Authority. DAC was also pushing for the resignation of Al Tronzo, a White man who was the head of the Authority. The dispute involved attempts to force the Housing Authority to re-hire three Black workers who were allegedly fired for civil rights activities. Utterback resigned as deputy director, but remained as legal counsel. Tronzo accused the DAC of "anarchy," because they were trying to take over by attending Authority board meetings. Interestingly, Attorney Utterback was among a group of prominent, upper middle class Blacks who worked the legal system to secure

---

81 In 1968, when I was working for H.J. Heinz Company, my boss, Harry Carroll, asked me to set up a program for Heinz to become engaged with the Black community. He was aware of the good reputation of Gulf Oil and wanted a program like theirs. I explained that all Gulf Oil did was spend thousands of dollars getting Black folks drunk and suggested that we should do something better. He agreed, and Heinz set up a program of free food distribution to the offices of the Poverty Program, a deposit to Dwelling House Savings and Loan in order to help it qualify for federal deposit insurance, and grants to Black organizations. Mr. Carroll also served on the board of the Sickle Cell Anemia Society. I point this out only to illustrate that Gulf Oil had a good reputation among Pittsburgh corporations and others were ready to follow its lead.

Black rights in the 1930s, 1940s, and 1950s. Time had recast him and others in his group as too old and conservative remnants of another era.

January 18: The H.K. Porter Company would be picketed by the Direct Action Coalition because it failed to live up to an agreement reached with DAC.

February 7—Headline: H.J. HEINZ SET TO MEET WITH DIRECT ACTION GROUP.

February 14—Headline: TRAFFORD AREA RESIDENTS SEEK AID OF PGH DAC. Trafford-area, well-to-do home owners accuse government officials of racial discrimination.

April 25—Headline: DAC WANTS BLACK FBI AGENTS HERE. Charles Harris, DAC president claimed that the FBI had no Black agents in Pittsburgh and few in the entire United States.

May 2: DAC filed a complaint with Civic Arena authorities, claiming that Whites get the best seats in the arena.

MAY 2—HEADLINE: BROWN LEAVES NAACP. Byrd Brown announced that he was leaving the post he had held for more than a decade, because he was running for U.S. Congressman in the 14th Congressional District. His run for office conflicted with the by-laws of the National NAACP. Brown was unsuccessful in his attempt to gain public office.

June 6: The Direct Action Coalition meets with Civic Arena authorities to demand more and better jobs for Blacks.

June 13—Headline: DAC PRESSURES CONGRESSMEN ON VOTER RIGHTS EXTENSION.

June 20—Headline: DAC WANTS ALL LEVELS BLACK COPS. They struggle with the Pittsburgh Police Department in efforts to secure higher-ranking jobs for Black police officers.

August 1: The Direct Action Coalition sought a Federal probe of the Fraternal Order of Police, claiming the union was racist, was against Blacks, and fostered discrimination against Black officers.

August 29—Headline: DAC DECLARES 'OPEN WAR' ON PORT AUTHORITY BOARD.

1971 Events

A careful examination of all available editions of the 1971 *Pittsburgh Courier* shows that civil rights activities continued at a high rate. Illustrative of the 37 articles published that year are the following:

January 9—Headline: CRISIS IN SCHOOLS BLASTED BY BLACK COALITION GROUP.

January 30—Headline: DAC HITS COUNTY COMMISSIONER ON RACIST DISCRIMINATION. The Direct Action Coalition complained that the Allegheny County commissioners promoted and condoned racism and discrimination at the Greater Pittsburgh Airport.

May 8: DAC endorses political candidates.

Clearly, the Pittsburgh civil rights movement did not die in 1968. However, 1970-1971 did bring a number of changes. Most dramatic was a shift in leadership from the National Association for the Advancement of Colored People and its action arm, The United Black Action Coalition to the Direct Action Coalition. When Charles Harris formed DAC, some of the top leaders in the NAACP left, thus depleting the strength of the United Black Action Coalition.

Former friends fell out as James McCoy, head of the United Black Protest Committee, challenged Byrd Brown for the presidency of the Pittsburgh NAACP. Although Brown won the election, it caused a further split in the leadership of the civil rights fraternity. Later, Brown was looking for new vistas to conquer when he decided to seek a seat in the U.S. Congress. He concentrated more and more on that quest, finally resigning from the NAACP in 1970.

Another apparent change in 1970 was that more and more of the civil rights activities were originating from groups in The Hill District. Little was heard from groups from the Northside, Homewood, and other Black communities. Some groups appear to have ceased functioning.

Asking when the Pittsburgh civil rights movement died is not the most relevant question. Although much diminished, efforts to gain equality still continued. The more cogent question seems to be "What was gained and what was lost through the movement?" This is the question I consider in the next chapter.

CHAPTER 25

The Civil Rights Movement in Retrospect

Looking Back—A Short View

A s I concluded each interview for my oral history project, I felt it was important to ask, "Was it worth it? Did significant changes take place? Did we accomplish what we set out to do? Did the Black community pay a price for the movement? With the exception of Dr. Charles Greenlee, all those I interviewed indicated, quite strongly, that the time and energy they expended had resulted in changes that were well worth the effort. Many said they would have done things differently, and some said the movement stopped too soon. Dr. Charles Greenlee, however, contended, "We, the Black community, had not made lasting gains in proportion to the amount of effort expended and that Pittsburgh was, in many ways, just as racist as it had been prior to the movement." His words proved prophetic when, in the 1990s, Dr. Ralph Bangs of the University of Pittsburgh published a series of reports on economic conditions in Pittsburgh and Allegheny County. Of 50 comparable cities in the United States, Pittsburgh was the most oppressive and most resistant to Black advancement. Thus, assessing whether significant, lasting changes were made is a complicated task. From the perspective of those I interviewed, the gains achieved by the late 1980s as the Civil Rights Movement came to an end were mixed.

In terms of employment, Blacks were now hired by banks, utility companies, hotels, schools, and retail establishments. Yet, few Blacks occupied management, executive, or board positions where policy decisions were made. The same was true in the news and entertainment industry where more Blacks were employed at local TV and radio stations. Yet, on-air Black reporters were assigned to weekend or late-night broadcasts. Those who made decisions about the content of programming were still White. Blacks could sit anywhere in movie theaters, but few movies had Black lead characters or featured themes relevant to Black lives. Blacks owned few theaters, a very small number of radio stations, and no televisions stations. When Black and White musician unions merged, Black musicians were hired less frequently.

In terms of retail establishments, Blacks could no longer be denied service. They could shop in department stores, eat in restaurants, and stay in major hotels. Yet, Blacks often reported receiving poor service.

In terms of government, Blacks held more positions in city and county government, including city and county councils. Yet, Pittsburgh has never had a Black mayor, and the vast majority of department heads in both the city and county government were White. There are more Blacks on the Pittsburgh police force, but their numbers diminished once the federal consent decree mandating the hiring of Blacks and women was lifted.

In terms of public education, Helen Faison was appointed interim superintendent of the Pittsburgh Public School System in 1999, the first Black to hold that position. More Black teachers and other professionals had been hired. Yet, the majority of the Board of Education was White and their views prevailed during the many bitter battles over equal education for Black children. Although Black youngsters could attend any school, the system still failed them miserably; the gap between Black and White student achievements remained very wide.

In colleges and universities, Blacks students and faculty were represented in more significant percentages than prior to the movement. Yet, most department chairs were White as were the Chairs of the most powerful committees. Most colleges and universities offered little in terms of academic courses that reflect the contributions of African Americans. Years would pass before a Black was appointed as a president of any higher education institution in the Pittsburgh area.

In terms of foundation funding, Black organizations had begun to receive more funding. Yet, the majority of board trustees, employees, and all foundation managers were White. The same was true of the committees that determined the approval of grant applications. POISE remained the only Black-controlled foundation, but its endowment was miniscule in comparison to those of White-controlled foundations.

Thus, while gains had been made in Pittsburgh, the higher up the organizational ladder one looked, the whiter the complexion in education, industry, and government. Blacks could see the top, but only through a still impenetrable glass ceiling.

In the push for integration into a White dominated society, Blacks suffered several important losses. Blacks abandoned the traditional Black communities as they moved to "better communities" in the suburbs. Black businesses suffered as Blacks were free to patronize White-owned establishments.

The truth is that integration was one of the causes of so many Black businesses folding. Add to this the fact that we, as Blacks, did very little to encourage our youth to become entrepreneurs. Instead, we encouraged them to go to school, get a good education, and then go to work for a White-owned company. For example, I was in a video store located in Wilkinsburg that was liquidating its inventory of films. When I asked the owner why he was closing, he responded:

> I can't compete with the White-owned video store a few doors away. I offer the same movies at the same price as the White guy. In fact, because I have so few customers, I am far more likely to have the movie they want in stock. My store is just as nice as his, and I try to treat all customers well. In spite of all this, I watch Black folks walk right by my store and go to the White man.

In the 1990s, a Black man opened an Athlete's Foot store on Homewood Avenue. I listened sadly as the owner told me that he was closing. "Why?" I asked. The owner told me, "I have the same stuff other stores have. Still, Black folks take a bus, drive a car, or get a jitney to travel to the mall and buy their stuff from the White-owned store. I am losing money each day. I can't even support my family."

Another example of our failure to support one another is the attempt of several folks to keep a supermarket in the Homewood area. When the Giant Eagle chain decided that they no longer wished to stay in the community, they sold the store to a Black employee. Blacks no longer came to the store, and it closed in a short time. The store re-opened under new management, but that incarnation soon failed for the same reasons. After being vacant for some time, the store re-opened under a new name, and was sponsored by a prominent Black church in response to the constant complaints of Blacks about not having a supermarket in the area. At the time of its opening, I was the host of *Black Talk* on a local radio station. The manager of the store and some of the church members appeared on my show on more than one occasion. Each day I was on the air—three hours per day, five days per week—I urged listeners to shop at the store. Despite the efforts of all involved, it became apparent that the store would soon close unless Blacks began to shop there. I began to hear the usual negative comments about the store, ranging from its being dirty to not having enough products to being too expensive. I decided to investigate, and went to the store several times, bought a bag of groceries, and compared my purchases with those from a Giant Eagle located in a nearby White neighborhood. I found no difference. On one occasion, I visited the Black market and 10 minutes later went to the White market. Only six Blacks were shopping in the Black market; dozens were patronizing the White store. It was so disheartening to see how the lessons of mistrust learned in slavery were still undermining our support for each other.

The Coliseum, a large banquet hall owned by John and Tina Brewer, sat in the large Black community of Homewood. Most days of the year, it sat vacant while Black-controlled organizations held their functions at White-owned establishments in White communities. One day, John Brewer and I were working with staff at the Carnegie Library Fine Arts Department to identify the thousands of photographs taken by the late Charles "Teenie" Harris, the renowned *Pittsburgh Courier* photographer. We were having difficulty identifying many of the venues where Black gatherings were held. Addressing the White staff, I said, "You're probably wondering why so many of events were held in the basements of churches. Quite simply, at the time most of these photos were taken, White-owned establishments refused to rent even to such prominent Black organizations as the NAACP and The Urban League." As such racism fell away, Blacks seemed to forget the discrimination suffered for generations. They turned their backs on Black communities and Black establishments.

During my interview with Byrd Brown, we reflected on what had been accomplished by the Pittsburgh civil rights movement. With a pensive tone, Byrd offered the following analysis:

> Power concedes nothing. Once the demonstrations and picketing stopped, Whites no longer felt threatened, so the walls went back up.

> Some of us became tired and exhausted. Some of us believed that passage of civil rights legislation meant that the job was done. Some of us got caught up in the same materialism as others and became satisfied with our little piece of the pie.

> We failed to realize what integration would do to us. We did not pay enough attention to our own communities. Many Blacks who could move did just that and abandoned their roots. We took two steps forward, but now we are bogged down in a swamp of racism,

and our young folks don't realize that the job was not completed. They think they got that good job through their own efforts. They don't realize what we went through in order to open the doors that they now casually walk through.

Blacks need to understand that the passage of civil rights legislation hasn't changed anything. This is what people coming up today do not understand. When we were still segregated in all walks of life, we had a sub-culture in which we depended upon ourselves. We had Wylie Avenue, Herron Avenue. We had all kinds of businesses, and we patronized those businesses. We had developed commercial and middle classes. Blacks were striving to move into the mainstream of society, but we had a greater sense of cohesion; a greater sense of respect; a greater sense of relatedness; a greater sense of self-respect, and respect for each other than we have now.

We no longer have a commercial middle class. When integration and desegregation came, everyone Black went downtown. So the small hotels in which we stayed went out of business; the small restaurants, like Dearing's Tea Room, went out of business. The Black shoemaker went out of business, as did the Black cleaners, and the Black drug stores. We are just now coming back, but we still don't have the number of Black-owned business we had in the 1940s and 1950s.

People don't realize that we are a commercial, mercantile nation and if Blacks are closed out of any aspect of that commercial market, we are disadvantaged. All you have to do is look around in the board room, into the businesses of America, and you can determine the degree to which we are disadvantaged. We have to overcome this; we have to do whatever is necessary to overcome these disadvantages. Otherwise, we are just talking slogans and singing songs.

It is important and incumbent upon us to realize that we must be supportive of each other in our neighborhoods, and we must develop neighborhoods that are viable and livable; otherwise, we will never overcome the problems of racism and discrimination that still exist today.

As a people, we made slight gains, or perhaps none at all, when you look at the number of people who benefited little from all our efforts. Many individuals "made it," but forgot how they got there. The level of racism today is just about the same, and soon it will be bubbling to the surface again. Blacks and Whites no longer seem interested in coming together to solve these issues. Black folks have become consumed with self-hatred.

Looking Back—A Longer View

I began writing *Voices* in 2001. Most of my interviews had been completed earlier, so the images and thoughts throughout the book reflect the comments of those involved in the Pittsburgh civil rights movement prior to 2001. Unfortunately, most of those individuals are now gone, so I cannot ask for their current views. And, even though I was close to most of the people I interviewed, I would not venture to speak for them now. I have, however, been able to ask several of the remaining interviewees if they would want to change their words. As I expected, their response was an immediate and vehement "No! That is what I felt at the time, and I don't want to change anything."

However, there can be no doubt that the world has changed since 2001. But in some ways, it has not changed much at all. Police still continue to kill unarmed Black men and most go unpunished. The most recent statistics I could find come from 2015, and I can't help but ask why these deaths are not tracked annually. At any rate, according to STASTICA.COM, 135 unarmed Blacks were killed by police in 2015; a number also cited in an NPR report. I was unable to find statistics on the number of police officers who were convicted for these shootings. I can recall only seven who were convicted of murder; 37 were convicted of lesser crimes.[82] While I could find no accurate accounting for the numbers of cities and municipalities that had to pay wrongful death settlements for police killing Blacks, the number is mind-boggling. The fact that anyone who owns a smart phone, also owns a video camera, has been instrumental in almost all the cases where officers have been convicted of wrong-doing. Interestingly, despite the fact that many police department members are required to wear body cameras, these devices are often not operative when the police arrest Blacks.

The killing of unarmed Black people is, in part, what started the BLACK LIVES MATTER movement. It began in 2013 after the acquittal of George Zimmerman in the shooting death of Black teenager, Travon Martin. It has since grown into a national organization, holding hundreds of demonstrations across the United States. This movement often joins with other protests across the country and, once again, young students, both Black and White, are taking to the streets of America to protest inequality. However, it appears that the movement has no national leadership. Nor has it become as far-reaching as the Civil Rights movement of the 1960s. Despite this, I am happy that the movement started, even though it appears that most White Americans have not embraced it. Is this, once again, the rejection of anything Black?

It always seems that when Blacks make some advance, no matter how large or small, there is a penalty to be paid. One example is the unexpected election of Barack Obama as the first African-American president of the United States of America. When he was elected, I wept out of happiness and what that might mean for Blacks. Yet, I also wept out of sadness, because my life experiences and my training as a social scientist and researcher, told me that Black people would pay dearly for their role in electing a Black man to the highest office in the land. White bigots had not expected him to win. I had heard their strident voices before the election. Many Whites did not vote in the first election, because, in my opinion, they did not expect him to win, especially over someone named Clinton. They did not expect that Blacks and young, hopeful White folks would vote for him. Nor did they expect him to win against the rich republican Mitt Romney in the next election.

Once elected, Obama's every effort to bring about change was thwarted by the White Republican party. No one stood against this concerted campaign to undermine the President's policies, even if United States citizens would have benefited from those policies. The civility with which the Office of the President had traditionally been treated was replaced with disgraceful rhetoric of hateful bigotry. When a White Republican representative publicly called Obama a liar, he was not censured by his colleagues, and he was applauded by many racists. The fact that he got away with such behavior was a sign of things to come.

---

82 These statistics are from a 2021 *USA TODAY* report by Rick Rowan.

Sadly, as I had predicted, the payback came with the election of Donald Trump, the most racist, homophobic, anti-immigrant, sexist person ever to occupy the White House. His blatantly racist rhetoric gave permission for others to freely express their bigotry. His blatantly abusive denigration of women opened pathways for renewed assaults on women's rights, and under the guise of "family values," state legislatures continue to wage war to overturn *Roe v Wade*. Despite this, a majority of women voters cast their ballots for him.

His rants against Mexican and South American immigrants "storming" into our country and "stealing" jobs from deserving American (read White) citizens fueled anti-immigration sentiments, which ultimately led to tearing children away from their parents and confining them to detention centers where all too many suffer neglect and abuse. Labeling COVID-19 a Chinese-promulgated disease led to an upsurge in violence against Asian Americans.

Aided and abetted by the White Republican party, especially those in the Senate, anti-Black sentiment is once again gaining traction. Outraged that enough Black voters cast their votes to overwhelmingly elect Joseph Biden, Donald Trump launched a completely unsubstantiated campaign of "voter fraud." Under the guise of "Voter Fraud Reform," many state legislatures are once again working to deny Blacks the right to vote. The specter of the Old South is again rearing its ugly head, with openly blatant racism back in vogue in the North as well. Remember, if northern Whites had not turned a blind eye to what was happening, the Jim Crow laws passed in the South after Reconstruction could not have been enacted.

In the face of these assaults on the civil rights on so many fronts and against so many groups, we would be wise to heed the words of Martin Niemöller, a prominent German Lutheran pastor and outspoken critic of Hitler:

> First they came for the socialist, and I said nothing because I was not a socialist. Then they came for the trade unionist, and I said nothing because I was not a trade unionist. Then they came for the communist, and I said nothing because I was not a communist. Then they came for the Jews, and I said nothing because I was not a Jew. Then they came for me, and there was no one left to speak for me.

During the civil rights movement, even the smallest bits of progress seemed monumental after nearly 400 years of subjugation and slavery. Yet, as I look at the racism unleashed by Donald Trump and his allies, I can't help but think my life's work may have all been in vain. Others from the old movement with whom I spoke, echoed the same sentiment, saying, "Hey didn't we already fix that?" Those of us who fought for civil rights in Pittsburgh had hoped we were laying a foundation upon which the next generation could build. Sadly, it seems that whatever gains we made recreated the Illusion of Inclusion. Those who followed took for granted the freedoms for which so many had sacrificed so much. We were lulled into a false comfort, thinking that the war, not just the battle, had been won. The election of Barack Obama seemed to be the final confirmation that the United States was shedding the immorality of its violent, racist past. As the election of Donald Trump made clear, the 50 years following the assassination of Martin Luther King, Jr. had merely been a hiatus during which the troops for social injustice were regrouping and gathering strength.

Epilogue

On October 14, 2008, I attended the memorial service of my friend and civil rights leader, Arthur Edmunds. As I looked around the church, I nodded silent acknowledgement of my compatriots who had also come to honor Art. Some mounted the steps to the altar to deliver words of praise for our fallen brother. As I watched my old friends, I noted that their gaits weren't as steady; their voices did not ring from the rafters of the church as they had done in the old days. For many of us, death is not too far away.

In that moment of sad reflection, I was filled with remorse that I did not complete this book in the 1990s when so many of our civil rights heroes were still alive. I pray now, that they know I have kept my promise to record our struggles.

I have been teaching for more than forty years. I always tell my students, "If you decide to battle injustice, do not take that decision lightly. Understand that being a warrior will cost you. Be certain you are willing to pay the price, because as surely as I stand here you *will* pay. No one really cares about the pain a warrior feels. In fact, many are surprised that a warrior feels *any* pain at all."

After a particularly hard-fought battle, a friend said, "You must be really happy. That was such an important victory." He was surprised when I replied, "I am sad, and I hurt. The problem with battles is not whether I win or lose. There is no taste of sweet victory. When I win, someone else loses. No matter how wrong the loser is they are still a human being and sometimes I pretty much have to destroy some part of them or their life. Don't get me wrong; I know that just as soon as the battle begins I still have do it. But there is no victory dance, no toast to success. I am left with an empty feeling. You see, in order to take up the battle I must move from my place of peace. Once the battle is over it takes a long time to find my 'center' again. Whether I win or lose, there is a penalty I must pay."

Still, we need a new generation of warriors who are willing to raise their voices against discrimination and injustice. The Internet offers a tremendous tool for uniting those willing to fight for a truly inclusive society. At the same time, it poses a tremendous threat, allowing those with racial prejudices to spread mistrust and hate. Left unopposed, they threaten to undermine any progress that has been made in the fight for civil rights and take us back to the rampant cruelty that devastated the lives of so many. We cannot afford to lapse again into the illusion of inclusion.

There is a popular saying among Black folks who consider themselves knowledgeable about the past attempts to achieve Black equality: "When the people demand it, a leader will arrive." Unfortunately, I do not believe that. Since the end of the movement, I have seen many troubling signs. Charges of "reverse discrimination" assert that affirmative action laws and practices discriminate against White males. I did not hear them raise their voices when the society engaged in hundreds of years of "forward discrimination" that was there for the benefit of White males, who still rule the country. Until we teach all students about "White Privilege," they will never understand that this country was established by a specific group of people who set up all the institutions to serve people who look like them. The fact is that each day, when we awaken, we either enjoy privileges or are denied those same privileges based simply on the color of our skin. These unearned privileges are not based on how hard you work or what you know; they are there because you were born White, male and economically privileged.

I also see disturbing trends among our Black youth, who seem to know and care little about that "old civil rights shit." Many have never heard of the important Black leaders who fought so hard for the rights they now enjoy. They see no need for us to have any leaders; everything is *cool!* Black studies programs across the nation are in trouble, because Black youngsters do not enroll in courses offered. Black-on-Black crime is at an all-time high. The prisons are bulging with intelligent young brothers whose lives are in shambles because they were chasing the ready dollars in illegal street pharmaceutical sales. Many of the gains we won during the movement are being stripped away, and we do nothing. It feels as if the journey must begin anew. History teaches us that movements like the past civil rights movement are cyclical. They say the movements always return. Ours is thirty years overdue.

I am an old man now. Many times, when I felt the need to take on some battle, I would pray, "God, if it is okay with you, I would just as soon not fight this battle. I am tired of fighting. Please give me a sign that someone else can take this one." The older I got, the more often I would ask to be allowed to take a pass. Yet, the message seemed to be, "No, my son, I want you to do this. I will let you know when it is time to rest." Now in my eighth decade, I fear that death will be the Creator's message that my work is finally done. I pray that before I'm gone I will see new leaders take up the cause of justice. I pray these new warriors will have the strength and courage to continue the vital work started by those whose voices have filled these pages.

I must continue to believe that as long as we breathe, there is hope.

Information Resources

Allen, James (author/editor) with Foreword and essays by Congressman John Lewis, and contributions by Hilton Als and Leon F. Litwack, Leon. *Without Sanctuary: Lynching Photography in America.* Twin Palm Publishers, 2004

Bennett, Lerone. *Forced into Glory*. Johnson Publishing Company, Chicago; 2000.

Bennett, Lerone. *Before the Mayflower*. Johnson Publishing Company, Chicago, 1961.

Franklin, John Hope. *The Emancipation Proclamation*. New York, 1963.

Franklin, John Hope, and Alfred A. Moss Jr. *From Slavery to Freedom*. New York: McGraw, Hill, 2000.

Glasco, Laurence. *The Civil Rights Movement in Pittsburgh: To Make this City 'Someplace Special.'* Unpublished monograph available at www.freedomcorner.org/downloads/glasco.pdf.

Huggins, Nathan, Martin Kilson, and Daniel Fox. *Key Issues in the African American Experience*. Harcourt Brace Jovanovich, 1971.

McGhee, Heather. *The Sum of Us: What Racism Costs Everyone and How We can Prosper Together*. Random House, 2021.

Proctor, Ralph. *Racial Discrimination against Black Teachers and Professionals in the Pittsburgh Public Schools System,* 1834-1973.Oakmont, PA: Learning Moments Press, 2021.

Ribeiro, Alyssa. M.A. Thesis. *A Period of Turmoil*. University of Pittsburgh, 2006.

Tolnay, Stewart E., and E.M. Beck. *A Festival of Violence: An Analysis of Southern Lynchings 1882-1930.* The Board of Trustees of the University of Illinois, 1995.

Trotter, Joe William, Jr. *The African American Experience*. Houghton Mifflin Company; 2001.

Learning Moments Press

Learning Moments Press is the publishing arm of the Scholar-Practitioner Nexus, an online community of individuals committed to the quality of education. Learning Moments Press features three series of books.

The Wisdom of Practice Series showcases the work of individuals who illuminate the complexities of practice as they strive to fulfill the purpose of their profession.

The Wisdom of Life Series offers insightful reflections on significant life events that challenge the meaning of one's life, one's sense of self, and one's place in the world.

The Social Context Series showcases the work of individuals who illuminate the macro socio-economic-political contexts within which education policy and practice are enacted.

Cooligraphy artist Daniel Nie created the logo for Learning Moments Press by combining two symbol systems. Following the principles of ancient Asian symbols, Daniel framed the logo with the initials of Learning Moments Press. Within this frame, he has replicated the Adinkra symbol for *Sankofa* as interpreted by graphic artists at the Documents and Design Company. As explained by Wikipedia, Adinkra is a writing system of the Akan culture of West Africa. *Sankofa* symbolizes taking from the past what is good and bringing it into the present in order to make positive progress through the benevolent use of knowledge. Inherent in this philosophy is the belief that the past illuminates the present and that the search for knowledge is a life-long process.

CPSIA information can be obtained
at www.ICGtesting.com
Printed in the USA
LVHW022327150122
708681LV00011B/727

9 781734 959468